Xinhao Wang
Rainer vom Hofe

Research Methods in Urban and Regional Planning

Xinhao Wang
Rainer vom Hofe

Research Methods
in Urban and Regional Planning

With 97 figures and 139 tables

AUTHORS:

Dr. Xinhao Wang
School of Planning
University of Cincinnati
Cincinnati, OH 45221-0016
USA
E-mail: xinhao.wang@uc.edu

Dr. Rainer vom Hofe
School of Planning,
University of Cincinnati,
Cincinnati,OH 45221-0016
USA
E-mail: rainer.vomhofe@uc.edu

ISBN 978-7-302-13785-6 **Tsinghua University Press, Beijing**
ISBN 978-3-540-49657-1 **Springer Berlin Heidelberg New York**

Library of Congress Control Number: 2007920896

© 2007 Tsinghua University Press, Beijing and Springer-Verlag GmbH Berlin Heidelberg
Co-published by Tsinghua University Press, Beijing and Springer-Verlag GmbH Berlin Heidelberg

Springer is a part of Springer Science+Business Media
springer.com

Cover design: Frido Steinen-Broo, EStudio Calamar, Spain
Printed on acid-free paper

Preface

Urban and regional planners develop and evaluate plans for communities—the places we live, work, interact, and entertain on a daily basis. Their responsibilities require skills of retrieving, analyzing and presenting data. One of the required courses in all planning programs is planning methods. While teaching such a course we feel the need for a text book that provides an up-to-date introduction to the fundamental methods related to planning and human services delivery. In specific, this book describes methods used in four areas: demographic analysis, economic analysis, land use analysis, and transportation analysis.

Many people have been helpful and supportive throughout this endeavor. Up front are our families who understood and supported us during the period. Andrea Yang, Rainer's wife and also a planner, edited various chapters. David Edelman and Wolfgang Preiser provided suggestions for the content of this book and excellent insights and guidance whenever we asked for. We are grateful for the release time that David Edelman, the School Director, gave us on behalf of the entire School of Planning faculty.

We would like to thank Dr. Stefan Rayer, Dr. Chen-Ping Yang and Dr. Zhongren Peng, who took time from their busy schedule to review various chapters. Dr. Rayman Mohamed used some preliminary chapters in his planning methods class and gave us valuable feedback. Their comments and suggestions significantly improved the book.

Our graduate students in the School of Planning, University of Cincinnati, S. Madi Fusco, Elisabeth Kramer, Tony Bonanno, Tatiana Kosheleva, and Nikita Jones prepared data, exercises, and edited the text. Many other students in the research method classes also commented to the manuscript.

We also wish to thank Dr. Donglu Shi, for his collaboration throughout the process.

Xinhao Wang and Rainer vom Hofe
Cincinnati, Ohio, USA

Contents

List of Figures

List of Tables

Chapter 1   Introduction: Planning Research Methods

1.1   Planning

Planning is a profession that is concerned with shaping our living environment. Frenchman (2000) observes that the profession of planning is alive and more plans have been made recently than ever before. As an example, a comprehensive plan sets the basis of land use policies and guides a community from where it is today to where we want it to be in the future. As the concept of sustainable development and the need for public involvement in planning by diverse groups become more widely accepted among politicians, policy-makers and the general public, it is critical to incorporate impact assessment and analysis into the planning and decision-making process. During such a process, planners bring stakeholders together (e.g., elected officials, business representatives, developers, community groups, residents, etc.) to set development goals and policies (e.g., what are we trying to achieve and how?). To do so, all stakeholders in a community should work together to analyze, compare, contrast and prioritize different development alternatives for a sustainable future (Smith et al., 2000; Wang, 2001). Planners, in particular, have the responsibility of gathering and evaluating available data, as well as accurately presenting future consequences of different action proposals to all stakeholders (Halls, 2001).

Alternatives of future actions are ultimately formulated from the evaluation of stakeholders' input on development goals and policies. Planning can take place at various scales. At the neighborhood scale, planning may help empower a community to deal with appropriate service deliveries, such as initializing a neighborhood revitalization project, creating a thriving, pedestrian-friendly environment, promoting mixed-use land developments and building an economically attractive environment for businesses.

Planning may also occur at a large geographic scale such as a metropolitan area. Regional planning is the term often used when the planning focus goes beyond the neighborhood level. Portland, USA, is often revered as an example of good planning on a larger geographic scale. Portland's planning success is partly attributable to the establishment of an "urban growth boundary" in conjunction with the implementation of a light rail system. Portland's successful revitalization of the Rose Quarter neighborhood, on the other hand, would be an example of good neighborhood planning.

Planners may work for the public sector (e.g., in the United States, city, county, state and federal governments), the nonprofit sector (e.g., neighborhood or special interest organizations), or the private sector (e.g., consulting firms). Planners' responsibilities vary widely. Planners may work as generalists, engaging in many types of issues for a specific geographic region, or they may be specialized in one subject field. The issues planners face may be related to land use, economic development, transportation, environment, urban design, housing or social equity.[1]

Independent of the geographic scales, the sectors, or the subject fields, all planning efforts have a strong commonality: planning professionals can affect the future of a community with their abilities to understand the history of the community, to respond to the forces for growth, and to anticipate the future of the social, economic, environmental and cultural status of a community. We cannot develop a plan for an area before we understand it (Isserman, 2000).

1.2 Planning Analysis

Responsible planning entails a solid understanding and competence of the comprehensive and complex community features, including the physical, economic, and social factors that influence a community's future. There are two broad entities that form the core of the planning profession: (1) the social, behavioral and cultural relationships between people and (2) the form and quality of the built or natural environment. An effective planner must have communication skills, expertise in one or more subject areas and dedication to the harmony between humans and the environment. In addition, the complexity of planning problems often requires planners to acquire qualitative and quantitative analytical skills in order to make sound, justified recommendations. It is necessary to understand how humans and the environment interrelate in order to plan long-term visions that would lead to a better future for a community.

The importance of planning analysis as the basis of the planning process has long been widely acknowledged (Bracken, 1981). Many research studies have explored the potential of using a geographic information system (GIS) to store spatial data, to perform interactive spatial analysis, to sketch a city and to display data and modeling results through maps and tables (i.e., Singh, 1999; Batty, et al., 1999; Brail and Klosterman, 2001). Klosterman (1999) elevated the GIS application by developing a scenario-based, policy-oriented planning support system (PSS), "What If?" that used GIS data to support community-based processes of collaborative planning and collective decision-making. To take the advantage of the development of computing technology, this textbook introduces several

---

[1] Association of Collegiate Schools of Planning, Guide to Graduate and Undergraduate Education in Urban and Regional Planning, 11th ed.

common methods in the planning analytical toolbox. We have written this book with the following objectives in mind.

The first objective is to present a wide variety of urban and regional planning analytical methods. The strength of this book lays in the detailed explanation of selected analytical methods. Since this is a text book on planning research methods, students will apply the methods with hands-on exercises using real world data. Planning professionals will also find the book is an invaluable reference.

The second objective is to present these selected analytical methods in a manner that will allow the readers to apply individual methods on their own. The book emphasizes the theoretical foundation, data requirement, assumptions, limitations, and constraints of the analytical methods, using practical examples. We want to bring theory, data gathering and result interpretation together and prepare the readers for the rather difficult task of collecting the "right" data and using the "right" methods.

The third objective is to emphasize how different subject areas in planning relate to each other. More specifically, we want to demonstrate how the result of the analysis of one subject area may feed as input into the analysis of another subject area. For instance, a population projection may be used in a land use analysis in order to answer a question "Is there enough land to accommodate the projected population growth in the region?"

This textbook sets itself apart from other planning textbooks in the fact that it uses a holistic approach of presenting and combining a wide variety of selected planning methods in one textbook. There are an astonishing number of analytical methods applicable to the study of urban and regional development and human service delivery. Therefore, in this textbook, we keep the focus limited to four fundamental pillars of planning methods: (1) demographic analysis, (2) economic analysis, (3) land use analysis, and (4) transportation analysis. This book provides an up-to-date introduction to the fundamental of the research methods that aid planners in answering the "who", "what", "where", and "how" questions about human activities in a community: "Who are the people living here?" (demographic analysis); "In what activities are people involved?" (economic analysis); "Where in the region do these activities occur?" (land use analysis); and "How are people and their various activities connected spatially?" (transportation analysis).

1.3   The Illustrative Study Area—Boone County, Kentucky, USA

In addition to the detailed explanation of individual methods, we constantly remind the readers of the interrelation of these four areas of planning analysis. This more holistic approach is necessary because most planning issues stem from a number of issues involving several planning disciplines. Examining strategies in preparing a comprehensive plan is an example that different planning disciplines intersect. Comprehensive plans, often the foundation for local planning, envision a community's future development. Comprehensive plans may describe and prioritize where development will occur, when development is expected to occur, and who will be part of or be affected by the future development. Using a variety of analytical methods provides the means to better understand the past and the present, in order to make educated recommendations regarding how to predict the future. Such prediction shapes strategies to direct future growth of population and employment opportunities, and to provide adequate land and efficient transportation facilities to meet the anticipated demand.

Throughout this book, we primarily use Boone County, Kentucky, USA as the region to illustrate the use of various methods in practical real-world scenarios (Fig. 1.1). Using the same geographical region enables us to demonstrate how several planning methods may intersect with each other. Boone County, the northernmost county in the Commonwealth of Kentucky, is just across the Ohio River from Cincinnati, Ohio. When it was officially established in 1799, Boone County was primarily a rural county. In its early days, the county was isolated from its neighbor Cincinnati by the Ohio River, despite their relative proximity. Farming was the predominant activity and crops could be easily transported on

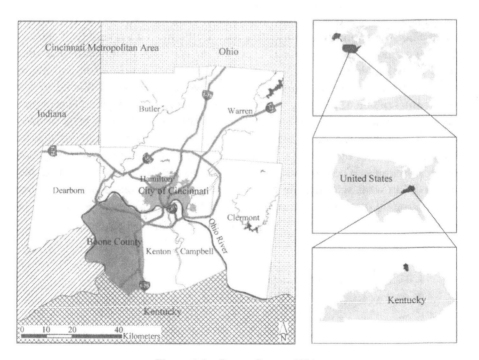

Figure 1.1 Boone County, USA

the Ohio River, which constitutes the northern and western border of the county. The average farm size for Boone County in the nineteenth century was around 100 acres, and cash crops included corn, soybeans, tobacco, and livestock. While agricultural activities were inherently a major part of Boone County's economy, it was the river trade that truly fueled the county's population growth, which increased modestly until the end of the nineteenth century. It wasn't until the twentieth century that Boone County's proximity to urban Cincinnati began to have inevitable effects. The industrial revolution was in full swing and Cincinnati provided many jobs, particularly in manufacturing, that paid good wages. Boone County's population started declining for decades as people migrated to Cincinnati for manufacturing jobs. This trend of migration began to reverse in the 1940s as integral transportation links were constructed within the county, including the Cincinnati/Northern Kentucky International Airport and Interstate Highway 71 and 75. The county's population is now expanding due to the increased accessibility. Today, Boone County is considered one of the fastest growing counties in Kentucky.[1]

Boone County has three incorporated cities: Florence, Union, and Walton. The 2000 Census indicates a total population of 85,991 with a total employment of 68,684.[2] This clearly shows that Boone County has not simply grown in terms of residents; it has also become an employment center. This is a result of being strategically located along I-71 and I-75; having the international airport and all of its support activities (e.g., couriers and messengers, storage and warehousing); having an over 100,000 square foot regional shopping mall with over 130 specialty retail stores; and being the home to some specialized manufacturing firms (e.g., frozen specialty foods and printing).

Despite it's recent rapid growth, parts of Boone County are still very rural. For example, the county enjoys a growing horse community in its rolling bluegrass hills. As one of the fifteen counties of the Cincinnati-Middletown metropolitan statistical area (MSA)[3], Boone County offers all the urban amenities while maintaining a relatively rural setting. However, Boone County is quickly growing out of its rural character. This growth, which has concentrated in the east of the county near the highway, is beginning to disseminate westward towards the more rural area. Since Boone County offers a large percentage of available land near urbanized Cincinnati, this rapid growth is projected to continue well into the future.

---

[1] Source: www.boonecountyky.org/history.htm.

[2] Source: Census Bureau and Bureau of Labor Statistics.

[3] The Cincinnati-Middletown OH-KY-IN Metropolitan Statistical Area includes the following counties: Dearborn, Franklin, and Ohio in Indiana; Boone, Bracken, Campbell, Gallatin, Grant, Kenton, and Pendleton in Kentucky; and Brown, Butler, Clermont, Hamilton, and Warren in Ohio. Source: Census Bureau, Metropolitan and Micropolitan Statistical Area Definitions.

1.4   Structure of the Book

This textbook is written as an introductory book for upper level undergraduates and graduate students. It includes mathematical equations at a level of complexity that non-mathematicians will be able to comprehend. As each new method is introduced, a scenario or application is presented. The best way to learn analytical methods is to study them in the context of an application-driven, real-world scenario. Since this textbook is an introductory text, it will not cover every analytical method in the greatest possible detail. Instead, it will provide students with enough conceptual and theoretical background to understand the principles and working mechanisms of the presented methods.

The book is divided into eight chapters. In addition to this chapter, Chapter 2 is a general presentation of the "three-step approach" of transforming observed phenomena (data) into constructive information which is used to help guide a decision-making process. The three steps are: data collection, data analysis, and data presentation. The distinction between different types of data, i.e., qualitative and quantitative data, the four levels of measurements, and the process of data aggregation are discussed. The discussion of data analysis focuses on basic statistical measurements, such as measures of central tendency and dispersion, and the basics of correlation and regression analysis. Part of the data analysis introduces the fundamentals of spatial analysis, including GIS which has increasingly been used in planning analysis. In the end of the chapter, the numerous ways of presenting data analysis results are described. Tables, charts, scatter diagrams, and maps are all ways to present data analysis results and findings in an appealing and easy to understand way.

Chapter 3 covers the fundamentals of demographic analysis, i.e., population size, distribution, composition (i.e., sex and age), and change over time. In the section on trend *extrapolation* methods, emphasis is placed on how past trends can be extrapolated into the near future for the sole purpose of projecting future population. The models discussed include easy to use extrapolation methods such as the share of growth and shift-share model, as well as more sophisticated population models such as the geometric and the logistic population model. The last section describes the principles of cohort-component model. Populations change naturally from births and death and through migration. Each of the three components is discussed in detail, including all the rates, i.e., fertility, survival, and migration rate. Each section brings empirical examples using Boone County's population and concludes with remarks on strengths and weaknesses of covered population models.

Chapter 4 is devoted to widely used analytical approaches built upon the concept of economic base analysis. The conceptual framework of the economic base theory is explained with cross-references to the Keynesian macroeconomic framework. We will start with the simple task of putting together a regional economic profile of Boone County, Kentucky. The state of Boone County's economy is assessed by studying the economic base of the county at two points in time and comparing the county's economy to the economy of a larger benchmark region. Based on the notion of an economic dichotomy, several methods are described that allow the division of a regional economy into a basic sector, which is export-oriented, and a non-basic sector, which is locally-oriented. These methods include location quotient and minimum requirement method. Location quotient is one of the most widely used economic tools in planning to distinguish basic and non-basic sectors. The economic base multiplier is discussed in detail as it provides the means of assessing the regional economic impacts with selected key variables, such as employment, following an initial change in the basic sector. This chapter concludes with the introduction of the shift-share analysis which focuses on explaining the reasons for economic growth or decline in selected industry sectors.

Chapter 5 is an introduction to the fundamentals of input-output analysis. The chapter stresses the importance of the input-output analysis as a valuable tool for planners in the context of economic development and its value as an instrument for economic impact analysis. The chapter begins by explaining the theoretical background of the input-output framework and how input-output tables can be derived from economic accounts of firms and businesses. The input-output table and its economic transactions are discussed in detail, which is followed by a step-by-step approach that shows how the input-output table and all its transactions can be used for building an economic impact model. The derivation of input-output based multipliers is described in the context of the type I output multiplier. The notion of the open versus the closed model is explained and subsequently the type II output multiplier is derived. Additionally, household income multipliers, income multipliers, household employment multipliers, and employment multipliers are calculated using the same database for the open, as well as the closed, economic framework. The chapter concludes with a discussion of assumptions and weaknesses of the input-output framework and the introduction of the social accounting matrix (SAM), which is an extension of the input-output framework.

Chapter 6 focuses on several aspects of land use analysis. Because of the close interrelationship of land with human activities, such as employment, residential, and recreational use, land use analysis plays a key role in rapidly growing areas with increasing demand for more land to be developed. Land use analysis provides the means to categorize current uses of land, to evaluate potential land use change within the existing legal framework, and to assess various impacts of proposed land use changes such as environmental, economic, traffic, services, or aesthetic impacts. This chapter begins with a manifestation of the land-human relationship and explains the concept of land use intensity. The increasing intensity of human activities is used as basis to explain the comprehensive phenomenon of societal change in the context of urbanization.

Different land classification schemes, which distinguish between different human activities at various levels of intensity, are introduced. Land use mapping is introduced as a way of graphically presenting the land-human relationship. Land suitability analysis is presented as a tool to identify developable land parcels under consideration of physical constraints (i.e., slope, soil, groundwater aquifer, and flood plain), access constraints (i.e., distances to roads, surface waters, sewer lines, or water lines), and cost/benefit of the development. Accordingly, land suitability analysis is described in detail as a systematic eight-step procedure to identify developable land. Considering the increasing availability of land use databases in a GIS format, the concepts of land suitability analysis are also explained using GIS.

Chapter 7 deals with the last of the four planning methods presented in this book—transportation analysis. There is much written on this subject by planners, economists and engineers alike, and we do not attempt to provide full coverage of transportation analysis. Today, transportation analysis, and therefore transportation models, are widely used and have achieved a high level of sophistication and complexity. Almost all larger metropolitan areas use transportation models to some extent. Transportation models often are developed and calibrated to reflect the very region-specific aspects of transportation systems. Nevertheless, many of these models are built on similar principles which often have a long-standing tradition in transportation analysis. As such, this chapter begins with an explanation of basic concepts in transportation analysis. For instance, the notion of nodes, links, traffic volume, average daily traffic (ADT), average peak hour traffic (PHV), and traffic analysis zones (TAZ) are described. The main part of this chapter is a description of what is commonly referred to as the traditional 4-step travel demand modeling process: trip production, trip distribution, mode choice, and trip assignment. This chapter must be seen as a basic, but essential, introduction to the traditional process of travel demand analysis. We want to emphasize the importance of understanding these basic principles of travel demand analysis for continued and more sophisticated studies in travel forecasting.

The significance of a holistic approach to analyze a study region is reemphasized in Chapter 8, which recaps and synthesizes previously discussed analytical planning methods. Although the chapter does not add much to concepts and principles of planning analytical methods, it is what we considered our favorite chapter. Like most planners, we prefer to actually get our hands dirty and do some real-world analysis instead of only talking about assumptions, strengths, and shortcomings of these methods. This last chapter brings together many planning methods presented throughout the book in an applied manner. Using a more holistic approach demonstrates how these four areas of planning analyses—demographic, economic, land use, and transportation analysis—can complement each other and therefore give analysts a more comprehensive understanding of the characteristics and dynamics of a community.

Along with the advancement of computers, we have seen many powerful software packages that can perform sophisticated planning analyses. In the literature, scholars have demonstrated the power of computers in planning application (Brail, 1987; Cartwright, 1993; Huxhold et al., 1997). Cartwright (1993) summarizes the advantages of spreadsheets as easy to program and easy to modify. Therefore, a user can be more likely to understand how a model works. For those experienced with spreadsheet software, none of these planning analyses will be much of a challenge; and, with the data provided everybody should be able to replicate the demonstrated analyses.

Section one shows the step-by-step approach of a cohort-component population projection for Boone County, including how to build the Boone County population pyramid, a straightforward task that sometimes can be quite a challenge to format. The next section demonstrates how land suitability analysis can be used for household allocation modeling. More specifically, how can we determine if there is enough land to accommodate the projected population growth, and if so, where would the proper locations for the new residential development be? A detailed example of an economic impact analysis for a hypothetical employment increase in Transportation and Warehousing sector in Boone County is described in the third section.

While commercially available software packages would simplify the task, we decided to do the entire input-output analysis in spreadsheet format. This should add more to the understanding of the working mechanism of input-output analysis. Such knowledge will help the readers to avoid errors when they interpret analytical results. Particularly, we show how to build an input-output table, which looks like the ones in standard textbooks, based on a commercially available database. The derivation of the output, income, and employment multipliers is demonstrated step-by-step, followed by an interpretation of results on this hypothetical impact scenario.

The last section concludes with an example on trip generation and trip distribution. We will use illustrative numbers to go through the process in spreadsheet. Readers will experience the meaning of balancing trip production and trip attraction. In the end, we will calculate the number of additional trips generated following the hypothetical employment increase and how these additional trips affect the trip generation in other traffic zones.

The chapters are arranged so that this textbook can be used in a course in the quarter system as well as the semester system. To permit an appropriate coverage of relevant analytical methods, we suggest chapters 3, 4, 6, and 7 be used as the core material. If time permits, chapter 5 might be helpful in explaining the nuts and bolts of economic impact analysis while chapter 8 brings detailed descriptions on how planning analytical methods can be carried out.

References

Batty, M., M. Dodge, B. Jiang and A. Smith. 1999. Geographical Information Systems and urban design. In: J. Stillwell, S. Geertman and S. Openshaw (eds). *Geographical Information and Planning.* Berlin: Springer-Verlag.

Bracken, Ian. 1981. *Urban Planning Methods: Research and Policy Analysis.* London: Methuen & Co. Ltd.

Brail, Richard K. and Richard E. Klosterman (eds). 2001. *Planning Support Systems: Integrating Geographic Information Systems, Models, and Visualization Tools.* Redlands: ESRI Press.

Brail, Richard K. 1987. *Microcomputers in Urban Planning and Management.* New Brunswick, NJ: Rutgers, The State University of New Jersey.

Cartwright, Timothy J. 1993. *Modeling the World in a Spreadsheet.* Baltimore, MD: Johns Hopkins University Press.

Frenchman, Dennis. 2000. Planning shapes urban growth and development. In: Lloyd Bodwin and Bishwapriya Sanyal (eds). *The Profession of City Planning.* New Brunswick, NJ: Center for Urban Policy Research, Rutgers, The State University of New Jersey.

Halls, P.J. 2001. Geographic information science: innovation driven by application. *Computers. Environment and Urban Systems*, 25(1), 1 – 4.

Huxhold, William E., Patrick S. Tierney, David R. Turnpaugh, Bryan J. Maves and Kevin T. Cassidy. 1997. *GIS County User Guide.* New York: Oxford University Press.

Isserman, Andrew M. 2000. Economic base studies for urban and regional planning. In: Lloyd Bodwin and Bishwapriya Sanyal (eds.). *The Profession of City Planning.* New Brunswick, NJ: Center for Urban Policy Research, Rutgers, The State University of New Jersey.

Klosterman, Richard E. 1999. The what if? collaborative planning support system. *Environment and Planning B: Planning and Design*, 26: 393 – 408.

Singh, R. R. 1999. Sketching the city: a GIS-based approach. *Environment And Planning B: Planning And Design*, 26: 455 – 468.

Smith, J., J. Blake and A. Davies. 2000. Putting sustainability in place: sustainable communities projects in Huntingdonshire. *Journal of Environmental Policy and Planning*, 2(3): 211 – 223.

Wang, Xinhao. 2001. Integrating water quality management and land use planning in a watershed context. *Journal of Environmental Management*, 61(1): 25 – 36.

Chapter 2   Data and Data Presentation

Planning is a process that designs a plan of action or evaluates the impact of a proposed action to achieve a desirable future. During this process planners often obtain the necessary data from different sources, analyze them efficiently and comprehensively, and present the results in easily understandable forms. The rationale for such a process is that public policy and decision makers derive their decisions based on the anticipated future from knowledge about the present and the past of a community. The three-step procedure—data collection, analysis, and presentation has the goal of accurately presenting the information to reflect what has happened and what may happen.

It is worthwhile to distinguish the difference between data and information. Through observations, experiments and measurements, we collect data about the objects we are interested in. In another word, data represents the facts about the objects. Although unavoidable, the affect of personal judgment should be kept to minimum. Ideally, data should be the same regardless of who collects them. In reality, data collection is both a science and an art. There is abundant literature discussing data and data collection. In this book, we will assume that data are available and represent real world phenomenon well.

Information is our interpretation of the data. This is the process of summarizing data into a form that people can easily understand what real world features those data may represent. Figure 2.1 illustrates the process of converting data into information. There are large quantities of data. Each data value describes one feature of the object which we are interested in. Data aggregation summarizes data into groups in order to reduce the data quantity to manageable categories. Data analysis explores and describes the distribution patterns within a category and the relationships between the categories to generate information. Finally, the presentation process applies various forms of media and formats to inform the analytical results to the audience. We will discuss the three components in detail in later sections.

Data can be numbers, text, photos or other forms of records that describe the status and behavior of a subject. Data are collected through various forms of research, such as surveys, observations, experiments, or interviews. A researcher can collect data as part of the project or use data collected by others, which is called secondary data. For example, we may use a survey method to collect data about people's opinions on a proposed shopping center. Figure 2.2 lists the data from a survey of 40 people. The data values are "For" or "Against". Some examples

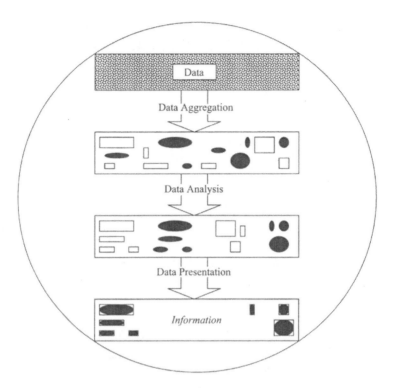

Figure 2.1   The process of converting raw data into information

For	For	For	Against	Against	Against	Against	For	Against	Against
For	For	Against	For	For	Against	Against	For	For	For
For	For	For	Against	For	For	For	For	Against	Against
Against	Against	Against	Against	For	For	Against	Against	For	Against

Figure 2.2   Survey data of 40 people on a proposed shopping center

of the data we will use in this book are population and economic numbers, land use maps and traffic counts.

2.1   Data

Data must first be organized by variables in order to be useful (De Vaus, 2002). For example, the data shown in Fig. 2.2 are all about people's opinions toward the proposed shopping center. The variable is therefore named as "attitude about the proposed shopping center." Using the variable terminology, data are the variable values obtained from observations. Variable values, which reflect the characteristic or quality of an object, can be text or numbers. To make a variable useful in a study the variable values must show variation. That is, the range of possible values should be wide enough to describe the differences. In the shopping center example, the variable has two values, "For" and "Against", that represent the differences of opinions.

Let's look at another example. When a planner prepares a community plan, one of the first tasks is to analyze the population characteristics. The United States Census Bureau conducts a census count every decade and publishes the results in summarized form. For example, the population in Boone County, Kentucky in 2000 was 85,991. Among them, 43,492 were female and 42,499 were male. These three numbers are derived from data about individuals. In this case, the 85,991 pieces of data were summarized into three numbers, which provide information about population in Boone County. The reduction from 85,591 to 3 is quite significant. Further, a reader can easily know the Boone County population size from these numbers, which would be difficult to derive from the original data.

This data can be further processed. For example, when we divide the ratio of female to male population:

$$\text{Ratio} = 43,492 \: / \: 42,499 = 1.02$$

Then, we can use this one number to describe that there are about 2% more females than males in Boone County. In this example, two variables were used from census—gender and county. For the gender variable, the possible values are male and female. For the county variable, the possible values are the collection of counties in the United States. In the end, a third variable, female to male ratio, is used to describe the gender composition in a county. This example shows a simple example of data process.

Figure 2.3 shows that data can be divided into two types—quantitative and qualitative. We can simply interpret the two data types as numeric and nonnumeric data (Babbie, 2004). Qualitative data, also called categorical data, describe the characters of the object of interest. The "For" or "Against" the shopping center are examples of qualitative data. Quantitative data are numerical values, which can be further divided into discrete and continuous data (Johnson

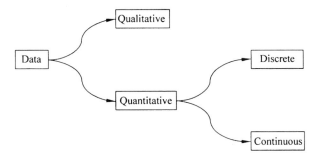

Figure 2.3   Illustration of data types

and Kuby, 2004). Discrete data are integers and continuous data have decimals. Discrete data normally are related to counts, such as the female population in a county. Continuous data are measures of certain features, such as the amount of residential land in a county measured in square kilometers. Different data types represent the variations of a variable with different detail levels, which is called level of measurement.

2.1.1 Level of Measurement

The basic requirement for the aggregation of a single variable data is that the categories resulting from the aggregation should be exhaustive and mutually exclusive. This means that any variable value should always belong to one and only one category. The categories can be represented in four levels of measurement from lowest to highest—nominal, ordinal, interval and ratio. These four levels reflect the different extents of measuring variation. Table 2.1 illustrates the progress of the four levels of measurement.

Table 2.1   The progress of the four levels of measurement

	Difference	Order	Known Difference	True Zero
Nominal	×			
Ordinal	×	×		
Interval	×	×	×	
Ratio	×	×	×	×

At the **nominal level of measurement**, the lowest level of measurement, the focus is to show the "difference" among variable values. An example of a nominal level of measurement is land use categories as shown in Table 2.2. Each land use code represents a land use category, such as urban, agricultural, or rangeland. Normally, the code is represented with a word or a letter. Even though sometimes numbers are used they still only reflect the difference. In Table 2.2 Tundra is represented with the number 8 and Forest Land with the number 4. It does not imply that Tundra is twice as large as Forest Land.

Table 2.2   Anderson Level I land use land cover classification

Code	Description	Code	Description
1	Urban or Built-up Land	6	Wetland
2	Agricultural Land	7	Barren Land
3	Rangeland	8	Tundra
4	Forest Land	9	Perennial Snow or Ice
5	Water		

At the **ordinal level of measurement**, variable values are expressed in categories that can be ranked. For any two values in different categories, one can tell which has a higher value. Table 2.3 lists population rates in the eight OKI counties. Warren and Boone Counties are labeled as "High Increase" and that for Campell and Kenton Counties are "Low Increase". The information from this level of measurement demonstrates that (1) Warren and Boone Counties have different population growth rates than the Campbell and Kenton Counties; (2) the difference between Warren and Boone Counties, or between Campbell and Kenton Counties are insignificant; and (3) Warren and Boone Counties grow at a faster rate than Campbell and Kenton Counties.

Table 2.3   1990 – 2000 population growth rates in OKI counties (ordinal level)

County	State	Population Growth Rates
Boone	Kentucky	High Increase
Butler	Ohio	Moderate Increase
Campbell	Kentucky	Low Increase
Clermont	Ohio	Moderate Increase
Dearborn	Indiana	Moderate Increase
Hamilton	Ohio	Low Decline
Kenton	Kentucky	Low Increase
Warren	Ohio	High Increase

At the **interval level of measurement**, a variable is measured with numerical values. The actual difference between two values has specific meaning. For example, the first zoning ordinance was introduced in New York City in 1916[1]. And, a similar ordinance was adopted in Shanghai in 1929 (Huang, 2001). This level of measurement can be interpreted as (1) the two cities adopted a zoning ordinance at different years (nominal level); (2) New York City adopted its zoning ordinance before Shanghai City (ordinal level); and (3) Shanghai adopted its zoning ordinance 13 years after New York City (interval level).

In addition to all the features of the interval level of measurement the **ratio level of measurement**, which is the highest level of measurement, implies that the values are measured against a meaningful zero value. For example, the highway length in municipality A can be described as twice as long as municipality B if the total highway length in municipality A is 500 kilometers and in municipality B it is 250 kilometers.

In the following example, we can see how to measure a variable at the four different levels. To measure the variable, population by county, at the ratio level,

---

[1] The 1916 Zoning Resolution became a model for urban communities throughout the United States. http://www.nyc.gov/html/dcp/html/zone/zonehis.html

we need to know exact population counts for each county. Part I of Table 2.4 contains 2,000 population for the eight OKI counties. For example, there are 85,991 people in Boone County, 845,303 in Hamilton County (where the City of Cincinnati is located) and 332,807 in Butler County. From those population numbers, we can see that Butler County is about 4 times as large as Boone County and Hamilton County is three times of Butler County. This ratio is meaningful because the number zero means no people living in a county.

Table 2.4 2000 population in OKI counties

County	State	Population 2000	County	State	Population 2000
Part I : Ratio Level			Part III : Ordinal Level		
Boone	Kentucky	85,991	Boone	Kentucky	Medium
Butler	Ohio	332,807	Butler	Ohio	Large
Campbell	Kentucky	88,616	Campbell	Kentucky	Medium
Clermont	Ohio	177,977	Clermont	Ohio	Medium
Dearborn	Indiana	46,109	Dearborn	Indiana	Small
Hamilton	Ohio	845,303	Hamilton	Ohio	Large
Kenton	Kentucky	151,464	Kenton	Kentucky	Medium
Warren	Ohio	158,383	Warren	Ohio	Medium
Part II : Interval Level			Part IV: Nominal		
Boone	Kentucky	− 91,986	Boone	Kentucky	A
Butler	Ohio	154,830	Butler	Ohio	B
Campbell	Kentucky	− 89,361	Campbell	Kentucky	A
Clermont	Ohio	0	Clermont	Ohio	A
Dearborn	Indiana	− 131,868	Dearborn	Indiana	C
Hamilton	Ohio	667,326	Hamilton	Ohio	B
Kenton	Kentucky	− 26,513	Kenton	Kentucky	A
Warren	Ohio	− 19,594	Warren	Ohio	A

Part II of Table 2.4 is an example of the interval level of measurement. We used Clermont as the base to compare 2000 population in the OKI eight counties. From the table, we can see that Boone County's population is less than that of Clermont County by 91,986 people while Butler County's population is 154,830 more than that of Clermont County. At this level of measurement, the number "0" for Clermont County does not mean zero population. It only represents a relative point of measurement. Therefore, we cannot derive the population ratio between any two counties.

If all we want to know is the order of the counties by population, we can measure the population variable at the ordinal level. As shown in Part III of Table 2.4, the counties are labeled "Large", "Medium", or "Small" according to county population. At this level, we can confidently say that Hamilton County is larger than Boone County, although we do not know by how many more people.

If the research only requires us to know which counties are similar in size, a measurement at the nominal level would be sufficient. In this case, we can assign letters "A", "B", and "C" to the three groups of counties. From Part IV of Table 2.4, we can quickly conclude that Boone County is similar in size to four other counties. Hamilton and Butler counties are similar in size and Dearborn County is unlike any of other counties in terms of population size. However, we are unable to tell which county is bigger.

There are two important issues related to the Levels of Measurement. First, the higher the level, the more effort is required for measurement, data storage and analysis; therefore, it will require more funding and time. In the country population example, little effort is required to compare the sizes of Boone County and Hamilton County at the nominal level—they are different (Part IV in Table 2.4). The variable value for Boone Country is "A" and the variable value for Hamilton Country is "B". However, it will require a lot more effort to compare the two counties at the ratio level. We must search for population data for the two counties (Part I in Table 2.4). With these data, we can say that the population size in Hamilton County is about 10 times as large as that in Boone County.

The second issue is that a measure at a higher level can be converted to a lower level while the other way is impossible. Let's use the county population example again. If all we know is at the nominal level of measurement, as shown in Part IV of Table 2.4, we cannot derive a higher level of measurement, such as knowing which group represents larger population size. On the other hand, once we have the numerical population values, we can measure population at any of the four levels. We would like to offer one word of caution about changing the level of measurement. As we see in Table 2.4, the conversion from interval level to ordinal level requires a researcher's judgment. We used a criterion that any county with population greater than 300,000 is a large county. Therefore, Butler County and Hamilton County are in the "Large" category. If we change the criterion to 170,000, then Clermont County also will be in the "Large" category.

With the knowledge of the level of measurement for a variable, we can decide how to interpret the variable data. Because computers are much more efficient with numbers than text, nominal variable values are often stored as numbers. When you know that a measure is nominal, you will only use the numerical values as category identifiers. The knowledge of the level of measurement also helps you decide what statistical analysis to use. Certain analysis, such as calculating the mean, would not be applicable to a variable at the nominal level of measurement. Now we have discussed the four levels of measurement. How do we decide when to use what level of measurement? For certain variables, it is easy to decide. For example, the land use variable can only be measured at the nominal level. For some other variables, the measurement can be made at several levels. Therefore, the decision should be made according to the goal of study. A rule of thumb is to use the lowest level of measurement that satisfies the study goal. If you are not sure then use a higher level than the one you think might be sufficient.

2.1.2   Data Aggregation

Data aggregation is a process of grouping individual variable values. There are many different options of data aggregation. Let's look at three of them. The first option is to group data based on the values of a single variable. We call this reclassification. The second option is to group data based on another variable. We call it sectoral aggregation. The third option of data aggregation is to group data by their spatial locations.

2.1.2.1   Reclassification

Reclassification is a process that aggregates data at the current or lower levels of measurement in order to reduce the data amount and achieve satisfactory analytical quality. For example, residential land in a municipality is measured at the nominal level as high density residential, rural density, residential, and medium density residential. If a study does not require the detail of different residential land uses we may reclassify these three values into a single value—residential land. This could significantly reduce the data size without affecting the analytical result.

For numerical variable values, there are different ways of reclassification. The most commonly used reclassification methods are cluster, quantile and equal interval. The cluster approach ranks data based on the values and measures the distance between two adjacent data pieces. The reclassification normally starts with the largest distance and moves down to the next largest distance. This process is repeated until the desired number of groups is reached. Using the quantile classification we will divide the data records into classes in a way that each group has an equal number of data pieces. Using the equal interval method we will first calculate the range of data values (maximum – minimum) and then divide the range by the number of groups to decide the break points.

Let's use the data in Table 2.5 to illustrate the three different classification methods. The table shows the 2000 population density by census tract in Boone County, Kentucky, USA. There are 16 census tracts in Boone County. We will reclassify the census tracts into four groups.

In Table 2.5, the "Tract" column stores the census tract identification number, the "Population" column is the 2,000 population. The census tracts are sorted by 2,000 population, from the lowest to highest. The "Order" column lists the rank order. When we use the quantile classification method, the rule is to assign equal numbers of census tracts to each group. In this case, four census tracts are assigned to each group, e.g., 16 tracts divided by 4 groups. The group assignment using the quantile method is stored in the "Quantile" column.

Table 2.5   2000 population by census tract in Boone County

Order	Tract	Population	Quantile	Equal Interval	Difference	Rank of Difference	Cluster
1	706.01	2,330	1	1			1
2	706.04	2,527	1	1	197	11	1
3	703.04	2,895	1	1	368	7	1
4	704.01	3,338	1	1	443	5	1
5	705.02	4,263	2	2	925	4	1
6	703.07	4,521	2	2	258	8	1
7	703.09	4,735	2	2	214	9	1
8	703.08	4,811	2	2	76	14	1
9	703.01	5,012	3	2	201	10	1
10	703.05	5,175	3	2	163	12	1
11	702	6,173	3	3	998	3	2
12	704.02	6,602	3	3	429	6	2
13	701	6,751	4	3	149	13	2
14	706.03	8,201	4	4	1,450	1	3
15	705.01	9,297	4	4	1,096	2	4
16	703.06	9,360	4	4	63	15	4

The rule of the equal interval method is to assign groups based on the data range. In the Boone County case, the lowest population is 2,330 and the highest population is 9,360. Therefore the range is 7,030 (= 9,360 – 2,330). When we divide the range by 4 groups, the data range for each group is 1,757.5 (7,030/4). Therefore, the break points for classification are 4,087.5, 5,845, and 7,602.5, respectively. The result of this classification method is stored in the "Equal Interval" column.

The rule for cluster classification is to divide data into groups at the largest difference between any two adjacent values. The column "Difference" in Table 2.5 saves the differences calculated from adjacent records. From which, we can see that the largest difference is 1,450, between census tracts 701 and 706.03. Consequently, the census tracts in Boone County are divided into two groups at this point. The first 13 census tracts are in Group One and the last three census tracts are in Group Two. Then we find the next largest difference is 1,096, between the 14th and the 15th census tracts. Therefore, we will break the second group here to make three groups. Similarly, we can separate the first group into two between the 10th and the 11th census tracts. Now we can stop the classification process since we have derived all four groups. Figure 2.4 displays the classification process graphically.

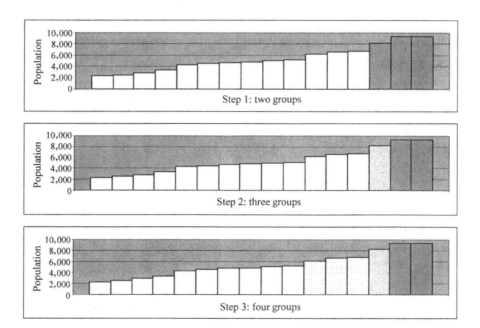

Figure 2.4   Classification process using the cluster method

The classification sometimes can be complicated by having to separate real differences from artificial differences imposed by the reclassification of a variable (Blackwell, 2001). The classification can even be subject to debate from the definition of each group category. For example, Robbin (2000) argues that the classification system for racial and ethnic data in the United States is a symbol of political conflict and the social construction of identity. The Office of Management and Budget (OMB) in 1977 issued Statistical Policy Directive Number 15, "Race and Ethnic Standards for Federal Statistics and Administrative Reporting." Four racial categories were established: American Indian or Alaskan Native, Asian or Pacific Islander, Black, and White. In addition, two ethnicity categories were established: Hispanic origin and Not of Hispanic origin (U.S. Census Bureau, 2000). The standards were revised in 1997.

The new standards have five categories for data on race: American Indian or Alaska Native, Asian, Black or African American, Native Hawaiian or Other Pacific Islander, and White. There are two categories for data on ethnicity: Hispanic or Latino, and Not Hispanic or Latino. OMB gave a reason for breaking apart the "Asian or Pacific islander" category into two categories as that under the old standards; Native Hawaiians comprise about three percent of the Asian and Pacific Islander population. By creating separate categories, the data on the Native Hawaiians and other Pacific Islander groups will no longer be overwhelmed by the aggregate data of the much larger Asian groups (OMB, 1997). The classification generally reflects a social definition of race recognized in the country.

2.1.2.2   Sectoral Aggregation

Sectoral aggregation is an example of grouping variable values based on the values of another variable. Depending on whether the variable we are interested in is discrete (count) or continuous, the aggregation is processed differently. For example, selected census variables for Boone County are listed in Table 2.6. The census tracts are classified into four groups based on the percent of renter occupied units. The "Population" variable represents the 2000 population for each census tract. The percent vacant unit is the third variable. In this case, population is an example of the discrete variable and "% of vacant units" is an example of continuous variable.

For a count variable such as "Population" in Table 2.6, we normally aggregate it by adding the data values. For example, we can add the population of the three census tracts where the percent of renter occupied units is less than 10. Table 2.7 shows the result that the total population in this group of census tracts is 12,594.

For a continuous variable we normally calculate the average value for the category. For example, we can calculate the mean percentage of vacant units for the census tracts with the same percent of renter occupied units. Table 2.8 shows the calculation for the less than 10% group.

Table 2.6   Boone County census data

Tract	% Renter Occupied Units	Population	% Vacant Units
701	4 (> – 31)	6,751	4.7
702	4 (> – 31)	6,173	4.9
703.01	4 (> – 31)	5,012	13.9
703.04	3 (21 – 30)	2,895	5.5
703.05	3 (21 – 30)	5,175	3.9
703.06	3 (21 – 30)	9,360	3.0
703.07	1 (<10)	4,521	5.3
703.08	3 (21 – 30)	4,811	6.7
703.09	1 (<10)	4,735	2.3
704.01	1 (<10)	3,338	7.2
704.02	2 (11 – 20)	6,602	4.0
705.01	3 (21 – 30)	9,297	7.5
705.02	2 (11 – 20)	4,263	8.0
706.01	2 (11 – 20)	2,330	10.7
706.03	2 (11 – 20)	8,201	9.2
706.04	2 (11 – 20)	2,527	4.9

Table 2.7   Aggregation of a discrete variable

Tract	% Renter Occupied Units	Population
703.07	1 (<10)	4,521
703.09	1 (<10)	4,735
704.01	1 (<10)	3,338
Total		12,594

Table 2.8   Aggregation of a continuous variable

Tract	% Renter Occupied Units	% Vacant Units
703.07	1 (<10)	5.3
703.09	1 (<10)	2.3
704.01	1 (<10)	7.2
Average		4.9

After we repeat the same calculations, we can derive the total population and mean percent of vacant units for all four groups in the country. The results are shown in Table 2.9.

Table 2.9   Total population and mean percentage of vacant units

% Renter Occupied Units	Number of Census Tracts	Population	% Vacant Units
1 (<10)	3	12,594	4.9
2 (11 – 20)	5	23,923	7.3
3 (21 – 30)	5	31,538	5.3
4 (> – 31)	3	17,936	7.8

2.1.2.3   Spatial Aggregation

Similar to the sectoral aggregation, spatial aggregation summarizes variable values based on another variable. Only this time the second variable represents a spatial dimension. Lets take a look at the map shown in Fig. 2.5. The sixteen census tracts in Boone County can be grouped into four County Census Divisions (CCDs). A CCD is a statistical area unit used by the U.S. Bureau of Census. The name of each CCD is based on a place, county, or well-known local name that identifies its location[1]. Through the spatial aggregation, the census tract level data can be summarized at the CCD level, as shown in Table 2.10.

---

[1] For further description of CCDs, visit the U.S. Census Bureau web site at: http://www.census.gov/geo/www/cob/cs_metadata.html

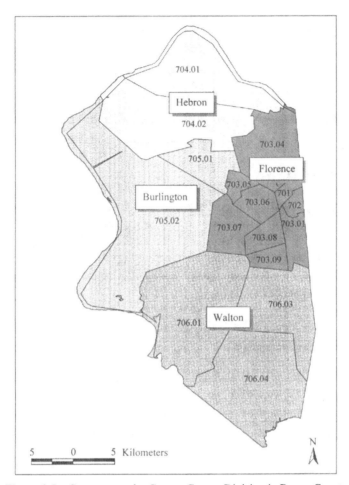

Figure 2.5   Census tracts by County Census Division in Boone County

Table 2.10   Census tracts by County Census Division (CCD) in Boone County

CCD_ Name	Number of Census Tracts	Area (sq · km)	Population	Population Density (people/ (sq · km))	Occupied Units	Renter Occupied Units	% Renter Occupied Units
Burlington	2	178.2	13,560	76	5,092	989	19
Florence	9	114.6	49,433	431	15,665	3,004	19
Hebron	2	139.8	9,940	71	4,305	1,082	25
Walton	3	233.1	13,058	56	6,196	2,971	48

The classification, sectoral aggregation, and spatial aggregation sometimes need to be used together in a study. Spencer (2004) gives an example in analyzing

23

antipoverty policies in the United States. The spatially concentrated poverty in U.S. is a major concern of the antipoverty policies. Some of the policies are place-based, such as to improve the infrastructure of a neighborhood. Other policies are people-based, which aims to empower the poor people. Spencer argues that a more powerful policy can be developed if the two dimensions—people and place—can be integrated in policy analysis. This is an example of classification being the basis for research on the multiple aspects of poor peoples' lives.

2.2 Data Analysis

Once data are collected and organized in a usable format, we need to summarize them for the purpose of generating ideas and supporting theories by identifying patterns, describing relationships and explaining causes. In this section, we will discuss four data analysis techniques that are applicable for analyzing quantitative data. In particular, they are: descriptive statistics, analysis of relationships, spatial analysis and comparative analysis.

2.2.1 Descriptive Statistics

Descriptive statistics provide simple ways to present large amounts of data with few limited summary variables. The two types of descriptive statistics commonly used in planning studies are: (1) measures of central tendency, which use one value to represent the average of a variable, and (2) measures of dispersion, which use one value to describe the extent of spread between the data points and the average.

2.2.1.1 Measures of Central Tendency

The three common measures of central tendency are mean, median and mode. The mean is calculated by adding the observed variable values and then dividing the total by the number of observations. Let's look at the % vacant units data in Table 2.6. A mean will tell us on average, what would be the proportion of renter-occupied units in a census tract. To calculate a mean, we need to add all the values together and divide the total by the number of values. The formula for calculating the mean can be expressed as:

$$\bar{x} = \frac{\sum x}{n} \tag{2.1}$$

where, $\bar{x}$ is the mean, $\sum x$ represents the total of x and n is the number of records. In the case of % vacant units in Boone County, there are 16 census tracts, $n = 16$. The sum of the percent vacant units of the 16 census tracts is 101.6%,

$$\sum x = 4.7\% + 4.9\% + 13.9\% + 5.5\% + 3.9\% + 3.0\% + 5.3\% + 6.7\%$$
$$+ 2.3\% + 7.2\% + 4.0\% + 7.5\% + 8.0\% + 10.7\% + 9.2\% + 4.9\%$$
$$= 101.6\%$$

Therefore the mean is 101.6% divided by 16, which is 6.3%,

$$\overline{x} = \frac{\sum x}{n} = \frac{101.6\%}{16} = 6.3\%$$

Median is the second measure of central tendency. By definition, median is the value of the data that occupies the middle position when the data are ranked. To derive the median, we need to rank the variable observations and find the value in the middle that divides the variable observations into two equal number groups. Therefore, for an odd number of observations, the single value in the middle position of the ranked variable values is the median. For an even number of observations, there are two values in the middle position of the ranked variable values and the mean of the two values is the median. Again, let's look at the % vacant units data in Table 2.6. We can sort the data records by the variable, % vacant units. The result is shown in Table 2.11. The two values in the middle, the 8th and 9th position, are 5.3% and 5.5%. The mean of the two values is (5.3% + 5.5%) / 2 = 5.4%. Therefore, the median of percent vacant units is 5.4%.

Table 2.11   Boone County census data sorted by %vacant units

Tract	% Vacant Units	Order	
703.09	2.3	1	
703.06	3.0	2	
703.05	3.9	3	
704.02	4.0	4	
701	4.7	5	
706.04	4.9	6	
702	4.9	7	
703.07	5.3	8	5.4%
703.04	5.5	9	
703.08	6.7	10	
704.01	7.2	11	
705.01	7.5	12	
705.02	8.0	13	
706.03	9.2	14	
706.01	10.7	15	
703.01	13.9	16	

It may be difficult to find the data record in the middle position when there are many data records. One simple approach is to calculate the depth of median (Johnson and Kuby, 2004):

$$d(\tilde{x}) = \frac{n+1}{2} \qquad (2.2)$$

where,

$d(\tilde{x})$ — the depth of the median;

n — the number of data records.

The calculation of median is different, depending if $d(\tilde{x})$ is an integer. If $d(\tilde{x})$ is an integer, one of the variable values is the median. If $d(\tilde{x})$ is not an integer, we need to use two variable values to calculate the median. When $d(\tilde{x})$ is an integer, let's use j to represent the position of the median. In this case, $j = d(\tilde{x})$. The variable value at the jth position is the median. When $d(\tilde{x})$ is not an integer, let's use j to represent the largest integer that is smaller than $d(\tilde{x})$ and k to represent the smallest integer that is larger than $d(\tilde{x})$. The two variable values needed are at the jth and kth positions. The median is the mean of the two values. We can illustrate this method to the data in Table 2.11.

$$d(\tilde{x}) = \frac{n+1}{2} = \frac{16+1}{2} = \frac{17}{2} = 8.5$$

The integer immediately smaller than 8.5 is 8 and the integer immediately larger than 8.5 is 9. Therefore, the median is the average of the 8th and 9th data values:

$$\tilde{x} = \frac{5.3 + 5.5}{2} = \frac{10.8}{2} = 5.4\%$$

The mode is the third measure of central tendency. It is the value or the category with the most frequent occurrence. From Table 2.6, we can see that two census tracts, 702 and 706.04, have 4.9% units being vacant. No other census tracts have same percent vacant units. In this case, the highest frequency is 4.9%, therefore, the mode for the percent vacant units is 4.9%.

Now we have calculated three different measures of central tendency. Figure 2.6 illustrates the original data and the three summary statistics—mean, median and mode. We can quickly notice that the three values are not the same. Most likely this is the result you will get for any dataset. It is very rare, although not impossible, that three measures are the same. Then which one is the best measure or which measure should we use in a study to represent a typical value? There is no simple answer to this question. It depends on the nature of your data and the purpose of your analysis (Babbie, 2002). You may remember that the mean is the arithmetic average value, the median is the value in the middle, and the mode is the most common value. If you know which of those features is the most important for your study, you should choose the appropriate measure accordingly. Otherwise, you may use all of them to describe your data, since they reflect different aspects of the same data. Collectively you may get a better understanding of the data.

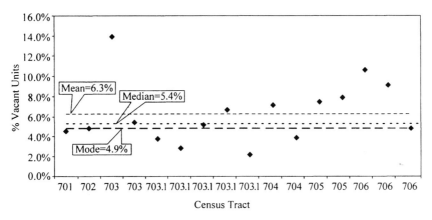

Figure 2.6   Comparison of mean, median and mode of percent of vacant units

We also need to understand the limitations of each of the three measures. The mean is sensitive to extreme values. A few very large or very small values may increase or decrease the mean significantly. In our example, the percent of vacant units (13.9%) in Census Tract 703.01 is much higher than other census tracts, contributes to the results of the mean value to be higher than the other two measures of central tendency. Should the percentage of vacant units in Census Tract 703.01 increase, while the variable values in all other census tracts remain the same, the mean of this variable would be even higher.

The median has its own limits. Assume a hypothetical city where 49% of residents travel one hour or longer to work every day and 48% residents only travel 5 minutes to work. About 3% residents travel 20 minutes to work. The median will be 20 minutes, which would hardly be a good representation of the travel time for the city residents.

Problems with the mode measure can be complicated. On the one hand, none of the variable values may occur more than others—a case that there is no mode. On the other hand, there may be multiple variable values that are equally popular— a case of multiple modes. Some people also call this as case of no mode.

We can conclude the discussion of measures of central tendency by saying that we need to carefully choose the measures of central tendency based on the research purpose. Knowing the differences will also help you understand people's choice of measures of central tendency in various studies. Finally, the limitations of these measures help us to see the needs for measures of dispersion.

2.2.1.2 Measures of Dispersion

Measures of dispersion are used to describe the variability of the distribution of data. The two common measures of dispersion are range and standard deviation. The range describes the difference between the smallest (L) and the largest (H) values of the data. In the case of % vacant units by census tract in Boone County, Tract 703.01 has the highest percentage, 13.9%, and Tract 703.09 has the lowest percentage, 2.3%. Therefore, the range is the difference between the two extremes, 11.6%.

$$\text{Range} = H - L = 13.9\% - 2.3\% = 11.6\%$$

While the range only uses the two extreme values to describe the data variability, standard deviation uses all data values in measuring data distribution around the mean. It is the square root of the squared deviations of the individual data about their mean.

Before we introduce the formula to calculate the standard deviation, we need to distinguish the difference between a sample and a population. Population is a collection of individuals or objects. Data analysis can help us to investigate the population properties. A sample is a subset of the population. Normally, the data we collect for analysis make up the sample. We can use data analysis to describe the sample. In statistical data analysis, this is called descriptive statistics. We can also estimate population properties from analyzing the sample data. This is called inferential statistics.

The following formula is for calculating the sample standard deviation:

$$s = \sqrt{\frac{\sum (x - \bar{x})^2}{n - 1}} \tag{2.3}$$

where,

    s — sample standard deviation;
    x — individual data in the sample;
    $\bar{x}$ — sample mean;
    n — sample size.

The formula for calculating the population standard deviation is:

$$\sigma = \sqrt{\frac{\sum (X - \mu)^2}{n}} \tag{2.4}$$

where,

    σ — population standard deviation;
    X — individual data in the population;

μ — population mean;

n — population size.

Applying these two formulas to the census tract data in Table 2.6, we derive that the sample standard deviation of the percent vacant units is 3.0% and the population standard deviation of the percent vacant units is 2.9%. Table 2.12 illustrates the calculation. For simplicity, we will first use the data as a sample for the calculation, and then use the same data as a population.

Table 2.12   Calculation of the mean and the standard deviation

Tract	% Vacant Units (x or X)	$(x - \bar{x})$ or $(X - \mu)$ (%)	$(x - \bar{x})^2$ or $(X - \mu)^2$ (%)
701	4.7	− 1.7	0.03
702	4.9	− 1.4	0.02
703.01	13.9	7.6	0.58
703.04	5.5	− 0.9	0.01
703.05	3.9	− 2.5	0.06
703.06	3.0	− 3.4	0.12
703.07	5.3	− 1.1	0.01
703.08	6.7	0.4	0.00
703.09	2.3	− 4.0	0.16
704.01	7.2	0.9	0.01
704.02	4.0	− 2.4	0.06
705.01	7.5	1.2	0.01
705.02	8.0	1.6	0.03
706.01	10.7	4.3	0.19
706.03	9.2	2.8	0.08
706.04	4.9	− 1.5	0.02
Total	101.7		1.39

From Table 2.12:

$$n = 16 \qquad \sum x = 101.6\% \qquad \bar{x} = 6.3\% \qquad (x - \bar{x})^2 = 1.38\%$$

Sample standard deviation

$$\sum (x - \bar{x})^2 / (n - 1) = 0.00092$$

$$s = \sqrt{\frac{\sum (x - \bar{x})^2}{n - 1}} = 3.0\%$$

Population standard deviation

$$\sum (X - \mu)^2 / n = 0.00086$$

$$\sigma = \sqrt{\frac{\sum (X - \mu)^2}{n}} = 2.9\%$$

The sample standard deviation is used in descriptive statistics as well as inferential statistics. In descriptive statistics, the sample standard deviation can

29

describe the distribution of the sample. In inferential statistics, the sample standard deviation can be used to estimate the population standard deviation. It is also used in making inference about other population parameters. Similarly, the population standard deviation can be used to describe the population distribution. With or without knowledge of a population's standard deviation can affect the methods used for two major applications of inferential statistics—parameter estimations and hypothesis testing (Johnson and Kuby, 2004).

Why do we need so many different types of descriptive statistics? To answer this question, we need to revisit the purpose of using descriptive statistics. As we mentioned earlier, the purpose of descriptive statistics is to describe a sample data with a few summary statistics. Each individual descriptive statistic can only describe one aspect of the characteristics of a group of values in the original dataset. Measures of central tendency alone cannot completely characterize a set of data. Two very different data sets may have similar measures of central tendency and different distribution. Depending on the purpose of a study, one descriptive statistic may be more suitable than others. Some studies may need to use multiple descriptive statistics to more fully describe the original data.

If the purpose of our study is to find an overall average value representing the data set, we are likely to use the mean. If the housing units are evenly distributed among the 16 census tracts, on average, 6.3% units are vacant. If we want to know the most common percent of vacant units by census tract in Boone County, we should use the mode. The median tells us that the percent vacant units in half of the census tracts are below and half are above 5.4%. Usually when people say average, they refer to the mean. In planning studies, we often use the median to represent the "average" for the reasons we mentioned earlier—the mean can be easily affected by one or a few data that are very much different from the rest. We call them outliers. The outliers will not affect the median. For example, let's assume a community with 500 households. If the income for 475 households have an annual income of $10,000 and the other 25 households, $100,000 each, the mean households will be:

$$\frac{475 \times 10,000 + 25 \times 100,000}{500} = \$14,500$$

This income figure is higher than 95% of the households in the community. For the same community, the median is $10,000, which is a more representative of the community.

2.2.2 Analysis of Relationships

The analysis of relationships involves more than one variable. The simplest form is bivariate analysis, in which the relationship of two variables is the focus. Here we discuss the commonly used bivariate analyses—correlation and regression. It is important to notice that correlation is used to determine if there is any relationship between two variables. Regression is used to determine how independent variable(s) affects a dependent variable. The following paragraphs briefly describe the two analyses. More detailed discussion can be found in almost any statistics text book.

The outcome of a correlation analysis is to calculate the strength and the direction of the linear relationship between two variables. A common correlation analysis is to calculate the linear correlation coefficient for ordered pairs of continuous numerical variables (measured at the interval or ratio level of measurement). The Pearson's product moment, $r, (-1$ to $+1)$ is a measure of the strength of a linear relationship between two variables. The formula to calculate r is expressed as:

$$r = \frac{\sum (x - \bar{x})(y - \bar{y})}{(n-1)s_x s_y} \tag{2.5}$$

where,

r — pearson's product moment;

n — sample size;

x — data for variable x;

$\bar{x}$ — mean of x;

s_x — standard deviation of x;

y — data for variable y;

$\bar{y}$ — mean of y;

s_y — standard deviation of y.

Figure 2.7 displays the relationship between the r value and the linear relationship. We need to pay attention to two aspects of the correlation coefficient. The sign represents the direction of the correlation. A negative value reflects a negative correlation, which means that the increase of values of the first variable is associated with the decrease of values of the second variable. A positive correlation indicates that the two variables change in the same direction. A value of zero means that the two variables do not have linear relationship. That is, the change of one variable is not linearly related to the change of the other variable. A value of 1 or -1 reflects that the linear relationship between the two variables is a perfect straight line. The closer the coefficient is to the two extreme values, the stronger the linear relationship between the two variables. In general, a correlation coefficient between 0.8 and 1 or between -1 and -0.8 is considered

Figure 2.7 Linear correlation coefficient and the strength of the linear correlation

as strong correlation. A value between −0.5 and 0.5 is an indication of weak correlation.

Let's use the data in Table 2.13 to examine the relationship between population density and the percentage of vacant units by census tract in Boone County. The r value is calculated as −0.37. The analysis indicates that the two variables are negatively related and the linear relationship is not very strong.

Table 2.13   Data for correlation analysis

Tract	Population Density (people/(sq·km)) (x)	% Vacant Units (y)	$x - \bar{x}$	$y - \bar{y}$	$(x-\bar{x})\cdot(y-\bar{y})$
701	1,468	4.7	1,010	− 1.7	− 16.96
702	1,470	4.9	1,012	− 1.4	− 14.51
703.01	425	13.9	− 33	7.6	− 2.48
703.04	73	5.5	− 385	− 0.9	3.29
703.05	892	3.9	435	− 2.5	− 10.68
703.06	851	3.0	394	− 3.4	− 13.35
703.07	229	5.3	− 228	− 1.1	2.49
703.08	481	6.7	24	0.4	0.09
703.09	623	2.3	166	− 4.0	− 6.66
704.01	51	7.2	− 406	0.9	− 3.48
704.02	88	4.0	− 369	− 2.4	8.75
705.01	432	7.5	− 25	1.2	− 0.29
705.02	27	8.0	− 430	1.6	− 7.06
706.01	24	10.7	− 433	4.3	− 18.72
706.03	152	9.2	− 305	2.8	− 8.54
706.04	30	4.9	− 427	− 1.5	6.27

$$\bar{x} = 457 \quad \bar{y} = 6.3\%$$
$$s_x = 488 \quad s_y = 3.0\%$$
$$n = 16 \quad \sum(x-\bar{x})(y-\bar{y}) = -81.86$$
$$r = \frac{\sum(x-\bar{x})(y-\bar{y})}{(n-1)s_x s_y} = \frac{-81.86}{(16-1)\times 488 \times 3.0\%} = -0.37$$

In summary, two variables x and y, may have no correlation, which means that the change of x is not associated with a definite change of y. If the change of x is always accompanied with a definite change of y, we say that x and y are correlated. If the change of x and change of y are linearly correlated, the correlation is called linear correlation. If x increases and y also increases, the correlation is positive. If x increases and y decreases, the correlation is negative. The linear correlation coefficient, r, measures the strength of the x-y "linear correlation". The r value of -1 or 1 is an indication of perfect linear correlation.

Figure 2.8 shows that as the population density increases, the percentage of vacant units decreases, which is an example of negative correlation. The distribution of points does not closely resemble a straight line, which is an indication of weak correlation. The graphic examination is consistent with the numerical calculation. A linear correlation coefficient of -0.37 is a weak negative correlation.

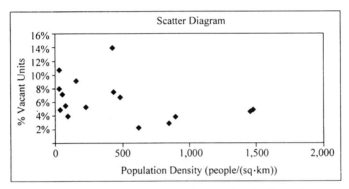

Figure 2.8 Distribution of census tract level population density and percent vacant units in Boone County, 2000

2.2.3   Regression Analysis

When two variables have a high linear correlation coefficient, we would feel comfortable to estimate the value of one variable based on our knowledge of the other variable. Regression analysis is one such estimation tool. The purpose of a linear regression analysis is to find a line of best fit or regression line. Finding "a line of best fit" means to find a straight line that minimizes the sum of all squared vertical distances (e.g., deviations) from the observed data points to the line. A criterion commonly referred to as "ordinary least square (OLS) criterion".[1] Once the intercept and the slope of the "best fit line" are derived from linear regression analysis, the value of the variable y can be estimated from a known value of the variable x. The variable x is called an "independent variable" and the variable y is called a "dependent variable" (Chatterjee et al., 2000).

---

① The ordinary least square method was developed by the German mathematician Carl Friedrich Gauss.

The population of two cities for the years between 1995 and 2000 indicates what is meant by fitting a straight line (Fig. 2.9). The first variable, *x*, is the year and the second variable, *y*, is the population. The graph shows that the population in Dodge City grew at a constant rate of 500 persons per year. A line of best fit will connect all data points. You can also easily imagine that you will basically never encounter an area that grew by exactly the same absolute number of persons for an extended period of time.

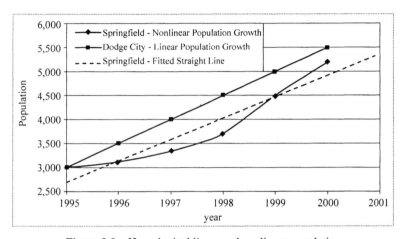

Figure 2.9   Hypothetical linear and nonlinear population

In the case of Springfield, population grew slower during the first three years and picked up to grow faster the last two years. The line connecting the data points is not linear. The dotted line represents a straight line for the Springfield data. We can see that finding a straight line to represent a nonlinear relationship always will be an approximation. For a given *x* value, the difference of the observed data value, *y*, and the calculated value, $\hat{y}$ (on the regression line), can be expressed as:

$$\varepsilon = y - \hat{y} \qquad\qquad (2.6)$$

where,

   y — the observed dependent variable value;

   $\hat{y}$ — the calculated dependent variable value (on the straight line);

   ε — the difference between the observed and calculated dependent variable values.

If the variables *x* and *y* are perfectly correlated, we can determine the exact value of variable *y* for any given value of variable *x* and ε will always be zero. This is case of Dodge City. We have recognized that this is unlikely in real world simply because time will never be the sole determinant of population. Many other factors, such as social and economic conditions, play a crucial role in population growth or decline. Thus, we should not expect that the error term (ε) be zero. Figure 2.10 is a graphic representation of the error term. The vertical distance from the x axis to the regression line, $\hat{y}$, represents the portion of y value that can be explained by the independent variable, x. ε, the vertical distance between the regression line and the observed value, y, for the same x value, represents the portion of y value that cannot be explained by x (Sanders and Smidt, 2000). The linear regression analysis is used to find such a straight line that minimizes the sum of squared errors:

$$\text{Minimize } \sum \varepsilon^2$$

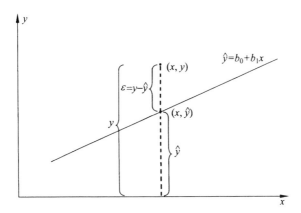

Figure 2.10   Illustration of the linear regression

This line is also called the best fit line, or the regression line, which is expressed as:

$$\hat{y} = b_0 + b_1 x \tag{2.7}$$

where,

$\hat{y}$ — the predicted value for variable y for a given x;

b_0 — the intercept of the line of best fit;

b_1 — the slope of the line of best fit.

Mathematically, a straight line is given by the linear function:

$$y = b_0 + b_1 \cdot x \tag{2.8}$$

where (x, y) represent arbitrary points on the line, b_0 is the y-intercept (y-value where the line crosses the y-axis), and b_1 is the slope (e.g., steepness) of the line. The formulas to calculate b_0 and b_1 are:

$$b_1 = \frac{\sum (x - \overline{x})(y - \overline{y})}{\sum (x - \overline{x})^2} \tag{2.9}$$

and
$$b_0 = \frac{\sum y - \left(b_1 \cdot \sum x \right)}{n} = \overline{y} - (b_1 \cdot \overline{x}) \tag{2.10}$$

The actual computational steps in estimating the regression line, e.g., the regression coefficients, are rather straight forward and can easily be done using a spreadsheet or a statistical software package.

For the Springfield example, we calculated coefficients b_0 and b_1 as:

$$b_0 = 2,253$$
$$b_1 = 444.3$$

The estimated straight line for Springfield's population statistics therefore is:

Population = 2,253 + 444.3(Year)

where the population is the estimated population for a particular year.

The observed population data and the population calculated with the line of best fit are displayed in Table 2.14.

Table 2.14   Estimation results: Springfield

Year	Observed Population Springfield	Estimated Population Springfield	Absolute Difference	Percent Difference (%)
1995	3,000	2,698	– 302	10.1
1996	3,100	3,142	42	– 1.4
1997	3,350	3,586	236	– 7.1
1998	3,700	4,030	330	– 8.9
1999	4,500	4,475	– 25	0.6
2000	5,200	4,919	– 281	5.4
2001	N/A	5,363	N/A	N/A
2002	N/A	5,808	N/A	N/A
2003	N/A	6,252	N/A	N/A

The goodness of fit can be seen by looking at the difference between the observed data and the estimated population values. The difference between the two is what cannot be explained by the explanatory variable, time. Accordingly, it is the part that is included in the error term, ε (Fig. 2.11).

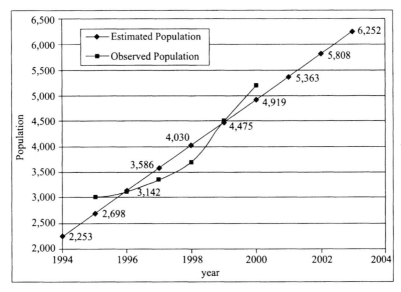

Figure 2.11   Observed versus estimated population data for Springfield

The goodness of fit can also be expressed by a single summary measure—the square of linear correlation coefficient, called the coefficient of determination, r^2—which ranges between 0 and 1. If all observed population data were on the straight line, a case of perfect fit, r^2 would be 1.0. The r^2 for Springfield is 0.91 stating that about 91% of the variation in population can be explained by time. The higher the coefficient of determination, r^2, the better fit of your straight line to observed population data.

2.2.4   Time Dimension

Sometimes it is important to calculate changes of variable values over time. Changes can be expressed as an absolute change or a percent change, as an average annual absolute change, or as an average annual percent change. Let us use x_t to represent the value in the beginning year and t_{t+n} for the ending year. The period between the beginning and ending year is n year. Also, let us use G_a for the absolute change, G_p for the percent change, g_a for the average annual absolute change, and g_p for the average annual percent change. The formulas to calculate the four changes are expressed as:

$$G_a = x_{t+n} - x_t \tag{2.11}$$

$$G_p = G_a / x_t = (x_{t+n} - x_t) / x_t \tag{2.12}$$

$$g_a = G_a / n = (x_{t+n} - x_t)/n \tag{2.13}$$

$$g_p = (x_{t+n} / x_t)^{1/n} - 1 \tag{2.14}$$

Using the total population for Boone County—57,589 for 1990 and 85,991 for 2000, we can assign the variable values as:

$$t = 1990$$
$$n = 10$$
$$t + n = 2000$$
$$x_t = 57,589$$
$$x_{t+n} = 85,991$$

The following section illustrates how to compute the population change rates. An **absolute change** is the difference between populations in the ending year and the beginning year:

$$G_a = x_{t+n} - x_t = 85,991 - 57,589 = 28,402$$

The result shows that Boone County's population grew by 28,402 people from 1990 to 2000. A positive G_a value represents an increase and while a negative value indicates a decline in the variable values.

A percent change reflects the magnitude of the absolute change in reference to the variable value at the beginning year:

$$G_p = G_a / x_t = 28,402/57,589 = 0.493 \text{ or } 49.3\%$$

The result shows that Boone County's population grew by exactly 49.3% from 1990 to 2000.

If we are interested in the average rate of change for a year during this period, we can calculate an **average annual absolute change**:

$$\text{AAAC} = G_a / n = 28,402/10 = 2,840$$

For this 10-year period, Boone County's population grew, on average, 2,840 persons per year.

We can also calculate the **average annual percent change** for this period:

$$\text{AAPC} = (x_{t+n} / x_t)^{1/n} - 1 = (85,991/57,589)^{1/10} - 1 = 1.0409 - 1 = 0.0409 \text{ or } 4.09\%$$

On average, Boone County's population grew by 4.09% every year between 1990 and 2000.

If the change rates can be derived from other studies, we can rearrange Eq. (2.11) to Eq. (2.14) to calculate the future value for a variable x_{t+1}, based on the present value, x_t :

$$x_{t+n} = G_a + x_t \tag{2.15}$$

$$x_{t+n} = x_t \cdot G_p + x_t = x_t \cdot (1 + G_p) \tag{2.16}$$

$$x_{t+n} = x_t + n \cdot g_a \tag{2.17}$$

$$x_{t+n} = x_t (1 + g_p)^n \tag{2.18}$$

2.2.5   Spatial Analysis

Spatial analysis is a critical part in planning analysis methods. Two spatial analysis methods are commonly applied in planning studies. They are buffering and overlaying. Most Geographic Information Systems have these functions. Buffering refers to the delineation of an area surrounding a target object with one or several fixed distances. Overlay analysis is the process of analyzing multiple data layers together for a specified location or area.

Let's use a hypothetical case to illustrate the two spatial analysis types. A developer, who is looking for suitable land for a residential development in Boone County, decides to use three criteria to identify potential developable land. The first criterion is that the land must be currently undeveloped. The second criterion is that the land is not too close to a highway (more than 400 meters away) and not too far from a highway (within 5 kilometers). The third criterion is that the slope should be less than 20%.

Figure 2.12 illustrates the process of identifying the available land. The buffering analysis is used twice to create a 400 m buffer and a 5 km buffer to the highways in Boone County. Next, the overlay analysis is used to identify the area between 400-meter and 5-kilometer buffers. Then the buffer area and the vacant land are overlaid to derive the vacant land within the buffer area. This overlaid area is further overlaid with the 20% slope data layer. The result of the last overlay analysis is the areas with less than 20% slope and between 400-meters and 5-kilometers to highways. Those land areas will be considered as potential land for future development.

This illustration shows only one example of all possible overlay analysis—to exclude or include certain areas. There are times when an overlay analysis is used to rank areas from the characteristics of multiple data layers. Such analysis has two versions, weighted overlay analysis and a simple overlay analysis. In a simple overlay analysis, each data layer is treated equally important. In a weighted overlay analysis, some data layers will be treated as more important than others by assigning them with more weights than others. A detailed discussion about weighed overlay analysis will be in Chapter 6, land use analysis.

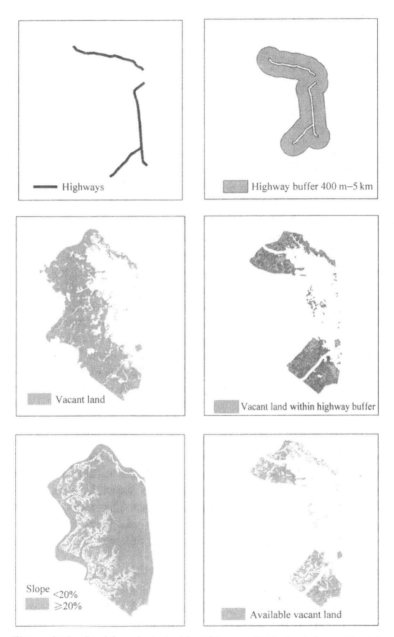

Figure 2.12 Spatial analysis in identifying available land for residential development

2.3   Presentation

Presentation is a process for you to communicate to a large audience. The communication is to present the data you have collected and the outcome from analyses you have conducted to your clients. The most common method of presentation is a written report. The text should clearly get across the message to your readers in a concise and straightforward fashion. In addition, you may use one or a combination of three methods discussed below to support the text.

2.3.1   Tabular Presentation

Presenting data in tables is an efficient way of summarizing data. A table may have one or more columns and one or more rows. One common way of using tables is to list the features of a set of objects. Those features can be numbers or text. Numbers are often used to summarize the numerical data and text is used to describe the characters or attributes. Table 2.15 summarizes the land uses in Boone County. The first row lists the names of the variables. In this case, they are the land use, size in square kilometers and proportion of the total area. Data for each land use type are stored in the rest of the rows. The primary purpose of such table is to summarize data for comparison. From the table, we can easily find that more than half of the land in Boone County is undeveloped. Most of the developed land is for commercial use.

Table 2.15   Land use in Boone County

Land Use	Size (sq · km)	Proportion (%)
Residential land	97	15.2
Commercial land	155	24.3
Vacant land	362	56.7
Other Urban land	24	3.8
Total	638	100

The second type of table is often used in statistical analysis, which summarizes the relationship between two variables. This type of table is normally called a contingency table. As shown in Table 2.16, the first column labels the class name for the first variable, age, in a 10-year interval. The first row labels classes the second variable, gender. Other cells in the table store the Boone County population by gender for each age cohort. From the table, we can easily see that the majority of residents in Boone County were younger than age 50. There were very few people who were above 80 years of age.

Table 2.16   Boone County 2000 population by gender and age

Age \ Gender	Female	Male	Total
0 – 9	6,618	7,006	13,624
10 – 19	6,306	6,719	13,025
20 – 29	5,645	5,629	11,274
30 – 39	7,543	7,182	14,725
40 – 49	7,206	7,184	14,390
50 – 59	4,642	4,629	9,271
60 – 69	2,596	2,398	4,994
70 – 79	1,960	1,422	3,382
80+	943	363	1,306
All ages	43,459	42,532	85,991

Sometimes, the same data can be presented as percentages, as shown in Tables 2.17 to 2.18. By expressing the data as percentage, we can easily interpret the number counts with a known range—0 to 100%. Table 2.17 indicates the percentage gender distribution by age cohort, where the row total sums to 100%. From the last row of the table, we can see that in the county as a whole, the female proportion is slightly higher than the male proportion, 50.5% vs. 49.5%. Only for ages below 20 are there more males than females. The gender distribution skews significantly for older ages, especially for aged 80 and above. In that age cohort, 72.2% people are female.

Table 2.17   Boone County 2000 population by gender and age (percent of row total)

Age \ Gender	Female	Male	Total
0 – 9	48.6	51.4	100.0
10 – 19	48.4	51.6	100.0
20 – 29	50.1	49.9	100.0
30 – 39	51.2	48.8	100.0
40 – 49	50.1	49.9	100.0
50 – 59	50.1	49.9	100.0
60 – 69	52.0	48.0	100.0
70 – 79	58.0	42.0	100.0
80+	72.2	27.8	100.0
All ages	50.5	49.5	100.0

By contrast, Table 2.18 shows the percentage age distribution by gender. Now, the column total sums to 100%. The table displays the distribution of female or male population by age. For example, the percentage of people aged 60 or over is quite small for both male and female.

Table 2.18   Boone County 2000 population by gender by age (percent of column total)

Age \ Gender	Female	Male	Total
0 – 9	15.2	16.5	15.9
10 – 19	14.5	15.8	15.2
20 – 29	13.0	13.2	13.1
30 – 39	17.4	16.9	17.1
40 – 49	16.5	16.9	16.7
50 – 59	10.7	10.9	10.8
60 – 69	6.0	5.6	5.8
70 – 79	4.5	3.3	3.9
80 +	2.2	0.9	1.5
All ages	100.0	100.0	100.0

Last, Table 2.19 indicates the percent age-gender distribution and therefore, the table total sums to 100%. In each cell, the percentage is calculated against the county total population. For example, the females of aged 0 – 9 is 7.7% of the county population.

Table 2.19   Boone County 2000 population by gender by age (percent of total)

Age \ Gender	Female	Male	Total
0 – 9	7.7	8.1	15.8
10 – 19	7.3	7.8	15.1
20 – 29	6.6	6.5	13.1
30 – 39	8.8	8.4	17.2
40 – 49	8.4	8.4	16.7
50 – 59	5.4	5.4	10.8
60 – 69	3.0	2.8	5.8
70 – 79	2.3	1.7	4.0
80 +	1.1	0.4	1.5
All ages	50.6	49.5	100.0

2.3.2   Graphic Presentation

People often say that a picture is worth a thousand words. And so does a graphic presentation. A graphic presentation refers to visual displays of numerical data, often referred to as charts. Five different types of charts are commonly used in data presentation: bar, pie, scatter, line and histogram. The choice of which charts to use depends on the types of data and what is the most important information you want a reader to notice. In general, a bar or a pie chart is used to display one discrete and one continuous variable, while scatter, line, and histogram charts are used for two continuous variables.

In a bar chart, the height of a bar depends on the magnitude of a variable value. Figure 2.13 is a bar chart made from the population data in Table 2.16. The bar height reflects the male and female population and the bars are grouped by the age cohort. Several pieces of information can be presented in a bar chart. From a bar, chart we can compare the male and female population for the same age cohort, which shows us a pattern. At young ages, there are more males than females: and at middle ages, the proportions of the two genders tend to be similar. At old age, there are more females than males. When we review the bars for male population at a different age cohorts, we see that the population decreases sharply in the 40 to 60 age cohorts. Lastly, we can examine both genders for all ages to conclude that the change patterns for both genders are similar, although to various extents. We see a population decrease from teens to twenties. This may be attributed to there being no major college in Boone County and people going to other places to pursue higher education. There are good job opportunities that attract people between the ages of 30 and 50 to the county. There may not be much for retirees, therefore, people move away after they have retired. Of course these are only speculations. Further population and economic analyses may support the observations or suggest other explanations.

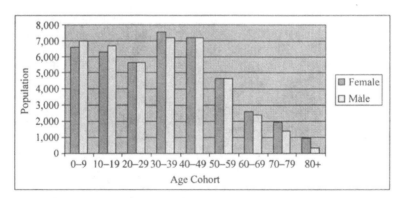

Figure 2.13 A bar chart of population by gender by age cohort

A pie chart is an effective presentation tool when we want to show the proportion of different components. Figure 2.14 is an example of land use composition in a community. From the label we can see that there are four land use types, namely residential land, commercial land, vacant land, and other urban land. We can quickly recognize from the size of the slices that vacant land makes up more than half of the land and the other urban land has the smallest portion of the four. Finally, the percentage values for each land use type give us exactly the percentage of each land use type. For instance, 15.2% land is used for residential purpose.

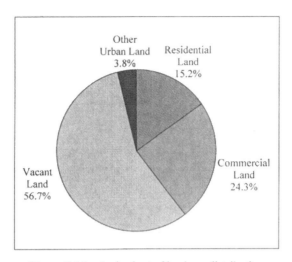

Figure 2.14   A pie chart of land use distribution

A scatter chart is also called a scatter diagram. Dots are plotted based on the values of two variables. Figure 2.15 exhibits a scatter diagram for the 2,000 census tract level data in Boone County. The x-axis is the population density in number of people per square kilometer and the y-axis is the percentage of vacant units. A scatter diagram is good for identifying outliers and patterns between two variables. In this example, three outliers deserve further analysis. One census tract has a much higher percentage of vacant units (14%) than other census tracts of similar population density. Two other tracts have very high population density (greater than 1,400 people per square kilometer). The rest of the census tracts demonstrate a general pattern that as the population density increases, the

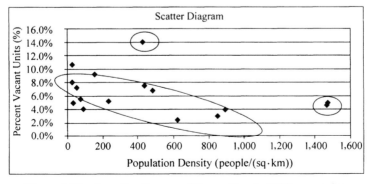

Figure 2.15   A scatter diagram of Boone County 2000 census data

percentage of vacant units decrease. That is, the low density areas are more likely to have higher percent vacant units.

A line graph is useful when the two variables of interest have a one to one relationship, that is, for each *x* value there is a corresponding *y* value. Figure 2.16 gives an example of a line graph using the data in Table 2.20. The *x*-axis is the number of rooms in an occupied unit, and the *y*-axis is the percent of households for renter—or owner—occupied units. From the chart we can easily make several observations: Fox example, there is only small proportion of units with 3 or fewer rooms are occupied by owners and a very small percentage of rental units for 7 or more room units.

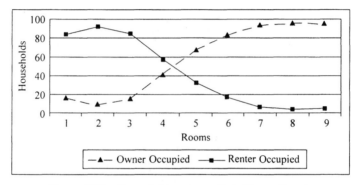

Figure 2.16   Occupied housing units in Boone County

Table 2.20   Percent of ownership by unit size

Rooms	Owner Occupied	Renter Occupied
1	16	84
2	8	92
3	15	85
4	42	58
5	67	33
6	84	16
7	93	7
8	96	4
9	96	4

A histogram displays the count or frequency by category for a continuous variable. To construct a histogram, the range of the variable is divided into a few categories and the number of records for each category is counted and presented by the height of a bar. Figure 2.17 gives an example of a histogram chart. The age is divided into 10-year cohorts. The 2,000 total population in Boone County is counted for each age cohort. From the histogram chart, we can see that majority of people in Boone County are younger than 50 years, with the 30 – 39 age cohort being the highest number. Such information can be quite important in other planning related decisions, such as housing, school, employment, health care etc.

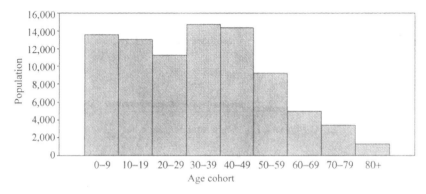

Figure 2.17   Population by age cohort

2.3.3   Map Presentation

2.3.3.1   Factors Affecting Map Design

Before we discuss ways of making and using maps, we need to be reminded that no map can truly represent real world entities. One reason is that we are using a 2-dimensional map to represent the 3-dimentional world. The other reason is that a map can only display a portion of the complex world. Therefore, the person who produces a map dictates what information a map should present.

Maps are often used in planning to display features with spatial significance such as location and geographical arrangement. From a map, we can read information about distance, direction, area, shape and spatial connection. To prepare a map for meaningful presentation, we must remember several factors that control the map design: map objective, generalization, scale, mode of use, and color and texture.

Map objective refers to how you intend to use the map. The map design varies depending on the use of the map, such as for a book or for a poster, folded or flat, black and white or colored, square or rectangular, and so on. The target audience is important because your map must be understandable by your intended readers, such as policy makers, technical committees or the general public. This controls the complexity of your map design.

Generalization refers to your selection of the information to be included in a map. A map is a generalized or simplified representation of reality. Since you can only effectively present certain aspects of the reality, you want to include only the information that serves the purpose of the map.

Maps use symbols to represent real world elements, such as rivers and streets. In order to do so, we need to use symbols that are in proportion to the real world phenomena. A map scale tells us the ratio between the symbol and the element it represents. For example, we can use a one centimeter long line on a map to represent a one kilometer highway at a scale of one centimeter to one kilometer, or 1 : 100,000. In addition to the ratio display, a map scale can be represented with a graphic scale bar, as shown in Fig. 2.18.

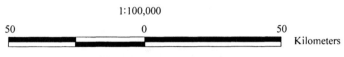

Figure 2.18 Scale ratio and scale bar

It is important to note that a map scale should be read as a fraction. That is, a 1 : 100,000 scale is smaller than a 1 : 1,000 scale. On a fixed size of map sheet, a smaller scale map will cover a lager area than a larger scale map.

Map scales dictate how much detail you are able to place on a piece of paper. For example, a line width of 0.1 mm represents a 100 m wide line at a scale of one to one million (1 : 1,000,000). The same line width represents a 1 m wide line at a scale of one to ten thousand (1 : 10,000). Therefore, the edge of a 9 m wide road can be properly represented at the 1 : 10,000 scale, it would be impossible to appear on the map at 1 : 1,000,000.

The mode of use is another factor that must be considered in map design. If you will display the map on your computer monitor, you may have a color palette of 256 colors to choose from. If you intend to prepare hard copy maps, you may have very limited color use. Even for the computer display, you need to consider the ability of human eyes to detect the tiny difference between similar colors. When the map reproduction is anticipated, you must consider the limitations on the color reproduction and pattern separation. Most journals limit maps to black and white only and gray scale normally does not reproduce well.

2.3.3.2 Map Elements

The most important map element is the map. The map title, scale bar, north arrow, and legend are the other basic elements. In addition, we can add elements, such as graphics, tables, or text to a map.

A map places various symbols at different places to represent real world features. By comparing the difference of symbols and by examining the place of symbols, a reader can learn the spatial placement and arrangement of real world features. The basic symbols used in maps are points, lines, polygons, and labels. Refer to the Boone County map shown in Fig. 2.19, we use lines to represent linear features, such as streams. The area-based features, such as census tracts, are represented as polygons.

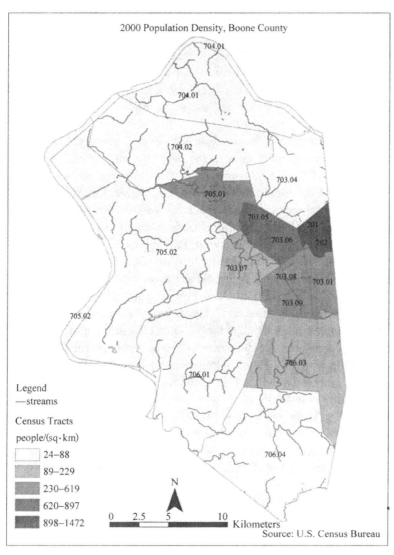

Figure 2.19   2000 population density by census tract in Boone County

2.4   Projections, Forecasts, or Estimates

Although the literature offers concrete definitions of projections, forecasts, and estimates, people often use them interchangeably without recognizing the immediate consequences.[1] As a foundation for the rest of this book we would

---

[1] For a detailed discussion on this matter, please see Smith et al. (2001), p. 3.

like to conclude this chapter by distinguishing the three terms.

Projection is a general term for mathematically derived statements based on predetermined assumptions. For example, if we assume the population growth will follow the same pattern as observed for the last 20 years, then the county's population will double in the next 10 years. The importance here is that we need to specify first all parameters we will use in calculations. For example, we have observed that a county's population grew by five percent in the past 10 years and assume that this growth will continue in the next 10 years. Or, we assume that birth, survival, and migration rates in the past 10 years will remain constant in the next 10 years. In any case, some prior judgments are necessary which start with the choice of the input data, e.g., the time period for which we select the data, and/or the parameters. The uncertainty of future events makes the "correct" choice of parameter values a precarious undertaking. For this very reason, it is a common practice to offer a variety of projections using different parameter values. Many demographic studies offer low, middle, and high series of projected population. The middle series is usually the projection based on parameters we believe will provide the most likely occurring population. A low series sets a lower bound and the high series sets a higher bound of future population.

Forecast, on the other hand, is the statement about the most likely occurring future. Here, the result—the forecast—is based upon personal judgment. For example, having projected future population for a county, using three different growth rates, you now have to decide what, according to your opinion, will be the most likely future population. In other words, you have to choose the one set of parameters that will lead to the most likely result based on what you believe. You make a hypothesis about the future and prepare your action accordingly. There is no guarantee that your hypothesis will be correct. However, an inadequate, or sometimes a wrong hypothesis, is better than no hypothesis (Rodwin and Sanyal, 2000).

An estimate, by definition, refers exclusively to past or present statistics. For example, population estimates are the most basic and most often required for planning analyses. The U.S. Census Bureau is legally required (under Title 13 of the U.S. Code) to produce detailed, sub-national population estimates which are used in federal funding allocations, setting the levels of national surveys, and monitoring recent demographic changes (U.S. Census Bureau). Population estimates serve a different purpose than projections or forecasts by filling in intercensal years—the years between two censuses. Using the decennial base count, estimates are derived from existing data such as births, deaths, federal tax returns, medicare enrollment and immigration collected from various sources. For example, if you are interested in this year's total population and its racial breakdown of a U.S. city, rather than going out and counting everybody you can try the U.S. Census Bureau's website and search for the estimates.

In general, based on the fact that you simply cannot know what the future will be like, you are always well advised to come up with a variety of projections. Offering a middle series, a high series, and a low series takes the burden off your shoulders to determine the most appropriate forecast. The dependence on technical approaches and inclusion of predetermined assumptions imbed two potential sources for errors: first, the right choice of projection model; second the selection of the right parameters and their values. Putting your projection in a range of possible outcomes always increase the level of confidence that the actually accruing future is within your projections. We will follow this terminological distinction and use the term "projection" when talking about future trends. On the other hand, "estimates" will be used exclusively when referring to past and present.

References

Babbie, Earl R. 2002. *The Basics of Social Research*, 2nd ed. Belmont, CA: Wadsworth.

Babbie, Earl R. 2004. *The Practice of Social Research*, 10th ed. Belmont, CA: Wadsworth.

Blackwell, Louisa. 2001. Women's work in UK official statistics and the 1980 reclassification of occupations. *Journal of the Royal Statistical Society: Series A (Statistics in Society)*, 164(2): 307 – 325.

Chatterjee, Samprit, Ali S. Hadi and Bertram Price. 2000. *Regression Analysis by Example*, New York: John Wiley & Sons, Inc.

De Vaus, D. A. 2002. *Analyzing Social Science Data*. London: SAGE.

Huang, Nan-zhen. 2001. *Urban Development History of Shanghai, China*. Available online at: http://hhhnz.freewebspace.com/.

Johnson, Robert and Patricia Kuby. 2004. *Elementary Statistics*, 9th ed. Belmont, CA: Thomson Learning.

Office Of Management And Budget (OMB). 1997. *Federal Register Notice: Revisions to the Standards for the Classification of Federal Data on Race and Ethnicity*. Washington DC: Executive Office of the President, Office of Management and Budget, Office of Information and Regulatory Affairs. Available online at: http://www.whitehouse.gov/omb/fedreg/1997standards.html.

Robbin, Alice. 2000. Administrative policy as symbol system: political conflict and the social construction of identity. *Administration & Society*, 32(4): 398 – 431.

Rodwin, Lloyd and Bishwapriya Sanyal. (eds.) 2000. *The Profession of City Planning: Changes, Images, and Challenges*. New Brunswick: Center for Urban Policy Research, Rutgers, The State University of New Jersey.

Sanders, Donald and Robert Smidt. 2000. *Statistics—A First Course*, 6th ed. New York: McGraw-Hill.

Smith, Stanley K., Jeff Tayman and David A. Swanson. 2001. *State and Local Population Projections: Methodology and Analysis*. New York: Kluwer Academic/Plenum Publishers.

Spencer, James H. 2004. People, places, and policy: a politically relevant framework for efforts to reduce concentrated poverty. *The Policy Studies Journal*, 32(4): 545 – 568.

U.S. Census Bureau. 2000. *Racial and Ethnic Classifications Used in Census 2000 and Beyond*, Washington DC: U.S. Census Bureau, Population Division. Last Revised: April 12, 2000 at 01:12:12 pm. Available online at: http://www.census.gov/population/www/socdemo/ race/racefactcb.html.

U.S. Census Bureau. 2001. Cartographic Boundary Files. Washington DC: U.S. Census Bureau, Geography Division, Cartographic Products Management Branch. Last Revised: April 19, 2005 at 02:12:09 pm. Available online at: http://www.census.gov/geo/www/cob/cs_ metadata.html.

U.S. Census Bureau. 2004. Terms and Definitions, Population Estimates: Concepts. Washington DC: U.S. Census Bureau, Population Division. Last revised: August 24, 2004 at 08:15:21 am. Available online at: http://www.census.gov/popest/topics/ terms/.

Chapter 3   Demographic Analysis

3.1   The Need for Demographic Analysis

Planning for the future requires, to some extent, making projections based on past observations The U.S. Census Bureau provides, as a routine procedure, national and state-level population projections.[1] State governments, often in cooperation with an external agency such as a university, do more geographically focused population analyses and projections. For example, the Urban Studies Institute at the University of Louisville, part of the Kentucky State Data Center (KSDC), is responsible for the periodical projection of future population trends at the state and county-level and for selected cities in Kentucky.[2] Dealing with the uncertainty of future estimated births, deaths, and migration patterns, the institute offers three simultaneous population projections at low, middle and high growth rates. Additionally, the institute makes a variety of past and present population estimates available online. For more geographically detailed population projections and estimates, local government agencies, such as city planning departments or county planning commissions, engage in all sorts of methods to evaluate past and present demographic trends.[3]

Generally, population projections are the base for many planning activities, such as producing land use and transportation plans, determining the direction of future economic development and providing guidance for housing, school, and shopping center developments. Population projections often become the center-piece of comprehensive plans and the future vision of localities. The importance of population estimates and projections in planning becomes apparent by looking at some selected, local planning issues:

Land use planning: General land use and specific development policies need to regularly address increasing population size. A town's conceptual image and physical appearance depends largely on future land use planning. Expected population growth patterns drive much of the decision-making processes such as designating more residential areas; finding the right combination of residential,

---

[1] Schedule of population and household projection releases by the U.S. Census Bureau: http://www.census.gov/population/www/projections/projsched.html. State Population projections by the U.S. Census Bureau: http://www.census.gov/population/www/projections/stproj.html.

[2] Urban Studies Institute at the University of Louisville: http://ksdc.louisville.edu/Projections2003.htm.

[3] Boone County, Kentucky, official website: http://www.boonecountyky.org/.

commercial, office, and industrial uses in mixed-use areas; and allocating parks and open spaces.

Transportation planning: Growing cities and metropolitan regions face the challenge of coping with increases in transportation demand. More automobiles on the streets and highways and higher demands for public transportation systems have their origins in growing populations.

Economic development: A growing economy creating sufficient employment opportunities, which in return allows a sustained increase in people's standard of living is central to economic development planning. A region's population and its growth trend is thus of major importance. For instance, a growing number of people will foster local retail sales, will be the basis of a qualified labor pool for expanding industries, and will be the basis of various tax incomes for state/local governments.[1]

Environmental planning: Planners constantly face the challenge of preserving nature and wildlife habitat while providing high quality spaces to meet the demand for human activities. Population analysis provides the base for searching the balance between human and nature.

Housing: Booming regions have tremendous demand for housing. Knowing the projected population increase for a specific time period will give some guidance to those who must accommodate this demand. Identifying demographic characteristics, such as persons per household, will add valuable information on the total future need of housing units.

Public services and facilities: Imagine that public services cannot keep pace with population increase. The direct result would be garbage-filled streets and bottlenecks in the provision of water and electricity. Planning ahead for anticipated population growth is essential in public services and facility plans.

Sustainable development: Sustainability can be defined as finding a level of economic development that does not compromise the economic vitality of future generations or the integrity of the natural environment. Population growth that, for instance, considers resource requirements environmental constraints would be a first step towards building a healthy and sustainable urban and regional environment. Translating the idea of *"Constrained Economic Growth"*[2], into holistic urban and regional planning would lead to sustainable community development. In the long run, intergenerational equity would be reached, in

---

[1] Following the principles of the economic base theory, increasing export demand for regionally produced goods and services may also contributes to a large extend to a region's economic prosperity.

[2] Batie Sandra, 1989: 1,084 – 1,085. "Sustainable Development: Challenges to the Profession of Agricultural Economics." *American Journal of Agricultural Economics*, December: 1,083 – 1,101. We recognize that advocates of the "Resource Maintenance Definition" of sustainable development among others argue for the separate maintenance of human and natural capital, since they are complements rather than substitutes (Daly and Cobb, 1989:72). The degree to which this separation is handled leads to the distinction of "weak" and "strong" sustainability.

which the demand of growing population is addressed with the most appropriate measures in transportation, land use, and economic plans that always consider environmental quality.

All these planning examples demonstrate the importance of understanding past and present demographic population characteristics, such as gender and age distributions and expectations of future population development. They emphasize how the analysis of past and present population statistics and future population developments can play a key role in a variety of planning and decision processes. For service deliveries by local governments, in transportation, land use or environmental planning, underestimating future populations can lead to shortages and a reduction of the quality of life. Overestimating future populations, on the other hand, may result in wasting local resources through costly oversupply of services.

Before we actually start analyzing past and present population characteristics, we first need to discuss the terms and definitions used by demographers and the components of changes in population trends.

3.1.1   Typology of Projection Methods

There is a wide range of population projection methods in the literature and there are several ways of classifying population projection methods. As a first distinction, we can clearly make a difference between **subjective** and **objective projections** (Armstrong, 1985). Subjective projections can be simply described as "wild guesses" and as such abstain from a rigorous systematic and methodological approach. They depend largely on feelings and intuitions and, at their best, can only reflect impressions on future population tendencies. Objective projections follow the quantitative approach of collecting data and applying a quantitative method to obtain a projected result.

Given the importance of population projections for the planning community, you can easily imagine that you would not risk your planning career by depending entirely on subjective projections. However, we must recognize that objective projections also rely, to some extent, on subjective elements. This includes the choice of the "correct" projection method and/or as mentioned before, the selection of the right parameters used in projections.

Some projection methods depend solely on historical trends (e.g., trend extrapolation models) while others account for various interrelationships of population statistics with non-demographic variables, such as regional employment, amenities and wage levels (e.g., structural population models). Figure 3.1 identifies three main population projection methods: trend extrapolation, cohort-component, and structural.

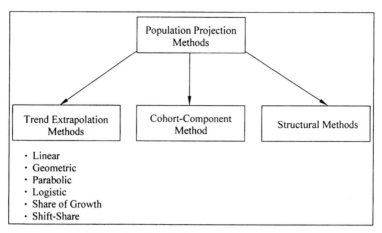

Figure 3.1 Population projection methods

Trend extrapolation methods observe historical trends and project them into the future. These methods are often used for small areas where disaggregated population statistics are not always available. They are powerful straightforward tools for projecting populations because they rely on a single, highly aggregated, data series. For instance, we can extrapolate the observed population trend for the past twenty years for Cincinnati into the near future. The different individual methods listed under this group (e.g., linear, geometric, etc.) refer simply to different mathematical approaches of finding the best fit for the observed data. An important thing to remember is that trend extrapolation does not account for any causes of these past observed trends. This is where the **cohort-component** [①] methods come into play. The most common version of the cohort-component methods uses sex-age-specific population cohorts and adjusts them for the three factors of population growth: births, deaths, and migration. Subdividing the sex-age-specific cohorts further by race/ethnicity increases the level of detail, but also increases the data requirements. The level of detail and the fact that it accounts for the components of population changes make this group the most frequently used population projection method. Accounting further for non-demographic factors leads us to the **structural models**. Beyond the scope of this textbook and often very complex in nature, models falling into this group explain population growth (dependent variable) through a variety of non-demographic (independent) variables such as employment, wage levels, and local amenities as well as land use and transportation models. [②]

Now that we have briefly described the three major categories of population

---

① According to relevant literature, the origins of the cohort-component method go back to Refs. (Carnan, 1985; Bowley, 1924; whelpton, 1928).

② A detailed discussion of structural models is offered by Smith et al. (2001).

projection methods, we will take a closer look at factors that affect the choice of methods. Each method represents a unique mix of characteristics, assumptions, and requirements. So how can you be sure to pick the most appropriate projection method? Surely, understanding the unique characteristics, assumptions, and requirements is an essential step towards making an educated choice, but there are many more factors that must be considered.

Subjective impressions: Although you have decided to go with an objective population projection, you may have a tendency of using one method over others. This might be because a method appears more elegant, more reliable, or you simply prefer to copy a "similar" study from a neighboring/close-by county for which you have a detailed description of the method.

Time constraint: Usually, people expect you to get the job done within a certain time. This is no exception when it comes down to doing a population projection. Your judgment on how long it will take to collect the data, do the analysis, and write a report will certainly influence your decision on what method to choose.

Technical skill level: People tend to avoid methods with which they feel uncomfortable with. Lack of adequate training, for example, can be one reason to choose a more straightforward approach over a more complex one.

Data availability: As a general rule, data are more widely and easily available for larger geographic regions. For the United States, the Census Bureau offers, for example, population estimates by age, sex, race, and Hispanic origin at the national, state, county, and sub-county level, such as census tract and block group.[1] State governments usually maintain population statistics on a regular basis, often associated with state universities. Generally, trend extrapolation methods usually have lower data requirements when projecting population totals. The cohort-component method on the other hand has higher data requirements by using sex-age-specific population cohorts.

Detail of analysis: Are you interested in total population changes or do you need to analyze the underlying causes for these population changes, such as migration, births, and deaths? The level of detail in your analysis can play a major role when choosing among simpler trend extrapolation techniques or the more data-intensive cohort-component model.

Purpose of the population projection: It makes a big difference if your supervisor asks in an informal way for a rough figure as a base for follow-up analyses or if your analysis will be posted on the county's planning commission website as part of the comprehensive plan.

Strengths and weaknesses: Every method has strengths (e.g., low data requirement), which may at the same time lead to weaknesses (e.g., low level of detail). Balancing the pros and cons might provide further guidance of what method might be most appropriate.

---

[1] Source: U.S. Census Bureau, Population Division: http://eire.census.gov/popest/estimates.php.

3.2 Demographic Analysis—Fundamental Concepts

For planners and demographers alike, population analyses do not begin with immediately applying sophisticated methods in population projections. Rather, most demographic analyses start with fundamental concepts, including:

(1) describing populations by their actual size,

(2) determining population distribution across predefined areas,

(3) creating sex, race, and age composition profiles of populations of interest, and

(4) calculating observable percent changes of selected population characteristics.

The point here is to get a thorough understanding of the population of interest by studying characteristics for periods where data are available. For planning purposes, these first demographic analyses can already give planners valuable and necessary information. Is the population of an area declining or increasing? By what rate is the area declining or increasing? With such information, school district superintendents could make some educated guesses about expected enrollment if they know the age composition of the area's population. For the provision of public services, such as police and fire protection or the local library, local governments use population statistics to avoid costly over or under provisions of needed services. This list of examples on how population statistics influence the planning decision process could be extended.

Let us focus on the first of the fundamental concepts of demographic analysis, the **population size**. Using 1990 and 2000 U.S. Census Bureau population statistics for Boone County we see immediately that the county is growing fast. Boone County had a population of 57,589 in 1990 and 85,991 in 2000.

While the concept of population size is straightforward, it is an important fact that, in general, people are counted according to their permanent place of residence. For example, someone living in a neighboring county and commuting daily to Boone County for work is not considered a resident of Boone County. As a result this person would, of course, not show up in Boone County's population size in Table 3.1. The so called "de jure" approach counts people only at their permanent place of residence.

Table 3.1 Boone County population size, 1990 and 2000

Boone County, Kentucky	1990	2000	Absolute Change	Percent Change
Male	28,111	42,499	14,388	51.2
Female	29,478	43,492	14,014	47.5
Total	57,589	85,991	28,402	49.3

Source: U.S. Census Bureau, Data Set: 1990 and 2000 Summary Tape File 1 (STF 1)

The next demographic concept deals with **population changes**. Generally, change can be expressed as: absolute change, percent change, average annual absolute change, or average annual percent change. In Chapter 2, we used the population totals for Boone County for 1990 and 2000 from Table 3.1 above (e.g., 57,589 and 85,991 respectively) to calculated the four different measures of changes:

Absolute change: subtract the 1990 population from the 2000 population:

$$85,991 - 57,589 = 28,402$$

Percent change: divide the absolute population change by the 1990 population to get percentages:

$$28,402 / 57,589 = 49.3\%$$

Average annual absolute change (AAAC): divide the absolute population change by the number of years between 1990 and 2000; here we have exactly 10 years:

$$AAAC = 28,402 / 10 = 2,840$$

Average annual percent change (AAPC): apply the geometric growth formula, Eq. (3.1) and solve for the growth rate, Eq. (3.2): [1]

$$Pop_{2000} = Pop_{1990}(1 + AAPC)^{Years} \qquad (3.1)$$

$$AAPC = [Pop_{2000} / Pop_{1990}]^{1/Years} - 1 \qquad (3.2)$$
$$AAPC = [85,991/57,589]^{1/10} - 1 = 1.0409 - 1 = 4.09\%$$

The next concept is **spatial distribution of population**, the spatial pattern of human settlements. We all know that human settlements are not evenly distributed. For example, California (35,484,453) is one of the most populated states, while North Dakota (633,837), South Dakota (764,309), Montana (917,621), and Wyoming (501,242) belong to the least populated states in the United States.[2] Another way of expressing uneven spatial distribution of population is in the form of population densities, usually defined as persons per unit area. These examples show the population distribution across political areas, namely states. Other political entities may include counties, cities, townships and school districts. Common non-political, geographic entities include the various statistical entities used by the U.S. Census Bureau. The smallest geographic unit for which

---

[1] Most of you will recognize that the process of computing annual growth rates is identical to the more familiar process of compounding in finance or accounting. Here, instead of population data, we would use future and present values to represent the compound rate.

[2] The numbers in parenthesis are the U.S. Census Bureau population estimates for 2003.

the Census Bureau tabulates 100-percent data is the census block. Several blocks clustered together form a block group, and the next higher level is census tract. Effective June 6, 2003, the Census Bureau began using metropolitan and micropolitan statistical areas within a "Core Based Statistical Area" (CBSA) classification when referring to larger urban agglomerations. Metropolitan statistical areas must have at least one urbanized area with a population of 50,000 or more. Micropolitan statistical areas must have at least one urban cluster with a population of at least 10,000 but less than 50,000.[1,2]

The map in Fig. 3.2 shows how the Year 2000 population is distributed in Boone County. It illustrates that the population is not evenly distributed

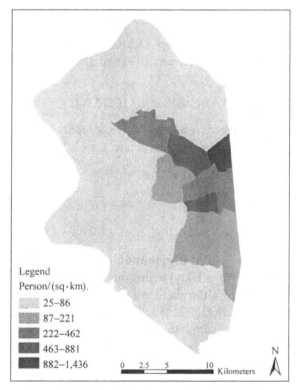

Figure 3.2 Boone County population distribution

---

① http://www.census.gov/population/www/estimates/00-32997.pdf.

② The six New England states use the same criteria for metropolitan and micropolitan statistical area definitions. A New England city and town area (NECTA) must have an urban core with a population of at least 2.5 million. Further subdivision of NECTAs is possible and referred to as New England city and town area divisions. The definition of boundaries is important in defining the area of interest for population analyses. Source: http://www.census.gov/population/www/estimates/metrodef.html.

throughout the county. A large share of the county's population (e.g., 23,551) lives in the east.

The last basic demographic concept refers to **population composition**. Commonly used population composition includes age and sex. Table 3.2 and Table 3.3 show the population composition for Boone County by age, sex, and race for the years 2000 and 1990.

Table 3.2   Boone County population by age, sex, and race, 2000

Boone County, Kentucky	White	Black or African-American	American Indian and Alaska Native	Asian including Pacific Islanders	Some other race, two or more races	Total
Total	81,822	1,306	200	1,137	1,526	85,991
Male:	40,347	716	88	544	804	42,499
0 to 4 years	3,240	60	8	57	137	3,502
5 to 9 years	3,461	67	7	40	110	3,685
10 to 14 years	3,301	61	8	40	67	3,477
15 to 19 years	3,023	34	7	24	54	3,142
20 to 24 years	2,421	67	4	23	76	2,591
25 to 29 years	2,787	82	7	42	85	3,003
30 to 34 years	3,350	73	8	84	69	3,584
35 to 39 years	3,618	69	8	83	75	3,852
40 to 44 years	3,578	77	10	47	37	3,749
45 to 49 years	3,020	61	10	39	23	3,153
50 to 54 years	2,520	27	6	28	29	2,610
55 to 59 years	1,887	22	2	15	14	1,940
60 to 64 years	1,344	3	2	8	8	1,365
65 to 69 years	1,020	9	1	9	8	1,047
70 to 74 years	829	1	0	5	4	839
75 to 79 years	553	1	0	1	5	560
80 to 84 years	243	0	0	0	3	246
85 years and over	152	2	0	0	0	154
Female:	41,475	590	112	593	722	43,492
0 to 4 years	3,065	71	11	61	139	3,347
5 to 9 years	3,242	59	7	46	104	3,458
10 to 14 years	3,151	44	12	32	70	3,309
15 to 19 years	2,811	36	8	22	63	2,940
20 to 24 years	2,361	45	9	23	52	2,490
25 to 29 years	2,921	47	7	56	69	3,100
30 to 34 years	3,411	53	10	86	61	3,621
35 to 39 years	3,804	55	11	84	49	4,003
40 to 44 years	3,699	66	9	70	35	3,879

Continued

Boone County, Kentucky	White	Black or African-American	American Indian and Alaska Native	Asian including Pacific Islanders	Some other race, two or more races	Total
45 to 49 years	3,087	41	9	34	17	3,188
50 to 54 years	2,646	26	6	30	22	2,730
55 to 59 years	1,862	15	5	13	18	1,913
60 to 64 years	1,388	9	4	15	3	1,419
65 to 69 years	1,156	7	3	9	7	1,182
70 to 74 years	1,092	3	1	8	6	1,110
75 to 79 years	773	5	0	2	4	784
80 to 84 years	522	3	0	1	1	527
85 years and over	484	5	0	1	2	492

Source: U.S. Census Bureau, Census 2000

We see immediately that we have one sub-table each for the male and the female population. This **sex (i.e., gender)** composition in Table 3.3 shows that there were slightly more females (e.g., 43,492) than males (e.g., 42,499) in Boone County in 2000.

Table 3.3   Boone County population by age, sex, and race, 1990

Boone County, Kentucky- Males	White	Black or African-American	American Indian and Alaska Native	Asian including Pacific Islanders	Some other race, two or more races	Total
Total	56,716	361	88	355	69	57,589
Male:	27,651	197	49	179	35	28,111
0 to 4 years	2,330	17	2	33	4	2,386
5 to 9 years	2,547	14	5	16	6	2,588
10 to 14 years	2,420	17	4	10	2	2,453
15 to 19 years	2,079	15	3	11	2	2,110
20 to 24 years	1,834	20	5	8	1	1,868
25 to 29 years	2,261	22	7	16	3	2,309
30 to 34 years	2,672	23	0	25	6	2,726
35 to 39 years	2,480	22	4	22	3	2,531
40 to 44 years	2,176	7	7	16	4	2,210
45 to 49 years	1,687	16	6	7	2	1,718
50 to 54 years	1,290	2	1	6	1	1,300
55 to 59 years	1,089	8	2	3	1	1,103
60 to 64 years	964	3	1	2	0	970
65 to 69 years	773	3	1	2	0	779
70 to 74 years	466	4	1	1	0	472

Continued

Boone County, Kentucky- Males	White	Black or African- American	American Indian and Alaska Native	Asian including Pacific Islanders	Some other race, two or more races	Total
75 to 79 years	282	1	0	0	0	283
80 to 84 years	177	3	0	0	0	180
85 years and over	124	0	0	1	0	125
Female:	29,065	164	39	176	34	29,478
0 to 4 years	2,249	12	2	23	3	2,289
5 to 9 years	2,339	13	1	16	5	2,374
10 to 14 years	2,282	14	6	6	6	2,314
15 to 19 years	2,003	9	3	7	5	2,027
20 to 24 years	1,915	11	2	12	1	1,941
25 to 29 years	2,480	16	2	20	3	2,521
30 to 34 years	2,935	16	1	39	4	2,995
35 to 39 years	2,527	20	6	10	3	2,566
40 to 44 years	2,256	13	2	19	3	2,293
45 to 49 years	1,665	10	3	6	1	1,685
50 to 54 years	1,277	5	4	6	0	1,292
55 to 59 years	1,152	8	3	4	0	1,167
60 and 61 years	1,093	2	3	5	0	1,103
65 to 69 years	912	5	1	1	0	919
70 to 74 years	683	3	0	1	0	687
75 to 79 years	541	4	0	1	0	546
80 to 84 years	432	2	0	0	0	434
85 years and over	324	1	0	0	0	325

Source: U.S. Census Bureau, Census 1990

Of major importance for planning purposes is the **age** composition of a population. As we mentioned already, demand for public services such as education, depends largely on the age structure of an area's population. Children and teenagers need to go to school and go to the playground after school. Young professional families have children and buy their first home. As people age, preferences and demands for public services change. Older people have usually higher demand for health care and nursing homes. We can easily see that the age structure of a population reveals important information on needs and demands of the population for planning purposes.

One term people often use to describe age groups is **age cohorts**. Usually, many demographic studies divide the population into five- or ten-year age cohorts. It reduces the number of total cohorts significantly compared to using one-year age cohorts. But it also reduces the level of detail by aggregating single years into multi-year age cohorts. In the example, the population of Boone County is divided into five-year age cohorts with the exception that the last age cohort includes all persons 85 years of age and over. Reading down the column labeled "total" for the female sub-table of Table 3.2, we can identify the following:

— the youngest age cohort 0 – 4 years has 3,347 members,

— the age cohort 35 – 39 years is the largest one with 4,003 females and

— the oldest age cohort of 85 years and over has 492 females.

Depending on what information you need, a table like this can provide the number of females of school age, the number of women of working age and the number of potential retirees living in the county.

Together, the **age-sex** composition of a population is often graphically represented in what is called a **population pyramid**. It is a double histogram of the sex-age structure where females are on the left side of the vertical zero line and males are on the right side. Each horizontal bar represents one age cohort, with the youngest age cohort at the bottom and the oldest age cohort at the top. The length of each bar is directly related to the number of persons it represents.

From Fig. 3.3, we see that there were more males than females in the youngest age cohort in Boone County, which is consistent with the worldwide observable phenomena that more males are born than females. The exact male/ female birth ratio is 1.05 stating that for every 100 female babies, there are 105 male babies born. The largest age group for both sexes in Boone County is that of age 35 – 39; thereafter the population cohorts decrease. Beginning with the age cohort 25 – 29, the number of females outweighs the number of males for all subsequent age cohorts, reflecting lower mortality rates for females at all ages. Also beginning

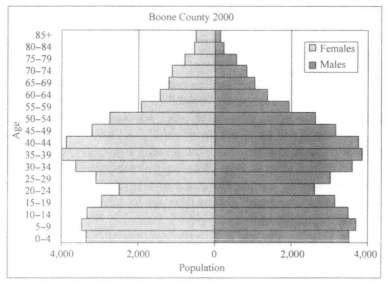

Figure 3.3 Population pyramid, Boone County, 2000

with the age cohort $60-64$, the number of persons per age cohort declines drastically, partly due to exponentially increasing mortality rates in these upper age cohorts. Another factor that contributes to this is maybe the fact that many older people move to retirement homes that are away from Boone County.

For interpreting county-level population pyramids one must be aware of two forces that simultaneously shape the form of pyramids. One is the **fertility rate**, which plays an important role in projecting population. Although national fertility rates are easily available in the United States, fertility rates also show region-specific variances.

A second, and for smaller areas, more important force is **in- and out-migration**. The irregularity in the population pyramid for Boone County beginning with the age cohorts $15-19$ can mainly be explained by age cohort specific migration rates. Later in this chapter you will see that this irregularity in the population age structure overlaps flawlessly with the county's age-specific migration rates. In other words, the observable decline, which begins with the age cohorts $15-19$, can be attributed largely to migration.

This section closes with the realization that describing one area's population according to its size, distribution, composition, and change will reveal a lot of information. These four basic population characteristics should give you enough guidance to avoid unnecessary and wrong conclusions in population projections. We recommend studying all possible aspects of your target population before actually doing the projections. The more you know about the population you are going to project, forecast, or estimate, the better.

3.3   Components of Change—Demographic Reasons for Population Change

Two simultaneous forces account for changes in population over time. First, population grows over time through births (B) and people moving into the target region (in-migrants; IM). Second, population declines through deaths (D) and people leaving the region (out-migrants; OM). Explaining observed and projected population changes through accounting for the individual components of change (births, deaths, and migration) sets the stage for probably the most basic formula in demography: the demographic balancing Eq. (3.3a) and Eq. (3.3b).

Demographic balancing equation is: [1]

$$P_{t+n} - P_t = B - D + (\text{IM} - \text{OM}) \tag{3.3a}$$

---

[1] Smith et al., 2001: 30.

The change in population between future year $t+n$ and initial year t is the result of the number of births (B) plus the in-migrants (IM), minus the number of deaths (D) and out-migrants (OM) for this specific time period of n years. The two population variables, P_{t+n} and P_t, are static measures and refer to the population statistics at one point in time. The four components of change measures are dynamic and quantify the number of births, deaths, and in- and out-migrants for that time period. Alternatively, in- and out-migrants could be netted out and referred to as "net migration (NM)". The demographic balancing equation can then be rewritten as:

$$P_{t+n} - P_t = B - D + \mathrm{NM} \qquad (3.3b)$$

where NM refers to net migration which is computed as: $\mathrm{NM} = \mathrm{IN} - \mathrm{OM}$.

The population statistic P can be the total population. As we will explore in greater detail in the section on the cohort-component method, the population is most commonly further disaggregated into sex and age cohorts.

Taking a second look at the demographic balancing equation we can immediately recognize that part of population changes, e.g., B and D, come mainly from the population itself, independent from outside forces. This is where the sex and age structure of the population play a crucial role. More women in the childbearing age means more births per time period, everything else being constant. On the other hand, populations with an old age structure are more likely to have a greater number of deaths per time period. Netting out births and deaths, we can refer to **natural population increase or decrease**. In the case where births outnumber deaths ($B > D$), the population is said to experience natural increase. However, when more people are dying than being born ($B < D$), population would naturally decrease.

People migrate for various reasons. Some people just need a move, some are looking for better regional amenities (e.g., weather, recreational value of region), and others simply get transferred through their jobs. The Sunshine State, Florida, is the most popular retirement state in the United States. The weather is the main factor. Younger people seem more likely to prefer San Francisco, New York, or Washington D.C. for professional reasons, or simply because these places are the "happening" place to live. The bottom line is that reasons for migration are very complex. A structural population model is one strain of models that accounts for other than pure demographic factors included in the demographic balancing Eq. (3.3a).

3.3.1 Fertility

The first component on the right-hand side of the demographic balancing Eq. (3.3) deals with B, also referred to as fertility. Technically, the term fertility denotes the number of live births, often expressed as the number of actual live births to women in a particular age cohort, symbolized by n. Many different fertility rates are used in the literature. Table 3.4 lists two of them. The age-specific birth rate $(_n\text{ASBR}_x)$ is the number of live births per 1,000 females in the same age cohort over an x year period. Fertility rates also can be presented as probabilities that a woman in this specific age cohort will give birth in x years period $P(_n\text{ASBR}_x)$. In this case, we talk about fertility rates f_n, where n refers to the age cohort n.

Table 3.4 Live births and fertility rates, Boone County, Kentucky, July 2003[1]

Age-specific Cohort of Mother	Age-specific Birth Rates[1] $(_n\text{ASBR}_x)$	Probability of Birth $(P(_n\text{ASBR}_x))$
10 – 14	52.4	0.0524
15 – 19	391.6	0.3916
20 – 24	491.7	0.4917
25 – 29	491.7	0.4917
30 – 34	287.8	0.2878
35 – 39	86.4	0.0864
40 – 44	9.5	0.0095
Total		1.8111

(1) per thousand females over a five-year period

Table 3.4 represents the age-specific birth rates statistics for Boone County, Kentucky.[1] Following this table, we immediately can identify that:

(1) the number of live births are reported for a five year period.

(2) the females are divided into five-year age cohorts.

(3) the age range of childbirth-giving women starts at 10 – 14 years and ends at 40 – 44 years.

(4) the majority of childbirth-giving females are 20 – 29 years of age. Whereby in the case of Boone county, the lower half of the twenty age cohort (e.g., 20 – 24 years) and the upper half of the twenty age cohort (e.g., 25 – 29 years) appear to have identical fertility rates.

From Table 3.4, we can conclude that fertility rates are very age specific, which is graphically emphasized in Fig. 3.4.

① Source: Kentucky Population Projections, July 2003, The University of Louisville Urban Studies Institute, Kentucky State Data Center.

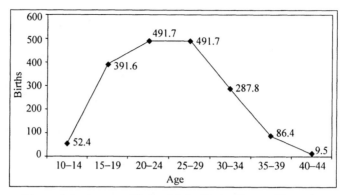

Figure 3.4 Age-specific live births, Boone County, Kentucky

There are many more factors that influence fertility rates. Among others, fertility rates vary geographically, culturally, and over time. According to the U.S. Central Intelligence Agency's (CIA, 2004) "The World Factbook", the United States' birth rate is estimated at 14.14 births/1,000 persons at midyear for the year 2003. For comparison, Ethiopia's birth rate for the same year is estimated at 39.81 births/1,000 persons and Germany's birth rate is at 8.6 births/1,000 persons indicating geographical and cultural variations in birth rates.

Looking at fluctuations of fertility rates over time, the United States exhibits some sharp changes. While the total fertility rate was slightly over 3.5 births per woman during the Baby Boom years in the late 1950s and early 1960s, it fell drastically by the mid-1970s to about 1.8 births per woman. Since the 1990s, the total fertility rate[1] per woman recovered slightly to a level of 2.0 – 2.1, which is the level required for the natural replacement of the population.[2]

While fertility rates differ across regions and fluctuate over time, it is important to recognize that these differences and fluctuations are not solely grounded in regional and cultural variations, but may be the result of a combination of complex economic, social, and other factors. This becomes apparent by comparing fertility rates across selected female subgroups for women 15 – 44 years old:[3]

(1) The general fertility rate (GFR) for all women was 61.4 births per 1,000 women.

(2) Hispanic women had the highest general fertility rate among all race and origin groups with 82.0 births per 1,000 women, while the GFR was significantly smaller for Asian and Pacific Islander women with 55.4.

---

[1] The total fertility rate refers to the average number of children that would be born per woman if all women lived to the end of their childbearing years and bore children according to a given fertility rate at each age.

[2] Source: U.S. Census Bureau, Fertility of American Women: June 2000 (P20-543RV). National Center for Health Statistics, National Vital Statistics Report, Vol. 47, No. 25.

[3] All fertility rates are reported as births per 1,000 women for the year 2002. Source: Fertility of American Women: June 2002, October 2003, U.S. Census Bureau.

(3) Women in the South are slightly more reproductive than women living in the Midwest with fertility rates of 67.0 and 55.6 births per 1,000 women respectively.

(4) Women in the labor force, of course, had lower fertility rates (47.4) than women not in the labor force (95.0).

(5) Women with an annual family income of under $10,000 had the highest fertility rate (84.5) versus women with a family income of more than $75,000, who had the lowest fertility rate (60.0).

(6) With respect to educational attainments, the lowest fertility rate is reported for women who graduated from college with an associate degree (51.6), while women who received a graduate or professional degree have a significantly higher fertility rate (84.9).

We see that fertility rates vary across geographic regions, and are dependent on economic and social factors and fluctuate over time. We further see that different data sources, for instance the CIA World Factbook and the National Center for Health Statistics (NCHS), use different definitions of fertility/birth rates. They all build upon the total number of live births (reported in the United States by the NCHS) and the corresponding population size for that specific area (reported by the U.S. Census Bureau). In the conclusion of this section on births and fertility, we will define in more detail the different fertility rates.

Crude birth rate (CBR): The crude birth rate used in the example is from the CIA World Factbook as the number of live births per 1,000 population.

$$CBR = (B/P) \times 1,000 \qquad (3.4)$$

where, B is the number of live births per year and P is the total midyear population.[1]

The National Center for Health Statistics announced on its 2003 National Vital Statistics Report (Vol. 52, No. 10) the lowest birth rate for the United States since national data have been available with a crude birth rate of 13.9. For the calculation, the NCHS used the reported live births during 2002 and the 2002 population estimate produced by the U.S. Census Bureau based on the 2000 census. Given all the necessary pieces of information, the crude birth rate formula[2] can be written as follows:

$$CBR = (4,021,726 / 288,368,706) \times 1,000 = 13.9$$

General fertility rate (GFR): The next logical step to improving the crude birth rate is by relating the number of births to the number of females in the

---

① Live births reports the number of babies born. Midyear population refers to the number of people alive at midyear, usually a calendar year.

② The number of births is taken from the National Vital Statistics Report, Vol. 52, No. 10, December 17, 2003: "Births: Final Data for 2002", p. 30, Table 1.

reproductive age group, mainly 15 – 44 years. The examples we used earlier to emphasize the influence of economic and social factors as determinants for differences in fertility rates used general fertility rates. The generic formula can be written as:

$$GFR = (B / FP_{15-44}) \times 1,000 \qquad (3.5)$$

where, B is the number of live births per year and FP_{15-44} is the age-specific female cohort of the population, or all women of age 15 – 44.

Using the GFR formula, the general fertility rate for all women of age 15 – 44 in the United States for the year 2002 can be computed as:[1]

$$GFR = (4,021,726 / 62,044,142) \times 1,000 = 64.8$$

Age specific birth rate (ASBR): The next step is to take all females in reproductive age for a specific area and divide them into age cohorts, for example, age cohorts of five years. This was done in Table 3.4 and the results are age-specific birth rates. For each age cohort of females, the ASBR is computed as the ratio of total births for that specific age group over the total number of females in this particular age group at midyear.

$$_n ASBR_x = (_n B_x /_n FP_x) \times 1,000 \qquad (3.6)$$

where x indicates the lower limit of the age cohort and n, the number of years in the age interval. B and FP refer, again, to the number of births and female population, respectively.

For example, $_n FP_x$ defines the age cohort that starts at age x and includes all females up to an age of $x + n$ years. $_5 FP_{20}$ therefore, defines the cohort of females age 20 – 24, which spans five years, at midyear. Table 3.4 reports the ASBR for the cohort $_5 FP_{20}$ to be 491.7. Meaning that for 1,000 women belonging to this age group, 491.7 will give birth over a five-year period.

Total Fertility Rate (TFR): Often, the literature refers to average number of births per woman. For example, earlier we reported that in the United States the average number of births per woman fluctuated between 2.0 and 2.1 during the 1990s. What people use here is called the total fertility rate. It is computed as the sum of all ASBR's. For example, Table 3.4 identifies the conditional probability— $P(_n ASBR_x)$ —that a woman will give birth given that she belongs to the age cohort 20 – 24 years with 0.4917. This probability refers to one woman

---

[1] Using births from the: National Vital Statistics Report, Vol. 50, No. 5 and the number of females of 15 – 44 years from the U.S. Census Summary File (SF1), the GFR is slightly different from the October 2001 release by the U.S. Census Bureau: GFR = 65.9 = (4,058,814 / 61,576,997) × 1,000. The difference is explained by the fact that at the earlier release date only preliminary data were available.

only and is conditional in that this woman must belong to that age-specific cohort. Accordingly, the total fertility rate for that specific woman would be adding all conditional probabilities for her entire reproductive lifespan:

$$\text{TFR} = \sum [P(_n\text{ASBR}_x)] \qquad (3.7)$$

From Table 3.4, we can calculate that the total fertility rate for Boone County, KY is 1.811. Although we know that the age-specific birth rates reported in Table 3.4 refer to the entire female population in Boone County at one point in time, namely 2003, for calculating the TFR, we now must interpret the table slightly different. Let us, for now, assume that we observe 1,000 women over their entire "hypothetical" reproductive lifespan. Meaning that in the beginning of their reproductive lifespan, all 1,000 women would be in the age group $10-14$. Together they would give 52 live births during these five years. Accordingly, the same 1,000 women would after five years enter the second age cohort of $15-19$ years and would give 392 live births. Analogously, adding all births together would tell us that over the reproductive lifespan of these specific 1,000 women, they would give 1,811 live births, assuming that no one left the cohort. In other words, the TFR refers to the number of babies born during women's reproductive years. In the case of Boone County, a woman on average will give birth to 1.8 babies in her life time.

Note that the TFR is based on hypothetical assumptions in that we now look at the entire lifespan of a group of women. We further assume that no one leaves this hypothetical cohort and the birth rates will not change over their lifespan. The TFR is also important when referring to the level necessary for natural replacement of the population; the replacement level fertility. According to the Census Bureau, approximately 2.1 births per woman are required for a population to maintain its current level in the long run. In the case of Boone County, KY, the TFR of 1.811 means that the population will naturally decline.

3.3.2   Mortality

A second component of change is people dying from one time period to the next. This can be either expressed in the form of **mortality or survival rates**. Table 3.5 lists the survival rates for Kentucky, as county-specific survival rates are not available for Kentucky.

The first column in Table 3.5 identifies the 5-year age cohorts. Columns two and three list the survival rates as the number of 5-year survivors per 1,000 male or females, respectively, by age cohort. Columns four and five express the same survival rates in form of probabilities for a person to survive from one age cohort to the next. For example, the entry for the female $25-29$ age cohort of 996.6 states that of 1,000 females of age $25-29$ (e.g., beginning age) 996.6 will

Table 3.5   Survival rates by age and sex, Kentucky, July 2003

Age-Specific Cohorts	Male	Female	Male	Female
Live births	992.4	993.4	0.9924	0.9934
0 – 4	996.7	997.5	0.9967	0.9975
5 – 9	998.8	999.2	0.9988	0.9992
10 – 14	997.2	998.5	0.9972	0.9985
15 – 19	992.9	997.3	0.9929	0.9973
20 – 24	992.9	997.4	0.9929	0.9974
25 – 29	991.8	996.6	0.9918	0.9966
30 – 34	989.6	995.3	0.9896	0.9953
35 – 39	985.9	993.2	0.9859	0.9932
40 – 44	980.3	989.1	0.9803	0.9891
45 – 49	970.9	983.5	0.9709	0.9835
50 – 54	954.0	973.0	0.9540	0.9730
55 – 59	925.6	957.0	0.9256	0.9570
60 – 64	883.0	932.0	0.8830	0.9320
65 – 69	823.6	897.0	0.8236	0.8970
70 – 74	750.8	850.4	0.7508	0.8504
75 – 79	639.2	765.3	0.6392	0.7653
80 – 84	498.5	637.3	0.4985	0.6373
85 +	297.6	381.4	0.2976	0.3814

survive the five-year period and enter the female age cohort of 30 – 35 (e.g., ending age). Expressed as a probability we can read the same entry in that there is a 0.9966 probability for a woman to reach age 30 assuming that she is in the 25 – 29 age cohort. The relationships of age, sex, and survival rates are graphically shown in Fig. 3.5. In Kentucky, females have higher survival rates at all ages. Both sexes show that with increasing age survival rates decline continuously. We also see immediately from the data that the first two age cohorts (e.g., 0 – 4 years and 5 – 9 years) show slightly lower survival rates which can be explained partly by higher infant and early childhood mortalities.

In the United States, the National Vital Statistics Report (NVSR) by the Department of Health and Human Services[1] reports annually life tables by age, race, and sex, which are the most detailed source available at present for survival rates. Among others, these tables report probabilities of dying between ages x and $x + 1$, number of people surviving to age x, and number dying between ages x to $x + 1$. Five-year survival rate tables can be derived from the life tables through aggregation of annual data into five-year age cohorts.

---

[1] http://www.cdc.gov/nchs/.

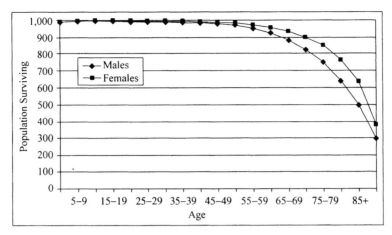

Figure 3.5   Population surviving by sex and age-specific cohort, Kentucky, July 2003

The NVSR also includes a table of survivorship by age, sex, and race in the United States from 1900 to 2000.[1] According to the table, the life expectancy rose significantly in this 100 year period. In 1900, 58.5% of the population reached age 50 and 13.5% survived to age 80. In 2000, 93.5% survived to age 50 and 51.0% of the population survived to age 80. However, while the first 50 years indicate a large reduction in infant mortality (infants born surviving the first year) from 87.6% in 1900 to 97.0% in 1950, the second half of the last century was characterized primarily by improvements in the surviving age of the older population.

Life expectancy in the United States is recorded in "The World Factbook" as 77.43 years for the total population in 2003. This refers to the average number of years to be lived by a group of people born in the same year, assuming constant mortality at each age in the future. For comparison, life expectancy in Ethiopia is 40.88 years, in Germany 78.54 years, and in China 71.96 years. These data are often used as a measure of overall quality of life in a country.

For the remainder of this section on mortality, we will focus exclusively on survival rates. It is important, however, to recognize that if we know the number of people surviving from one time period to the next, we immediately know the number of people dying for this specific time period and vice versa.

Life Table Survival Rates: Official life tables were introduced as early as the 1660s in London by the Englishman John Graunt[2]. In the United States they have been prepared since the beginning of 1900, first for every ten years and

---

[1] Source: National Vital Statistics Report, December 19, 2002, Vol. 51, No. 3, p. 38, Table 10. Survivorship by age, rage, and sex: Death registration States, 1900 – 1902 to 1919 – 1921, and United States, 1929 – 1931 to 2000; http://www.cdc.gov/nchs/data/nvsr/nvsr51/nvsr51_03.pdf.

[2] Smith et al., 2001: 52.

since 1945 on an annual basis. Today, annual or decennial life tables are available at national and state-level. Table 3.6 shows an abridged version of the U.S. life table for the entire population.

Table 3.6 Abridged life table for the total population, United States, 2000[1]

Age	Probability of Dying Between Ages x to $x+n$ $(_nq_x)$	Number Surviving to Age x (l_x)	Number Dying Between Ages x to $x+n$ $(_nd_x)$	Person-Years Lived Between Ages x to $x+n$ $(_nL_x)$	Total Number of Person-Years Lived Above Age x (T_x)	Expectation of Life at Age x (e_x)
0 – 1	0.00693	100,000	693	99,392	7,686,810	76.9
1 – 4	0.00131	99,307	130	396,916	7,587,418	76.4
5 – 9	0.00082	99,177	82	495,668	7,190,502	72.5
10 – 14	0.00104	99,095	103	495,278	6,694,833	67.6
15 – 29	0.00341	98,992	338	494,200	6,199,555	62.6
20 – 24	0.00479	98,654	473	492,113	5,705,355	57.8
25 – 29	0.00494	98,181	485	489,702	5,213,242	53.1
30 – 34	0.00578	97,696	565	487,130	4,723,539	48.3
35 – 39	0.00806	97,132	783	483,813	4,236,409	43.6
40 – 44	0.01182	96,349	1,139	479,070	3,752,596	38.9
45 – 49	0.01773	95,210	1,688	472,085	3,273,527	34.4
50 – 54	0.02576	93,522	2,409	461,940	2,801,442	30.0
55 – 59	0.03968	91,113	3,615	447,124	2,339,510	25.7
60 – 64	0.06133	87,498	5,366	424,879	1,892,377	21.6
65 – 69	0.09217	82,131	7,570	392,758	1,467,498	17.9
70 – 74	0.13838	74,561	10,317	348,168	1,074,739	14.4
75 – 79	0.20557	64,244	13,207	289,331	726,571	11.3
80 – 84	0.31503	51,037	16,078	215,947	437,240	8.6
85 – 89	0.46111	34,959	16,120	133,503	221,293	6.3
90 – 94	0.61506	18,839	11,587	62,766	87,790	4.7
95 – 99	0.75434	7,252	5,470	20,388	25,024	3.5
100 years and over	1.00000	1,781	1,781	4,636	4,636	2.6

(1) Source: National Vital Statistics Report, December 19, 2002, Vol. 51, No. 3, p. 38.

Column 1, Age-specific intervals $(x \text{ to } x+n)$: Reports the exact interval— n—between two ages—x and $x+n$—as indicated. For example, "5 – 9" indicates the five year interval between the fifth and tenth birthday. In this example, n indicates a five year interval and x equals the beginning age of the age cohort. Exceptions are the first two age cohorts age $0-1$ and $1-4$ and the last age cohort $100+$.

Column 2, Probability of dying between ages x to $x+n$ $(_nq_x)$: Refers to the proportion of people alive at age x (beginning of the interval) and will not reach age $x+n$ (end of the interval). For instance, $_5q_{10} = 0.00104$ tells us that the proportion of the total population in the United States dying after their tenth birthday and before reaching their fifteenth birthday is 0.00104. Meaning that out of every 100,000 people in this cohort, 104 will die before reaching age fifteen.

Column 3, Number surviving to age x (l_x): Shows the number of the surviving members of 100,000 people at age x. Beginning with 100,000 life births in column three, 97,132 will complete their 35th year of life and 1,781 will have a 100 year birthday party.

Column 4, Number dying between ages x to $x+n$ $(_nd_x)$: Reports the number of all the people dying from 100,000 life births between exact ages x to $x+n$. Following Table 3.6 we can identify that in the United States 693 babies will die in their first year of life and 13,207 people will die between ages 75 to 80.

Column 5, Person-years lived between ages x to $x+n$ $(_nL_x)$: Refers to the total of person-years lived between ages x to $x+n$. Important for deriving person-years lived is knowing when people die during a particular age interval. For instance, people belonging to the age cohort $35-40$ who reach their 40th birthday would contribute five-person years each. People dying between ages 35 to 40 would contribute less than five person-years lived depending on when they died. In case they died exactly on their 37th birthday, they count as two person-years, if they died in between birthdays, they count for the whole years and partial years they lived.

Column 6, Total number of person-years lived above age x (T_x): Is the summation of the total of person-years lived between ages x to $x+n$ (e.g., $_nL_x$) and that of all subsequent age intervals. For instance, the aggregated total of person-years lived above age 35 (e.g., 4,236,409) is the sum of all intervals of person-years lived between ages x to $x+n$ (e.g. column 5) starting with interval 35 to 40.

Column 7, Expectation of life at age x (e_x): Indicates the remaining lifetime in years for persons reaching the exact age x. According to the abridged life table for the total population of the United States, persons of age 35 are expected to have an average remaining lifetime of 43.6 years.

The relationships among the different variables included in Table 3.6 and described thereafter can also be expressed in mathematical terms.

Column 2, the probability of dying between ages x to $x+n$ $(_nq_x)$ can be calculated as:

$$_nq_x = {_nd_x}/{I_x}$$

Knowing the number of people surviving between ages x to $x+n$, the number dying between ages x to $x+n$ can be expressed as:

$$_nd_x = I_x - I_{x+n}$$

The person-years lived between ages x to $x+n$ $(_nL_x)$ can be expressed as

$$_nL_x = T_x - T_{x+n}$$

Data in a life table can then be used to calculate survival rates as:

$$_nS_x = {_nL_{x+n}}/{_nL_x} \tag{3.8}$$

where $_nS_x$ is the survival rate, $_nL_{x+n}$ and $_nL_x$ are the numbers of two successive person-years lived for the corresponding successive age intervals taken from the life table.

For the total U.S. population, for example, the survival rate from the age interval $35-40$ to $40-45$ is computed as:

$$_5S_{35} = {_5L_{35+5}}/{_5L_{35}} = 479,070/483,813 = 0.9902$$

When we plan to project population for male and female, we can find separate life tables for male and female and for different target areas. The structures of the life tables are exactly the same so is the calculation of the survival rates. Moving the decimal point three positions to the right, we now can compare this national level survival rate (e.g. 990.2) with the numbers reported for the same age interval in the Kentucky survival rate table. For males, the corresponding survival rate is reported as 989.6 and for females it is 995.3. Observed discrepancies in survival rates between the U.S. population and Kentucky are very small and can be explained through:

(1) different target years. The United States rates refer to the year 2000, while the Kentucky rates are for 2003.

(2) different levels of aggregation. We are comparing sex-specific rates (e.g., female and male in Kentucky) with aggregated rates for the entire U.S. population.

(3) different target areas. Here, we compare state-level with national-level survival rates.

Conceptually similar to the Age-Specific Birth Rates $(_nASBR_x)$ are Age-Specific Death Rates $(_nASDR_x)$ which play an important role as a starting point for the construction of life tables. They are calculated as the ratio of the number of deaths $(_nD_x)$ between age x and age $x+n$ over the population $(_nP_x)$. Subscript n refers to the time period of n years.

$$_n\text{ASDR}_x = {_nD_x} / {_nP_x} \qquad (3.9)$$

Like fertility rates, ASDRs use the mid-interval population, preferably from census data. Mid-interval population is commonly used when averaging population. Alternatively, the population can refer to the number of people at the beginning of a period. For constructing life tables it is assumed that deaths are spread out evenly over the entire time-period, n.

3.3.3 Migration

The last two components of the demographic balancing equation account for the fact that people relocate. People move within the same county to a different residence, to a different county within the same state, between states, or even internationally. Generally, talking about moving or movers implies a change in location. People moving within a town from one end to the other end and staying within the same jurisdictional boundary are referred to as local movers and are not considered to be migrants. To qualify as a migrant, a person must move across jurisdictional boundaries. Although, for people living close to county or state boundaries, this can also imply just moving a few blocks away.

Depending on the attractiveness of a place, which among others includes amenities, availability of jobs, and recreational activities, etc., some places have positive net migration rates, indicating that more people move into the region than leave it. On the other hand, less attractive and declining regions show negative net migration rates. It is important to recognize that although net migration shows whether a region gains or loses population due to migration, it does not implicitly indicate how many people are actually migrating in and out. Depending on the depth of your analysis and data availability, you might want to account for in- and out-migration separately or simply use net migration data.[1] The U.S. Census Bureau provides data on migration in the United States at national, state and county levels.[2] Table 3.7 shows that Americans indeed are still on the move. Forty-six percent of Americans ages 5 years and over,

---

[1] In the concept of planning in general and in population projection for planning purposes in particular, net migration is sufficient most of the time. For a more detailed discussion on the pros and cons of gross versus net migration please see chapter 6 of Smith, Tayman, and Swanson.

[2] Data Source: Census 2000 PHC-T-23. Migration by Sex and Age for the Population 5 Years and Over for the United States, Regions, States, and Puerto Rico: 2000 at: http://www.census. gov/population/www/cen2000/migration.html.

Table 3.7 Gross and net migration by sex for the population 5 years and over for the United States and Kentucky, 2000

Geographic Area	Population 5 years and over	Same residence (nonmovers)	Total movers	Different residence 5 years ago					
				Different residence in same geographic area	Domestic Migration[1]			From abroad[2]
					Inmigrants	Outmigrants	5-year net migration	
United States	262,375,152	142,027,478	120,347,674	112,851,828	(X)	(X)	(X)	7,495,846
Male	128,160,479	68,381,473	59,779,006	55,767,900	(X)	(X)	(X)	4,011,106
Female	134,214,673	73,646,005	60,568,668	57,083,928	(X)	(X)	(X)	3,484,740
Kentucky	3,776,230	2,112,135	1,664,095	1,299,535	318,579	284,452	34,127	45,981
Male	1,838,610	1,019,192	819,418	629,222	163,929	144,452	19,477	26,267
Female	1,937,620	1,092,943	844,677	670,313	154,650	140,000	14,650	19,714

(1) Outmigrants and 5-year net migration are not included in total movers.

(2) This category includes movers from foreign countries, as well as movers from Puerto Rico, U.S. Island Areas, and U.S. minor outlying islands.

or 120,347,674 people, moved in the period from 1995 to 2000. Of these 120 million movers, only a small portion (7,495,846 people or approximately 6 percent) qualify as migrants. At the state-level for Kentucky, for example, 44% (1,664,095 people) of Kentucky's population moved in the same five-year period, of which 318,579 moved into the state and 284,452 left the state resulting in net migration of 34,127 people. Additionally, 45,981 people moved in from abroad.

While calculating fertility and survival rates is usually done based on area-specific data, for computing in/out and net migration rates, the choice of the appropriate population base is not that straightforward. In the case of out-migration, we can apply the areas of interest population as base but what can be applied in the case of in-migration rates? Definitely, these rates are somewhat independent of the target area. Of course, some areas, like San Francisco, are attractive enough to attract people. But in most cases, in-migration rates depend to a larger extent on the population statistics from where these people are migrating. This problem is well recognized in the literature; nevertheless, most studies applied for simplicity the population of the area under consideration as the denominator without differentiating between in/out and/or net migration rates.[1]

The general net migration rate is of the following form:

$$_n\text{mr}_x = (_n M_x / P_x) \times 1,000 \qquad (3.10)$$

where $_n\text{mr}_x$ is the migration rate under consideration (e.g., in, out, or net migration rate), $_n M_x$ is the corresponding number of in/out or net migrants between time period x to $x+n$, and P_x is the population total in beginning year x. In the case of calculating migration rates, the population total in beginning year x is preferred in the literature versus using midyear or end of interval population.

For Kentucky and Boone County, we can apply the migration rate formula and compute all rates as follows: [2]

The results in Table 3.8 show that Boone County has significantly larger migration rates than Kentucky. Kentucky experienced, from 1995 – 2000, a population increase due to net migration of almost 9 persons per 1,000 population, while Boone County's population grew by 119 persons per 1,000 population. A direct and logical conclusion from observed magnitudes of migration rates is that in the case of Boone County, in-migration plays a crucial role in population growth. In the case of Kentucky, which exhibits a slowly growing population, in-migration is a less significant factor of population growth.

---

[1] Smith et al., 2001: 105.

[2] The U.S. Census Bureau used in its 1995 – 2000 migration rate estimation the 1995 – 2000 net migration as the numerator and the approximated 1995 population as the denominator. Multiplying this rate by 1,000 then refers to rates per 1,000 population. Source: http://www.census.gov/prod/2003pubs/censr-7.pdf.

Table 3.8   Migration rate example, Kentucky and Boone County, 1995 – 2000[1]

Kentucky	Number of Persons	Rates (per 1,000 Population)
Total Population (1995)	3,887,427	
Total Population (2000)	4,041,769	
Inmigrants (1995 – 2000)	318,579	81.95
Outmigrants (1995 – 2000)	284,452	73.17
Gross Migration (1995 – 2000)	603,031	155.12
Net Migration (1995 – 2000)	34,127	8.78
Boone County	Number of Persons	Rates (per 1,000 Population)
Total Population (1995)	70,017	
Total Population (2000)	85,991	
Inmigrants (1995 – 2000)	25,232	360.37
Outmigrants (1995 – 2000)	16,896	241.31
Gross Migration (1995 – 2000)	42,128	601.68
Net Migration (1995 – 2000)	8,336	119.06

(1) Sources: http://ksdc.louisville.edu/kpr/pro/Summary_Table.xls and http://www.census.gov/prod/2003pubs/censr7.pdf.

Referring back to the problem of the correct population choice for the denominator in computing the migration rates, using the population under consideration will have different effects in both cases. Generally, the literature recommends using the population under consideration as the denominator for decreasing or slowly growing populations. Thus in the case of Kentucky, using Kentucky's population will not introduce a large error in computing migration rates. However, in the case of Boone County, the argument might be that in-migration by far outweighs other migration forces, and that this in-migration is independent of the target areas population. Therefore, a situation where choosing Kentucky's or even the United State's population might be the better denominator for calculating migration rates. For example, the net migration rate for Boone County can be recalculated using Kentucky's population as denominator:

$$\text{net migration rate} = (8{,}336 \, / \, 3{,}887{,}427) \times 1{,}000 = 2.14$$

This example shows that by using Kentucky's larger population, we get a significantly smaller net migration rate. Overall, using Kentucky's population will help smooth out the otherwise significant impact of a large number of in-migrants which migrated, to a large extent, independent of Boone County's existing population. But keep in mind, when we are projecting future net migration in Boone County, we must use the population of Kentucky as the basis for calculating the number of in migrants.

3.4   Trend Extrapolation Methods

Extrapolating past trends into the future is the main idea behind all the trend extrapolation methods. This idea is appealing for small-area population projections with low data requirements, low costs, and easy application. Observing how the population grew/declined for the past years, we project future population assuming that these observed trends will continue into the near future. For example, Boone County's, Kentucky population increased in each consecutive year between 1990 and 2000 (Table 3.9). Continuing past trends into the future will, therefore, lead to projecting the population as growing in the future.

Table 3.9   Population of Boone County, Kentucky, 1990 – 2000[1]

Year (n)	Index Number	Observed Population (Pop_n)	Total Absolute Growth	Average Annual Absolute Change(AAAC)	Total Percent Growth	Average Annual Percent Change (AAPC)
1990	1	57,589				
1991	2	60,574	28,402	2,840	49.32	4.09
1992	3	62,897				
1993	4	65,318				
1994	5	67,554				
1995	6	70,017				
1996	7	72,860				
1997	8	76,162				
1998	9	79,818				
1999	10	83,349				
2000	11	85,991				

(1) Source of data: http://ksdc.louisville.edu/kpr/popest/ice9000.xls.

A fast and straight forward approach to getting a first impression on the overall past population trend can be obtained here by plotting the population on a simple graph with time on the horizontal axis and population on the vertical axis. Although population projection(s) are usually based on a mathematical model, it is particulary the graphical presentation the helps better understand population trends over time. The case of Boone County is clear cut in that the population grew continuously in the past as indicated in Fig. 3.6. The trend could be more complex in that population both increased and decreased during the period in which data are available.

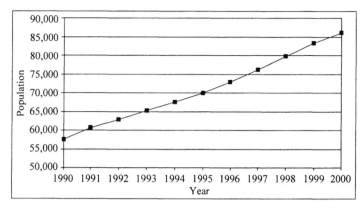

Figure 3.6   Population of Boone County, Kentucky, 1990 – 2000

We start describing population extrapolation models with simple average annual absolute population changes (AAAC) and/or average annual percent changes (AAPC) based on population statistics at two points in time. For instance, having the census population statistics for an area for the Census 1990 (Boone County: 57,589) and the Census 2000 (Boone County: 85,991) is sufficient to immediately compute two estimates: (1) the estimate for the observed annual population growth expressed as persons per year (AAAC) and (2) the estimate for the constant annual rate the population grew over the time period for which data are available (AAPC). For Boone County, the AAAC is derived by dividing the absolute population growth by the number of years:

$$\begin{aligned}
\text{AAAC} &= (\text{Pop}_{2000} - \text{Pop}_{1990})/n \\
&= (85,991 - 57,589)/10 \\
&= 2,840
\end{aligned} \tag{3.11}$$

Based on the same information, the AAPC is calculated using the geometric growth rate formula as:

$$\begin{aligned}
\text{AAPC} &= (\text{Pop}_{2000}/\text{Pop}_{1990})^{(1/n)} - 1 \\
&= (85,991/57,589)^{(1/10)} - 1 \\
&= 4.09\%
\end{aligned} \tag{3.12}$$

With this information readily available, we can have a quick and simple population projection for 2001, assuming that the observed average annual absolute/ percent changes will continue for the following year. More specifically, applying the average annual absolute change, the population for 2001 is projected as:

$$\begin{aligned}
\text{Pop}_{2001} &= \text{Pop}_{2000} + n \cdot (\text{AAAC}) \\
&= 85,991 + 1 \times (2,840) \\
&= 88,831
\end{aligned}$$

where, Pop refers to the population in the corresponding years, n is the number of years to project in the future, and AAAC is the average annual absolute change of the area's population. Overall, the population follows a linear growth pattern, depending solely on the calculated average annual absolute change for the period data are available.

Analogously, we can apply the already computed average annual percent change (AAPC) rate as follows:

$$\text{Pop}_{2001} = \text{Pop}_{2000} \cdot (1 + \text{AACP})^{n}$$
$$= 85,991 \times (1 + 0.0409)^{1}$$
$$= 89,508$$

where, Pop again refers to the population in the corresponding years, n is the number of years to project in the future, and AAPC is the growth rate expressing average annual percent changes of the area's population. what is important here is that the population grows annually by the same rate, namely by 4.09 percent. The difference in projected Boone County population for the years 2001 – 2010 using the AAAC and the AAPC is shown graphically in Fig. 3.7.

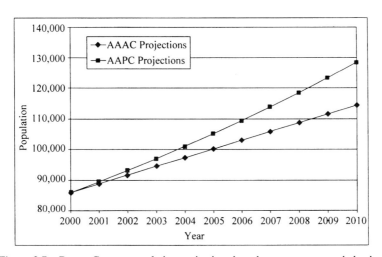

Figure 3.7   Boone County population projections based on average annual absolute change and average annual percent change, 2001 – 2010

3.4.1   Share of Growth Method

Ratio methods, such as the share of growth and the shift-share methods, are among the easiest extrapolation methods and are therefore popular among planners and demographers. The underlying principle of the share of growth as well as the shift-share method is a comparison of the smaller area's population to the population of a larger area, such as comparing a county to a state or a metropolitan area. In particular, the share of growth method observes the smaller area's share of population growth for a past time period—the base period. Assuming that this observed share of growth remains constant and knowing the larger area's projected population for the future target year, we can project the smaller area's future population. The share of growth method is expressed as:

$$Pop_{m,ty} = Pop_{m,ly} + \left[\frac{(Pop_{m,ly} - Pop_{m,by})}{(Pop_{n,ly} - Pop_{n,by})} \right] (Pop_{n,ty} - Pop_{n,ly})$$

$$= Pop_{m,ly} + growthshare(Pop_{n,ty} - Pop_{n,ly}) \qquad (3.13)$$

where,

Pop_m — population of smaller area;

Pop_n — population of larger comparison region;

ty — target year, i.e., year to be projected;

ly — launch year, i.e., later year of base period;

by — base year, i.e., earlier year of base period;

growthshare — share of growth.

An example of Boone County demonstrates the share of growth method. The needed data are listed in Table 3.10.

Table 3.10   Boone County and Kentucky population statistics, 1990 – 2000[1]

Year	Kentucky	Boone County
1990	3,686,891	57,589
2000	4,041,769	85,991
2010	4,374,591	

(1) Source: Kentucky State Data Center, Summary table for Kentucky and Counties: http://ksdc.louisville.edu/kpr/pro/Summary_Table.xls.

The base period in the example is the period from 1990 to 2000. The observed share of growth for this ten-year period is calculated as:

$$growthshare = \frac{Pop_{Boone,2000} - Pop_{Boone,1990}}{Pop_{KY,2000} - Pop_{KY,1990}} = \frac{85,991 - 57,589}{4,041,769 - 3,686,891} = 0.08$$

Assuming this share of growth of 0.08 for Boone County to remain constant in the future and knowing Kentucky's population for 2010, we can project Boone County's population for the year 2010 as:

$$Pop_{Boone,2010} = Pop_{Boone,2000} + growthshare \cdot (Pop_{KY,2010} - Pop_{KY,2000})$$
$$= 85,991 + 0.08 \times (4,374,591 - 4,041,769)$$
$$= 85,991 + 26,626$$
$$= 112,617$$

Although the share of growth method is very simple in its application, there are situations where the share of growth method cannot be applied. Imagine a situation where, for instance, a county with a declining population is situated in an otherwise growing state. If we predict the population for the larger area to increase faster than previously observed, then the share of growth would predict the smaller area to decline faster as observed for the projection period. One can justly argue that this is a very unlikely assumption. The share of growth method must be applied with care in cases where smaller and larger areas' populations are not moving in the same direction.

3.4.2   Shift-Share Method

Rather than using shares of growth, the shift-share method uses the smaller area's share of total population in the base year and in the launch year. These two population shares and the projected population for the larger comparison region for the target provide the means for applying the shift-share method as:

$$Pop_{m,ty} = Pop_{n,ty} \left[\frac{Pop_{m,ly}}{Pop_{n,ly}} + \left(\frac{years_{pp}}{years_{bp}} \right) \left(\frac{Pop_{m,ly}}{Pop_{n,ly}} - \frac{Pop_{m,by}}{Pop_{n,by}} \right) \right]$$
$$= Pop_{n,ty} \left[share_{ly} + \left(\frac{years_{pp}}{years_{bp}} \right) (share_{ly} - share_{by}) \right] \qquad (3.14)$$

where,

Pop_m — population of smaller area;

Pop_n — population of larger comparison region;

ty — target year, i.e., year to be projected;

ly — launch year, i.e., later year of base period;

by — base year, i.e., earlier year of base period;

$share_{ly}$ — population share in launch year;

$share_{ly}$ — population share in base year;

$years_{pp}$ — number of years in the projection period;

$years_{bp}$ — number of years in the base period.

Using again the population data from Table 3.10, we can project Boone County's population for the year 2010 using the shift-share method as:

$$\text{Pop}_{\text{Boone,2010}} = \text{Pop}_{\text{KY,2010}} \left[\frac{\text{Pop}_{\text{Boone,2000}}}{\text{Pop}_{\text{KY,2000}}} + \left(\frac{\text{years}_{2000-2010}}{\text{years}_{1990-2000}} \right) \left(\frac{\text{Pop}_{\text{Boone,2000}}}{\text{Pop}_{\text{KY,2000}}} - \frac{\text{Pop}_{\text{Boone,1990}}}{\text{Pop}_{\text{KY,1990}}} \right) \right]$$

$$= 4,374,591 \times \left[\frac{85,991}{4,041,769} + \left(\frac{10}{10} \right) \times \left(\frac{85,991}{4,041,769} - \frac{57,589}{3,686,891} \right) \right]$$

$$= 4,374,591 \times \left[0.02128 + \left(\frac{10}{10} \right) \times (0.02128 - 0.01562) \right]$$

$$= 117,851$$

The example of the shift-share method assumes linearly changing shares for the projection period. Alternatively, the population shares can follow a nonlinear growth pattern over time. Notable of the shift-share method is also that the last term in parenthesis, i.e. the shift-term, can be negative. This is always the case where the population shares of the smaller region declined over the base period. One implication of declining population shares is that for particularly long projection periods, the smaller area's population projection can turn out to be negative, which is not possible. We must evaluate the projected population with caution. Often, a comparison of the outcome of the population projection with the small area's population growth/decline for the base period can give some first clues as to whether or not the outcome of the population projections using ratio methods (e.g., share of growth and shift-share method) leads to reasonable results. Here, a good knowledge of the small and larger areas' past and present population trends will be a useful guide for interpreting the projection results.

The remainder of this section on extrapolation methods deals with more complex population models that use regression analysis to project future population trends. We use a hypothetical example to demonstrate the rationale behind regression analysis for population projections. We then introduce four different population models: (1) the linear population model, (2) the geometric population model, (3) the parabolic population model and (4) the logistic population model.

3.4.3   Linear Population Model

In addition to simple ratio methods described above, trend extrapolation models can use regression analysis to fit a line to observed population data. Because of its computational and conceptual ease, the linear population model as expressed in Eq. (3.15) is the most widely used population model:[1]

---

[1]   Klosterman, 1990: 9; Smith et al., 2001: 167.

$$\text{Pop}_n = \alpha + \beta \cdot T_n \tag{3.15}$$

where,

Pop_n — estimated population for a given year n;

α — intercept of the linear regression model;

β — slope coefficient of the linear regression model;

T_n — the index number for year n.

The main assumption on which the linear model is based is straight forward: the population growth follows a linear pattern, meaning that the population will grow by the same number of people every consecutive year, expressed by the slope, β. The graphic solution is represented by fitting a straight line as "closely as possible" to observed population data, as indicated in Fig. 3.8. Using the calculated linear trend line, future population projections will then be exactly on the line.

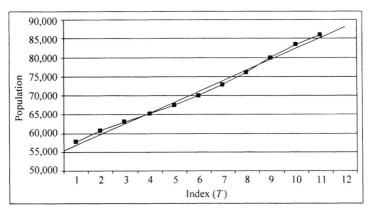

Figure 3.8   The linear trend line for Boone County, KY population data

As Fig. 3.8 indicates, the fitted straight line is an approximation of the observed population, but none of the observed data points (■) may actually lie on the straight line. The regression line has been fitted to observed population data for Boone County following the "least square criterion". As common in time series analysis, we supplemented the actual years (n), 1990, 1991, $\cdots$, 2000 with index numbers (T), e.g., 1, 2, $\cdots$, 10, 11, to simplify the computational process of estimating the regression line for the eleven years of available data for Boone County.

For a linear population trend line, the slope β indicates the calculated annual absolute population growth. In other words, it determines the number of people by which population grows/declines annually. Therefore, to determine a particular linear population trend line, we need to calculate the parameters α and β,

Research Methods in Urban and Regional Planning

which we will discuss now in greater detail. To demonstrate the computational process by hand, we are using Boone County's population statistics and the following linear regression model:

$$P = \alpha + \beta \cdot T + \varepsilon \qquad (3.16)$$

The computational steps deriving the two parameters α and β are rather straight forward and outlined in detail in Table 3.11.

Table 3.11   Linear population trend line computations, Boone County, KY[1]

Original Data			Deviations from Mean Values		Necessary Cross-products	
Observed Population, Pop	Year, n	Index Numbers, T	Population, p	Index Number, t	$p \cdot t$	t^2
57,589	1990	1	− 13,514	− 5	67,568	25
60,574	1991	2	− 10,529	− 4	42,115	16
62,897	1992	3	− 8,206	− 3	24,617	9
65,318	1993	4	− 5,785	− 2	11,569	4
67,554	1994	5	− 3,549	− 1	3,549	1
70,017	1995	6	− 1,086	0	0	0
72,860	1996	7	1,757	1	1,757	1
76,162	1997	8	5,059	2	10,119	4
79,818	1998	9	8,715	3	26,146	9
83,349	1999	10	12,246	4	48,985	16
85,991	2000	11	14,888	5	74,442	25
Totals 782,129		66	4	0	310,867	110

(1) Henceforth we adopt the convention of letting the lowercase letters p and t denote deviations from mean values for population statistics and index numbers.

(2) Population Mean: 71,103

(3) Index Number Mean: 6

As Table 3.11 shows, the table can be broken down into three distinct sections:

(1) the first three columns, including the original observed population data, the corresponding years (1990 – 2000), and the index numbers (1 – 11).

(2) the two successive columns, four and five, containing deviations from the mean values for the population (Pop) and the index number (T). Note that these deviations are denoted using lower case letters, e.g., p and t. Column four contains the deviations of the individual population statistics from the population mean. For example, − 13,514 is the difference between number of people in

Boone County in year 1 and the mean population for the 11 years, e.g., $(57,589 - 71,103) = -13,514$. Analogously, column five contains the deviations for the index number from their mean value, e.g., 6. For instance, the first deviation is computed as: $1 - 6 = -5$. To control the correctness of your computations, the sum of all deviations from the means must always equal zero.

(3) the last two columns, column six and seven, involve taking cross-products. Column six is the cross-product of the population deviation times the index number deviation (e.g., $p \cdot t$). For instance, 67,568 is the product of $-13,514$ and -5. The last column, seven, is the squared index number deviations (e.g., t^2). For instance, the first value 25 is $(-5)^2$.

What remains is plugging the results from Table 3.11 into the intercept and slope coefficient formulas:

$$\hat{\beta} = \frac{\sum (\text{Pop} - \overline{\text{Pop}}) \cdot (T - \overline{T})}{\sum (T - \overline{T})^2} = \frac{\sum p \cdot t}{\sum t^2} \qquad (3.17)$$

where,

$\overline{\text{Pop}}$ — the mean of Pop;

$\overline{T}$ — the mean of T;

p — the deviations from $\overline{\text{Pop}}$;

t — the deviations from $\overline{T}$;

$\sum$ — the summation expression (e.g., column total).

The intercept formula uses the fact that the straight line passes through computed mean values $\overline{\text{Pop}}$ and $\overline{T}$:

$$\hat{\alpha} = \overline{\text{Pop}} - \hat{\beta} \cdot \overline{T} \qquad (3.18)$$

For Boone County, the slope coefficient is estimated as

$$\hat{\beta} = \frac{\sum p \cdot t}{\sum t^2} = \frac{310,867}{110} = 2,826$$

The intercept $\hat{\alpha}$ can be computed using the estimated slope parameter, $\hat{\beta}$, and the mean values:

$$\hat{\alpha} = \overline{\text{Pop}} - \hat{\beta} \cdot \overline{T} = 71,103 - 2,826 \times 6 = 54,146$$

Inserting the parameter results into the linear population model for Boone County gives us the estimated population model:

$$\text{Pop} = 54,146 + 2,826 \cdot T$$

Research Methods in Urban and Regional Planning

Given that the estimated population model has been derived by using index numbers, for projecting Boone County's population for future years we have to use index numbers as well. For instance, we use 12 for the year 2001, 13 for 2002, 14 for 2003, and so on. Using the appropriate index numbers and the estimated linear population model, Boone County's population for the year 2001, 2002, and 2003 can be computed as follows:

$$\widehat{Pop}_{2001} = 54,146 + 2,826 \times 12 = 88,058$$

$$\widehat{Pop}_{2002} = 54,146 + 2,826 \times 13 = 90,884$$

$$\widehat{Pop}_{2003} = 54,146 + 2,826 \times 14 = 93,710$$

Of course, the projection period can be extended further into the future with the assumption that a linearly growing population remains constant. However, future projections must be interpreted with caution, as they usually become more and more unreliable. This is due to the fact that the assumption of a linear growth rate might not hold over an extended period of time.

Using the estimated linear population model we can also calculate the population for years for which we have observed population data. For instance, we can calculate the population for the year 2000 as:

$$\widehat{Pop}_{2000} = 54,146 + 2,826 \times 11 = 85,232$$

Comparing the estimated population value of 85,232 with the observed population value of 85,991 for the year 2000, we notice that the estimated value underestimates the observed population by 759 people. Referring back to Fig. 3.8 this also can be seen in that the fitted regression line lies below the actual population for the year 2000. To achieve consistency of the estimated population value and observed population value for the last year population data are available—the launch year—Smith et al. (2001) recommend the inclusion of an *adjustment factor*. They calculate the adjustment factor (ADJUST) as the difference of estimated and observed population for the launch year, or:

ADJUST=observed Pop_{2000} – estimated Pop_{2000}

Adding the adjustment factor to the linear population model for Boone County then shifts the fitted regression line upwards by 759 people and thus achieves consistency of estimated and observed population for the last year data were available. The general adjusted linear population model is:

$$Pop = \alpha + \beta \cdot T + ADJUST \tag{3.19}$$

And, for Boone County, the adjusted linear population model is defined as

$$Pop = 54,146 + 2,826 \ T + 759$$

Using the adjusted linear population model, Boone County's population for years 2001, 2002, and 2003 can be recalculated as follows:

$$\widehat{Pop}_{2001} = 54,146 + 2,826 \times 12 + 759 = 88,817$$

$$\widehat{Pop}_{2002} = 54,146 + 2,826 \times 13 + 759 = 91,643$$

$$\widehat{Pop}_{2003} = 54,146 + 2,826 \times 14 + 759 = 94,469$$

The sole purpose of the adjustment factor is to match estimated and observed population for the last year data were available. Particularly in cases where the estimated population for the launch year differs significantly from the observed population, the exclusion of the adjustment factor can lead to unjustifiable overestimated/underestimated populations for the years to come. We cannot say with certainty whether or not the inclusion of the adjustment factor will improve the population projections after all.

3.4.4   Geometric Population Model

In many cases population data do not exhibit linear growth patterns when plotted on a simple scatter plot. Under certain circumstances, populations might grow or decline following constant growth rates. For example, a population might grow/ decline at a rate of approximately 4%. Note the difference, while linear models assume constant absolute population growth, for instance the population will grow incrementally by 2,500 people per time period, geometric population models assume the population grows/declines at a constant growth rate, expressed in percent. For instance, a population of 1,000 growing at a rate of 10% will grow by 100 people between year one and two, by 110 people between year two and three and by 121 people between year three and four. As you easily can see, the rate of growth remains constant at 10%, but the absolute numerical value increases every year by 100, 110 and 121 in the first three years. The direct conclusion of applying constant growth rates is that population grows slowly in earlier years but grows considerably faster in later years.

Using the simplified example, the growth rate, r, is defined as:

$$r = \frac{Pop_{n+1} - Pop_n}{Pop_n} = \frac{121 - 110}{110} = 0.1 \text{ or } 10\%$$

where:

r — constant growth rate;

Pop_n — population in year n;

Pop_{n+1} — population in year $n+1$.

The constant growth rate, r measures the rate of growth between year n and year $n+1$.

We now extend the simple example from before to a total of 19 years, use an initial population of 1,000, a constant growth rate of 10%, and plot the linear versus the geometric curve. The constant incremental growth for the linear line is set at 200 people per year. Figure 3.9 graphically shows the difference between a linear and a geometric population growth curve. We see that the linear model predicts a higher population until year 16. The population projected with a geometric model exceeds the linear model projection after year 16. The more years we would move to the right side of the graph, the larger the difference between linear and geometric model estimates would become.

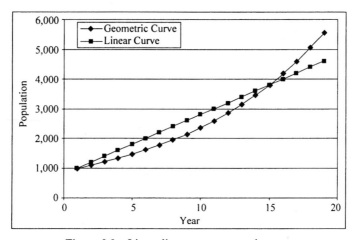

Figure 3.9   Linear line versus geometric curve

The compound rate formula

The growth rate is also commonly known as the compound rate. Here, the generic compound formula is:

$$FV_n = PV \cdot (1 + i)^n$$

where,

FV_n — future value;

PV — present value;

i — compound interest rate;

n — number of years, e.g., time.

Through substitution of FV_n with Pop_n (i.e., projected population in year n), PV with α (e.g., initial population), $(1 + i)$ with β (e.g., constant population growth factor), and n with T_n (the index number for year n) the compound rate formula takes the form of the geometric population model discussed in this section.

The general equation for the geometric growth curve is:

$$\text{Pop}_n = \alpha \cdot \beta^{T_n} \qquad (3.20)$$

where,

Pop_n — population in year n;

T_n — index number for year n;

β — constant population growth factor;

α — initial population.

While the estimation procedure was relatively straight forward in the case of the linear model, the geometric population model requires one additional step to be able to use the "ordinary least-square" criterion to estimate the two parameters. The geometric equation needs to be transformed into a linear form. This is done by taking logarithms:

$$\text{Pop}_n = \alpha\beta^{T_n}$$
$$\log(\text{Pop}_n) = \log(\alpha\beta^{T_n})$$
$$\log(\text{Pop}_n) = \log(\alpha) + \log(\beta) \cdot T_n$$

where,

$\log(\beta)$ — slope of the population trend line in logarithmic form;

$\log(\alpha)$ — intercept of the trend line with the y-axis in logarithmic form;

$\log(\text{Pop}_n)$ — log value of the predicted population.

Table 3.12 below shows the necessary steps to estimate the two regression parameters using the "ordinary least-square" criterion. The sole difference to the

Table 3.12   Geometric population curve computations, Boone County, KY

	Observed Population, Pop	Logarithm of Obs. Population, log (Pop)	Index Numbers, T
	57,589	4.7603	1
	60,574	4.7823	2
	62,897	4.7986	3
	65,318	4.8150	4
	67,554	4.8297	5
	70,017	4.8452	6
	72,860	4.8625	7
	76,162	4.8817	8
	79,818	4.9021	9
	83,349	4.9209	10
	85,991	4.9345	11
Totals	782,129	53.3328	66

linear model is now that we have to take the logarithmic of observed population values as indicated in the second column.

The population mean, $\overline{\text{Pop}} = 71{,}103$ and the mean index, $\overline{T} = 6$.

	Deviations from Mean Values		Necessary Cross-products	
	Population, $\log(p)$	Index Number, t	$\log(p) \cdot t$	t^2
	− 0.0881	− 5	0.4405	25
	− 0.0662	− 4	0.2646	16
	− 0.0498	− 3	0.1494	9
	− 0.0334	− 2	0.0668	4
	− 0.0188	− 1	0.0188	1
	− 0.0032	0	0.0000	0
	0.0141	1	0.0141	1
	0.0333	2	0.0666	4
	0.0537	3	0.1610	9
	0.0725	4	0.2898	16
	0.0860	5	0.4301	25
Totals	0	0	1.9017	110

Otherwise, all computations to derive the regression parameters are identical to the linear regression described earlier. Again, we use index numbers, calculate the deviations to the mean values (e.g., log (p) and t), and compute the necessary products in column six and seven.

The regression line coefficients are then calculated as:

$$\log(\hat{\beta}) = \frac{\sum \log(p) \cdot t}{\sum t^2} = \frac{1.9017}{110} = 0.0173$$

$$\log(\hat{\alpha}) = \log(\overline{\text{Pop}}) - \log(\hat{\beta}) \cdot \overline{T} = 4.8484 - 0.0173 \times 6 = 4.7447$$

Using the estimated regression coefficients, we can develop Boone County's geometric population model based on observed data for the years 1990 to 2000 as follows:

$$\log(\text{Pop}_n) = 4.7447 + 0.0173 \cdot T_n$$

Note that the estimated population model for Boone County is still in the logarithmic form. Although the model can be used to project Boone County's population for future years, it is important to recognize that these population projections will also be in their logarithmic form. Before getting meaningful population projections, we must convert the estimated population values back by taking the antilogarithm, the inverse operation of the logarithm. For instance, Boone County's population can be projected using the estimated regression model in logarithmic form for the years 2001, 2002, and 2003: [1]

$$\log(\widehat{\text{Pop}}_{2001}) = 4.7447 + 0.0173 \times 12 = 4.9522 \implies 10^{4.9522} = 89,571$$

$$\log(\widehat{\text{Pop}}_{2002}) = 4.7447 + 0.0173 \times 13 = 4.9695 \implies 10^{4.9695} = 93,208$$

$$\log(\widehat{\text{Pop}}_{2003}) = 4.7447 + 0.0173 \times 14 = 4.9867 \implies 10^{4.9867} = 96,994$$

Immediately you see that the results in their logarithmic form (e.g., 4.9522) have no direct meaning for planning purposes. Given that we used the base 10 logarithm, we get population projections by taking the inverse, or the antilogarithm, which is done as 10^{Pop_n}. [2]

Alternatively, we can write the geometric population model in its original form by taking the antilogarithms of the estimated regression line:

$$\text{Pop}_n = 55,553 \times 1.0406^{T_n}$$

The advantage of doing so is that we now have the population model in a form containing the constant annual population growth rate, r. For Boone County, the constant annual growth factor $(\hat{\beta})$ is 1.0406. The actual growth rate is then computed as (growth factor—1.0) and equals 0.0406 for Boone County. This indicates that between 1990 and 2000, the population in Boone County grew annually by a constant rate of 4.06%.

In a last step, we now project Boone County's population based on the geometric population model:

$$\widehat{\text{Pop}}_{2001} = 55,553 \times 1.0406^{12} = 89,571$$

$$\widehat{\text{Pop}}_{2002} = 55,553 \times 1.0406^{13} = 93,208$$

$$\widehat{\text{Pop}}_{2003} = 55,553 \times 1.0406^{14} = 96,994$$

Using either the geometric model or the transformed logarithmic version of the geometric model will result in identical population projections. Furthermore, the projections are slightly higher than the projections using the linear population model. The geometric model with its constant growth rate assumes faster growing populations in the later years.

---

[1] Please note that presented results have been calculated in a spreadsheet using more than 10 digits after the decimal points. Given that presented logarithm values indicate only 4 digits after the decimal point, some discrepancies to the final population projections will become apparent by recalculating the population projections using the rounded four digits after the decimal point values.

[2] The general form of the logarithm is: $y = \log_a(z) \Leftrightarrow a^y = z$, where a is called the base.

We conclude this section with the inclusion of the adjustment factor into the geometric population model for Boone County as:

$$Pop_n = 55,553 \times 1.0406^{T_n} + ADJUST$$

In similar fashion to the linear population model, the ***adjustment factor*** guarantees that the observed population for the last year data were available, i.e., year 2000 for Boone County, matches the estimated population for this particular year. The adjustment factor again for Boone County for 2000 is calculated as:

$$ADJUST = \text{observed Pop}_{2000} - \text{estimated Pop}_{2000} = 85,991 - 86,075 = -84$$

Based on the adjusted geometric population model, the projected population for Boone County for 2001, 2002, and 2003 is:

$$\widehat{Pop}_{2001} = 55,553 \times 1.0406^{12} - 84 = 89,487$$
$$\widehat{Pop}_{2002} = 55,553 \times 1.0406^{13} - 84 = 93,124$$
$$\widehat{Pop}_{2003} = 55,553 \times 1.0406^{14} - 84 = 96,910$$

3.4.5 Parabolic Population Model

The main assumption for the parabolic population model, like for the geometric model, is that under certain circumstances the population of an area is not expected to follow a linear growth path. The general equation for the parabolic curve is given in Eq. (3.21):

$$y = a + b_1 \cdot x + b_2 \cdot x^2 \tag{3.21}$$

The equation can be rewritten in Eq. (3.22) as a population model:

$$Pop_n = \alpha + \beta_1 \cdot (T_n) + \beta_2 \cdot (T_n^2) \tag{3.22}$$

where,

Pop_n — population in year n (dependent variable);

α — intercept;

β_1 and β_2 — coefficients of the parabolic curve;

T_n — index number for year n.

The more specific reason for choosing a parabolic over, for example a geometric population model, lies in the fact that the parabolic population model allows the incremental population growth (e.g., annual change in population expressed as people per year) to increase or decrease over time. (Remember that in a geometric model which assumes a constant growth rate over time, the annual population increase or decline expressed in people per year is always increasing).

This change in functional flexibility comes from the use of a linear and a nonlinear component in the parabolic model. Generally, the parabolic population curve is a quadratic function. As such, the signs (e.g., plus or minus) of estimated parameters determine if a population incrementally grows (declines) at increasing or decreasing rates. Given that we have two parameters to be estimated and each can have a positive or a negative sign, there are four different growth rate cases (Table 3.13).

Table 3.13   Effects of the signs of slope parameters on population growth/decline

Case	Sign of Linear Slope Parameter (β_1)	Sign of Nonlinear Slope Parameter (β_2)	Effects on Population Growth
I	positive	positive	increasing incremental population growth concaves upward
II	positive	negative	decreasing incremental population decline concaves downward
III	negative	positive	decreasing incremental population growth concaves upward
IV	negative	negative	increasing incremental population decline concaves downward

The effects of the signs of the parameters β_1 and β_2 can easily be graphed by expanding the square term Time^2 by ($\beta_1 / 2\beta_2$) and rewriting the parabolic population as:

$$\text{Pop}_n = \beta_2\left(T_n + \frac{\beta_1}{2\beta_2}\right)^2 + \alpha - \frac{\beta_1^2}{4\beta_2} \tag{3.23}$$

This is shown graphically below (Fig. 3.10). But note that only positive values for population and time are allowed.

Altogether, the parabolic model has three coefficients: the intercept with the y-axis, α, the coefficient for the linear term, β_1, and the coefficient for the nonlinear component, β_2. The parabolic curve can be estimated using ordinary least-square (OLS) regression techniques. However, adding a second variable (e.g., Time^2) to the right-hand side of the equation adds substantial computational complexity. Rather than doing the computation by hand as with the first two population models, we need to use a statistical software package. For example, we use SPSS software package to get the estimated regression coefficients for the

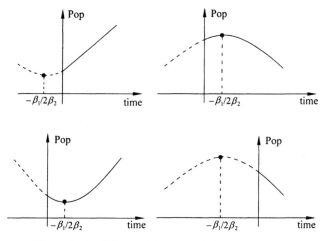

Figure 3.10   Effects of the signs of slope parameters

parabolic population model using the Boone County population data for 1990 to ·2000. The three estimated parameters are:

$$\hat{\alpha} = 56,017$$

$$\hat{\beta}_1 = 1,962$$

$$\hat{\beta}_2 = 72$$

We now use these three estimated parameters and set up the Boone County parabolic population model:

$$\text{Pop}_n = 56,017 + 1,962 \cdot T_n + 72 \cdot T_n^2$$

Given that the slope parameters are both positive, the parabolic model for Boone County projects a population increase at an increasing rate. In particular, Boone County's population based on the parabolic model is projected as

$$\widehat{\text{Pop}}_{2001} = 56,017 + 1,962 \times 12 + 72 \times 144 = 89,929$$

$$\widehat{\text{Pop}}_{2002} = 56,017 + 1,962 \times 13 + 72 \times 169 = 93,691$$

$$\widehat{\text{Pop}}_{2003} = 56,017 + 1,962 \times 14 + 72 \times 196 = 97,598$$

The annual absolute increases in population growth are 3,762 and 3,906 between 2001 and 2002 and between 2002 and 2003, respectively.

We again have the choice of including an adjustment factor into the population model. As already demonstrated, the adjustment factor is calculated as the difference of the observed population for Boone County in 2000 and the projected population for the same year using the parabolic population model. Here, the adjustment factor is calculated as: $85,991 - 86,312 = -321$. In the next step, we add the adjustment factor to the parabolic population of Boone County.

$$\text{Pop}_n = 56,017 + 1,962 \cdot T_n + 72 \cdot T_n^2 - 321$$

And with the adjusted parabolic population model, the population projections for Boone County for 2001, 2002, and 2003 are calculated as:

$$\widehat{\text{Pop}}_{2001} = 56,017 + 1,962 \times 12 + 72 \times 144 - 321 = 89,609$$

$$\widehat{\text{Pop}}_{2002} = 56,017 + 1,962 \times 13 + 72 \times 169 - 321 = 93,371$$

$$\widehat{\text{Pop}}_{2003} = 56,017 + 1,962 \times 14 + 72 \times 196 - 321 = 97,276$$

The population models discussed so far have one thing in common. They all allow unlimited population growth or decline. In other words, there are no boundaries. Populations could grow indefinitely. Alternatively, unlimited decline would lead to the extinction of a population in a region. To avoid this fallacy, demographers apply contain upper and/or lower limits or boundaries to population models.

You can easily imagine that any region has limited carrying capacity, which is determined by the boundary of land area and other factors. The term carrying capacity, in this context, refers to the maximal population size that an area can support without reducing its ability to support the population in the future.[①] We will discuss the carrying capacity in further detail in Chapter 6. Setting an upper limit avoids projecting population growths that are beyond a region's carrying capacity.

Many towns, cities, or counties face the challenge to provide the necessary infrastructure (e.g., roads, water, sewer, and electricity among others), schools, libraries, housing, jobs, and recreational facilities for a growing population. On the other hand, places rarely die out completely and become ghost towns. Independent of socio-economic and political trends, people are attached to places where they grew up and spent their childhood. It is therefore implausible to anticipate that a population declining trend will lead to a population that will vanish over time.

The idea of setting upper ceilings and lower bounds to an area's population growth/decline is realized in several different population models: the logistic model, the modified exponential model, and the Gompertz model. However, in practice these models are rarely applied because setting ceilings is notoriously difficult to do. If the pasts do not provide reasonable upper and lower limits, setting ceilings is more often guessing than a methodological approach. In the following section we discuss one of these "constraint" population models—the s-shaped logistic population model.

---

① Source: Population, Sustainability, and Earth's Carrying Capacity: A framework for estimating population sizes and lifestyles that could be sustained without undermining future generations, Gretchen C. Daily and Paul R. Ehrlich (1992), http://dieoff.org/page112.htm.

3.4.6   Logistic Population Model

The general form of the s-shaped logistic curve was first introduced by P. F. Verhurst, a Belgian mathematician in the 19th Century. Its popularity for population projections during the first part of the 20th century has been promoted by the work of Raymond Pearl and Lowell Reed (Klosterman, 1990). Although conceptually striking, the logistic model requires predetermining upper/lower population boundaries, which makes it less used than simpler models. Nevertheless and for populations with changing growth rates, the logistic population model still may deliver accurate population forecasts. This model may be of use, in particular, when an initial period of slow growth is followed by a period of rapid growth, which finally leads to a period of stagnating growth that levels off at an upper bound.[①]

Keyfitz (1968) gave the equation for a logistic curve as

$$Y = \frac{c}{1 + a \cdot e^{-bX}} \tag{3.24a}$$

where,

X — the independent variable;
Y — the dependent variable;
a and b — parameters;
c — growth ceiling constant.

Setting $c \to c, a \to a \cdot c$, and $e^{-b} \to b$, we can simplify the logistic curve as

$$\begin{cases} Y = \dfrac{1}{\dfrac{1}{c} + ab^X} \\[2ex] \dfrac{1}{Y} = \dfrac{1}{c} + ab^X \end{cases} \tag{3.24b}$$

We then get the logistic curve equation in a form that is familiar to us. It is important that although the predetermined growth ceiling is set at a parameter value, c, in the logistic curve function, the growth limit is given as its reciprocal value, $1/c$.

The population logistic model can thus be written as

$$\frac{1}{\text{Pop}_n} = \frac{1}{c} + \alpha \cdot \beta^{T_n} \tag{3.25}$$

where,

Pop_n — Population in year n;

---

① Smith et al., 2000: 170 – 171.

T_n — Index number for year n;

β — constant population growth factor;

α — parameter;

$1/c$ — reciprocal of the preset upper asymptotic population ceiling.

The logistic curve is applicable for scenarios with an upper growth limit of the population, as well as scenarios with a lower growth limit. The difference depends solely on the value of the β parameter. For $0 < \beta < 1$, we have the case of an upper growth limit, for $\beta > 1$ we have analogously, a lower growth limit. This is graphically shown in Fig. 3.11. We can rewrite the logistic population model Eq. (3.25) as

$$\text{Pop}_n = \frac{c}{1 + \alpha \cdot c \cdot \beta^{T_n}} \tag{3.26}$$

and for a large T_n :

when $0 < \beta < 1$, β^{T_n} approaches zero, Pop_n approaches c;

when $\beta > 1$, β^{T_n} approaches infinity, Pop_n approaches zero.

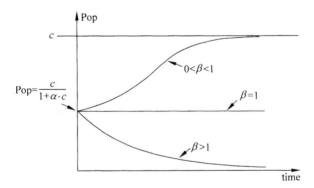

Figure 3.11   Effects of parameter β on population projections in the logistic model

We can transform the logistic curve to the linear form by taking the logarithms of Eq. (3.25):

$$\log\left(\frac{1}{\text{Pop}_n} - \frac{1}{c}\right) = \log(\alpha) + \log(\beta) \cdot T_n$$

where,

$\log(\beta)$ — slope of the population trend line in logarithmic form;

$\log(\alpha)$ — intercept of the trend line;

$\log(1/\text{Pop}_n - 1/c)$ — log of the difference between the inverse of the population size and the inverse of the population ceiling.

101

The transformation of the logistic population model using logarithms allows us to apply the linear regression technique for population projection. Let us assume that Boone County's upper growth limit is 250,000 people,[①] the model solution is illustrated in Table 3.14.

For Boone County, the parameter estimates are:

$$\log(\hat{\beta}) = \frac{\sum \log\left(\frac{1}{p} - \frac{1}{c}\right) \cdot t}{\sum t^2} = \frac{-2.6599}{110} = -0.0242$$

$$\log(\hat{\alpha}) = \log\left(\frac{1}{\overline{\text{Pop}}} - \frac{1}{c}\right) - \log(\hat{\beta}) \cdot \overline{T}$$

$$= -4.994 - 0.0242 \times 6 = -4.8492$$

The parameters $\hat{\alpha}$ and $\hat{\beta}$ then can be estimated by taking the antilogarithms of above parameter estimates.

$$\hat{\beta} = \text{anti}\log(\log\hat{\beta}) = \text{anti}\log(-0.0242) = 10^{-0.0242} = 0.9458$$

$$\hat{\alpha} = \text{anti}\log(\log\hat{\alpha}) = \text{anti}\log(-4.8492) = 10^{-4.8492} = 0.0000142$$

The final logistic population model for Boone County, KY, including the parameter estimates is

$$\frac{1}{\text{Pop}_n} = \left(\frac{1}{250,000} + 0.0000142 \times 0.9458^{T_n}\right), \text{or}$$

$$\text{Pop}_n = \frac{1}{\frac{1}{250,000} + 0.0000142 \times 0.9458^{T_n}}$$

Using this model, we can then project Boone County's population for the years 2001, 2002, and 2003 as follows:

$$\frac{1}{\widehat{\text{Pop}}_{2001}} = \frac{1}{250,000} + 0.0000142 \times 0.9458^{12} = 0.00001125 \Rightarrow \widehat{\text{Pop}}_{2001} = 88,856$$

$$\frac{1}{\widehat{\text{Pop}}_{2002}} = \frac{1}{250,000} + 0.0000142 \times 0.9458^{13} = 0.00001086 \Rightarrow \widehat{\text{Pop}}_{2002} = 92,070$$

$$\frac{1}{\widehat{\text{Pop}}_{2003}} = \frac{1}{250,000} + 0.0000142 \times 0.9458^{14} = 0.00001049 \Rightarrow \widehat{\text{Pop}}_{2003} = 95,331$$

---

① The upper growth limit is set at 250,000 people because Boone County is fast growing and because Boone County is partly rural with a large potential for future growth.

Table 3.14   Logistic population model calculations

Observed Population (Pop)	Reciprocal Population Value (1/Pop)	Reciprocal Difference (1/Pop − 1/c)	Log of Difference (log(1/Pop − 1/c))	Index Numbers (T)
57,589	0.00001736	0.00001336	− 4.874	1
60,574	0.00001651	0.00001251	− 4.903	2
62,897	0.00001590	0.00001190	− 4.924	3
65,318	0.00001531	0.00001131	− 4.947	4
67,554	0.00001480	0.00001080	− 4.966	5
70,017	0.00001428	0.00001028	− 4.988	6
72,860	0.00001372	0.00000972	− 5.012	7
76,162	0.00001313	0.00000913	− 5.040	8
79,818	0.00001253	0.00000853	− 5.069	9
83,349	0.00001200	0.00000800	− 5.097	10
85,991	0.00001163	0.00000763	− 5.118	11
Totals 782,129			− 54.938	66

Upper Population Limit (c): 250,000
Reciprocal Upper Limit ($1/c$): 0.000004
log ($1/Pop - 1/c$) Mean: − 4.994
Mean Index Number: 6

	Deviations from Mean Values		Necessary Cross-products	
	from Population, $\log(1/p - 1/c)$	from Index Number, t	$\log(1/p - 1/c)\cdot t$	t^2
	0.1203	− 5	− 0.6014	25
	0.0915	− 4	− 0.3662	16
	0.0698	− 3	− 0.2095	9
	0.0478	− 2	− 0.0956	4
	0.0279	− 1	− 0.0279	1
	0.0064	0	0.0000	0
	− 0.0178	1	− 0.0178	1
	− 0.0452	2	− 0.0904	4
	− 0.0748	3	− 0.2244	9
	− 0.1027	4	− 0.4108	16
	− 0.1232	5	− 0.6160	25
Totals	0	0	− 2.6599	110

Note that the projected population for Boone County based on the logistic model is calculated as its reciprocal value and needs to be converted back, which is shown on the right-hand side.

Similar to the previous models, we can adjust the logistic population model and recalculate the population projections for Boone County. Using the estimated logistic population model, the projected population for the year 2000 is 85,693. Thus, the logistic population model must be adjusted by 298 upwards. This is done in the easiest way by simply adding 298 to the outcome of the "unadjusted" logistic population model, or:

$$\widehat{Pop}_{2001} = 88,856 + 298 = 89,154$$
$$\widehat{Pop}_{2002} = 92,070 + 298 = 92,368$$
$$\widehat{Pop}_{2003} = 95,331 + 298 = 95,629$$

The same outcome is achieved by incorporating the adjustment factor into the logistic population model. In the logistic model where population is expressed in its reciprocal value, the adjustment term is calculated as:

$$ADJUST = \frac{1}{\text{estimated Pop}_{2000}} - \frac{1}{\text{observed Pop}_{2000}}$$
$$= \frac{1}{85,693} - \frac{1}{85,991}$$
$$= 0.000000041$$

Incorporating the adjustment factor into the logistic population model, the adjusted model becomes:

$$\frac{1}{Pop_n} = \frac{1}{250,000} + 0.0000142 \times 0.9458^{T_n} + 0.000000041$$

Also, note that the inclusion of the adjustment factor will move the upper (or lower) limit upwards (or downwards) by the value of the adjustment factor.

Over the past few pages, you have been introduced to six different population extrapolation methods. Two of them use simple ratios and four are based on more complex regression analysis. We further see that these four more complex methods use the "least-square criterion" to estimate the regression parameters. In Table 3.15 we compare population projections using all six different models for Boone County, KY for the years 2001 through 2010. If applicable, an adjustment factor is included (e.g., as shown in the four regression models). For a better comparison of each model's functional forms and characteristics, we summarized some key concepts of these extrapolation models into Table 3.16.

As a first impression, all projected results seem to be reasonable considering the fast population growth of Boone County during the 1990's. The share of growth

Table 3.15   Comparison of "adjusted" population projections for Boone County, KY

Year	Share of Growth	Shift-Share	Linear	Geometric	Parabolic	Logistic
2001	–	–	88,817	89,487	89,609	89,154
2002	–	–	91,643	93,124	93,371	92,368
2003	–	–	94,469	96,910	97,276	95,629
2004	–	–	97,295	100,849	101,326	98,934
2005	–	–	100,121	104,947	105,519	102,278
2006	–	–	102,947	109,213	109,857	105,656
2007	–	–	105,773	113,651	114,338	109,064
2008	–	–	108,599	118,270	118,963	112,497
2009	–	–	111,426	123,076	123,732	115,949
2010	112,617	117,851	114,252	128,078	128,645	119,416

method and the linear population model are at the low end of projections with 112,617 and 114,252 for 2010 respectively. The parabolic and geometric models have the highest ones with 128,645 and 128,078 for 2010. As mentioned earlier, models that rely on growth rates, such as the geometric and parabolic population models, have faster growing populations in later years which is clearly apparent in Table 3.15. But how can we determine which model provides the "best" results?

As a first step, you can visually examine observed population data to identify the growth pattern. Of course, having only few data points on a scatter plot makes it difficult to identify a pattern. Data for a longer time period could readily help identify if the visually observed pattern is of linear or geometric nature.

A more sophisticated input evaluation criterion uses the coefficient of relative variation (CRV). This is based on the idea of finding the curve that provides the closest match to observed historic data; this method compares the actual trend in observed historic data to the assumed trend for each extrapolation method. In other words, We compare the observed historic data to the estimated data derived from a trend curves. The CRV is defined as the ratio of the standard deviation to the mean:

$$CRV = \frac{\text{standard deviation}}{\text{mean}} = \frac{s}{\bar{x}} \qquad (3.27)$$

As a common measure of dispersion, it measures how dispersed our data are around a measure of central tendency, e.g., the mean. The closer the curve fits the historic population data, the less dispersed the data, which corresponds to a lower CRV. For Boone County, the CRV calculations are in Table 3.17. Please note that for these calculations only the historic data (for the index numbers 1 through 11) are included.

Following the criteria that the lowest CRV provides the best fit to observed population data, the logistic curve would be the best choice. However, our

Table 3.16 Summary characteristics of selected extrapolation methods

Model	Population Model	Regressand	Regressors	Estimated Parameters
Share of Growth	$\text{Pop}_{m,ty} = \text{Pop}_{m,ty} + \text{growthshare}(\text{Pop}_{n,ty} - \text{Pop}_{n,ty})$	N/A	N/A	N/A
Shift-Share	$\text{Pop}_{m,ty} = \text{Pop}_{n,ty}\left[\text{share}_{ty} + \left(\dfrac{\text{years}_{pp}}{\text{years}_{bp}}\right)(\text{share}_{ty} - \text{share}_{by})\right]$	N/A	N/A	N/A
Linear	$\text{Pop}_n = \alpha + \beta \cdot T$	Pop_n	T_n	α, β
Geometric	$\text{Pop}_n = \alpha \cdot \beta^{\text{Time}}$	$\log \text{Pop}_n$	T_n	$\log \alpha, \log \beta$
Parabolic	$\text{Pop}_n = \alpha + \beta_1 \cdot \text{Time} + \beta_2 \cdot \text{Time}^2$	Pop_n	T_n and T_n^2	α, β_1, β_2
Logistic	$1/\text{Pop}_n = 1/(c + \alpha \cdot \beta^{\text{Time}})$	$\log(1/\text{Pop}_n - 1/c)$	T_n	$\log \alpha, \log \beta$

Continued

Model	Characteristics
Share of Growth	small target area grows/declines according to a *predetermined and constant population growth share* of the smaller area in comparison to a larger region—requires population projection of larger comparison region
Shift-Share	small target area population is determined based on base year and launch year population shares of the smaller area to a larger region—requires population projection of larger comparison region
Linear	*constant absolute growth* increments $\beta : \text{Pop}_{n+1} - \text{Pop}_n$ population increase: $+\beta$; population decline: $-\beta$
Geometric	*constant growth factor* $\beta = 1 + r$, where r is growth rate, e.g., $\text{Pop}_{n+1}/\text{Pop}_n = \text{constant} = 1 + r$ "the rise of the increment in population is related to the size of the population and increasing" ratio between increment in population / total population = constant
Parabolic	*increasing/decreasing growth increments* depending on β_1 and β_2 β_1: constant linear growth component, e.g., $\text{Pop}_{n+1} - \text{Pop}_n = \text{constan}$ β_2: constant non-linear growth; constant in second differences depends on β_2: if $\beta_2 < 0 \rightarrow$ concave downwards sloping if $\beta_2 = 0 \rightarrow$ linear if $\beta_2 > 0 \rightarrow$ concave upwards
Logistic	*constant ratio of increments for reciprocal*, $(1/\text{Pop}_n)$, of population values constant factor: $(1/c - 1/\text{Pop}_{n+1})/(1/c - 1/\text{Pop}_n) = \text{constant} = 0.9458$ s-shaped curve with upper growth limit of $1/c$ where upper asymptotic growth limit equals c *growing* populations: $\alpha > 0$ and $0 < \beta < 1$ *declining* populations: $\alpha > 0$ and $\beta > 1$

Table 3.17   Evaluation of population projections[1]

	Observed Population data	Linear	Geometric	Parabolic	Logistic
pop. limit	–	–	–	–	250,000
Alpha (α)	–	54,146	55,553	56,017	0.00001415
Beta (β_1)	–	2,826	1.0406	1,962	0.9458
beta 2 (β_2)	–	–	–	72	–
1	57,589	56,972	57,809	58,052	57,525
2	60,574	59,798	60,157	60,230	60,028
3	62,897	62,624	62,600	62,552	62,604
4	65,318	65,451	65,142	65,019	65,253
5	67,554	68,277	67,788	67,629	67,973
6	70,017	71,103	70,541	70,383	70,764
7	72,860	73,929	73,405	73,281	73,622
8	76,162	76,755	76,386	76,323	76,547
9	79,818	79,581	79,488	79,509	79,536
10	83,349	82,407	82,716	82,839	82,585
11	85,991	85,233	86,075	86,312	85,693
Standard Deviation (σ)	9,403.81	9,372.99	9,371.43	9,396.67	9,355.21
Mean (μ)	71,102.64	71,102.64	71,100.73	71,102.64	71,102.71
CRV	–	13.1823	13.1805	13.2156	13.1573
MAPE	–	0.9238	0.4744	0.4703	0.5850

(1) Projections in Table 3.17 do not include adjustment factors.

calculations also show that all CRVs are extremely close to each other, indicating that in the case of Boone County, each of the four extrapolation methods listed in Table 3.17 would provide, at least for short-term projections, similar results. But be aware that with longer projection horizons the gap between the individual population projection models widens and the choice among different population models becomes more significant.

The most commonly used evaluation criterion is the mean absolute percentage error (MAPE). The MAPE is an output evaluation criterion and compares projected population values to the observed population statistics.[1] For Boone County, we would compare the projected values to the observed values for index numbers 1 through 11. The MAPE is the average value of the sum of absolute values of errors expressed in percentage terms and can be written as:

[1] The literature alludes numerous other measures of forecast errors: (1) mean error (ME), (2) mean absolute error (MAE), (3) mean percentage error (MPE), (4) root mean square error (RMSE), (5) Theil's U statistic, and (6) Theil's delta statistic.

$$\text{MAPE} = \frac{1}{n}\sum_{i=1}^{n} |\text{PE}_i|,$$

(3.28)

and

$$\text{PE} = \frac{\hat{y}_i - y_i}{y_i} \cdot 100$$

where,

y_i — observed population values;

$\hat{y}_i$ — forecasted population values;

n — total number of observations;

PE — percentage error.

As you can see, the MAPE is calculated by averaging the percentage difference between the calculated values and the original observations. The result is an indication of the accuracy of the model when applied to the initial data set. The more closely the calculated values are to the observed values, the smaller the MAPE, and therefore, the better the model.

Going back to Table 3.17, we can see that the computed mean absolute percentage errors range from 0.4703 to 0.9238 for the four models. Based on the output evaluation criterion, the parabolic curve indicates the lowest MAPE. All MAPEs can be considered to be very low and very close to each other, making the final model choice less straightforward. While we have applied the MAPE to historic data, e.g., 1990 to 2000, its drawback is that we cannot apply it to check future projections simply because we do not have future census data. For this reason, MAPEs are normally calculated for comparing projection values with census numbers once the latter becomes available. For instance, we could check 1997 Boone County population projections for the year 2000 with actual census 2000 data.

Based on the observed Boone County population data and using the visual, the input evaluation, and the output evaluation criteria, there is strong evidence that the more complex population models do not clearly out perform the simpler linear population model. Thus, using more sophisticated models is not necessarily a guarantor for better projections. For Boone County, the observed population values indicate an unmistakable growth trend. Even more, by visual observation, we already can conclude that all individual observations lie very close to a linear trend line. This particular circumstance is the reason that any of the six extrapolation methods will produce reasonable population projections. However, such a clear-cut case, as with Boone county, is not the rule of thumb. Usually, the computed coefficients of relative variation (CRV) and mean absolute percentage errors (MAPE) provide at least some decision guidelines for which model to choose. Nevertheless, both methods require estimated and observed population data and as such can only be done for time periods for which population data are available.

Remark on R^2 values

Using statistical software packages and having the computer do the curve fitting, as part of the output, you will usually get a R^2 value. As we have already discussed, the R^2 measures the amount of variation in the observed population values as explained by time. Therefore, the higher the R^2, the better the fit of your estimated straight regression line to observed data.

R^2 values are only appropriate for comparing different population projection models when the regressands, e.g., the population variable on the left-hand side of the linearly transformed population regression model, are identical.[1] Given that the population extrapolation models vary widely in their regressands, the R^2 does not provide the means for a comparison of the goodness-of-fit of different extrapolation models. In other words, an R^2 from a regression using absolute population as a dependent variable (Pop_n) cannot be compared to the R^2 of the geometric model which uses population in logarithmic form ($\log(\text{Pop}_n)$).

3.5 Cohort-Component Method

A second main method for many state and local governments to project an area's population is the cohort-component method. The cohort-component method provides detailed demographic information on why and how the population changes.

The **first step** in the cohort-component method is to divide the population into age and sex cohorts. Further stratification depends primarily on needs and data availability and could be done according to race and ethnicity. More detailed subdivisions could follow, for instance, the racial and ethnic breakdown used in the 2000 Census.

In the **second step**, fertility, mortality, and migration rates, are applied to each individual cohort. For each cohort we will project how the population will change over a predetermined time period. Then we can answer questions like:

(1) How will the cohort of female of age $20-24$ years change over the next five years?

(2) What is the projected change in the total male population for a 10-year time period?

(3) How is the area's population as a whole projected to change?

Before we get started, there are some more considerations that need to be taken into account. First, all age-groups must be uniform in that the years in the cohorts (n) are identical. Very often, cohort-component models divide the population into five-year age cohorts. This level of detail keeps data and

---

[1] Gujarati,1995: 171.

computational requirements within manageable limits while still providing sufficient details. Second, the number of years in the projection intervals (z) should relate to the number of years in the cohorts (n). For instance, using five-year age cohorts would logically suggest projecting for five-year periods (e.g., $n = z$). The advantage is that one specific age cohort, e.g., 25 – 29 years, would advance over a five-year projection period to the next age cohort, e.g., 30 – 34 years. This is shown in Fig. 3.12 below.

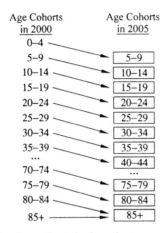

Figure 3.12   Age cohorts in the cohort-component model

And of course, all rates used in the cohort-component model must be adjusted to reflect five-year projection periods. For instance, the fertility rate for a particular female age-group, e.g., 491.7 for the age group of 20 – 24 years in Boone County, must reflect the appropriate time interval. Problems may arise when projecting five year age cohorts for let us say a three year time period as there is a clear mismatch of projection period and age cohort definition. However, using five-year age cohorts would also allow multiples of five-year projection intervals, for instance, 10 years, 15 years, etc.

Earlier in this chapter, we have referred to the individual components of change as births, deaths, and in- and out-migration. We further have discussed the individual rates that reflect these components namely fertility, survival, and migration rates. In this section, we now pull all required data for Boone County together and will develop a cohort-component model for the county. For Boone County, things are simplified, in that fertility, survival, and net migration rates by age and sex are available online at the Kentucky State Data Center & Kentucky Population Research (KSDC/KPR) at the University of Louisville Urban Studies Institute. The center provides these data for each of the 120 counties in Kentucky. The time interval (n) is five years. Particularly, we will project the 2000 Boone County population into the year 2005. The population is broken down into age-sex cohorts. The youngest five-year age group is 0 – 4 years, the oldest group lumps together all people over the age of 85. Furthermore, in the sample model we will be using net migration rates.

Table 3.18 contains the rates for the male population in Boone County and Table 3.19 contains the rates for the female population. It is noteworthy that fertility rates apply only for the female population of age 10 through 44, where the age is measured at the beginning of the five year interval.

Table 3.18   Male age-specific survival and migration rates per 1,000 persons

Beginning Age 2000	Ending Age 2005	Survival Rates	Net Migration Rates
Live Births	0 – 4	992.4	113.1
0 – 4	5 – 9	996.7	213.0
5 – 9	10 – 14	998.8	120.0
10 – 14	15 – 19	997.2	29.8
15 – 19	20 – 24	992.9	– 2.2
20 – 24	25 – 29	992.9	350.5
25 – 29	30 – 34	991.8	321.1
30 – 34	35 – 39	989.6	162.4
35 – 39	40 – 44	985.9	155.2
40 – 44	45 – 49	980.3	49.3
45 – 49	50 – 54	970.9	94.0
50 – 54	55 – 59	954.0	76.6
55 – 59	60 – 64	925.6	2.6
60 – 64	65 – 69	883.0	– 12.1
65 – 69	70 – 74	823.6	48.2
70 – 74	75 – 79	750.8	74.7
75 – 79	80 – 84	639.2	49.2
80 – 84	85 – 89	498.5	13.1
85 +	90 +	297.6	143.2

Table 3.19   Female age-specific fertility, survival, and migration rates per 1,000 persons

Beginning Age 2000	Ending Age 2005	Fertility Rates	Survival Rates	Net Migration Rates
Live Births	0 – 4	–	993.4	113.1
0 – 4	5 – 9	–	997.5	213.0
5 – 9	10 – 14	–	999.2	120.0
10 – 14	15 – 19	52.4	998.5	21.4
15 – 19	20 – 24	391.6	997.3	21.3
20 – 24	25 – 29	491.7	997.4	385.2
25 – 29	30 – 34	491.7	996.6	255.2
30 – 34	35 – 39	287.8	995.3	122.8

Continued

Beginning Age 2000	Ending Age 2005	Fertility Rates	Survival Rates	Net Migration Rates
35 – 39	40 – 44	86.4	993.2	160.6
40 – 44	45 – 49	9.5	989.1	10.2
45 – 49	50 – 54	–	983.5	142.4
50 – 54	55 – 59	–	973.0	67.5
55 – 59	60 – 64	–	957.0	18.0
60 – 64	65 – 69	–	932.0	– 12.1
65 – 69	70 – 74	–	897.0	48.2
70 – 74	75 – 79	–	850.4	74.7
75 – 79	80 – 84	–	765.3	49.2
80 – 84	85 – 89	–	637.3	13.1
85 +	90 +	–	381.4	143.2

Once the necessary population data and the age-specific fertility, survival, and net migration rates are collected and the model is conceptually prepared (e.g., deciding on the cohort breakdown and the time interval), we are ready to do all calculations in a spreadsheet. We will complete the model for the female population in Table 3.20. The cohort-component model is broken down into three parts:

(1) Columns one and two contain the initial female population in Boone County in 2000 ($_n F_x^{2000}$) broken down by age cohorts.

(2) Columns three to six include the age-specific survival, net migration, and fertility rates. We divided all initial rates from Tables 3.18 and 3.19 by 1000.

(3) Columns seven to thirteen contain the results from the calculations. These are:

① surviving female population in 2005 ($_n SF_{x+z}^{2005}$ — column seven),

② female deaths from 2000 to 2005 ($_n DF_x^{2000-2005}$ — column eight),

③ net migrating female population between 2000 to 2005 ($_n NMF_{x+z}^{2000-2005}$ — column nine),

④ female population in childbearing age ($_n ARF_x^{2005}$ — column ten),

⑤ number of projected births between 2000 to 2005 ($_n B_x^{2000-2005}$ — column eleven),

⑥ projected female population in 2005 ($_n F_{x+z}^{2005}$ — column twelve),

⑦ age cohorts in 2005.

Note that the first age cohort in future year 2005 is the 5 – 9 year cohort and the oldest age-group is 90 years and older. This is due to the fact that all female children of age 0 – 4 have moved after five years into the next higher age cohort, e.g., 5 – 9 years. The age cohort 0 – 4 in 2005 will be filled exclusively through births between 2000 and 2005.

Table 3.20 Female cohort-component module

Age in 2000	Female Pop. $_5F_x^{2000}$	Survival Rates $_5sr_x$	Net Migration Rates $_5nmr_x^{2000-2005}$	Fertility Rates $_5ASBR_x^{2005}$	Adjusted Fertility Rates $_5abr_x^{2005}$	Survive to 2005 $_5SF_{x+z}^{2005}$	Deaths 2000–2005 $_5DF_x^{2000-2005}$	Migrate 2000–2005 $_5NMF_{x+z}^{2000-2005}$	At Risk Female Pop. $_5ARF_x^{2005}$	Births 2000–2005 $_5B_x^{2000-2005}$	Projected Female Pop. $_5F_{x+z}^{2005}$	Age in 2005
1	2	3	4	5	6	7	8	9	10	11	12	13
0 – 4	3,347	0.9975	0.2130	–	–	3,339	8	713	–	–	4,052	5 – 9
5 – 9	3,458	0.9992	0.1200	–	–	3,455	3	415	–	–	3,870	10 – 14
10 – 14	3,309	0.9985	0.0214	0.0524	0.2220	3,304	5	71	3,377	750	3,375	15 – 19
15 – 19	2,940	0.9973	0.0213	0.3916	0.4417	2,932	8	63	2,999	1,324	2,995	20 – 24
20 – 24	2,490	0.9974	0.3852	0.4917	0.4917	2,484	6	959	3,446	1,694	3,443	25 – 29
25 – 29	3,100	0.9966	0.2552	0.4917	0.3898	3,089	11	791	3,886	1,515	3,881	30 – 34
30 – 34	3,621	0.9953	0.1228	0.2878	0.1871	3,604	17	445	4,057	759	4,049	35 – 39
35 – 39	4,003	0.9932	0.1606	0.0864	0.0480	3,976	27	643	4,632	222	4,619	40 – 44
40 – 44	3,879	0.9891	0.0102	0.0095	0.0048	3,837	42	40	3,897	19	3,876	45 – 49
45 – 49	3,188	0.9835	0.1424	–	–	3,135	53	454	–	–	3,589	50 – 54
50 – 54	2,730	0.9730	0.0675	–	–	2,656	74	184	–	–	2,841	55 – 59
55 – 59	1,913	0.9570	0.0180	–	–	1,831	82	34	–	–	1,865	60 – 64
60 – 64	1,419	0.9320	– 0.0121	–	–	1,323	96	– 17	–	–	1,305	65 – 69
65 – 69	1,182	0.8970	0.0482	–	–	1,060	122	57	–	–	1,117	70 – 74
70 – 74	1,110	0.8504	0.0747	–	–	944	166	83	–	–	1,027	75 – 79
75 – 79	784	0.7653	0.0492	–	–	600	184	39	–	–	639	80 – 84
80 – 84	527	0.6373	0.0131	–	–	336	191	7	–	–	343	85 – 89
85+	492	0.3814	0.1432	–	–	188	304	70	–	–	258	90 +
Total	43,492					42,092	1,400	5,050	26,295	6,283	47,142	

	Live Births 2000 – 2005 by Sex	Survival Rates $_5sr_x$ by Sex*	Projected Population by Sex	Child Deaths 2000 – 2005	Age in 2005
Female	3,065	0.9934	3,045	20	0 – 4
Male	3,218	0.9924	3,194	24	0 – 4
Total	6,283		6,238	45	
* Sex Ratio	1.05				

Total Projected Female Pop. F_{2005}

50,187

3.5.1   The Mortality Component

The first calculation we compute the female population likely to survive to the year 2005. Conceptually, the mortality component is presented in Fig. 3.13 below.

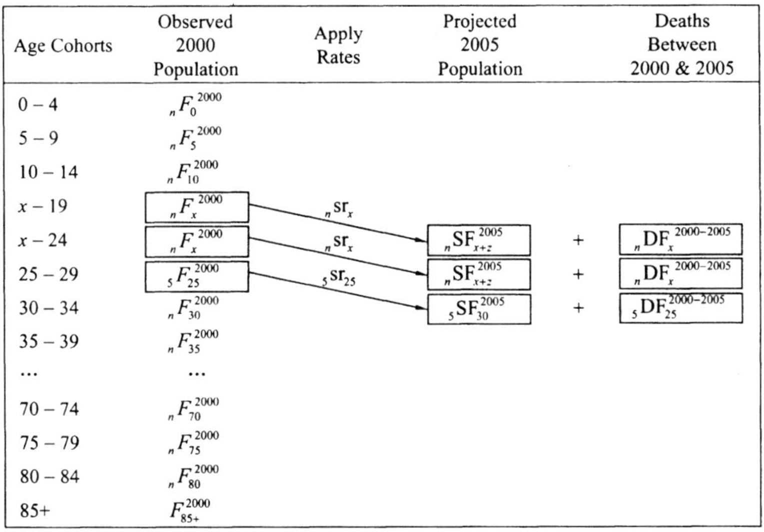

Age Cohorts	Observed 2000 Population	Apply Rates	Projected 2005 Population	Deaths Between 2000 & 2005
0 – 4	$_nF_0^{2000}$			
5 – 9	$_nF_5^{2000}$			
10 – 14	$_nF_{10}^{2000}$			
x – 19	$_nF_x^{2000}$	$_n\mathrm{sr}_x$		
x – 24	$_nF_x^{2000}$	$_n\mathrm{sr}_x$	$_n\mathrm{SF}_{x+z}^{2005}$ +	$_n\mathrm{DF}_x^{2000-2005}$
25 – 29	$_5F_{25}^{2000}$	$_5\mathrm{sr}_{25}$	$_n\mathrm{SF}_{x+z}^{2005}$ +	$_n\mathrm{DF}_x^{2000-2005}$
30 – 34	$_nF_{30}^{2000}$		$_5\mathrm{SF}_{30}^{2005}$ +	$_5\mathrm{DF}_{25}^{2000-2005}$
35 – 39	$_nF_{35}^{2000}$			
...	...			
70 – 74	$_nF_{70}^{2000}$			
75 – 79	$_nF_{75}^{2000}$			
80 – 84	$_nF_{80}^{2000}$			
85+	F_{85+}^{2000}			

Figure 3.13   The mortality component of the cohort-component model

Depending on the age-specific survival rate ($_n\mathrm{sr}_x$), the female population from the initial year 2000 ($_nF_x^{2000}$) either will move in the beginning of 2005 into the next age cohort ($_n\mathrm{SF}_{x+z}^{2005}$) or will not survive from 2000 to 2005 ($_n\mathrm{DF}_x^{2000-2005}$).

Computationally, this first step is done by multiplying the launch year female population in 2000 by its age-specific survival rate:

$$_n\mathrm{SF}_{x+z}^{2005} = {}_nF_x^{2000} \cdot {}_n\mathrm{sr}_x, \tag{3.29}$$

where,

$_nF_x^{2000}$ — female population in 2000;

$_n\mathrm{SF}_{x+z}^{2005}$ — surviving female population in 2005;

$_n\mathrm{sr}_x$ — age-specific survival rate, beginning age x, for five years age cohorts;

x — youngest age in a specific age cohort;

n — number of years in a specific age cohort (e.g., five years);

z — number of years in the projection interval (e.g., 2000 – 2005).

For the female age cohort 25 – 29 years in 2000, the surviving population in 2005 is

$$_5\text{SF}_{30}^{2005} = {_5}F_{25}^{2000} \cdot {_5}\text{sr}_{25} = 3,100 \times 0.9966 = 3,089$$

Taking the difference between the initial female population in 2000 and the surviving female population for that corresponding age cohort in 2005 will give us the number of female deaths in Boone County during the five-year projection period:

$$_n\text{DF}_x^{2000-2005} = {_n}F_x^{2000} - {_n}\text{SF}_{x+z}^{2005} \tag{3.30}$$

where,

$_n\text{DF}_x^{2000-2005}$ — number of female deaths between 2000 and 2005, age cohort x.

For the female age cohort, $25-29$ in 2000, the number of females not surviving to the year 2005 would be projected as

$$_5\text{DF}_{25}^{2000-2005} = {_5}F_{25}^{2000} - {_5}\text{SF}_{30}^{2005} = 3,100 - 3,089 = 11$$

It should be emphasized that the youngest age cohort $0-4$ years in the projection year, 2005, is derived solely from cumulated births occurring between 2000 and 2005. This is described in detail in the fertility component section. Also, the oldest age cohort in 2005 now includes females aged 90 years or older. To be consistent with the 2000 age cohort definition, the two oldest age cohorts in 2005 (e.g., $85-89$ and $90+$) can be combined into one age cohort labeled $85+$. Alternatively, one could combine the two oldest age cohorts of the launch population (e.g., $80-84$ and $85+$ in 2000) into one cohort. The surviving population in the target year (e.g., $85+$ in 2005) is calculated by multiplying this combined population by the survival rate of the oldest population.

3.5.2 The Net Migration Component[①]

The second part of the calculations concentrates on deriving the net migrating female population for Boone County for the years 2000 to 2005. Calculating female net migrants versus calculating female in-migrants and female out-migrants has the advantage that it only requires one set of migration rates. However, by doing the net migration calculations, it is of importance to note whether the net migration rates refer to the initial launch year population or to the surviving target year population. Both approaches are possible and the choice is dependent upon how the net migration rates were derived, which is either by using the initial launch year population as the denominator or the surviving target year

---

[①] Conceptually, there is no difference between calculation net migration and in- and out-migration separately. In the example of Boone County, the choice between net migration and in- and out-migration calculations has been made dependent on data availability.

population as the denominator. In Boone County, the migration rates are per age-specific female cohort at the beginning of the five-year period.[1]

Another important and vital factor is the appropriate choice of the at-risk population. This addresses why people in- or out-migrate, which can depend upon socioeconomic factors internal or external to the area. First, it is theoretically justifiable that out-migration depends upon internal factors and therefore, also upon the area's population. Here, the population at risk, the population used to calculate the number of out-migrants, is the area's own population. The same logic does not hold for in-migration. The literature argues[2] that in-migration depends on factors external to the area of interest and, therefore, the appropriate choice of the population at risk to in-migrate should not be the area of interest. In the case of in-migration, the more appropriate population at risk is the population outside of the area under consideration. This can be, for example, the "adjusted U.S. population", which is derived by subtracting the area of interest's population from the U.S. population for a particular year. However, using, for example, the adjusted U.S. population as the population at risk to in-migrate to the area of interest explicitly implies that the in-migration rates must have been derived based on the adjusted U.S. population.

The choice of the appropriate population at risk is also necessary for calculating net migration rates. However, the choice can be different depending upon wether more people in-migrate than out-migrate or vice versa. Imagine a fast growing region with clearly far more people moving into this region than leaving it. In this situation, with in-migration being predominant, the net migration rates should be calculated using a population as base that lies outside the region, e.g., for example the adjusted U.S. population as previously described. Now picture a region which is losing population or growing at a very low rate. Here, net migration rates can be calculated based on the region's own population.

In practice, however, a far simpler approach is often used for calculating net migration rates. Net migration rates can easily be calculated as residuals by rearranging age-sex-specific demographic balancing equations. The only information necessary is the age-sex-specific population (P) for an area at two points in time (e.g., 1995 and 2000) and the number of deaths (D) and births (B) between these two points in time. We may then estimate the number of net migrants per age cohort x as:

$$_n\text{NM}_{x+z}^{1995-2000} = {}_nP_{x+z}^{2000} - {}_nP_x^{1995} - {}_nB_x^{1995-2000} + {}_nD_x^{1995-2000} \qquad (3.31)$$

While in practice this is straightforward, we must keep in mind that conceptually net migration rates derived from residuals do not represent real probabilities, as is the case with fertility and survival rates.

---

[1] Source: http://ksdc.louisville.edu/kpr/pro/assumptions.htm.

[2] Smith et al., 2001:104 – 105.

The net migration rates for Boone County are listed under column four in Table 3.20. The Kentucky State Data Center calculated the rates using (1) the county's own population as the at-risk population and (2) the population at the beginning of the five-year time period. The calculations are again straight forward and are shown graphically in Fig. 3.14.

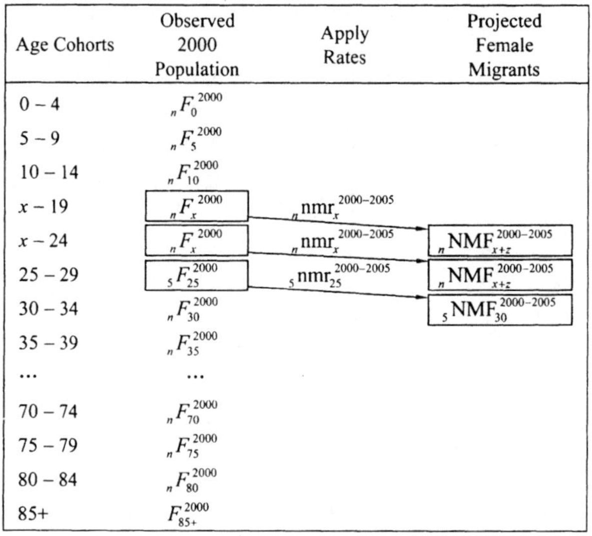

Age Cohorts	Observed 2000 Population	Apply Rates	Projected Female Migrants
0 – 4	$_nF_0^{2000}$		
5 – 9	$_nF_5^{2000}$		
10 – 14	$_nF_{10}^{2000}$		
x – 19	$_nF_x^{2000}$	$_n\text{nmr}_x^{2000-2005}$	
x – 24	$_nF_x^{2000}$	$_n\text{nmr}_x^{2000-2005}$	$_n\text{NMF}_{x+z}^{2000-2005}$
25 – 29	$_5F_{25}^{2000}$	$_5\text{nmr}_{25}^{2000-2005}$	$_n\text{NMF}_{x+z}^{2000-2005}$
30 – 34	$_nF_{30}^{2000}$		$_5\text{NMF}_{30}^{2000-2005}$
35 – 39	$_nF_{35}^{2000}$		
...	...		
70 – 74	$_nF_{70}^{2000}$		
75 – 79	$_nF_{75}^{2000}$		
80 – 84	$_nF_{80}^{2000}$		
85+	F_{85+}^{2000}		

Figure 3.14   The net migration component of the cohort-component model

For Boone County, the age-specific number of female migrants is derived using the equation:

$$_n\text{NMF}_{x+z}^{2000-2005} = {}_nF_x^{2000} \cdot {}_n\text{nmr}_x^{2000-2005} \qquad (3.32)$$

where,

$_n\text{NMF}_{x+z}^{2000-2005}$ — female population migrating between 2000 and 2005 per age cohort x;

$_nF_x^{2000}$ — female population in 2000, age cohort x ("at-risk population");

$_n\text{nmr}_x^{2000-2005}$ — net migration for age cohort x.

Again using the sample age cohort of females aged 25 – 29 in Boone County from Table 3.20, we calculated the number of female migrants for this age cohort as:

$$_5\text{NMF}_{30}^{2000-2005} = {}_5F_{25}^{2000} \cdot {}_5\text{nmr}_{25}^{2000-2005} = 3{,}100 \times 0.2552 = 791$$

Of the females aged 30 – 34 in Boone County in 2005, 791 will be in-migrants.

3.5.3   The Fertility Component

The last portion of the cohort-component model calculates the number of births per age-specific female cohort. In particular, how many babies will be born to women of childbearing age, e.g., also referred to as women at risk. The outcome of these calculations will be used to project the number of females and males that go into the first age cohort $0-4$ years in the target year 2005.

The fertility component of the model requires three individual steps which are

(1) to project the number of births per female age cohort;

(2) to aggregate all births and allocate this aggregated total between male and female births;

(3) to apply the survival rates to the cumulated male and female live births, projecting the number of males and females that will survive to the target year and form the youngest age cohort (e.g., $0-4$ years in 2005).

The age-specific birth rates reported by the Kentucky State Data Center for Boone County are for a five-year period at the end of the five-year period. This requires adjusting the launch year female population in childbearing age by deaths and migration for the five-year period. The individual steps are graphically represented for the female cohort aged $25-29$ in Fig. 3.15. The individual components are described following Fig. 3.15.

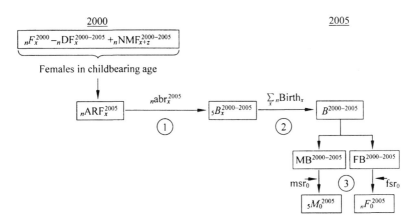

Figure 3.15   Fertility component of the cohort-component model

We see that the female population aged $25-29$ is in a **first step** adjusted for deaths and migration and form the so-called at-risk female age cohort (ARF) aged $25-29$. This at-risk female age cohort is then used to calculate the number of births per age cohort. Transforming this idea into equations we get:

$$_n\text{ARF}_x^{2005} = {}_nF_x^{2000} - (0.5 \cdot {}_n\text{DF}_x^{2000-2005}) + {}_n\text{NMF}_{x+z}^{2000-2005} \tag{3.33}$$

119

$$_nB_x^{2000-2005} = {}_n\mathrm{ARF}_x^{2005} \cdot {}_n\mathrm{abr}_x^{2005} \qquad (3.34)$$

$$_n\mathrm{abr}_x^{2005} = \frac{({}_n\mathrm{ASBR}_x^{2005} + {}_n\mathrm{ASBR}_{x+5}^{2005})}{2} \qquad (3.35)$$

where,

$_n\mathrm{ARF}_x^{2005}$ — at-risk female population at the end of the projection interval, age cohort x;

$_nB_x^{2000-2005}$ — births between 2000 and 2005, age cohort x;

$_n\mathrm{abr}_x^{2005}$ — adjusted birth rate, age cohort x;

$_n\mathrm{ASBR}_x^{2005}$ — age-specific birth rate, age cohort x.

Equation (3.33) determines the at-risk female population by adjusting the female launch year population ($_nF_x^{2000}$) for deaths ($_n\mathrm{DF}_x^{2000-2005}$) and female net migration ($_n\mathrm{NMF}_{x+z}^{2000-2005}$). The adjustment of the deaths per female cohort by the factor 1/2 needs some more explanation. The assumption is that on average, a woman of childbearing age will stay half of the projection interval (e.g., $n/2$) in one age cohort and half in the next higher age cohort. For a five-year interval, a woman age 27 will stay three more years in the 25 – 29 cohort and the two remaining years in the 30 – 34 cohort. The direct result is that not all women belonging to the 25 – 29 cohort at the beginning of the interval will die at age 25 – 29 which requires adjusting the number of female deaths per cohort.

Equation (3.34) then calculates the projected births per age cohort by multiplying the at-risk female population ($_n\mathrm{ARF}_x^{2005}$) by the corresponding adjusted birth rate ($_n\mathrm{abr}_x^{2005}$).[1] In section 3.3, we have discussed the age-specific birth rate ($_n\mathrm{ASBR}_x^{year}$). The concept for adjusting the age-specific birth rates is the same as for deaths. Women, on average, will only stay half of the projection interval (e.g., $n/2$) before moving into the next higher age cohort. For instance, the average age for women aged 25 – 29 years is 27.5 years, the middle year of this specific age cohort. On average, a woman will therefore stay 2.5 years in the age cohort 25 – 29 years before she advances into the age cohort 30 – 34 years, meaning that women spend half their time in one age cohort and the other half in the next higher age cohort.

---

[1] Given that the adjusted fertility rate is derived from age-specific birth rates, we alternatively also refer to it as the adjusted birth rate ($_n\mathrm{abr}_x^{2005}$).

For Boone County females aged 25 – 29 in 2000, the births are computed as (see also column 10 and 11, Table 3.20):

$$_5\text{ARF}_{25}^{2005} = {}_5F_{25}^{2000} - (0.5 \times {}_5\text{DF}_{25}^{2000-2005}) + {}_5\text{NMF}_{30}^{2000-2005}$$
$$= 3,100 - (0.5 \times 11) + 791 = 3,886$$

$$_5B_{25}^{2000-2005} = {}_5\text{ARF}_{25}^{2005} \cdot {}_5\text{abr}_{25}^{2005} = 3,886 \times 0.3898 = 1,515$$

$$_5\text{abr}_{25}^{2005} = \frac{{}_5\text{ASBR}_{25}^{2005} + {}_5\text{ASBR}_{30}^{2005}}{2} = \frac{0.4917 + 0.2878}{2} = 0.3898$$

The **second step** combines all births per age cohort into one aggregated figure, total births in Boone County between 2000 and 2005 ($B^{2000-2005}$). Having a cumulative figure for births in Boone County, we split the total births based on the historic male/female sex ratio at birth into cumulative male and female live births ($\text{MB}^{2000-2005}$ and $\text{FB}^{2000-2005}$).

This is done as follows:

$$B^{2000-2005} = \sum_x {}_nB_x^{2000-2005} \tag{3.36}$$

$$\text{MB}^{2000-2005} = \left[\frac{1.05}{1+1.05}\right] B^{2000-2005} \tag{3.37}$$

$$\text{FB}^{2000-2005} = \left[\frac{1}{1+1.05}\right] B^{2000-2005} \tag{3.38}$$

where,

$B^{2000-2005}$ — cumulative births between 2000 and 2005;

$\text{MB}^{2000-2005}$ — cumulative male births between 2000 and 2005;

$\text{FB}^{2000-2005}$ — cumulative female births between 2000 and 2005;

1.05 — historic male/female sex ratio at birth[1].

The idea here is to derive the total number of male and female babies born separately to women in Boone county of childbearing age between 2000 and 2005. In return, these two totals, e.g., $\text{MB}^{2000-2005}$ and $\text{FB}^{2000-2005}$, will be adjusted for infant mortality and finally, be used to build the youngest age cohort aged 0 – 4, in the target year 2005. Before we go to the last step, let us do the calculations of female and male births in Boone County. Beginning with step two, the actual calculations are added underneath Table 3.20.

---

[1] Source: http://www.odci.gov/cia/publications/factbook/print/us.html.

$$B^{2000-2005} = \sum_x {}_n B_x^{2000-2005} = 750 + 1,324 + 1,694 + 1,515 + 759 + 222 + 19$$

$$= 6,283$$

$$\mathrm{MB}^{2000-2005} = 6,283 \times \left[\frac{1.05}{1+1.05} \right] = 6,283 \times 0.5122 = 3,218$$

$$\mathrm{FB}^{2000-2005} = 6,283 \times \left[\frac{1}{1+1.05} \right] = 6,283 \times 0.4878 = 3,065$$

The calculations project a total of 3,218 male and 3,065 female births between 2000 and 2005 to all women of childbearing age in Boone County.

The fact that not all newborns will survive to the target year 2005 is shown in **step three**, where we adjust the number of male and female live births for infant mortality. This is done analogously to all other age cohorts, in that the cumulative live births are multiplied by a sex-specific survival rate.

$$_n F_0^{2005} = \mathrm{FB}^{2000-2005} \cdot {}_n \mathrm{sr}_0 \qquad (3.39)$$

where,

$_n F_0^{2005}$ — youngest female age cohort aged $0-4$ in 2005;

$_n \mathrm{sr}_0$ — survival rate for the age cohort $0-4$.

We then compute the females in Boone County aged $0-4$ in 2005 as:

$$_5 F_0^{2005} = 3,065 \times 0.9934 = 3,045$$

Boone County is projected to have 3,045 females in the youngest age cohort aged $0-4$ in 2005.

3.5.4 Bringing All Components Together

So far, we have calculated the surviving female population, the net migrating female population, and the female births surviving to the year 2005. Now we are ready to bring all these individual pieces together in one equation in order to project the age-specific female population in 2005. But note that this final equation is not applicable for the youngest age cohort aged $0-4$ in 2005 which comes exclusively form the fertility component:

$$_n F_{x+z}^{2005} = {}_n \mathrm{SF}_{x+z}^{2005} + {}_n \mathrm{NMF}_{x+z}^{2000-2005} \qquad (3.40)$$

Column twelve in Table 3.20 shows these final calculations. For Boone County, the projected female population aged $30-34$ years in 2005 is:

$$_5F_{30}^{2005} = {}_5SF_{30}^{2005} + {}_5NMF_{30}^{2000-2005} = 3,089 + 791 = 3,881\text{ }^{(1)}$$

The sum of all these projected age-specific cohorts in column twelve, Table 3.20, plus the result form the youngest age cohort aged $0-4$ in 2005 from the fertility component will give us the final result, the cumulative projected female population for Boone County in the target year 2005:

$$F^{2005} = \sum_x {}_nF_{x+z}^{2005} + {}_5F_0^{2005} = 47,142 + 3,045 = 50,187 \qquad (3.41)$$

where,

F^{2005} — cumulative female population in 2005;

x — youngest age in a specific age cohort in 2005, e.g., $0-4, 5-9, 10-14$, etc.;

z — number of years in the projection interval (e.g., $2000-2005$).

The projected female population in Boone County for 2005 totals 50,187.

All calculations above refer to the female part of the cohort-component model. To get a complete small area model for Boone County, the same calculations need to be repeated for the county's male population. They are identical to what has been described for the female population. They are even simplified in that the male calculations do not include the fertility component. To show a complete cohort-component for Boone County, we added age-specific calculations for the male population in Table 3.21 without further elaborations. Adding total projected female and male population from the two cohort-component models will then give us Boone County's total projected population for the year 2005. It is calculated as:

$$P^{2005} = F^{2005} + M^{2005} = 50,187 + 49,266 = 99,453 \qquad (3.42)$$

Hamilton and Perry (1962) proposed a short version of the cohort-component method, which apply **cohort-change ratios** (CCR) to the beginning population. These cohort-change ratios are usually calculated from the last two censuses. Given that censuses in the United States are ten years apart, the Hamilton-Perry method often projects five-year age groups in ten year intervals. Mortality and migration are combined into a single rate rather than treating them separately. Further simplification is possible by using child-woman ration instead of the age-specific birth rates in the fertility component. While the Hamilton-Perry method may be given preference where data are not readily available to build a more complex cohort-component model, a potential source of error is the use of constant growth rates—which in the case of particularly fast growing regions, can overestimate future populations.

---

① The difference of one female in this equation is due to rounding in the table.

Table 3.21 Male cohort-component module

Age in 2000	Male Pop. $_5M_x^{2000}$	Survival Rates $_5sr_x$	Net Migration Rates $_5nmr_x^{2000-2005}$	Survive to 2005 $_5SM_{x+z}^{2005}$	Deaths 00 to 05 $_5DM_x^{2000-2005}$	Migrate 00 to 05 $_5NMM_{x+z}^{2000-2005}$	Projected Male Pop. $_5M_{x+z}^{2005}$	Age in 2005
1	2	3	4	5	6	7	8	9
0 – 4	3,502	0.9967	0.2130	3,490	12	746	4,236	5 – 9
5 – 9	3,685	0.9988	0.1200	3,681	4	442	4,123	10 – 14
10 – 14	3,477	0.9972	0.0298	3,467	10	104	3,571	15 – 19
15 – 19	3,142	0.9929	– 0.0022	3,120	22	– 7	3,113	20 – 24
20 – 24	2,591	0.9929	0.3505	2,573	18	908	3,481	25 – 29
25 – 29	3,003	0.9918	0.3211	2,978	25	964	3,943	30 – 34
30 – 34	3,584	0.9896	0.1624	3,547	37	582	4,129	35 – 39
35 – 39	3,852	0.9859	0.1552	3,798	54	598	4,396	40 – 44
40 – 44	3,749	0.9803	0.0493	3,675	74	185	3,860	45 – 49
45 – 49	3,153	0.9709	0.0940	3,061	92	296	3,358	50 – 54
50 – 54	2,610	0.9540	0.0766	2,490	120	200	2,690	55 – 59
55 – 59	1,940	0.9256	0.0026	1,796	144	5	1,801	60 – 64
60 – 64	1,365	0.8830	– 0.0121	1,205	160	– 17	1,189	65 – 69
65 – 69	1,047	0.8236	0.0482	862	185	50	913	70 – 74
70 – 74	839	0.7508	0.0747	630	209	63	693	75 – 79
75 – 79	560	0.6392	0.0492	358	202	28	386	80 – 84
80 – 84	246	0.4985	0.0131	123	123	3	126	85 – 89
85 +	154	0.2976	0.1432	46	108	22	68	90 +
Total	42,499			40,899	1,600	5,173	46,072	

Cummulative Live Births 2000 – 2005 MB_{00-05}	Survival Rates $_5ST_{2000}$	Projected Male Pop. M_{2005}	Child Deaths 00 to 05	Age in 2005
3,218	0.9924	3,194	24	0 – 4

Total Projected Male Pop. M_{2005}

49,266

3.6   Concluding Remarks

The population models have one thing in common. They assume that observed population trends can be carried over into the near future. As we have seen, this is repeatedly done for the population trend extrapolation methods by

(1) Gathering population data for the past years,

(2) Plotting these observed population data onto a scatter plot and inspecting them visually,

(3) Extrapolating observed trends into the near future, either using simple ratio methods as the share of growth or shift-share method or the more complex regression models such as the linear, geometric, parabolic, or logistic population model.

The strength of all trend extrapolation methods undoubtedly lie in their small data requirement. In most cases, total population figures for a number of past years will be sufficient to obtain an area's population projections for future years. This low data requirement makes extrapolation models very attractive for small areas where historical population data are not always readily available at a more detailed level.

Regarding the required modeling skills, trend extrapolation models vary significantly. While share of growth and shift-share models are conceptually and computationally easy to understand and implement, regression models such as the logistic model, involve higher mathematical skills. Nevertheless, understanding the linear transformation of the more sophisticated extrapolation models makes them easy to apply as the linear model.

On the other hand, extrapolation models have severe drawbacks. Given their use of limited and highly aggregated data, they lack any information about the different components of projected population growth/decline. In other words, we get no explanation on theoretical grounds for these projected population changes. The attractiveness of the very low data requirement, therefore, must be acknowledged as an intrinsic limitation to the projected results. Further, the use of highly aggregated data for past years treats factors like the area's economic, housing, and/or recreational attractiveness as external to the method.

Another difficult task is the choice of the appropriate timeframe for selecting past population statistics. If available, should we use populations for the last 10, 20, or even 50 years? This decision is less problematic for areas where data show a slow but steady growth pattern. The choice is more challenging for fast-growing areas or for areas with alternating population growth and decline patterns. What if the area grew generally at a slow rate for the last 50 years, but suddenly seven years ago began to decline? While typically the heaviest reliance is on the more recent data, there is no guarantee that the population will continue to decline. Other data might be of particular help for choosing the appropriate period of past years. For instance, improvements in the area's economic environment might have already indicated a turn in population growth. If this is the case, choosing only the last seven years would erroneously lead to further projected population decline while we know from outside sources that the population may more likely start growing again.

Another shortcoming of trend extrapolation methods is that they do not allow the ability to play out different future scenarios. For instance, how will population projections change if economic conditions, birth rates, migration patterns, and other factors change? We want to reemphasize that extrapolation models rely upon the assumption that observed past conditions are assumed to continue in the future. This assumption may or may not hold. As a direct consequence, the further into the future we project, the less reliable the extrapolation models become. The likelihood of a continuation of observed past population trends is greater when projecting only a few years into the future as when projecting population trends for as many as 20 – 30 years into the future. Therefore, population projections that go too far into the future must be read with reservation.

We want to conclude this section on extrapolation methods with the remark that in many cases, practitioners often use the simple and straight forward population models. Also in favor of extrapolation models is the fact that there is virtually no evidence that more complex methods outperform extrapolation models.

Population analysis is a challenging task and by far more than just running some population models. As Rayer puts it: [1]

"The real challenge in population analysis is describing and projecting populations within 'reasonable' limits. We spend 90% of our time making sure the data make sense and if they do not, we make adjustments."

Computationally, the cohort-component method is easy and straightforward. Once the required data and rates are collected, its computations can be done using a spreadsheet. Cohort-component methods are widely used at all government levels. Its popularity mainly goes back to the amount of detail provided by the model. The breakdown of the target population into cohorts allows zooming in on specific parts of the population, e.g., females of age 30 to 34. For each of these cohorts, the components of the model, e.g., births, deaths, and migration, explain the reasons for population changes over time.

For many areas, the question is not only by how much the total population is projected to change over the next five years. For better planning, many local governments want to understand:

(1) Why is the population changing? Are the reasons for the expected changes mainly driven by births, deaths, and/or in- and out migration?

(2) How is the population changing? Is the population aging? Is the racial composition of the population changing?

While many of these questions can be answered directly from the

---

[1] Quote from personal communication with Dr. Stefan Rayer.

cohort-component model, it also means that with more detailed models the data requirements increase significantly. For a detailed population projection, population data by sex, age, and race/ethnicity as well as all fertility, survival, and in- and out- migration rates must be available. The computational requirements, time, and costs increase with the level of detail.

For planning purposes, many planning agencies will not get involved in the process of collecting and verifying data and computing the individual birth, survival, and migration rates. As planners, we prefer using readily available population data and rates to set up a cohort-component model. Using readily available data and rates provided by various governmental agencies, we are incorporating all assumptions into the cohort-component model. For example, the Boone County net migration rates were derived by using the area's own population as the population base. As such, we cannot use the adjusted U.S. population as the population at risk of migrating. Another example would be if the individual birth, survival, and migration rates have been calculated using the base population at the beginning, in the middle, or at the end of a specific time interval. For instance, had the survival rate been constructed using the base population at the beginning of a time interval, all following calculations must use the target population at the beginning of this particular time interval for consistency. For planners using pre-calculated rates can mean a higher degree of dependability on the assumptions made by the data collecting and rate calculating agency.

A last but critical point is the fact that all individual rates are calculated using historic data. Assuming that the observed trends in the components of growth and the demographic composition of the population remain constant for future time periods, we use rates computed from historic data and apply them to project future population growth. For instance, the computed birth rates based on the number of live births for the last period data available are used for projecting births for the next time period. The main assumption here is similar to that from the population trend models: past population trends can be carried on into the near future.

Each population projection method discussed in this chapter is applicable under certain situations. The choice of appropriate method should be a combination of purpose, time-money constraints, level of detail, and data availability. The most important of all is to ensure that input data are correct and reasonable. In reality, researchers spend most their time working on the data rather than running the models. Keep in mind that for population projections, you will spend hours and hours making sense out of your input data and in many cases, changes to the collected data are necessary before they can be used for population modeling purposes.

In general, there is virtually no evidence that more complex population methods, such as cohort-component and structural models, provide better population projections. Each method has strengths and weaknesses and each is based on a set of assumptions, which have an impact on the results. What more complex models do offer, however, is the ability to play out different future scenarios by using altering migration, birth, or survival rates. In addition, all these different rates applied in the cohort-component method could be trended themselves. For instance, observing migration rates on an annual basis for a longer period of time would allow to project migrations rates for future time periods.

Given that it is almost impossible to tell which of the described population projection methods would achieve "more accurate" projections under given conditions, it is very common to apply a mixture of different methods. Using averages derived from a mixture of methods is a more conservative way of projecting future population. The fact is that long-term trends are likely to regress towards the mean. In addition, it is common to provide an interval of projected populations rather than offering one exact population projection (e.g., point estimator). Calculating a series of low, middle, and high population projections allows to project populations within a range of values. Usually the middle series reflects what you believe is the most likely occurring population trend.

Projection errors decrease with population size. This is why many agencies use a stepwise approach of projecting populations. In a stepwise approach, state totals are calculated first. In a second step, county totals are calculated and the sum of all county totals must equal the state total. If not, adjustments to the county totals are made until their total equals the state total. More detailed calculations at the county-level, for instance, individual age cohorts are included in the third step. These more detailed projections are controlled by the county total.

Review Questions

1. What is the difference between population projections, forecasts, and estimates? From the U.S. Census Bureau website, are the inter-decennial population figures for the years 1991 – 1999 projected, forecasted, or estimated? Describe why?

2. Choosing the most appropriate projection method can depend on a variety of factors. Name at least five factors you think should be considered when choosing a projection method.

3. Briefly describe the four fundamental concepts of demographic analysis.

4. According to the demographic balancing equation, there are three components of change. Name these three components of change and explain how these components are being accounted for in the cohort-component model.

5. Trend extrapolation methods are very popular to project populations. Explain the rational behind all these extrapolation models. Explain the main

conceptual difference between the group of trend extrapolation models and the cohort-component method.

6. Under what circumstances would you consider the geometric population model as being appropriate to project population growth or decline? What does the slope coefficient of the geometric population model express? And what is the most obvious and important difference between the geometric population model and the logistic population model?

7. For each of the four trend extrapolation models discussed in chapter 3, we provided an adjusted form of the model. Explain the rational behind the inclusion of the adjustment factor into the model.

8. Describe in detail the net migration component of the cohort-component method. For a region that is losing population, what would you choose as denominator for calculating the net migration rate: the region's population or the population outside the region? Explain why.

9. What are the strengths and weaknesses of the cohort-component method?

10. Under what circumstances would you prefer an extrapolation model over a cohort-component model?

Exercises

You are hired as a planner for a small urban county, Sunshine County, and one of your first tasks is to update the county's demographic profile and to provide the county government with "reasonable" population projections until the year 2010.

1. Your first analysis is the graphical presentation of the county's population using a population pyramid (for detailed instructions on how to build a population pyramid, see Chapter 8). The county population data are listed in Table 3.22. What detailed information on Sunshine County does the population pyramid exhibit?

2. Calculating average annual absolute change (AAAC) and average annual percent change is a quick way of examining past observed population trends. Using the population data for the last twenty years, calculate the AAAC and AAPC for Sunshine County and interpret your results. In addition, project the county's total population for the year 2010 using the AAAC and AAPC.

3. A more sophisticated way of projecting populations uses trend extrapolation models. Using the data from Table 3.23, estimate the linear and geometric population model for Sunshine County. Compare your results with the AAAC and AAPC from above and project the county's total population for the year 2010 using both the linear and geometric extrapolation models.

4. Another quick way of projecting an area's future total population applies ratio methods, such as the share of growth and the shift-share method. Project the 2010 Sunshine County population using both the share of growth and the shift-share method, based on the information provided in Table 3.24.

Table 3.22 Sunshine County population by sex and age, 2000

Sunshine County, 2000	Male	Female
Total Population	19,185	19,856
Under 5 years	1,512	1,364
5 to 9 years	1,509	1,437
10 to 14 years	1,476	1,357
15 to 19 years	1,492	1,490
20 to 24 years	1,543	1,665
25 to 29 years	1,450	1,504
30 to 34 years	1,410	1,475
35 to 39 years	1,507	1,600
40 to 44 years	1,525	1,660
45 to 49 years	1,399	1,466
50 to 54 years	1,184	1,238
55 to 59 years	840	860
60 to 64 years	649	712
65 to 69 years	542	576
70 to 74 years	432	482
75 to 79 years	346	391
80 to 84 years	222	298
85 years and over	147	281

Table 3.23 Annual total population data for Sunshine County, 1980 – 2000

Year	Total Population	Year	Total Population
1980	26,065	1991	31,531
1981	26,611	1992	32,475
1982	26,759	1993	33,356
1983	27,283	1994	34,125
1984	27,794	1995	34,947
1985	27,917	1996	36,017
1986	28,453	1997	36,967
1987	28,976	1998	37,620
1988	29,682	1999	38,419
1989	29,992	2000	39,041
1990	30,508		

Table 3.24 Comparison of Sunshine County population to a benchmark region

Year	Benchmark Region	Sunshine County
1990	360,000	30,508
2000	400,000	39,041
2010	425,000	

5. The cohort-component model requires more detailed data than previous methods. Using Tables 3.22 and 3.25, which provide data on population by sex and age, birth rates, survival rates, and migration rates, set up the female cohort-component module and project the female age-specific population for the year 2010.

Table 3.25   Survival, birth, and net migration rates for Sunshine County, 2000 – 2005

Beginning Age in 2000	Ending Age in 2005	Survival Rates[2]		Net Migration Rates[3]		Birth Rates[4]
		Male	Female	Male	Female	
Live births[1]	0 – 4	992.4	993.4	26.7	6.7	–
0 – 4	5 – 9	996.7	997.5	147.3	127.3	–
5 – 9	10 – 14	998.8	999.2	96.7	76.7	–
10 – 14	15 – 19	997.2	998.5	73.8	53.8	64.9
15 – 19	20 – 24	992.9	997.3	135.2	115.2	363.4
20 – 24	25 – 29	992.9	997.4	112.4	92.4	551.1
25 – 29	30 – 34	991.8	996.6	– 14.5	– 14.5	488.3
30 – 34	35 – 39	989.6	995.3	68.9	48.9	240.6
35 – 39	40 – 44	985.9	993.2	98.9	78.9	75.2
40 – 44	45 – 49	980.3	989.1	23.3	3.3	7.2
45 – 49	50 – 54	970.9	983.5	86.6	66.6	–
50 – 54	55 – 59	954.0	973.0	7.4	– 12.6	–
55 – 59	60 – 64	925.6	957.0	61.4	41.4	–
60 – 64	65 – 69	883.0	932.0	52.0	32.0	–
65 – 69	70 – 74	823.6	897.0	48.4	28.4	–
70 – 74	75 – 79	750.8	850.4	123.2	103.2	–
75 – 79	80 – 84	639.2	765.3	117.3	97.3	–
80 – 84	85 – 89	498.5	637.3	214.1	194.1	–
85 +	90 +	297.6	381.4	69.7	49.7	–

(1) Cumulative live births during the 5-year period.
(2) Total survivors (those who do not die) per 1,000 persons over a 5-year period.
(3) Rates are per 1,000 persons at the beginning of the 5-year period.
(4) Total live births per 1,000 females over a 5-year period.

References

Armstrong, J.S. 1985. *Long-range Forecasting: From Crystall Ball to Computer*. 2nd. ed. New York, NY: John Wiley.
Batie, Sandra. 1989. Sustainable development: challenges to the profession of agricultural economics. *American Journal of Agricultural Economics*, 1,083 – 1,101.

Boone County, Kentucky. 2004. Official Website. Available online from http://www.boone-countyky.org/. Accessed September 2004.

Bowley, A. L. 1924. Birth and population in Great Britain. *The Economic Journal,* 34: 188 – 192.

Cannan, E. 1895. The probability of a cessation of the growth of population in England and Wales during the next century. *The Economist Journal,* 5: 506 – 515.

Central Intelligence Agency (CIA). 2004. The World Factbook: United States. Internet; Available from http://www.odci.gov/cia/publications/factbook/print/us.html. Accessed September 2004.

Daily, Gretchen C. and Paul R. Ehrlich. 1992. Population, Sustainability, and Earth's Carrying Capacity: A Framework for Estimating Population Sizes and Lifestyles that Could Be Sustained without Undermining Future Generations. Available online from http://dieoff.org/page112.htm. Accessed September 2004.

Daly, Herman E. and John B.Cobb, Jr. 1989. *For the Common Good.* Boston, MA: Beacon Press.

Gujarati, Damodar N. 1995. *Basic Econometrics.* 3rd. ed. New York: McGraw-Hill, Inc.

Hamilton, C. and J. Perry. 1962. A short method for projecting population by age from one decennial census to another. *Social Forces,* 41: 163 – 170.

Kentucky State Data Center. 2003. Kentucky Population Estimates: Intercensal Population Estimates, 1991 – 1999. Available online from http://ksdc.louisville.edu/kpr/popest/ice9000.xls. Accessed September 2004.

Kentucky State Data Center. 2003. Kentucky Population Projections. Available online from http://ksdc.louisville.edu/Projections2003.htm. Accessed September 2004.

Kentucky State Data Center. 2003. Kentucky Population Projections: Assumptions and Methodology. Available online from http://ksdc.louisville.edu/kpr/pro/assumptions.htm. Accessed September 2004.

Kentucky State Data Center. 2003. Kentucky Population Projections: Middle Projection Series. Available online from http://ksdc.louisville.edu/kpr/pro/Middle_Series.xls. Accessed September 2004.

Kentucky State Data Center. 2003. Kentucky Population Projections: Populations 1990 – 2000, with Middle, Low, and High Projections 2005 – 2030. Available online from http://ksdc.louisville.edu/kpr/pro/Summary_Table.xls. Accessed September 2004.

Kentucky State Data Center. 2004. Available online from http://ksdc.louisville.edu/. Accessed September 2004.

Keyfitz N. 1968. *An Introduction to the Mathematics of Population.* Reading, MA: Addison-Wesley.

Klosterman, Richard E. 1990. *Community Analysis and Planning Techniques.* Savage, MD: Rowman and Littlefield Publishers, Inc.

National Center for Health Statistics. 1999. Births and deaths: preliminary data for 1998. *National Vital Statistics Report,* 47(25). Available online from http://www.cdc.gov/nchs/data/nvsr/nvsr47/nvs47_25.pdf. Accessed September 2004.

National Center for Health Statistics. 2001. Births: final data for 2000. *National Vital Statistics Report,* 50(5). Available online from http://www.cdc.gov/nchs/data/nvsr/ nvsr50/nvsr50_05.pdf. Accessed September 2004.

National Center for Health Statistics. 2002. United States life tables, 2000. *National Vital*

Statistics Report, 51(3), Available online from http://www.cdc.gov/nchs/data/nvsr/nvsr51/ nvsr51_03.pdf. Accessed September 2004.

National Center for Health Statistics. 2002. Births: preliminary data for 2002. *National Vital Statistics Report*, 51(11). Available online from http://www.cdc.gov/nchs/products/pubs/ pubd/nvsr/51/51-12.htm. Accessed September 2004.

National Center for Health Statistics. 2004. Available online from http://www.cdc.gov/ nchs/. Accessed September 2004.

Smith, Stanley K., Jeff Tayman and David A. Swanson. 2001. *State and Local Population Projections: Methodology and Analysis*. New York: Kluwer Academic/Plenum Publishers.

Smith, Stanley K. and Stefan Rayer. 2004. *Florida Population Studies*, Bureau of Economic and Business Research (BEBR), 37(2). Bulletin 138.

U.S. Census Bureau. 2000. Fertility of American Women: June 2000 (P20 – 543RV). Available online from http://www.census.gov/prod/2001pubs/p20 – 543rv.pdf. Accessed September 2004.

U.S. Census Bureau. 2000. Migration by Sex and Age for the Population 5 Years and Over for the United States, Regions, States, and Puerto Rico: 2000 (PHC-T-23). Available online from http://www.census.gov/population/www/cen2000/phc-t23.html. Accessed September 2004.

U.S. Census Bureau. 2000. Summary File 1(SF1). Available online from http://factfinder. census.gov/servlet/DTGeoSearchByListServlet?ds_name=DEC_2000_SF1_U& state=dt. Accessed September 2004.

U.S. Census Bureau. 2002. State Population Estimates by Selected Age Categories and Sex: July 1, 2002. Available online from http://www.census.gov/popest/archives/2000s/ vintage_2002/ST-EST2002-ASRO-01.html. Accessed September 2004.

U.S. Census Bureau. 2003. Domestic Migration across Regions, Divisions, and States: 1995 – 2000. Available online from http://www.census.gov/prod/2003pubs/censr-7.pdf. Accessed September 2004.

U.S. Census Bureau. 2004. Metropolitan and Micropolitan Statistical Area Definitions. Available online from http://www.census.gov/popest/estimates.php. Accessed September 2004.

U.S. Census Bureau. 2004. Population Estimates. Available online from http://www. census.gov/ popest/estimates.php. Accessed September 2004.

U.S. Census Bureau. 2004. Population Estimates Terms and Definitions. Available online from http://www.census.gov/popest/topics/terms/. Accessed September 2004.

U.S. Census Bureau. 2004. Schedule of Population and Household Projection Releases. Available online from http://www.census.gov/population/www/projections/projsched.html. Accessed September 2004.

U.S. Census Bureau. 2004. State Population Projections. Available online from http: //www. census.gov/population/www/projections/stproj.html. Accessed September 2004.

Whelpton. 1928. Population of the United States, 1925 to 1975. American Journal of Sociology 34: 253 – 270.

Chapter 4 Understanding Your Regional Economy —The Economic Base Theory

4.1 Introduction to Economic Models

Imagine that a car manufacturer is planning to build a car distribution center in the greater Cincinnati metropolitan region. Strategically, this would be a good choice for the car manufacturer, given that Interstate Highway 75 (I-75) is the main artery of the national car industry and Ohio lies in the midst of it. Economically, this would be great for the region, in that it would provide jobs and income for its workforce and new activities for regional businesses to supply the car manufacturer with goods and services.

Envision another scenario in which a national fast-food chain considers building a manufacturing plant in the greater Cincinnati region to produce the buns and patties for our well-loved "Juicy Burgers". The fast-food chain talks about creating 800 new jobs but expects a tax incentive package in return from the local government to smooth out their initial investment.

What do both scenarios have in common? Obviously, they would be highly welcome by

(1) the regional workforce, particularly those seeking employment with these businesses;

(2) the construction industry, which could gain additional contracts for building the distribution center and the plant;

(3) regional businesses and firms, which might expect an increase in demand for their goods boosting their overall level of business activities;

(4) the city and county governments, who may, in the long-run, benefit from additional tax revenues (e.g., corporate income tax).

Planners throughout the region busily consider the implications of these scenarios. Land use planners, working for the local and regional governments, would think about where to locate these two new industries. At the same time, their colleagues in the transportation department would examine the proposed locations for these new industries to ensure that they are strategically located so as not to add to traffic congestion. Economic development (ED) planners would use the opportunity to predict how industry output, employment, and income for residents and the government might be affected by this increase in **economic activities**. More specifically, ED planners might develop an impact analysis using **multipliers** to estimate changes in the regional economy (e.g., output, employment, and income) resulting from the proposed car distribution center or the fast-food chain's manufacturing plant. Clearly, in the case of the fast-food chain the **direct effect** on the labor market would be the creation of 800 new jobs. But what would be the **indirect effects** of this new plant on other businesses in the region? The 800 new jobs will create new income that will be spent, at least partly, within the region on housing, clothes, food, entertainment, and other items. In return, this will create more jobs in other regional businesses. Multipliers are one way to estimate the **total effects** on employment, for example, as a result of the new fast-food chain's manufacturing plant.

In this chapter, we will explore how the **economic base theory** can increase our understanding of how a regional economy works and how economic development processes shape regional economies. Although economic base theory—like other theories—is a simplified abstraction of reality, it can nevertheless be a useful platform for understanding how data can be used to analyze economic development processes and evaluate competing development strategies. We will start with a brief introduction of the origins of the economic base theory. A description of the structure of macroeconomic models in general will be followed by presentation of the economic base model. We will then focus on how you can evaluate the state of a regional economy based on readily available economic indicators and the application of the economic base theory. In particular, we will focus on location quotients, calculate the economic base multiplier, and use shift-share analysis for explaining observed patterns of economic growth or decline. Boone County, Kentucky, will once again serve as the study region.

4.2   The Economic Base Theory

The economic base theory has a longstanding tradition in planning and geography. The first appearance of the idea of an economic base can be traced back to 1659 when Pieter De la Court (1618 – 1685), a Dutch cloth merchant, published his manuscript on the prosperity of his home city of Leiden entitled: "t Welvaren der Stadt Leiden (the prosperity of the city of Leiden)".[1] In his manuscript, De la Court saw the wealth of Leiden as the direct result of the city's export-oriented industries: the University of Leiden and the manufacturing industries. De la

---

[1] Earlier publications by De la Court were initialed "V.D.H." which stands for Van den Hove, the Dutch translation for De la Court. De la Court's main publication Interest van Holland ofte Gronden van Hollands welvaert [The true interest and political maxims of the Republic of Holland and West-Friesland] was published in 1662 and has since been regarded as a milestone in the promotion of free market competition and the republic state. De la Court's ideas have translated into several languages and they even influenced the constitutional conventions of the United States of America in 1780. De la Court's homepage can be found at: http://www.childandfamilystudies.leidenuniv.nl/index.php3?c=268.

Court recognized that the inflow of foreign financial resources into a city will ultimately increase the city's overall economic activities.

De la Court's idea was later picked up and made popular by, among others, the German political scientist Werner Sombart (1863 – 1941).[1] In his work, Sombart shaped the concepts of "Städtegründer and Städtefüller ", which were translated by the American economic historian Frederick Nussbaum's (1933) as "town builders" and "town fillers".[2] Town builders leverage a town's prosperity by the means of trade; whereas town fillers provide the goods and services that are locally demanded. Sombart's 1916 first published volume of "Der Moderne Kapitalismus (modern capitalism)" presented a limited qualitative concept of the basic (export) v. non-basic (local) economic sectors. However, in the third volume with the same title, Sombart (1927) provided the first known, quantitative approach for identifying export employment shares.

The first appearance of the economic base theory in a textbook most likely occurred in 1939. In their textbook, *Principles of Urban Real Estate*, Homer Hoyt and Arthur Weimer presented the economic base theory as a methodical approach to determining basic employment and calculating the ratio between basic and service employment.[3] The authors substituted the words basic and service employment for Sombart's town-building and town-filling activities. As we will see later, Hoyt and Weimer's approach is still widely used in economic base analysis.

While Hoyt and Weimer are rightfully given much credit for the advancement of the economic base model, many other scholars contributed to its current popularity. Richard Andrews, Walter Isard, and Stan Czamanski, for instance, wrote several papers on the topic in the 1950s and 1960s.[4] We would not want to conclude this section without mentioning the work of Charles Tiebout (1924 – 1968). In his 1962 publication, Charles Tiebout added much to the credibility of the economic base theory by providing a mathematical proof that the economic base multiplier is equivalent to the Keynesian multiplier used by

---

[1] Günter Krumme, Werner Sombart and the Economic Base Concept, *Land Economics*, 44(1), February 1968, pp.112 – 116.

[2] Günter Krumme gives Werner Sombart the credit for phrasing the expressions " Städtegründer and Städtefüller ". Frederick Nussbaum used among others Sombart's three volumes "Der Moderne Kapitalismus" for bringing main ideas of the economic history of Europe to a larger American audience in his book "*A History of the Economic Institutions of Modern Europe*", published in 1933. He literally translated the expressions Städtegründer and Städtefüller as town builder and town filler.

[3] Andrew M. Isserman. Economic Base Studies for Urban and Regional Planning, In: Lloyd Rodwin and Bishwapriya Sanyal, eds. *The Profession of City Planning: Changes, Images, and Challenges, 1950 – 2000*. Center for Urban Policy Research, New Brunswick, NJ. Copyright © 2000 by Rutgers, The State University of New Jersey, Center for Urban Policy Research.

[4] For more on this topic, please see Isserman's, "*The Profession of City Planning*", which is an excellent source of early references on the economic base theory.

economists. This is an association we will come back to when explaining the underlying principles of the economic base theory.[1]

4.3   Understanding Your Regional Economy

Charles Tiebout showed us how the theoretical construct of the export base model, rooted in Keynesian macroeconomic theory, is related to the economic base theory; and therefore, the Keynesian multiplier is similar, in concept, to the economic base multiplier. Based on original work by Richard F. Kahn (1931), Maynard Keynes developed a multiplier framework, which allows assessment of total changes in economic activity that result from changes in exogenous spending, such as government expenditure and business investment. Following the rationale that initial exogenous spending leads to additional economic transactions within the region, Keynes reasoned that this expected increase in demand for regional goods and services has to be a "multiple" of the initial change in exogenous demand (Keynes, 1936).

Starting with Tiebout's conclusion, this section presents a version of a Keynesian macroeconomic model as a way to visualize a regional economy. In particular, we will recognize in this simplified framework **who** are the actors in a regional economy and **how** they relate to each other. We will then show how the macroeconomic model leads to the economic base model.

The most widely used approach for creating a visual image of a regional economy is based on the **circular flow of income and expenditure** as shown in Fig. 4.1. In this snapshot of an economy, we can identify three economic agents or decision makers: (1) firms and businesses, (2) households, and (3) the government. The selling and buying activities of decision makers takes place in three markets. In the **commodity market** they exchange goods and services for money. Trade of financial assets occurs in the **financial market** where people might, for example, buy assets to earn interest. And, the **factor market** provides firms and businesses with the necessary factors of production, such as capital and labor.

The lower left part of the loop represents the **flow of income**: households receive income from firms and businesses for providing the factors necessary for production. In particular, firms and businesses pay wages and salaries for labor, interest for capital, rent for land, and profit for entrepreneurial activities. Households own the factors of production, and therefore the combined outlays of the firms constitute aggregated household income.

---

[1] Charles Tiebout (1962), *The Community Economic Base Study*, Supplementary Paper #16, Published by the Committee for Economic Development (CED).

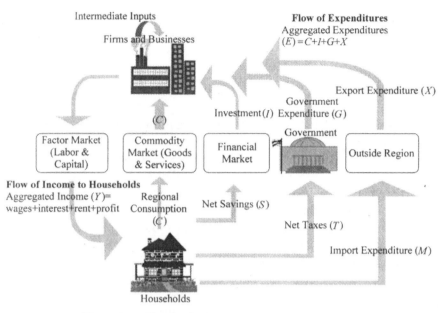

Figure 4.1   The circular flow of income and expenditure

The upper right side of the loop indicates a matched **flow of expenditures**: household consumption, investment spending, government purchases, and exports create **final demand** for locally produced goods and services. **Regional consumption** (*C*) represents spending by households for goods and services, such as food, clothing, and education. The purchase of a house is excluded from household consumption and listed under investment spending. **Investment spending** (*I*) refers to the creation of capital stock. It contains three subcategories: (1) fixed investment such as when a firm replaces worn-out machinery or a university builds a multipurpose field hall; (2) residential investment, the purchase of a house by households; and (3) inventory investment, businesses' inventory of unsold goods, for example, unsold automobiles at a car dealership. Investment is financed by **net household savings** (*S*). **Government expenditures** (*G*) consist of all the goods and services bought by various levels of governments, including highways, military equipment, and government investment. Government expenditure is financed by **net tax revenues** (*T*). This is called net tax revenues because it is the revenues that remain after transfer payments (e.g., social security benefits) and interest payments (e.g., government bonds) have been made. The final category on the expenditure side of the economy accounts for trade—both domestic (trade with other regions within the country) and foreign (trade with other countries). Households spend some of their income on **imports** (*M*)—the purchase of foreign-made goods and services. Similarly, people, institutions, and firms located outside of a region demand regionally produced goods and services—**export expenditures** (X). The **net export** (NX) is obtained by subtracting the value of imports from the value of exports.

The **flow of income** considers total income in the economy as the combined outlays of firms and businesses to factors of production owned by households. On the other side, the **flow of expenditures** measures aggregated spending on the economy's output of goods and services by all economic agents; within and outside of the region. Both sides form the national income accounting. Following the rules of national income accounting, both the flow of income and expenditures must ultimately lead to the same result; **the gross regional product** (GRP) or the monetary value of all regional economic activities. In both cases, the goal is to calculate a single summary measure that captures the level of regional economic activities. Real gross regional product—real GRP—measures the total regional economic activity on the final demand side, or

$$\text{real GRP} = C + I + G + \text{NX} \tag{4.1}$$

where,

C — the level of household consumption of regionally produced commodities;

I — the level of regional investment in physical capital;

G — the level of total government spending;

NX— represents total net exports (i.e., exports minus imports).

Using net exports implies that regional spending on imports is subtracted from real GDP as dollars leaving the region because imports do not add to the level of regional economic activities—called a **leakage**. Exports, on the other side, add to regional economic activities as inflowing dollars positively stimulate regional output—called an **injection**.

Similarly, the level of regional economic activities can also be calculated using the value added approach, indicated on the left-hand side of Fig. 4.1, or

$$\text{value added GRP} = \text{wages} + \text{interest} + \text{rent} + \text{profit} \tag{4.2}$$

Both approaches, if done correctly, must ultimately lead to the same level of total regional economic activities. Both measure the flow of dollars in the regional economy.

Using the information from this illustration we now can calculate the most fundamental form of the Keynesian multiplier (KM). For simplicity, we assume an economy with no government, no exports, and no imports. Under this situation, the economy is in equilibrium, where expenditures (E) equal income (Y):

$$E = Y \tag{4.3}$$

This equilibrium follows from the simple fact that every dollar of expenditure must have been earned. The next step is to define aggregate expenditure (E) as the sum of consumption (C) and investment (I), or:

$$E = C + I \tag{4.4}$$

and aggregate income (Y) as the sum of consumption (C) and savings (S), or:

$$Y = C + S \tag{4.5}$$

where, income (Y) is now measured in terms of household spending. With the absence of government and imports, savings represents a leakage in the system because income going to savings is the money not spent on regionally produced goods and services, and therefore, does not foster regional economic growth. In this simplified economy, an increase in aggregated savings (as opposed to consumption) would lead to a decline of economic activities. Investment (I) is determined exogenously. It is the policy variable that will be used later to determine changes in the equilibrium level of aggregate output.

The equilibrium condition of the commodity market implies:

$$Y = C + I \tag{4.6}$$

which is the result of substituting Eq. (4.4) into Eq. (4.3). The level of household consumption (C) depends upon various factors such as household income, household wealth, the interest rate, and expectations households have about the future. One way of representing consumption (C) is as a function of income (Y), or:

$$C = f(Y) = a + \text{mpc} \cdot Y \tag{4.7}$$

where,

a — the level of autonomous spending independent of income (e.g., housing and food);

mpc — the marginal propensity to consume. It is the fraction of each additional dollar earned that households will spend on consumption.

Substituting Eq. (4.7) into Eq. (4.6) we get:

$$Y = a + \text{mpc} \cdot Y + I \tag{4.8}$$

Solving this equation in terms of Y we get:

$$Y - \text{mpc} \cdot Y = a + I \tag{4.9}$$

$$Y \cdot (1 - \text{mpc}) = a + I \tag{4.10}$$

$$Y = \left(\frac{1}{1 - \text{mpc}} \right)(a + I) \tag{4.11}$$

where, $\left(\dfrac{1}{1 - \text{mpc}} \right)$ is called the Keynesian investment multiplier. Because a

(independent autonomous spending) is assumed to be predetermined and fixed—called a parameter—the expected change in income (output) results solely from a change in investment, independent of regional income, or:

$$\Delta Y = \left(\frac{1}{1 - \text{mpc}} \right) \cdot \Delta I \qquad (4.12)$$

where,
  ΔY — the expected change in income (output);
  ΔI — the exogenous change in investment—the injection into the economy.
  In this rather simplistic framework, households either spend a proportion of their income, according to the marginal propensity to consume (mpc), or save their income, corresponding to the marginal propensity to save (mps). Given that households can either spend their income or save it, we can conclude that:

$$\text{mpc} + \text{mps} = 1 \qquad (4.13)$$

where, mps or $(1 - \text{mpc})$ refers to the leakage of regional income—the savings. Rewriting Eq. (4.12) as:

$$\left(\frac{1}{1 - \text{mpc}} \right) = \frac{\Delta Y}{\Delta I} = \frac{\text{change in income (ouput)}}{\text{chang in investment}} \qquad (4.14)$$

We can define the Keynesian multiplier as the ratio of a change in income (output) to some exogenous change in investment.

For students familiar with calculus, the Keynesian multiplier can alternatively be derived by taking the partial derivative with respect to investment, or

$$Y = \left(\frac{1}{1 - \text{mpc}} \right)(a + I) \qquad (4.11)$$

$$\frac{\partial Y}{\partial I} = \left(\frac{1}{1 - \text{mpc}} \right) \qquad (4.15)$$

leading to the same result as in Eq. (4.14).

The **economic base theory** explains regional economic growth through the level of a region's export activities. The larger the external demand for a region's goods and services, the larger the economic stimulus. These non-regional expenditures lead to a multiplying effect of regional output, expressed through the economic base multiplier. Regional firms and businesses welcome exogenous increases in demand for their products and, assuming an absence of supply or capacity constraints, attempt to meet this increase in demand. In return, the regional firms and businesses increase their own demand for inputs from other regional suppliers, called intermediate inputs, and, for labor and capital, the factors of production.

The next round of economic impacts leads the regional suppliers to increase their own demand for intermediate inputs, labor, and capital and so on. The result is a chain reaction set in place through an injection of exogenous demand.

The chain reaction is additionally amplified through increases in aggregate household spending. This is made possible because an increase in regional output leads to an increase in demand for labor, which in turn leads to an increase in household income. In return, households will spend a fraction of this additional income on regionally produced goods and services, that alone increases demand. The round-by-round effect that follows an increase in exogenous demand is captured by a single summary measure— the economic base multiplier.

The economic base model is illustrated in Fig. 4.2. The economic base model divides total economic activities for a region—the right-hand side of the illustration—into either basic activities or non-basic activities. **Basic activities** include all regionally produced goods and services sold to people and businesses outside the region. This includes, of course, all goods and services leaving the region. But, it also includes all goods and services that are purchased by people out of town within the region where they are produced. The hotel industry is an example. A tourist from San Francisco staying in a hotel in Cincinnati, Ohio, increases regional exports (X). The important distinction is in the case of the tourist, payments made by the tourist come from outside Cincinnati. While for

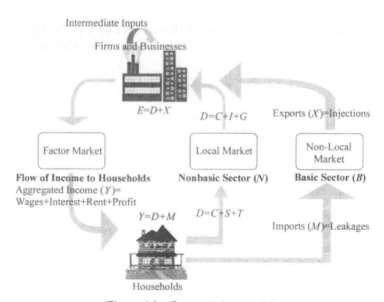

Figure 4.2 Economic base model

Cincinnati this inflow—injection—increases regional economic activities, for San Francisco on the other hand it is an outflow—leakage—of income.

Non-basic activities by definition include all purchases of regionally produced goods and services by local residents. As Fig. 4.2 indicates, these regional expenditures (D) are household driven and refer to goods and services used by the region itself. Grocery stores, real estate brokers, automobile repair shops, and banks provide goods and services usually referred to as non-basic activities. In the case of large corporations, for instance a national food or restaurant chain, the distinction between basic and non-basic activity is much fuzzier as some of the regional expenditures leave the region for some headquarters outside the regions. In this context, the food industry and restaurants, usually a typical regional or non-basic activity, takes on the character of a basic activity. Today's food and banking have become increasingly non-local.

In the economic base model, imports (M) play the same role as savings play in the Keynesian macroeconomic model. Imports represent the leakage of the economy, in that regional income leaves without further contributing to regional economic activities. Contrarily, export activities bring new dollars into the regional economy, increase regional production of goods and services, and fuel regional economic growth—it is the economic base for regional economic growth. In the context of regional economic development and following the principles of economic base theory, politicians and ED planners can encourage regional economic growth by: (1) promoting exports (i.e., increasing injections), and (2) encouraging import substitution (i.e., decreasing leakages).

An easy approach to deriving the economic base multiplier (BM) uses the dichotomy of basic and non-basic activities. In an economy where all activities are classified as non-basic (N) and basic (B), total regional activities (T) can be defined as:

$$T = N + B \tag{4.16}$$

While basic activities (B) are determined by exogenous sources (outside the region), non-basic activities (N) can be written as a function of total regional activities (T), or

$$N = f(T) = c + (\text{mpp} \cdot T) \tag{4.17}$$

where,

c— the level of autonomous domestic spending independent of total regional activities;

mpp — the marginal propensity to purchase regional products. It defines the fraction households will assign to domestic/local expenditures (D) of each additional dollar they earn.

Substituting Eq. (4.17) into Eq. (4.16) and solving this equation in terms of T for B gives us the simplest form of the economic base multiplier (BM) as:

$$T = c + (\text{mpp} \cdot T) + B \tag{4.18}$$

$$T - (\text{mpp} \cdot T) = c + B \tag{4.19}$$

$$T \cdot (1 - \text{mpp}) = c + B \tag{4.20}$$

$$T = \left(\frac{1}{1 - \text{mpp}}\right)(c + B) \tag{4.21}$$

where $\left(\dfrac{1}{1 - \text{mpp}}\right)$ is the economic base multiplier. We see immediately that the economic base multiplier is very similar to the Keynesian multiplier Eq. (4.11). Analogously, the economic base multiplier measures the change in total regional activities (ΔT) that results from an exogenous change in basic activities (ΔB) — the initial export stimulus as:

$$\Delta T = \left(\frac{1}{1 - \text{mpp}}\right) \cdot \Delta B \tag{4.22}$$

The alternative way of deriving the economic base multiplier using calculus is:

$$T = \left(\frac{1}{1 - \text{mpp}}\right)(c + B) \tag{4.21}$$

$$\frac{\partial T}{\partial B} = \left(\frac{1}{1 - \text{mpp}}\right) \tag{4.23}$$

Charles Tiebout was the first to recognize the close relationship between the economic base and the Keynesian multiplier. Following the economic dichotomy of the economic base theory, households either spend an additional dollar of income on imports (M) or on regional/local products (D). Expenditure on imports is expressed as the marginal propensity to import, mpm. Expenditure on domestic/local products is expressed as the marginal propensity to purchase regional products, mpp. Given that each additional dollar must be spent on either imports or regional products, we can specify that:

$$\text{mpp} + \text{mpm} = 1 \tag{4.24}$$

We may also express the marginal propensity to purchase regional products, mpp, as the ratio of non-basic activities to total regional activities, or:

$$\text{mpp} = \frac{\text{non-basic activities}}{\text{total regional activities}} = \frac{N}{T} \qquad (4.25)$$

This allows us to rewrite the multiplier as:

$$\text{BM} = \left(\frac{1}{1 - N/T} \right) \qquad (4.26)$$

We will now write the BM in a form that is well-recognized in the planning literature. From Eq. (4.16) we recognize that:

$$T = N + B \qquad (4.27a)$$

Dividing Eq. (4.27a) through T, we can rewrite the equation as:

$$1 = \frac{N}{T} + \frac{B}{T} \qquad (4.27b)$$

Next we rearrange Eq. (4.27b):

$$\begin{cases} 1 = \dfrac{N}{T} + \dfrac{B}{T} \\[2ex] \left(\dfrac{1}{1 - N/T} \right) = \left(\dfrac{1}{B/T} \right) \end{cases} \qquad (4.27c)$$

We recognize from Eq. (4.26) that the left-hand side of Eq. (4.27c) defines the economic base multiplier. Throughout planning-relevant literature, the economic base multiplier, BM is expressed as the ratio of total regional activities over basic economic activities, or:

$$\text{BM} = \frac{1}{B/T} = \frac{T}{B} \qquad (4.28)$$

Alternatively the economic base multiplier can be derived following the step-by-step procedure outlined for the Keynesian multiplier.[1] The starting point, again, is the initial equilibrium condition of aggregate expenditures (E) equals aggregate income (Y), or

$$E = Y \qquad (4.29)$$

[1] Follows Schaffer, Chapter 2, p. 6, Illustration 2.2, "The pure export-base model."

Aggregate expenditure (E) is defined as the sum of domestic production (D) and exports (X), or:

$$E = D + X \qquad (4.30)$$

Note that exports (X) replaced investment (I) as exogenous source for economic growth. Aggregate income (Y) is the sum of domestic expenditure (D) and imports (M), or:

$$Y = D + M \qquad (4.31)$$

Imports in the economic base model represent the leakage. In an economic dichotomy with only a regional and a non-regional market, domestic production and domestic expenditure are identical. D refers both to the regional purchases of regionally produced goods and services and the non-basic (N) or regional market activities.

Combining Eqs. (4.28), (4.29), and (4.30), we can write:

$$Y = Y - M + X \qquad (4.32)$$

where, exports (X) as the exogenous driving-force for economic growth, imports (M) as the endogenous leakages, and aggregate income (Y) as a measure for regional economic performance. Expressing imports in terms of aggregate income, or

$$M = f(Y) = \text{mpm} \cdot Y \qquad (4.33)$$

We can derive the economic base multiplier as:

$$Y = Y - (\text{mpm} \cdot Y) + X \qquad (4.34)$$

$$Y - Y + \text{mpm} \cdot Y = X \qquad (4.35)$$

$$Y = (1/\text{mpm}) \cdot X \qquad (4.36)$$

And, the economic base multiplier is:

$$\frac{\partial Y}{\partial X} = \left(\frac{1}{\text{mpm}} \right) \qquad (4.37)$$

The similarity between Eqs. (4.21) and (4.35) is obvious when replacing aggregate income (Y) by total regional activities (T), exports (X) by base activities (B), and the marginal propensity to import (mpm) by ($1 - \text{mpp}$).

4.4   Assessing the State of a Regional Economy

4.4.1   Compiling a Regional Economic Profile

Performing a local or regional economic profile is a first and essential step towards an up-to-date description of the state of the economy. There are several ways of doing this, all of which will give you a brief introduction to the indicators of local/regional economic and social conditions. Indicators included in the regional economic profile can include, but are not limited to:

Population statistics: population size, growth, and population composition (sex, age, and race); components of population change, median age, educational attainments, marital status, etc.

Household, family, and individual statistics: average household size, average family size, family structures, poverty rates, individuals below poverty level, families below poverty level, poverty rates, etc.

Housing statistics: total housing units, owner-occupancy rate, renter-occupancy rate, vacancies, median housing values, median of selected monthly owner costs, etc.

Economic statistics: median household income, median family income, population in labor force, employed and unemployed population, population not in labor force, personal income (e.g., net earnings, transfer payments, and dividends) by place of residence, per capita income by place of residence, means of transportation to work, mean travel time to work, etc.

Industry characteristics: employment by industry or by occupation, average earnings per job, earnings by place of work/industry (e.g., wages and salaries, other labor income, proprietors' income).

Natural physical resources: climate, environmental amenities, primary resources, such as water, forests, minerals, etc.

Built physical resources: communication, and transportation, and utility infrastructures.

A methodical and in-depth analysis of the region's economic and social conditions to identify the region's strengths, weaknesses, and opportunities for future economic development should not be limited to economic and industry characteristics. Information on the region's geographic, demographic, housing, or quality of life indicators will supplement each economic profile with valuable information. It is widely perceived that firms and businesses make their location decisions based upon more than purely economic factors, such as labor and energy cost, access to input and output markets, availability, price, and quality of local inputs. Location factors such as regional amenity features, climate, availability of built and natural physical resources (e.g., communication and transportation infrastructure, proximity to ocean, mountain, or state parks), and educational attainments of the population also may influence the region's competitiveness for attracting new businesses. To fully understand a region's comparative advantage and competitive position, it is, therefore, essential to include factors describing the larger physical and natural resources of your region.

Additionally, it is very helpful to compare your region's selected economic and social key indicators to that of a larger **benchmark** economy of which the region is a part. The benchmark region, for instance, may be a metropolitan statistical area (MSA), a state, or even the nation. Looking at key indicators for two geographic regions at a time allows you to immediately evaluate the comparative attractiveness of your region as an industrial and residential location. For example, Table 4.1 presents a variety of key variables included in an economic profile for Boone County. Comparing Boone County with Kentucky, we see instantly that the population in Boone County is on average younger and better educated than the overall population in Kentucky. Fewer families and individuals fall below the poverty level in Boone County (e.g., 4.4% in Boone County versus 12.7% in Kentucky). The cost of buying and owning a house is higher in Boone County; however, this is accompanied by correspondingly higher median household income levels in Boone County. Of the population 25 years and over, a larger share is in the labor force for Boone County than for Kentucky (e.g., 73.1% versus 60.9%), and Boone County registers lower unemployed labor force figures (2.3% versus 3.5%). Overall, we can conclude that Boone County is a prospering county in Kentucky, which performs above the state level in most selected key indicators.

Table 4.1 Highlights from the 2000 economic and social profiles, Boone County, KY[1]

	Boone County		Kentucky	
	Number	Percent (%)	Number	Percent (%)
Population Characteristics[2],[3]				
Total population	85,991	100.0	4,041,769	100.0
Male	42,499	49.4	1,975,368	48.9
Female	43,492	50.6	2,066,401	51.1
Median age (years)	33.4	(×)	35.9	(×)
Under 5 years	6,849	8.0	265,901	6.6
18 years and over	61,347	71.3	3,046,951	75.4
25 years and over	54,050	62.9	2,645,093	65.4
65 years and over	6,941	8.1	504,793	12.5
High school graduate or higher (25 years and older)	46,094	85.1	1,961,397	74.1

Continued

	Boone County		Kentucky	
	Number	Percent (%)	Number	Percent (%)
Bachelor's degree or higher (25 years and older)	8,564	22.8	271,418	17.1
Disability Status (population 21 to 64 years)	8,442	16.5	557,971	24.0
Household, Family, and Individual Characteristics[(2),(4)]				
Average household size	2.73	(×)	2.47	(×)
Average family size	3.17	(×)	2.97	(×)
Families below poverty level	1,042	4.4	140,519	12.7
Individuals below poverty level	4,785	5.6	621,096	15.8
Housing Characteristics[(2),(5)]				
Total housing units	33,351	100.0	1,750,927	100.0
Occupied housing units	31,258	93.7	1,590,647	90.8
Owner-occupied housing units	23,212	74.3	1,125,397	70.8
Renter-occupied housing units	8,046	25.7	465,250	29.2
Vacant housing units	2,093	6.3	160,280	9.2
Median value (dollars)	131,800	(×)	86,700	(×)
Median of selected monthly owner costs	(×)	(×)	(×)	(×)
With a mortgage	1,103	(×)	816	(×)
Not mortgaged	243	(×)	214	(×)
Economic Characteristics[(2),(4),(6)]				
Median household income (dollars)	53,593	(×)	33,672	(×)
Median family income (dollars)	61,114	(×)	40,939	(×)
Per capita income (dollars)	23,535	(×)	18,093	(×)
Population 16 years and older	64,033	100.0	3,161,542	100.0
In Labor Force (civilian and armed forces)	46,791	73.1	1,926,731	60.9
Employed	45,338	70.8	1,817,381	57.5
Unemployed	1,453	2.3	109,350	3.5
Not in labor force	17,242	26.9	1,234,811	39.1
Mean travel time to work in minutes (16 years and older)	24.4	(×)	23.5	(×)
Personal income by place of residence (dollars)	2,548,401	100.0	98,214,681	100.0
Net earnings (dollars)	2,000,735	78.5	63,927,483	65.1
Transfer payments (dollars)	217,453	8.5	16,583,202	16.9
Dividends (dollars)	330,213	13.0	17,703,996	18.0
Unemployment rate 2002	3.6		5.6	

Continued

	Boone County		Kentucky	
	Number	Percent (%)	Number	Percent (%)
Industry Characteristics[7],[8]				
Employment by industry	70,007	(×)	1,717,978	(×)
Average earnings per job (dollars)	35,912	(×)	29,407	(×)
Earnings by place of work (dollars)	2,876,699	100.0	68,851,883	100.0
Wages and salaries (dollars)	2,429,653	84.5	54,349,107	78.9
Other labor income (dollars)	277,420	9.6	7,150,156	10.4
Proprietors' income (dollars)	169,626	5.9	7,352,620	10.7
Five Largest Employers in the County:				
Delta Air Lines – Air Carrier	5,500			
COMAIR – Air Carrier	5,000			
Board of Education – Public School System	2,000			
DHL Airways – Air Freight Center	1,800			
GAP/Babnana Republic	1,722			
Geography Characteristics[9]	Boone County		Kentucky	
Land area, 2000 (square miles)	246		39,728	
Persons per square mile, 2000	349.2		101.7	
Metropolitan Statistical Area	Cincinnati-Middletown,OH-KY-IN MSA			

(1) Sources: all data were accessed in April 2004.

(2) U.S. Census Bureau, State and County Quickfacts, DP-1. *Profile of General Demographic Characteristics*: 2000. Census Summary File 1 (SF1);

(3) U.S. Census Bureau, State and County Quickfacts, DP-2. *Profile of Selected Social Characteristics*: 2000. Census Summary File 3 (SF3);

(4) U.S. Census Bureau, State and County Quickfacts, DP-3. *Profile of Selected Economic Characteristics*: 2000. Census Summary File 3 (SF3);

(5) U.S. Census Bureau, State and County Quickfacts, DP-4. *Profile of Selected Housing Characteristics*: 2000. Census Summary File 3 (SF3);

(6) U.S. Department of Commerce, Bureau of Economic Analysis (BEA), Regional Economic Accounts, *CA 05 Regional Economic Profile*, 2000;

(7) U.S. Department of Commerce, Bureau of Economic Analysis (BEA), Regional Economic Accounts, *CA 30 Regional Economic Profile*, 2000;

(8) U.S. Department of Labor, Bureau of Labor Statistics (BLS), *Quarterly Census of Employment and Wages* (QCEW), 2002;

(9) U.S. Census Bureau, *State and County QuickFacts*, 2000.

A next step to shed more light on the regional economic profile is to study the industry mix of a region. Identifying **major industries** helps to answer the question of whether your region's economic prosperity is driven largely by one or two main industries or the result of a wide variety of different industries. The breakdown of regional employment by industry (Table 4.2) helps to identify strengths and weaknesses of the regional economy.

Table 4.2   Boone County and Kentucky employment by industry, 2002

2002 NAICS Code	2002 NAICS Title	Boone County Employment	Employment Boone Co. (%)	Kentucky Employment	Employment Kentucky (%)
11	Agriculture, Forestry, Fishing and Hunting	79	0.11	7,558	0.44
21	Mining	35	0.05	19,501	1.14
22	Utilities	481	0.69	6,706	0.39
23	Construction	2,230	3.19	83,289	4.85
31 – 33	Manufacturing	10,360	14.80	275,466	16.03
42	Wholesale Trade	5,166	7.38	71,507	4.16
44 – 45	Retail Trade	8,724	12.46	212,458	12.37
48 – 49	Transportation and Ware-housing	12,855	18.36	76,588	4.46
51	Information	1,657	2.37	31,745	1.85
52	Finance and Insurance	4,506	6.44	63,321	3.69
53	Real Estate and Rental and Leasing	934	1.33	19,688	1.15
54	Professional, Scientific, and Technical Services	1,341	1.92	56,712	3.30
55	Management of Companies and Enterprises	995	1.42	13,451	0.78
56	Administrative and Support and Waste Mgmt.	4,233	6.05	84,912	4.94
61	Educational Services	267	0.38	12,901	0.75
62	Health Care and Social Assistance	2,897	4.14	189,627	11.04
71	Arts, Entertainment, and Recreation	489	0.70	17,747	1.03
72	Accommodation and Food Services	5,821	8.31	135,372	7.88
81	Other Services (except Public Administration)	1,733	2.48	45,768	2.66
92	Public Administration	5,107	7.29	292,125	17.00
99	Unclassified	97	0.14	1,536	0.09
Total		70,007	100.00	1,717,978	100.00

Source: Bureau of Labor Statistics (BLS), *Quarterly Census of Employment and Wages* (QCEW), 2002.

Boone County appears to be highly specialized in transportation and warehousing. Not surprising given that Boone County houses the Cincinnati/ Northern Kentucky International Airport. Again, data on employment by industry can be compared to a larger benchmark region. For example, manufacturing makes up 14.8% of the county's employment compared to 16.0% in Kentucky statewide. Although manufacturing is the second largest industry sector in the county, the Boone County data do not necessarily indicate that it is particularly specialized in manufacturing. But note that this conclusion only holds when comparing Boone County with Kentucky at the two-digit level of establishment aggregation using the North American Industry Classification System (NAICS) code. Using a different benchmark region and a different level of industry aggregation might alter the finding. Graphically, this can be emphasized in a chart as shown in Fig. 4.3.

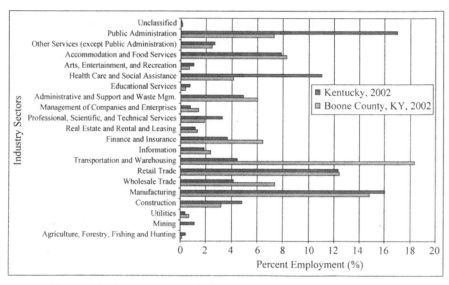

Figure 4.3   Boone County and Kentucky employment by industry, 2002

Another common practice in compiling a regional economic profile is to evaluate selected key indicators over time. For example, what were the industry sectors that experienced the largest growth for a particular time period? Observing past trends in selected variables might allow us to draw some preliminary conclusions about what to expect in the near future.

Trend data can be reported in tables or graphically, as demonstrated in the bar charts. In particular for Boone County, Figure 4.4 shows that all sectors exhibited a growth in absolute employment except the Federal Government. Transportation and public utilities show the largest increase in employment of 8,082 employers, demonstrating once again its importance for the regional economy.

It is arguable whether recently observed trend patterns will continue without changes in the future. At least for short-term predictions, historical growth patterns may give some guidance to identifying upcoming needs and opportunities for regional economic development. An economic profile containing economic and social indicators, a comparison of the region with an

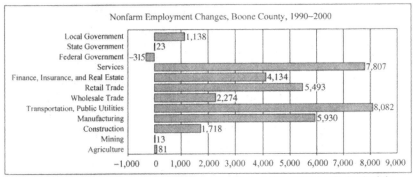

Source: Bureau of Economic Analysis (BEA), Local Area Personal Income Bureau of Labor Statistics,
Quarterly Census of Employment and Wages, 2000.

Figure 4.4   Industry employment changes for Boone County, 1990 – 2000

appropriate benchmark region, and an evaluation of historic growth patterns
highlights what challenges and opportunities a region may face in encouraging
and sustaining business development. It helps and supports the decision process
in regional economic development planning while helping firms and residents in
their location decisions.

4.4.2   Preliminary Consideration

The usefulness and appropriateness of the results of an economic base analysis
and its analytical tools and techniques depend heavily on such factors as the
choice of size of the study region, the selected benchmark region for comparison,
the chosen measurement units or the economic indicators, and the level of detail
used in the classification system of establishments.

4.4.2.1   The Study and Benchmark Region

While the definition of **study region** comes straight from the research question, the
choice of a study region plays a crucial role in terms of availability of useful data
and interpretation of the results of the economic base analysis. Usually,
government agencies provide economic and social data at different geographic
levels. Most commonly in the United States, data are provided at the national,
state, and county level. The U.S. Census Bureau provides data on population and
housing characteristics (e.g., Census 2000 summary file 3, SF 3) by census tract
and block group. Economic data published by the U.S. Census Bureau's
Economic Census are available at the larger ZIP code level. The Bureau of Labor
Statistics reports employment and wages in the Quarterly Census of Employment
and Wages program at the county, metropolitan statistical area, state, and
national levels. Annual income and employment data, published by the Bureau of
Economic Analysis (BEA), are also available for counties, MSAs, states, and

the nation or specific BEA-defined economic areas, which usually are larger multi-county areas. By identifying the study region, attention should be paid to data availability, particularly, when applying the economic base concept at the community level. Tiebout[1] mentioned in his paper on community economic base analysis that practically any size area is appropriate for an economic base study. Further, he recommends study of the larger economic area, which contains the community of interest as part of the community economic base analysis. Results at the community level are more viable when accompanied by additional knowledge of the larger economic area.

Besides the problem of data availability, the size of the study region must be considered in interpreting results from an economic base study. Smaller study regions generally have smaller economies and tend to be more specialized in fewer products compared with larger regions. For example, Boone County's economy is smaller than the economy of the Cincinnati-Middletown Metropolitan Statistical Area[2] of which Boone County is a part. Further, the location of the Cincinnati/Northern Kentucky International Airport in the county explains its specialization in transportation. This has two immediate implications for Boone County.

First, **the more a regional economy is specialized in the production of particular products, the more the region tends to import from the outside the region.** Boone County is highly specialized in transportation and warehousing (e.g., NAICS sector 48 – 49 in Fig. 4.3). With a large share of the labor force employed in these industries, Boone County might not be self-sufficient in other sectors. It must import other non-transportation and warehousing goods and services as needed. Money leaving the region for imports reduces the level of intra-regional or non-basic economic activities resulting in a smaller multiplier. At the same time, this high degree of specialization in transportation and warehousing leads to large exports of these sectors' services, boosting basic activities also leading to smaller multipliers (see also Fig. 4.2).

Secondly, **smaller regions usually have smaller multipliers.** In this context, size can refer to the region, population, employment, and other indicators. Comparing Boone County with the nation, one would expect the nation to be self-sufficient in most aspects. A higher level of self-sufficiency means fewer imports and more non-basic activities—most of the money is captured by the nation. This higher intensity of intra-national activities leads to higher multipliers. Conversely, smaller regions, like Boone County, depend to a larger extent on imports, which decrease the amount of intra-regional activities and results in smaller multipliers.

As we have already seen earlier, a common practice in economic base

---

[1] Charles Tiebout (1962), *The Community Economic Base Study*.

[2] The Cincinnati-Middletown Metropolitan Statistical Area includes fifteen counties in Ohio, Kentucky, and Indiana. Boone County is one of the seven Kentucky counties included in the Cincinnati-Middletown MSA.

analysis is using a **benchmark region** for comparison. A benchmark region is also widely used for determining the level of basic activities. Therefore, the choice and the size of the benchmark regions play crucial roles in the magnitude of the economic base multiplier and other outcomes of economic base analyses. Before deciding on a benchmark region, one should pay close attention to the purpose of the study. Does it make sense to compare Boone County with the nation? Or, would Kentucky or the Cincinnati MSA be the better benchmark region? In practice, smaller regions like counties are often compared with larger regions like MSAs or states. Usually, the smaller region is always an integral part of a larger benchmark region. It just would not make as much sense to compare Boone County with the state of California as it would to compare it to the state of Kentucky of which it is a part. Alternatively, one might call on the Cincinnati MSA or the Midwest as the benchmark region. It is important to recognize that each benchmark region has its own structural industry composition and its own strengths and weaknesses. By comparing Boone County with the Cincinnati MSA (a suburban-urban metropolitan area), one might draw different conclusions than from a comparison of Boone County to the state of Kentucky (which includes other metropolitan areas as well as rural areas).

4.4.2.2   Economic Indicator or Units of Measurement

There is no general rule as to which unit of measurement is the best for a particular situation. Each indicator has its strengths and weaknesses and is, by itself, insufficient to fully describe the state of a regional economy. In practice the choice of selecting the appropriate economic variable to use for the analysis is influenced by the availability of data. Often, the range of data on indicators available for smaller areas is limited.

Employment is probably the most commonly used economic indicator in any regional economic analysis. This is partly because it is easy to conceptualize that 12,855 people were employed in the transportation and warehousing sector in Boone County in 2002. Whereas, it is more difficult to interpret a county's economic activities when saying that its annual wage payments totaled 652.6 million dollars for 2002. Its status as the most widely available economic data series also influences the choice of employment as an indicator.

Although employment data are readily available through the Bureau of Labor Statistics, the Bureau of Economic Analysis, and the Census Bureau, as Table 4.3 indicates, the definition of **employment** is not necessarily the same among different agencies providing the data.

Generally, employment data can be provided by place of residence or place of work. **Employment by place of residence data** takes into account where members of the work force live. It divides the region's resident population into those in the labor force (those working or searching for work) and those not

155

Table 4.3   Total employment, Boone County, KY, 2001

	Total Employment, Boone County, KY 2001
Bureau of Labor Statistics (BLS)	
Quarterly Census of Employment and Wages	68,684
Bureau of Economic Analysis (BEA)	
Local Area Personal Income	81,919
Census Bureau	
County Business Patterns	55,444

in the labor force. The population in the labor force is further subdivided into employed and unemployed. To be considered unemployed and in the labor force, one must be without a job and actively looking for one. Those outside the labor force are both without a job and not seeking employment. Referring back to Table 4.1, of the 64,033 persons sixteen years and older in Boone County, 46,791 persons are in the labor force and 17,242 are not in labor force. Note that employment by place of residence does not necessarily match employment by place of work. Some people hold more than one job, particularly when counting part-time jobs. Others commute to work outside their region of residence. Some common and widely used sources for employment by place of residence data in the U.S. are:

(1) The Census Bureau, Decennial Census, Summary File 3 (SF3) (http://www.census.gov/Press-Release/www/2002/sumfile3.html);

(2) Bureau of Labor Statistics (BLS), Local Area Unemployment Statistics (LAUS) Program (http://www.bls.gov/lau/home.htm).

Employment by place of work refers to the actual number of jobs in a geographic area. Employment is commonly categorized by establishment according to their primary type of activity. Unfortunately, the definitions of employment by place of work published by the Census Bureau, the Bureau of Labor Statistics, and the Bureau of Economic Analysis differ substantially among agencies as already indicated in Table 4.3.

The **Bureau of Labor Statistics** and the State Employment Security Agencies (SESAs) cooperatively offer the Quarterly Census of Employment and Wages program.[1] Employment and wage data are available at the national, state, and county levels classified by establishment (disclosure restrictions may apply for confidentiality reasons). It includes workers covered by State Unemployment Insurance (UI) laws or federal employees covered by the Unemployment Compensation for Federal Employees (UCFE) program. Monthly employment counts every worker who received pay for the period that includes the 12th of each month. Quarterly wages include the complete compensation paid for the

[1] Source: http://www.bls.gov/cew/cewover.htm.

corresponding period. The statistics are incomplete in that they do not include the self-employed, proprietors, domestic workers, unpaid family workers, railroad workers covered by the railroad unemployment insurance system, and members of the armed forces. The BLS data do account for civilian government employees.

Quarterly employment and wage data are available on the BLS website. To access these data, go to the **Employment and Unemployment** menu and select **State and Local Employment.** From this page you can access the **Quarterly Census of Employment and Wages** (QCEW). Detailed QCEW statistics on employment and wage series are available for 1975 – 2000 on the Standard Industrial Classification (SIC) basis and from 2001 forward on the NAICS basis. In addition, 1990 – 2000 data are available on reconstructed NAICS basis. To access **Current Employment and Wages** (CEW) from the BLS website, go to the **Geography** menu and select **State and Local Employment.** From this page, you will have access to the CEW data.

The BEA makes employment and wage data available at the national, state, and county levels as part of its local area personal income estimates. The data are also available on the Regional Economic Information System (REIS) CD-ROM.[1] The BEA uses BLS data for its estimates and makes adjustments to account for employment and wages not covered, or only partially covered, by the State UI and UCFE programs. Among others, the BEA corrects employment and wages for the following establishments: farms, farm labor contractors, private households, private elementary and secondary schools, religious membership organizations, railroads, military, U.S. residents who are employed by international organizations and by foreign embassies, nonprofit organizations, students and their spouses employed by colleges or universities, elected officials of the judiciary, interns employed by hospitals and by social service agencies, and insurance agents classified as statutory employees.[2]

To access BEA data on Local Area Personal Income, Select **State and Local Personal Income.** From this page, access the **Interactive Table** and select **Local Area Annual Estimates.** Local Area Personal Income data include among others: (1) detailed county tables by NAICS industry for total full-time and part-time employment (series CA25) for 2001 forward, (2) detailed county employment by SIC industry (series CA25) for 1969 – 2000, and (3) wage and salary summary estimates from 1969 onwards (CA34).

The Census Bureau publishes employment and payroll data in its County Business Patterns (CBP).[3] The economic censuses collect economic data every five years from Federal administrative records and from survey information of

---

[1] For more information: http://www.bea.gov/bea/regional/articles.cfm.

[2] Source: http://www.bea.gov/bea/regional/articles/lapi2001/alternative_measures.cfm#N_4_.

[3] Source: http://www.census.gov/epcd/cbp/view/cbpview.html.

business establishments. Employment data reported in the CBP are usually lower in magnitude (see Table 4.3) when compared with BLS data because the CBP data do not include most government employees who are part of the BLS data. They only include government employees working in government hospitals, depository institutions, federal and federally sponsored credit agencies, liquor stores, and wholesale liquor establishments. The CBP data further exclude some agricultural production employees and household employees. Nevertheless, the CBP data are more complete with respect to educational and membership organizations and of small nonprofit organizations in other industries. One last difference is that the CBP data report employment for the month of March whereas BLS employment is the average of monthly data.

To get U.S. Census Bureau county business patterns data, select **Business**, select **County Business Patterns**. Employment and payroll data are available: ① at the county, state, national, ZIP, or MSA level on a NAICS basis for 1998 forward and ② at the county, state, national, or ZIP level on a SIC basis for 1994 – 1997.

While employment is the most popular economic indicator, in terms of giving a complete picture of the economy of a region, it has some significant shortcomings:

(1) Employment by place of work counts the number of jobs by establishment regardless if they are full- or time-part. Such figures may mask under-employment levels, skewing the real level of regional economic activity as some persons hold two part-time jobs or some persons only work seasonally.

(2) Technological progress and human development lead to substantial productivity increases. As such, employment figures may not correspond to output levels. The introduction of computers in the production process, —for example, the computerization of a car manufacturing assembly line—may increased the amount of goods and services produced, while, at the same time, the labor force in that particular sector stagnates or decreases.

(3) Measuring regional economic activity based on employment figures also does not account for government transfer payments and other non-job related income. Using only employment data, the level of economic activities in regions with higher levels of poverty, and therefore, higher levels of social security payments, is underestimated.

Income and earnings data indicate the amount of money circulating in the regional economy rather than the number of persons employed. The data addresses some of the shortcomings of employment statistics described earlier by: (1) accounting for full-time, part-time, and seasonal employment, (2) recognizing the fact that different jobs are paid differently, and (3) including non-job related income sources. However, the interpretation of this data is less straight forward than that of jobs. The use of dollar values rather than job numbers means that one must pay particular attention to exactly what the dollar values represent.

Income is a good measure to use when a study concerns the region's standard of living. It serves as the basis for calculating the per capita income, per family income, and per household income indicators. While the numerator—the aggregated personal income—remains the same in all three measures, the denominator changes accordingly to population, number of families, and households respectively. There are two major sources for U.S. personal income data: the Bureau of Economic Analysis (BEA) and the U.S. Census Bureau.

The **BEA** lists personal income by place of residence. The BEA defines personal income as:[1]

	earnings by place of work
−	personal contributions for social insurance
+	adjustments for residence[2]
=	net earnings by place of residence
+	investment (dividends, interest , and rent)
+	transfer payments (social security payments, pensions, welfare)
=	**personal income by place of residence**

It includes all sources of income—monetary and non-monetary (e.g., food stamps), but excludes individual social security contributions. Personal income as reported by the BEA converts earnings by place of work data into earnings by place of residence. As such it qualifies as an appropriate measure— together with local area cost of living—for a region's quality of life. The personal income data by the BEA are available at the national, state, county and metropolitan statistical area level. Personal income by place of residence data (CA05) from 1969 – 2000 are available under the 1987 SIC; from 2001 forwards, data are available under the NAICS.

For median household income, household, family, and per capita income indicators, and poverty rates, the U.S. Census Bureau might be the right gateway. In contrast to the BEA definition of personal income, the Census Bureau's money income definition excludes nonmonetary income sources and includes personal contributions for social insurance.

Earnings data are available by place of work and indicate an industry sector's contribution to regional income. Earnings by place of work are the largest contributor to personal income. Alternatively, earnings data are published by government agencies as wages, payroll, or earnings by industry. As we have already seen in the case of employment, there is no unique definition of earnings across government agencies. Although wages and payroll are similar concepts, the definitions as applied to compilation of data do not necessarily

---

[1] http://www.bea.gov/bea/regional/articles/lapi2001/intro.cfm.

[2] Adjusts regional earnings for the net inflow of earnings of inter-area commuters. For example, a person living in Boone County and working in Hamilton County, Ohio brings her earnings back home to Boone County. In contrast, persons that commute to Boone County for work leave the region with their earnings.

159

match. Usually, payroll is the more comprehensive definition for money compensation than wages. Ways and payroll are discussed below.

The Bureau of Labor Statistics (BLS) publishes total and average wages under its Quarterly Census of Employment and Wages program.[1] The BLS defines wages according to when the compensation was paid, regardless of when services were performed. Included in total compensation payments are bonuses, stock options, severance pay, the cash value of meals and lodging, tips and other gratuities, and, if applicable, employer contributions to deferred compensation plans (e.g. 401(k) plans).[2] Average wages are defined as the ratio of total annual wages over annual average employment. Depending on annual average employment, the ratio of full-time to part-time employment plays a crucial role in the level of average annual wages.

The BLS Current Employment Statistics (CES) program makes **earnings of workers** on non-farm payrolls available to the public.[3] Earnings data are derived from reports of gross payrolls based on the pay before deductions—such as Social Security, unemployment insurance, withholding tax, bonds, and union dues—are taken.[4] They include overtime pay, shift premiums, and payments for holidays, vacations, and sick leave. Excluded are bonuses, commissions, tips, and payments in kind (the value of free rent, fuel, or meals).

The BEA reports **earnings by place of work** and **earnings by industry** together with personal income in its **personal income by major source and earnings by industry** series (CN05). The BEA defines earnings by place of work as the sum of:[5]

wages and salary disbursements
+ other labor income
+ proprietors' income
= **earnings by place of work**

Wage and salary disbursements are the actual employers' compensation, including bonuses, commissions, pay-in-kind, incentive payments, and tips. It is a measure of gross disbursements, measured before deductions, such as social security contributions and union dues. Other labor income mainly consists of employer contributions to employee retirement plans, private group health and life insurance plans, privately administered workers' compensation plans, and supplemental unemployment benefit plans. Proprietors' income includes the return for business owners from sole proprietorships, partnerships, and tax-exempt cooperatives. This includes profit or other compensation paid to proprietors or

---

[1] Source: http://www.bls.gov/cew/home.htm.

[2] Source: http://www.bls.gov/cew/cewbultn02.htm.

[3] Source: http://www.bls.gov/sae/home.htm.

[4] Source: http://www.bls.gov/opub/hom/homch2_b.htm.

[5] Source: http://www.bea.gov/bea/regional/definitions/.

partners. Earnings by place of work are reported as an aggregate for each region. Earnings by industry, on the other hand, identify each industry sector's contribution to regional income and as such give us more detailed information on a region's strengths, weaknesses, and opportunities for future economic growth.

The U.S. Census Bureau lists **payroll** statistics, together with employment, in its County Business Patterns (CBP). The Census Bureau defines payroll as the sum of salaries, wages, tips, commissions, bonuses, vacation allowances, sick-leave pay, employee contributions to qualified pension plans, and the value of taxable fringe benefits. It is measured before deductions, such as Social Security, income tax, or insurance, are made. Proprietors' income is excluded. The CBP report the first quarter and annual payroll at the county, state, and national level.[1]

There are many more units of measurement that can be used in an economic profile. For example, data measuring industry output—e.g., **sales** data—might be of particular interest for local governments in projecting tax revenues. Although sales data are conceptually straight forward and constitute an appropriate measure of regional economic transactions, they are used infrequently, as they raise the concern of double-counting. Industries sell goods and services to households, governments, and outside the region and receive payments in return. Industries also sell goods and services to other industry sectors in the region, called intermediate inputs. In order to avoid double counting, these inter-industry transactions within the region must be subtracted from the total reported sales; otherwise, they will inflate the level of regional economic activities. For instance, in the sale of motherboards and soundcards from a computer parts manufacturer to an establishment that assembles computers, the sales of the motherboards and soundcards to the assembly establishment do not count towards total regional sales as they do when measuring the gross state product (GSP). Otherwise, the value of these same computer components would be listed twice: once by the computer part manufacturer and once by the computer assembly plant. Only final sales to consumers are listed under this rubric to avoid double counting. Sales data will become of major importance when discussing the input-output framework in Chapter 5.

4.4.2.3   The Level of Detail—the Economic Aggregation

Since the 1930's, economic data, such as employment and earnings by place of work have been collected, aggregated, and categorized in the U.S. following the SIC. Under the demand-oriented SIC, establishments are categorized according to their predominant type of economic activity. An establishment is a single economic unit engaged in the production process of goods and services. It can be a farm, a factory, or a grocery store. A company or an enterprise can consist of

---

[1] Source: http://censtats.census.gov/cbpnaic/cbpnaic.shtml.

more than one establishment. Industrial classification groups all establishments together based upon their major economic activity.

The original SIC was developed in the United States during a time when the nation's economic activities were dominated by manufacturing. To keep up with the economy's changing industrial composition—the appearance of new industries and diminishing of others—the SIC has been revised frequently, most recently in 1987. In 1997, due to major changes in the structure of the economy, for instance, the emergence of advanced technology industries (e.g., wireless telecommunication, internet publishing, fiber optic cable manufacturing, and reproduction of computer software), the NAICS was introduced. Not only does the NAICS expand the number of individual industries from 1,004 in the SIC system to 1,170 in the NAICS, in contrast to the demand-oriented SIC system, the NAICS is based on an economic production-oriented conceptual framework. In this sense, the NAICS, groups establishments together that have similar processes producing goods and services regarding their use of material inputs, capital equipments, and labor rather than their similarity in output as in the SIC.

The 1987 SIC is a hierarchical system. At the highest level of aggregation, it arrays the economy into eleven divisions, A through K (see Table 4.4). Divisions are divided into 83 two- digit major groups that are further subdivided into

Table 4.4 The 1987 U.S. Standard Industrial Classification System[1]

Major Division	1987 SIC Code	Industrial Sector
A	01 – 09	Agriculture, Forestry, and Fishing
B	10 – 14	Mining
C	15 – 17	Construction
D	20 – 39	Manufacturing
E	40 – 49	Transportation, Communication, and Utilities
	45	Transportation by Air
	451	Air Transportation, Scheduled, and Air Courier
	4512	Air Transportation, Scheduled
	4513	Air Courier Services
F	50 – 51	Wholesale Trade
G	52 – 59	Retail Trade
H	60 – 67	Finance, Insurance, and Real Estate (FIRE)
I	70 – 88	Services
J	90 – 97	Public Administration
K	99	Nonclassifiable Establishments

(1) Source: http://www.osha.gov/cgi-bin/sic/sicser5 and http://www.census.gov/epcd/naics/issues2.

416 three-digit industry groups. At the largest level of detail, the SIC systems covers 1,004 four-digit industries.

For example, division E covers "Transportation, Communication, and Utilities" (SIC code 40 – 49). "Transportation by Air" (SIC code 45) is one major group within division E. Among others, it includes, at the three-digit level the industry group "Air Transportation, Scheduled, and Air Courier" (SIC code 451). At the four-digit or highest level of detail, this particular industry group 451 covers industries "Air Transportation, Scheduled" (SIC code 4512) and "Air Courier Services" (SIC code 4513).

Classification of an economy into eleven divisions does not reveal much detail about individual industry activities. Breaking down divisions into major industry groups allows one to draw a more detailed picture of the regional economy. For smaller geographical areas, a more detailed break down which identifies industry groups or individual industries known to be located in the area may provide interesting insight into the local economy. For example, one would expect that Boone County, site of the Cincinnati/Northern Kentucky International Airport, would be highly specialized in air transportation. At the division-level, this specialization is not available, as air transportation is aggregated into the Transportation, Communication, and Utilities division. The two-digit level identifies Air Transportation as an individual industry group. More detailed information could then be included in an analysis at the three- and four-digit level. However, for reasons of confidentiality, this detailed level of information is not always readily available.

Introduced in 1997, the NAICS shown in Table 4.5 has already seen a revision in 2002. As its name says, NAICS is the standard classification system in Canada, Mexico, and the United States. Like its predecessor, the SIC, the NAICS is of hierarchical structure. The total number of industries covered under the NAICS is 1,179. The NAICS manual of the Bureau of Labor Statistics identifies 20 sectors, 100 sub sectors, 317 four-digit industry groups, 725 five-digit NAICS industries, and 1,170 six-digit industries.[1] Structural differences between the NAICS and SIC systems are summarized in Table 4.6.

The reorganization of the industries under the production-oriented NAICS gives the data greater economic meaning. Data produced under NAICS are more suitable than SIC data for calculating economic indicators that combine input and output measures, such as productivity, unit labor costs, and employment-output ratios.[2] Under the NAICS, the SIC divisions of Manufacturing and Services have been completely restructured. Additional sectors have been introduced to reflect the modern economy. For example, an information sector has been created covering Publishing Industries (formerly Manufacturing in the SIC), Broadcasting

---

[1] Source: www.bls.gov/cew/cewbultn02.htm.

[2] Source: Development of the NAICS, http://www.census.gov/epcd/www/naicsdev.htm.

Table 4.5 The 2002 North American Industry Classification System

2002 NAICS Code	2002 NAICS Title
11	Agriculture, Forestry, Fishing and Hunting
21	Mining
22	Utilities
23	Construction
31 – 33	Manufacturing
42	Wholesale Trade
44 – 45	Retail Trade
48 – 49	Transportation and Warehousing
481	Air Transportation
4811	Scheduled Air Transportation
51	Information
517	Telecommunication
5172	Wireless Telecommunications Carriers (except Satellite)
51721	Wireless Telecommunications Carriers (except Satellite)
517211	Paging
517212	Cellular and Other Wireless Telecommunications
52	Finance and Insurance
53	Real Estate and Rental and Leasing
54	Professional, Scientific, and Technical Services
55	Management of Companies and Enterprises
56	Administrative and Support and Waste Management and Remediation Services
61	Educational Services
62	Health Care and Social Assistance
71	Arts, Entertainment, and Recreation
72	Accommodation and Food Services
81	Other Services (except Public Administration)
92	Public Administration
99	Unclassified

Table 4.6 NAICS and SIC structural differences

Level of Detail	NAICS	SIC
Letter	–	Division
Two-digit	Sector	Major Group
Three-digit	Sub-sector	Industry Group
Four-digit	Industry Group	Industry
Five-digit	NAICS Industry	–
Six-digit	U.S. Industry	–

and Telecommunications (formerly Transportation, Communication, and Utilities), Motion Picture and Sound Recording industries, Information Services and Data Processing, and Libraries (all formerly classified as Services). Hotels and Other Lodging, Eating and Drinking Places form the new Accommodation and Food Services industrial category. Wholesale and retail industries have also been redefined. Updates on the NAICS are scheduled on a five-year basis.

Meanwhile, government agencies have completely converted the publication of economic data from the SIC code to the NAICS code. However, data prior to 1997 are still listed under the SIC system. This means that economic time series analysis confronts the difficult task of matching data from two different classification systems. In order to allow users to compare the two systems, the U.S. Census Bureau publishes a 1997 NAICS and 1987 SIC correspondence table (http://www.census.gov/epcd/www/naicstab.htm). In 2002, the 1997 NAICS underwent its first major revision, in which six of the twenty sectors were substantially revised. Tables matching the 2002 NAICS to the 1997 NAICS, as well as the 2002 NAICS to the 1987 SIC system, are available at the Census website (http://www.census.gov/epcd/naics02/).

4.5   Economic Base Analysis Techniques

So far we have examined a region's economy by evaluating readily available economic indicators. We have evaluated the most recently available economic and socioeconomic indicators, observed them over time, and compared a region's performance indicators to that of a benchmark region. We have discussed the economic base model as a way of conceptualizing the economic activity of a region. In this section, we will begin to apply analytical tools and techniques that fall under the category of economic base analysis. We will learn to analyze and describe the strengths and weaknesses of an economy, its specialization, and its level of diversity. Particularly where data availability constrains the use of more complex economic models, e.g., input-output or regional econometric models, economic base analysis techniques can become powerful decision making tools.

In order to begin, we need to divide the economy into basic and non-basic sectors. Recall that the basic sector is the engine of economic growth and depends on economic conditions outside the region, and the non-basic sector supports the basic sector and depends largely on local economic conditions.

4.5.1   The Survey Method

Conceptually, the most straightforward approach of dividing an economy into a non-basic and basic sector would be to conduct an extensive business survey.

Surveying local establishments, for example through mail questionnaires or telephone interviews, on whether produced goods and services are sold locally or exported outside the region would be the most direct way to either classify their activities as basic or non-basic and should provide the most accurate method of categorization.

Despite its conceptual simplicity, the survey method is rarely used, for good reasons. First, a widespread business survey requires time, money, and trained stuff. Depending on the number of regional businesses, the effort of conducting the survey may not be justified when compared with the usefulness of the survey results. Second, the accuracy of the outcome might be questionable considering the sensitivity of businesses to the questions asked regarding employment and sales. Businesses may not be willing to participate, and a lowered participation rate may decrease the accuracy of the data.

Instead of a full survey, sampling provides a means of classifying businesses with less effort. For larger areas with a vast number of businesses (the population), it is faster and more efficient to study a sample (subset of the population) instead of conducting a full census. When evaluating and studying the sample, we make inferences about the overall population while considering potential sampling errors. Stratified sampling, for instance, is one way to achieve an even representation of all regional businesses. Stratified sampling divides the population (e.g., all firms and businesses) into categories, or strata. For instance, we easily can divide businesses according to the North American Industry Classification System. Then, we draw a random sample from each stratum (e.g., agriculture, mining, utilities, and so on). The survey approach can further be simplified by taking into account that some businesses serve mostly the local market (e.g., local government), while others are purely export oriented (e.g., hotel and lodging). Pre-classification of some industry sectors will reduce the number of strata to those sectors that obviously serve entirely local or non-local markets.

4.5.2 The Assumption Method

The assumption approach is simple, quick, and inexpensive. The assumption approach simply assumes economic activities—industry sectors— as either being completely basic or completely non-basic. It is widely perceived that the Agriculture, Mining, Manufacturing, State and Federal Governments sectors are entirely basic activities and as such depend solely on factors outside the region. All remaining activities, basically the Utilities, Construction, Local Government, and service industries sectors, are assumed to be non-basic, depending only on local economic conditions. For Boone County, Table 4.7 demonstrates the use of the assumption method.

Unfortunately, one can never clearly divide economic activities into completely basic or non-basic activities. Referring to Table 4.7, Transportation Equipment

Table 4.7 Assumption method, Boone County, KY, 2002[1]

NAICS Code	2002 NAICS Title	Total Employment	Basic Employment	Non-basic Employment
11	Agriculture, Forestry, Fishing and Hunting	79	79	–
21	Mining	35	35	–
22	Utilities	481	–	481
23	Construction	2,230	–	2,230
238	Specialty Trade Contractors	1,569	–	1,569
31 – 33	Manufacturing	10,360	10,360	–
311	Food Manufacturing	1,498	1,498	–
323	Printing and Related Support Activities	935	935	–
326	Plastics and Rubber Products Manufacturing	1,770	1,770	–
333	Machinery Manufacturing	1,545	1,545	–
336	Transportation Equipment Manufacturing	1,317	1,317	–
42	Wholesale Trade	5,166	–	5,166
423	Merchant Wholesalers, Durable Goods	2,935	–	2,935
424	Merchant Wholesalers, Nondurable Goods	1,965	–	1,965
44 – 45	Retail Trade	8,724	–	8,724
445	Food and Beverage Stores	1,114	–	1,114
452	General Merchandise Stores	2,312	–	2,312
48 – 49	Transportation and Warehousing	12,855	12,855	–
481	Air Transportation	7,710	7,710	–
4811	Scheduled Air Transportation	7,652	7,652	–
492	Couriers and Messengers	2,236	2,236	–
493	Warehousing and Storage	1,183	1,183	–
51	Information	1,657	–	1,657
511	Publishing Industries (except Internet)	1,156	–	1,156
52	Finance and Insurance	4,506	–	4,506
522	Credit Intermediation and Related Activities	2,249	–	2,249
53	Real Estate and Rental and Leasing	934	–	934
54	Professional, Scientific, and Technical Services	1,341	–	1,341
55	Management of Companies and Enterprises	995	–	995
56	Administrative and Support and Waste Mgmt.	4,233	–	4,233
561	Administrative and Support Services	4,078	–	4,078
61	Educational Services	267	–	267
62	Health Care and Social Assistance	2,897	–	2,897
621	Ambulatory Health Care Services	1,055	–	1,055
71	Arts, Entertainment, and Recreation	489	–	489
72	Accommodation and Food Services	5,821	–	5,821
722	Food Services and Drinking Places	5,186	–	5,186
81	Other Services (except Public Administration)	1,733	–	1,733
811	Repair and Maintenance	943	–	943
92	Public Administration	5,107	1,434	3,673
92	Federal Government	1,161	1,161	–
92	State Government	273	273	–
92	Local Government	3,673	–	3,673
99	Unclassified	97	–	97
	Total	70,007	24,763	45,244

(1) Source: Bureau of Labor Statistics, Quarterly Census of Employment and Wages, 2002

Manufacturing is classified as basic. In particular, the 1,317 persons employed by establishments categorized under NAICS code 336 produce transportation equipment that is entirely exported outside the county. This assumption also means that all transportation equipment purchased by the larger Cincinnati / Northern Kentucky International Airport is imported from outside the county. This case clearly demonstrates that assuming all manufacturing industries are entirely basic will create substantial errors and ultimately lead to biased conclusions. Deciding on whether transportation equipment manufacturing should be classified as either basic or non-basic depends solely on the judgment of the researcher. In the case of Boone County, we will use the common practice of assuming that all manufacturing activities are basic sector activities. However, we must also acknowledge that in reality, the presence of the Cincinnati / Northern Kentucky International Airport, a consumer of transportation equipment, indicates that the assumption may ignore some locally consumed manufactured goods.

In another example, we assumed Transportation and Warehousing (a service activity) to be a basic activity. Our assumption revises the common approach of assuming all service-related industries perform non-basic activities. We make this adaptation in recognition that the majority of travelers using the Cincinnati / Northern Kentucky International Airport are not from Boone County. Additionally, most of the incoming and outgoing freight does not stay or originate in the Boone County.

These two examples show that the common practice of assigning all Agriculture, Mining, Manufacturing, State and Federal Government activity to the basic sector raises the question of accuracy in the results. Although commonly assigned to the non-basic sector, many service sector can be mainly basic activities under certain cirtumstances. This shows that only very few industry sectors can be clearly categorized as either basic or non-basic and that the assumption method by itself is of limited use dividing an area's economy into basic and non-basic activities. However, one useful application of the assumption method is to combine it with the survey method or as we will see later with the location quotient method. Identifying strata that are clear cut basic activities (such as Tourism, Hotel and Lodging) or non-basic activities (such as Local Government and Motion Picture Theaters) can substantially reduce the amount of survey work. Further, in-depth knowledge of the area's firms and businesses can improve the accuracy of the assumption method.

4.5.3   The Location Quotient Method

The location quotient (LQ) method is probably the most popular and widely used economic base analysis technique. Location quotients are applicable when identifying an area's industrial specialization relative to a benchmark region, often the nation. In this section, we use Boone County, Kentucky, as the study region and compare its economy to the National economy. We will refer to Boone County's economy as **regional economy**. Alternatively and as you will see in many other publications, the study region's economy may often be referred to as *local economy*.

Tiebout[1] also named LQs **coefficients of specialization**. For instance, we already know that Boone County is specialized in Transportation and Warehousing. We will later confirm this preliminary conclusion by evaluating the location quotient of transportation and warehousing. Observing location quotients over time will give us some insight into whether a regional industry is losing ground or gaining in strength. For example, a vast shopping mall, developed in the late 1970s in Florence, Boone County, attracts people from all over the Cincinnati area. By observing location quotients of the retail industry over time, we can look at whether the retail industry has developed into one of the economic driving forces (or specializations) of Boone County.

In contrast to the previously described assumption method, where an industry sector is assumed to be either basic or non-basic, the location quotient allows industry sectors to be divided into basic and non-basic activities. The location quotient method compares an industry's share of regional economic activity to the nation's share of economic activity for that industry. Although employment is the most common measure of economic activity, income and earnings data are also frequently used. Using employment as an example, the location quotient compares the share of regional employment in industry *i* with the share of national employment in industry *i*.

4.5.3.1　Calculation of Location Quotients

Location quotients are calculated at one point in time using the following formula:

$$\text{LQ}_i = \left(\frac{e_i}{e}\right) \bigg/ \left(\frac{E_i}{E}\right) = \frac{\text{share of regional employment in industry } i}{\text{share of national employment in industry } i} \qquad (4.38)$$

where, in the case of employment,

e_i — regional employment in industry *i*;

e — total regional employment (all sectors);

E_i — employment in industry *i* of the benchmark region (i.e., the nation);

E — total employment of the benchmark region.

More specifically, the location quotient can be described as the ratio of an industry's share of regional employment over its share of national employment.

---

[1]　Tiebout, 1962: 47.

It must be noted that the results of the location quotient method are highly influenced by the choice of the benchmark region. Generally, a more self-sufficient benchmark region is a better reference region. Meaning that, for calculating location quotients, larger geographic areas such as states and the nation are preferred.

The resulting location quotient may be interpreted in the following manner:

(1) **Location Quotients > 1.0**: $(e_i / e) > (E_i / E)$. The region has a greater share of employment (or earnings, etc) in industry i than the benchmark region. At least part of a region's employment in industrial sector i is engaged in basic activities. It is also assumed that for the region, industry i produces more goods and services than can be consumed locally, and therefore exports this excess production. The higher the LQ is, the greater the region's specialization in this industrial sector. In this case, the regional industry i is comprised of a basic and non-basic employment. While we generally assume that all excess production is exported, we must be aware of special cases where the entire production can be considered being a basic activity. For example, an establishment producing windshields for an automobile manufacturer will deliver all the windshields to where the automobile manufacturer assembles the cars. This activity should be considered entirely basic, if the windshield manufacturer and car manufacturer are not located next to each other (i.e., within the same economic region).

(2) **Location Quotients = 1.0**: $(e_i / e) = (E_i / E)$. The region's share of employment in industry i is equal to that of the benchmark region. It is assumed that the region is completely self-sufficient and neither exports nor imports the goods or services of this industry. All employment is considered non-basic.

(3) **Location Quotients < 1.0**: $(e_i / e) < (E_i / E)$. If industry i has a smaller share of employment than the benchmark region—the region falls below the level of self-sufficiency and needs to import to meet local demand for that particular industry sector's goods and services. All employment is considered non-basic.

Location quotients for Boone County are summarized in Table 4.8. Before going into greater detail about what location quotients can reveal or tell us, some remarks about the assumptions and development of the data in summary Table 4.8 are necessary. Our goal is to divide a region's economy into basic and non-basic activities, at a level of detail sufficient to identify the region's economic specializations. First, we use the assumption approach and assign clear-cut industries to either the basic or the non-basic sector. In particular, we assign all employment in Agriculture (11), Mining (21), Accommodation (721), Federal Government (92) and State Government (92) to the basic sector, while Local Government (92) employment is considered to be entirely non-basic. Second, to capture more detailed information on basic activities we decide to use the three-digit classification level for all sectors that indicate basic activities. For

Table 4.8 Location quotients and basic employment for Boone County, KY, 2002[1]

NAICS Code	2002 NAICS Title	Area Employment (e_i)	US Employment (E_i)	Location Quotient (LQ_i)	Basic Employment (b_i)	Nonbasic Employment (n_i)
	Total Employment	70,007	128,233,919		24,478	45,529
11	Agriculture, Forestry, Fishing and Hunting[2]	79	1,155,890	0.125	79	0
21	Mining[2]	35	505,979	0.127	35	0
22	Utilities	481	592,152	1.488	158	323
23	Construction	2,230	6,683,553	0.611	0	2,230
31 – 33	Manufacturing	10,360	15,209,192			
311	Food Manufacturing	1,498	1,532,478	1.791	661	837
314	Textile Product Mills	365	194,385	3.439	259	106
322	Paper Manufacturing	708	543,379	2.387	411	297
323	Printing and Related Support Activities	935	707,566	2.421	549	386
325	Chemical Manufacturing	686	924,737	1.359	181	505
326	Plastics and Rubber Products Manufacturing	1,770	846,766	3.829	1,308	462
333	Machinery Manufacturing	1,545	1,221,816	2.316	878	667
336	Transportation Equipment Manufacturing	1,317	1,820,170	1.325	323	994
N/A	Other Manufacturing	1,536	7,417,895	0.379	0	1,536
42	Wholesale Trade	5,166	5,617,456			
423	Merchant Wholesalers, Durable Goods	2,935	2,981,513	1.803	1,307	1,628
424	Merchant Wholesalers, Nondurable Goods	1,965	2,006,466	1.794	870	1,095
425	Wholesale Electronic Markets, etc.	266	629,478	0.774	0	266
44 – 45	Retail Trade	8,724	15,018,588			

Continued

NAICS Code	2002 NAICS Title	Area Employment (e_i)	US Employment (E_i)	Location Quotient (LQ_i)	Basic Employment (b_j)	Nonbasic Employment (n_i)
442	Furniture and Home Furnishings Stores	376	539,759	1.276	81	295
443	Electronics and Appliance Stores	472	527,907	1.638	184	288
447	Gasoline Stations	510	895,547	1.043	21	489
451	Sporting Goods, Hobby, Book, and Music Stores	525	667,119	1.442	161	364
452	General Merchandise Stores	2,312	2,814,249	1.505	776	1,536
453	Miscellaneous Store Retailers	603	963,711	1.146	77	526
N/A	Other Retail Trade	3,926	8,610,296	0.835	0	3,926
48 – 49	Transportation and Warehousing	12,855	3,989,116			
481	Air Transportation	7,710	561,291	25.161	7,404	306
488	Support Activities for Transportation	831	514,560	2.958	550	281
492	Couriers and Messengers	2,236	567,288	7.220	1,926	310
493	Warehousing and Storage	1,183	510,539	4.244	904	279
N/A	Other Transportation and Warehousing	895	1,835,438	0.893	0	895
51	Information	1,657	3,364,485			
511	Publishing Industries (except Internet)	1,156	958,746	2.209	633	523
518	Internet Service Providers	245	436,750	1.028	7	238
N/A	Other Information Services	256	1,968,989	0.238	0	256
52	Finance and Insurance	4,506	5,678,156			
522	Credit Intermediation and Related Activities	2,249	2,668,892	1.544	792	1,457
N/A	Other Finance and Insurance (D)	2,257	3,009,264	1.374	614	1,643
53	Real Estate and Rental and Leasing	934	2,028,109			
531	Real Estate	352	1,382,381	0.466	0	352

Continued

NAICS Code	2002 NAICS Title	Area Employment (e_i)	US Employment (E_i)	Location Quotient (LQ_i)	Basic Employment (b_i)	Nonbasic Employment (n_i)
532	Rental and Leasing Services	582	645,728	1.651	229	353
54	Professional, Scientific, and Technical Services	1,341	6,654,743	0.369	0	1,341
55	Management of Companies and Enterprises	995	1,695,554	1.075	69	926
56	Administrative and Support and Waste Mgm.	4,233	7,589,300			
561	Administrative and Support Services	4,078	7,271,717	1.027	108	3,970
562	Waste Management and Remediation Services	155	317,583	0.894	0	155
61	Educational Services	267	1,951,003	0.251	0	267
62	Health Care and Social Assistance	2,897	13,395,715	0.396	0	2,897
71	Arts, Entertainment, and Recreation	489	1,798,621	0.498	0	489
72	Accommodation and Food Services	5,821	10,197,329			
721	Accommodation[2]	636	1,772,296	0.657	636	0
722	Food Services and Drinking Places	5,185	8,425,033	1.127	586	4,599
81	Other Services (except Public Administration)	1,733	4,246,011			
811	Repair and Maintenance	943	1,238,075	1.395	267	676
N/A	All Other Services	790	3,007,936	0.481	0	790
92	Federal Government[2]	1,161	2,758,627	0.771	1,161	0
92	State Government[2]	273	4,485,071	0.111	273	0
92	Local Government[2]	3,673	13,412,941	0.502	0	3,673
99	Unclassified	97	206,330	0.861	0	97

(1) Source: Bureau of Labor Statistics, Quarterly Census of Employment and Wages, 2002

(2) assigned to either basic or nonbasic sector using the assumption approach.

instance, manufacturing sub-sectors (e.g., three-digit level) that are basic activities or specializations of Boone County are listed individually. The remaining sub-sectors and sectors where data restrictions applied for reasons of confidentiality are all lumped together. In the case of manufacturing, they are labeled "Other Manufacturing". Lumping all manufacturing sub-sectors into one higher manufacturing sector (e.g., two-digit level) not only leads to a loss of sectoral information, but in the case of Boone County would result in a lower estimate of basic employment in manufacturing.

Now let us turn our attention to some specific location quotients and how to interpret them. For example, the Utility sector in Boone County has a location quotient of 1.488. The location quotient for utilities is calculated as

$$LQ_{utilities} = \frac{481/70,007}{592,152/128,233,921} = 1.488$$

This implies that Boone County's utility industry also supplies neighboring counties with utilities. On the other hand, the county is far away from being self-sufficient in the provision of health care and social assistance as indicated by this industry's location quotient of 0.396.

For the vast shopping mall in Boone County with approximately 130 specialty stores on over 924,000 square feet of retail space[1], we further break down the retail sector into its sub-sectors. Using the three-digit NAICS, it becomes apparent that Boone County is indeed specialized in retail activities commonly located in shopping malls, such as furniture and home furnishing stores (442), electronic and appliance stores (443), sporting goods, hobby, and music stores (451), and general merchandise stores (452). All of these sectors have location quotients of greater than one indicating that people from outside the country frequent these stores.

This example further emphasizes the importance of going beyond the two-digit level of industrial classification. It is at the more detailed three-digit level of aggregation that we can immediately see Boone County's strength in several retail sub-sectors and its shortfalls in some other retail sub-sectors. By considering only the more aggregated two-digit level of industrial aggregation, this particular piece of information is lost. Comparing Table 4.9 below, location quotients for Boone County using the two-digit industry classification, with Table 4.8, location quotients for Boone County using the three-digit industry classification— indicates the loss of detail by using only the two-digit classification. Particularly for smaller areas with a relative small number of firms and businesses, the more detailed level of industrial classification reveals important information on the

---

[1] Source: http://www.tripsouth.com/shopping/ky-shopping.shtml.

Table 4.9   Location quotients using two-digit industry classification, Boone County, 2002

NAICS Code	2002 NAICS Title	Area Employment (e_i)	US Employment (E_i)	Location Quotient (LQ_i)	Basic Employment (b_i)	Nonbasic Employment (n_i)
	Total Employment	70,007	128,233,919		18,883	51,124
11	Agriculture, Forestry, Fishing and Hunting[1]	79	1,155,890	0.125	79	0
21	Mining[1]	35	505,979	0.127	35	0
22	Utilities	481	592,152	1.488	158	323
23	Construction	2,230	6,683,553	0.611	0	2,230
31–33	Manufacturing	10,360	15,209,192	1.248	2,057	8,303
42	Wholesale Trade	5,166	5,617,456	1.685	2,099	3,067
44–45	Retail Trade	8,724	15,018,588	1.064	525	8,199
48–49	Transportation and Warehousing	12,855	3,989,116	5.903	10,677	2,178
51	Information	1,657	3,364,485	0.902	0	1,657
52	Finance and Insurance	4,506	5,678,156	1.454	1,406	3,100
53	Real Estate and Rental and Leasing	934	2,028,109	0.844	0	934
54	Professional, Scientific, and Technical Services	1,341	6,654,743	0.369	0	1,341
55	Management of Companies and Enterprises	995	1,695,554	1.075	69	926
56	Administrative and Support and Waste Mgm.	4,233	7,589,300	1.022	90	4,143
61	Educational Services	267	1,951,003	0.251	0	267
62	Health Care and Social Assistance	2,897	13,395,715	0.396	0	2,897
71	Arts, Entertainment, and Recreation	489	1,798,621	0.498	0	489
72	Accommodation and Food Services	5,821	10,197,329	1.046	254	5,567
81	Other Services (except Public Administration)	1,733	4,246,011	0.748	0	1,733
92	Federal Government[1]	1,161	2,758,627	0.771	1,161	0
92	State Government[1]	273	4,485,071	0.111	273	0
92	Local Government[1]	3,673	13,412,941	0.502	0	3,673
99	Unclassified	97	206,330	0.861	0	97

(1) assigned to either basic or nonbasic sector using the assumption approach

175

area's economic strengths, weaknesses, and opportunities for economic growth. Sometimes for small areas, however, data availability at the more detailed level (because of business confidentiality) becomes a limitation that hinders a more detailed economic analysis.

The presence of the larger Cincinnati / Northern Kentucky International Airport is reflected by a location quotient of 25.161 for the air transportation sub-sector (NAICS 481). Again, this highlights the significance of a more detailed analysis at the three-digit level of industrial classification. Such information is not available using the two-digit level of industrial classification where we cannot distinguish between transportation and warehousing (NAICS 48 – 49). The detailed classification helps explaining the presence of firms and businesses that clearly have a major contribution to the regional economy, such as the shopping mall in Florence and the Cincinnati / Northern Kentucky International Airport.

In the next step, the location quotient can then be used to calculate basic or excess employment for an industry i as:

$$b_i = \left(1 - \frac{1}{LQ_i}\right) \cdot e_i \qquad (4.39)$$

where,

b_i — area basic employment in industry i.

For instance, Boone County's basic employment in machinery manufacturing (NAICS 333) is calculated as

$$b_{mach.mfg.} = \left(1 - \frac{1}{2.316}\right) \times 1,545 = 878$$

Out of a total of 1,545 employed in machinery manufacturing, 878 persons work to produce exports. Using the location quotient to derive export employment for location quotients smaller than 1.0 results in negative employment figures. This can easily be shown by evaluating the term $1/LQ_i$, which is larger than 1.0 for LQ's < 1.0. For example, the construction industry has a location quotient of less than 1.0. Using the basic employment calculation results in:

$$b_{construction} = \left(1 - \frac{1}{0.611}\right) \times 2,230 = -1,420$$

Negative employment does not really mean anything in this context, but one could interpret the negative employment figure as the number of workers needed in industry i (e.g., the example construction) to become self-sufficient; or to have a location quotient of exactly 1.0. In the example of Boone County, we have left out all basic employment calculations for industries with location quotients of less than 1.0.

Estimation of basic employment

Regional employment in industry i is the sum of basic and non-basic employment, or:

$$e_i = b_i + n_i \qquad (4.40)$$

Defining self-sufficiency by comparing a region's economy with that of the nation, we can describe non-basic employment in industry i as:

$$n_i = \left(\frac{E_i}{E} \right) \cdot e \qquad (4.41)$$

Where (E_i / E) is the share of industry i in national employment; a measure to define self-sufficiency in industry i. Substituting Eq. (4.41) into Eq. (4.40) then results in an expression that allows us to calculate basic employment without using location quotients:

$$b_i = e_i - \left(\frac{E_i}{E} \cdot e \right) \qquad (4.42)$$

Dividing both sides of the equation by E_i and rearranging the equation allows us to calculate export employment without using location quotients:

$$\frac{b_i}{E_i} = \frac{e_i}{E_i} - \left(\frac{E_i}{E} \cdot \frac{e}{E_i} \right) \qquad (4.43)$$

$$b_i = \left(\frac{e_i}{E_i} - \frac{e}{E} \right) \cdot E_i \qquad (4.44)$$

This term can be rearranged further:

$$b_i = \left(\frac{e_i \cdot E_i}{E_i} - \frac{e \cdot E_i}{E} \right) = \left(1 - \frac{e \cdot E_i}{e_i \cdot E} \right) \cdot e_i = \left(1 - \frac{1}{LQ_i} \right) \cdot e_i \qquad (4.45)$$

Bringing it all together in one step, we thus can write:

$$n_i = \left(\frac{E_i}{E} \right) \cdot e \Rightarrow \text{ for } n_i = e_i \Rightarrow LQ_i = 1.0 \Rightarrow \left(\frac{e_i}{e} \right) = \left(\frac{E_i}{E} \right) \qquad (4.46)$$

Dividing both sides of the equation again gives us the expression of the location quotient:

$$\left[\left(\frac{e_i}{e} \right) \Big/ \left(\frac{E_i}{E} \right) \right] = 1.0 = LQ_i \qquad (4.47)$$

Once we understand how the location quotient is derived and how it can be used to calculate basic employment in industry i, the assumptions and short-comings of the economic base techniques are easy to understand.[1]

But before we discuss the assumptions of the location quotient approach, let us rewrite the location quotient formula as:

$$LQ_i = \left(\frac{e_i}{e}\right)\Big/\left(\frac{E_i}{E}\right) = \left(\frac{e_i}{E_i}\right)\Big/\left(\frac{e}{E}\right) \qquad (4.48)$$

Rearranging the location quotient formula allows us to define the region's consumption and production shares. The consumption share (e/E) is expressed as the region's proportion of total national employment; the production share (e_i/E_i) is determined as the region's proportion of national employment in industry i. We now can conclude that the region is exporting its excess production if the production share exceeds the consumption share, or $(e_i/E_i) > (e/E)$. Analogously, the region must import if its production share falls short relative to the consumption share, or $(e_i/E_i) < (e/E)$. Identifying consumption and pro-duction shares will help us understand the assumptions and shortcomings of the location quotient approach and modification suggestions. In the remainder of this section, we will focus on the assumptions imbedded in the location quotient method and we will see how these assumptions affect the magnitude of the LQ and, thus, the calculated level of regional basic employment. The necessary information needed to modify the locations quotients in the examples is listed in Table 4.10.

Table 4.10 Additional information of Modification of the Location Quotient Method, Boone County, KY[1]

	Boone County	The Nation
Employment in 2002		
Employment in Information Sector	1,657	3,364,485
Total Employment	70,007	128,233,921
Personal Income in 2001 (thousands of dollar)	2,702,447	8,677,490,000
Wages in 2002 (thousands of dollar)		
Wages in Information Sector	59,580	188,758,526
Total Wages	2,514,100	4,714,374,741

(1) Sources: Bureau of Economic Analysis, CA05N data series; Bureau of Labor Statistics, quarterly census of employment and wages.

---

[1] Tiebout (1962) criticized the shortcomings already in much detail in his *The Community Economic Base Study*, p.48.

4.5.3.2   Assumptions and Limitations of Location Quotients

Assumption 1: Constant consumption pattern assumption

Defining the regional consumption share as e/E—the region's proportion of total national employment—implies that employees (used as a surrogate for consumers) in both the region and the nation exhibit equal consumption behavior. It simply means that the demand for health care services, going to movies, buying CDs, or going out for dinner is identical in the study region (Boone County) and the benchmark region (the nation).

This is intuitively flawed; for example, as we would expect a region in Florida, with a large percentage of retirees to have a higher demand for health care services than the nation as a whole. On the other hand, we might expect the same Florida region to exhibit a lower demand for primary education than that of the nation. Regional differences in consumption patterns become even more obvious by considering where people go scuba diving, sailing, or winter skiing. There are more cross-county skiers in Vail, Colorado (a mountain resort area) than on the Keys in Florida (an area of island beach resorts). We would, therefore, assume that the demand for winter sport accessories would be higher in Colorado than in Florida. Alternatively, the number of persons owning a yacht is larger in Florida than in Colorado. Furthermore, wealth is not distributed evenly across the nation. Richer counties, such as suburban Westchester, New York outside of New York, City, probably have a higher demand for luxury items, such as jewelry or 42 inch plasma TVs, than the rest of the nation.

These examples clearly show that the demand for goods and services is area-specific and assuming an equal consumption pattern between a study region and its benchmark region is a potential source for errors. While there is no clear-cut solution for this issue, the literature[1] recommends replacing employment data with income data to estimate the consumption share in the location quotient formula:

$$e/E \Rightarrow y/Y \qquad (4.49)$$

where, y and Y are regional and national income by industry respectively. The rationale is that consumption is better reflected through income than through employment data. Rewriting the initial location quotient definition by using personal income, we can recalculate Boone County's information location quotient (LQ_{inf}) as:

$$LQ_{inf} = \left(\frac{e_{inf}}{y}\right) \bigg/ \left(\frac{E_{inf}}{Y}\right) = \left(\frac{1,657}{2,702,447}\right) \bigg/ \left(\frac{3,364,485}{8,677,490,000}\right) = 1.581$$

$$(4.50)$$

---

[1] Klosterman, 1990, *Community Analysis and Planning Techniques*, p. 138.

which clearly differs from the purely employment-based location quotient of 0.902 (see Table 4.8), which is below the level of self-sufficiency. However, using income-based location quotient, Boone County now appears to be specialized in providing information services and exporting excess capacities.

Assumption 2: Constant labor productivity assumption

The production share term e_i / E_i in the rearranged location quotient formula implies equal labor productivity—defined as the ratio of total output over the number of workers or the number of hours worked—across regions. For example, we can read this as one food service industry worker in Boone County generates the same amount of output as a worker does in any part of the nation. This is just never the case as. The output of the food service industry depends largely on the region's wealth, the attractiveness of the region as a tourist destination, and the level of automation. Restaurants, for example, may wash their dishes by hand or use largely automated dish washers. Output is the same, namely clean dishes. But, the labor productivity (output per worker) is different for labor intensive versus capital intensive production. Again, the location quotient approach can be refined. Here, we are substituting earnings data (w) for employment data:[1]

$$e_i / E_i \Rightarrow w_i / W_i \tag{4.51}$$

By doing so, we are taking for granted that the level of regional earnings is a better reflector of regional labor productivity than employment. Remember that wages and salaries are a large component of regional earnings. In the following example of Boone County, we substitute the industry-specific employment through the industry's total annual wages implying that regional labor productivity is reflected in regional wage rates:

$$LQ_{inf} = \left(\frac{w_{inf}}{y}\right) \Big/ \left(\frac{W_{inf}}{Y}\right) = \left(\frac{59,580}{2,702,447}\right) \Big/ \left(\frac{188,758,526}{8,677,490,000}\right) = 1.014 \tag{4.52}$$

It turns out that the location quotient for information in Boone County changes again significantly. The location quotient is now 1.014, indicating that the county is self-sufficient with respect to information services.

Another approach of addressing the labor productivity assumption listed in the literature[2] is by using an industry-specific value added[3] parameter (v_i):

---

[1] Schaffer, 1999, *Regional Impact Models*, p. 10.

[2] Issermann (1977), *The Location Quotient Approach to Estimating Regional Economic Impacts*, p. 38.

[3] Value added is defined as the value of a firm's output minus all the intermediate inputs purchased from other firms. It contains wages, interest, rent, profits, and indirect taxes.

$$e_i / E_i \Rightarrow v_i(e_i / E_i) \tag{4.53}$$

where v_i is calculated as the sector's regional value added over its national value added. The idea is the same as before where we have replaced employment with earnings (e.g., using annual wages). Wages and salaries, which at least for labor-intensive industries is the largest contributor to value added, are a better way of accounting for regional labor productivity than employment.

For both adjustments, the presumption is that regional wage rates reflect regional labor productivity. However, this is arguable as regional wage rates are also determined by regional differences in the cost-of-living. For instance, corresponding wage rates will reflect the higher cost of living in New York City as compared to Flagstaff, Arizona. Therefore, a university professor in New York City is likely to earn more than her colleague in Flagstaff so that she may afford the same standard of living. Now decide for yourself, is it appropriate to conclude that the professor in New York City is much more productive than her colleague in Flagstaff based on the difference in salaries?

Assumption 3: No cross-hauling
Cross-hauling describes the fact that a region simultaneously exports and imports the same goods and services. Obviously, some people in Detroit, home to General Motors, Chrysler and Ford headquarters, are driving Japanese, and German and other imported cars. Thus, we can conclude that, while Detroit exports its excess production of cars, it imports cars to meet local consumer preferences at the same time.

The location quotient approach assumes that local demand is met first through local production. The region is assumed to import only if the region falls short of meeting all regional demand. Excess capacities are exported after all regional demand is satisfied through regional production. While conceptually straight forward, there is little that can be done to offset the cross-hauling effects. In every industry sector where cross-hauling is common—basically all sectors that are not solely focusing on local demand—exports are underestimated and so is the level of regional basic activities. A common alternative is to do the economic base analysis using a more detailed level of industrial classification. The idea is that a higher level of disaggregation (e.g., four-, five-, or six-digit NAICS code) partly counterbalances for the possibility that exports and imports cancel at a highly aggregated level of (e.g., two- digit NAICS code). A good example to demonstrate this "offsetting effect" is the retail industry in Boone County (Table 4.11).

At the two-digit level, retail trade in Boone County has a location quotient of 1.064. The region seems to be self-sufficient in that its residents purchase all goods and services offered by retailers locally. Additionally, basic employment

Table 4.11   Retail Trade, Boone County, KY

NAICS Code	2002 NAICS Title	Area Employment (e_i)	US Employment (E_i)	Location Quotient (LQ_i)	Basic Employment (b_i)	Non-basic Employment (n_i)
44 – 45	Retail Trade	8,724	15,018,588	1.064	525	8,199
445	Food and Beverage Stores	1,114	2,869,978	0.711	0	1,114
452	General Merchandise Stores	2,312	2,814,249	1.505	776	1,536

of 525 persons is possible as nonresidents, e.g., people out-of-town, shop Boone County's retail stores as well.

At the three-digit level, it is a completely different story. Boone County is specialized in General Merchandise Stores (NAICS 452). The majority of employees fall into the non-basic employment category with a total of 1,536 workers. The remaining 776 employees are counted under basic employment serving non-residents who like to shop in Boone County. At the same time, Boone County falls short of meeting the local demand for food and beverage stores, as the LQ of 0.711 indicates. This example illustrates the method's dependency on the degree of aggregation of the data.

At the two-digit level of industry classification, Boone County has a basic employment of 525; while at the three-digit level, basic employment in the General Merchandise Store sub-sector augments basic employment to 776. This is an increase of 47.8% by only considering these two selected sub-sectors. Accounting for all seven sub-sectors of Retail Trade listed in Table 4.8 would further increase basic employment. By doing this across all industry sectors for the county, you would find that basic employment figures are highly underestimated, which in return inflates the economic base multiplier.

Assumption 4: Self-sufficiency of the benchmark region

So far we have assumed that the benchmark region, e.g., the nation, is self-sufficient. This implies that the benchmark region consumes all of what is being produced and neither exports nor imports. Therefore, net national exports—determined as exports minus imports—for any industry sector is assumed to be zero. But we all know that this is rarely the case, particularly for manufacturing industries. Consider, for example, that there are few places on this planet where we are not able to get a McDonald's Hamburger and a can of Coca Cola. There are many other industry sectors that simultaneously export and import internationally, e.g., cross-hauling. A good example is automobile manufacturing. People all over the world drive American cars as well as domestically produced autos. Many Americans also prefer imported cars, such as Mercedes and Porsche over Chevrolet and Lincoln. This leads to both an underestimation of basic employment in the nation and an overestimation of national non-basic employment.

But what does this imply for the location quotient approach? The Printing Industry in the nation (NAICS 323) is a net exporter of its product, which is indicated by the fact that its exports exceed its imports.[1] With part of the industry's output being sold overseas, many workers in printing are engaged in international export production, which in return overestimates the denominator E_{pr}/E in the location quotient formula:

$$LQ_{pr} = \left(\frac{e_{pr}}{e}\right) \bigg/ \left(\frac{E_{pr}}{E}\right) \tag{4.54}$$

Note that for the purposes of calculating regional industry's location quotient, we assume that the benchmark region is self-sufficient in that sector and that we count only employment for national domestic consumption. But because national employment in printing (E_{pr}) includes both, non-basic and basic (international employment) employee, this overstates national employment in printing (E_{pr}). As a result, the denominator (E_{pr}/E) increases, causing the location quotient (LQ_{pr}) to decrease. The bottom line here is that in the case of the printing industry, its national employment share is overestimated leading to an underestimation of regional basic employment in the industry.

To demonstrate the impacts of exporting and importing, we have selected two manufacturing industries from Boone County, namely printing and related support activities (NAICS 323) and plastic and rubber products manufacturing (NAICS 326). For simplicity in remainder of this subsection, we will call these two sectors printing and rubber/plastic. Data on these sectors' net export values and values of shipments are available through the International Trade Administration (ITA) of the U.S. Department of Commerce (www.ita.doc.gov). These trade data are compatible with the employment data as they were tabulated following the NAICS concordance and are available down to the six-digit level. Value of shipments[2] covers the received net selling values free of board (f.o.b.) of all products shipped. The data and the adjusted employment figures are listed in Table 4.12.

---

[1] Source: International Trade Administration (ITA).

[2] Source: http://quickfacts.census.gov/qfd/meta/long_58619.htm.

Table 4.12 National employment export adjustments[1]

NAICS Code	2002 NAICS Title	US Employment (E_i)	US Net Exports (million \$)	Value of Shipments (million \$)	US Non-basic Employment (Non-basic $-E_i$)	US Basic Employment (Basic $-E_i$)
323	Printing and Related Support Activities	707,566	724	100,792	702,483	5,083
326	Plastics and Rubber Products Manufacturing	846,766	− 1,142	170,717	852,430	− 5,664

(1) Source: http://www.ita.doc.gov/td/industry/otea/industry_sector/tables_naics.htm.

One possible approach of addressing the self-sufficiency assumption of the benchmark region is to break down national employment in industry i into its basic and non-basic components:[1]

$$E_i = E_i^{\text{basic}} + E_i^{\text{non-basic}} \tag{4.55}$$

Knowing the export volume of an industry sector will allow us at least to estimate the sector's basic and non-basic activities (e.g., employment). In return we can adjust the national employment in industry i (E_i) by replacing it through the estimated non-basic national employment in this industry i.

$$E_i \Rightarrow E_i^{\text{non-basic}} \tag{4.56}$$

Using the example of printing activities, we adjust national employment in printing (E_{pr}) as follows:

$$E_{\text{pr}}^{\text{basic}} = \left(E_{\text{pr}} \cdot \frac{\text{net export in printing}}{\text{value of shipments in printing}} \right)$$
$$= \left(707,566 \times \frac{724}{100,792} \right)$$
$$= 5,083 \tag{4.57}$$

$$E_{\text{pr}}^{\text{non-basic}} = E_{\text{pr}} - E_{\text{pr}}^{\text{basic}}$$
$$= 707,566 - 5,083$$
$$= 702,483 \tag{4.58}$$

In this context, net export's share of total industry shipments gives us an approximation of how many persons are employed in the basic sector for the nation. Therefore, basic national employment in printing is estimated as total national employment in printing times the ratio of net export over value of shipments. The result indicates that 5,083 persons employed by the printing industry work for

[1] Klosterman, *Community Analysis and Planning Techniques*, p. 140.

export markets. We then subtract basic employment form national employment in printing (E_{pr}) and get the non-basic employment of 702,483.

Finally, we can adjust the location quotient for printing in Boone County (LQ_{pr}) by replacing national employment in printing (E_{pr}) with national non-basic employment in printing $(E_{pr}^{non\text{-}basic})$:

$$LQ_{pr} = \left(\frac{e_{pr}}{e}\right) \Big/ \left(\frac{E_{pr}^{non\text{-}basic}}{E}\right) = \left(\frac{935}{70,007}\right) \Big/ \left(\frac{702,483}{128,233,921}\right) = 2.438 \qquad (4.59)$$

As a result, the location quotient in Boone County increases from 2.421 (see Table 4.8) to 2.438, which in return will increase the printing sector's basic employment. The absolute change of 0.017 (0.7%) comes from the fact that a small portion of the value of shipments is exported (i.e., net export). The larger the share of net exports of the value of shipments, the larger the expected change in the location quotient and vice versa.

We conclude this section with three more remarks. First, net export data, as used in the example, are available for manufacturing-related activities only. The reason is that most service-related activities are predominantly oriented towards the national market. For instance, Americans buy computers, clothing, and food items from China, but Americans will have a hard time buying health care or warehousing in China. Some exceptions to this more general rule are that communication, utilities, finance, and insurance services are traded to some extent between the United States and Canada. Some services in the United States are increasingly provided offshore by places like India, for instance, costumer services by phone.

Second, in the case of a negative net export value—where imports exceed exports for an industry sector—the change in location quotient is the opposite of the above example. Conceptually, this means that nationwide there is not enough employment in industry i (E_i) to satisfy all demand, which understates national employment in industry i (E_i). In return this overestimates regional basic employment and inflates the location quotient in industry i. The plastic/rubber industry included in Table 4.12 is an example of an industry with a negative net export (e.g., $-1,142$). The location quotient (LQ_{pl}) adjustment for plastic/rubber can be recalculated as:

$$LQ_{pl} = \left(\frac{e_{pl}}{e}\right) \Big/ \left(\frac{E_{pl}^{non\text{-}basic}}{E}\right) = \left(\frac{1,770}{70,007}\right) \Big/ \left(\frac{852,430}{128,233,921}\right) = 3.803$$

resulting in a decrease in the LQ_{pl} from 3.829 to 3.803. As you can see, the direction of change for values of negative net exports is just the opposite of the change for values of positive net exports.

Finally, the four adjustment procedures we have discussed can be applied individually or cumulatively. For instance, using a more detailed level of industrial classification already increases the accuracy of the basic employment estimation. However, probably due to the tremendous increase in data requirements and computational complexity; in practice, few adjustments are actually applied to basic employment estimation.

The benchmark region caveat
An additional issue of which to be aware is the importance of the choice of benchmark region on the outcome of any economic base analysis. This choice defines the denominator in the location quotient formula, and, therefore, has a large impact on the magnitude of the location quotient and on the level of basic employment. To demonstrate this, we calculated the LQs for manufacturing in Boone County using (1) the Nation and (2) Kentucky as benchmark regions. The results are summarized in Table 4.13.

Table 4.13 Location quotient comparison by using alternative benchmark regions

	Boone County	Kentucky	The Nation
Manufacturing Employment	10,360	275,466	15,209,192
Total Employment	70,007	1,717,978	128,233,921
Location Quotients	–	0.923	1.248

Using the nation as benchmark region, the location quotient for manufacturing (LQ_{mfg}) is calculates as:

$$LQ_{mfg} = \frac{10,360/70,007}{15,209,192/128,233,921} = 1.248$$

The alternative use of Kentucky as the benchmark region significantly alters the location quotient as the example below shows:

$$LQ_{mfg} = \frac{10,360/70,007}{275,466/1,717,978} = 0.923$$

As this particular case demonstrates, the choice of the benchmark region has a significant impact on the outcome for the location quotient. In particular, using the nation as the reference region, Boone County appears to be specialized in manufacturing with excess production assumed to be exported. Choosing Kentucky as reference region alters the outcome. In this case, Boone County appears not to be self-sufficient in manufacturing products and we would conclude that the county needs to import manufacturing products in order to meet local demand.

Despite the shortcomings of location quotients, they are still widely used simply because they are conceptually easy to understand, simple to apply, and require a minimum of time and effort to find the appropriate data. However, their ease in use can lead to tremendous misinterpretations and one must critically evaluate all calculated location quotients. In order to avoid the embarrassment of presenting erroneous location quotients, combining the assumption and the location quotient method can help identifying conceptual errors. Some industry sectors are more easily and accurately assessed using the assumption method as they clearly serve either the regional or nonregional markets. Regardless of the outcome of the location quotient method, adjustments should be made based on your specific knowledge of the local industry. Among others, sectors that are often pre-specified as either purely basic or non-basic are:

local government = non-basic.

state and federal governments = basic.

hotel and lodging = basic; but local conventions, weddings, flower shows, and other local events may be partly considered non-basic activities.

real estate = non-basic; but high growth areas may have location quotients greater than one.

construction = non-basic; but area's with a larger population growth than observed nationwide can have location quotients greater than one.

food services and drinking places = non-basic; but predominantly tourist areas (e.g., Orlando, Florida) can be more basic than non-basic activities.

tourist industry = basic; but tourist locations also attract local visitors.

The exact assignment of employment to either basic or non-basic activites depends much on your common sense. In the case of local governments it is probably not difficult to imagine that they serve only their local residents. On the other hand, you will not stay in a hotel in your hometown while your apartment is next door. Thus, hotel and lodging are usually entirely basic activities. More difficult is the task for food services and drinking places. Generally, we would assume that they serve primarily local customers. You most certainly will not open a restaurant targeting people out of town. However, there are some clear cases where the food services and drinking places can have a large basic component. Orlando, Florida, is one of the cities that mainly lives off of tourism. Assigning all food services and drinking places to the non-basic sector would lead to underestimate basic activities in Orlando. Another example would be Ithaca, New York, a small town with a large out of town student body attending Cornell University. There are a large number of restaurants and bars in the college town next to campus. Although the students live in Ithaca, many of them receive supported from their parents, with the money coming from outside of the town. Thus, some of the restaurants and bars may be classified as basic activities.

We conclude this section with the understanding that location quotients are still very popular among planners as they allow a quick and inexpensive assessment of an area's economic strengths and weaknesses and opportunities for further economic growth. A solid knowledge of a region's economy and on-site interviews can help to improve the location quotient method and avoid drawing incorrect conclusions.

4.5.4 Minimum Requirement Method

The minimum requirement (MR) method, first introduced by Ullman and Dacey in 1960[1], is very similar conceptually to the location quotient method. Rather than comparing a study region to the national or state economy, the minimum requirement method compares the study region to **a set of similar comparison regions**. Using employment as an example, the minimum requirement method compares a study region's employment shares for industry i (e_i/e) to the employment shares for the same industry i of a whole set of similar regions, based on a variety of selection criteria. Using selection criteria guarantees that these selected regions are suitable for serving as comparison regions.

In the example, we have selected comparison counties using the following criteria:

(1) They must be comparable in population size to the study region, Boone County;

(2) They must be part of a larger metropolitan statistical area and, therefore, exhibit some urban characteristics;

(3) They must be located in the Midwest.

Following the selection criteria, we have identified six counties that we will use for comparison with Boone County to demonstrate the minimum requirement method. There is no specification for the number of areas needed for an adequate comparison. The general rule is: the more the better. Tiebout[2] lists this number as 100, but also mentions that this increases the possibility of including some mavericks—counties that exhibit some unusual economic patterns because of peculiar regional circumstances.

The minimum requirement method works as follows:

(1) select several similar regions for comparison using a set of selection criteria (e.g., population size, location, part of a metropolitan statistical area, etc.).

(2) calculate all industry sector's employment shares for the study region (e_i/e) and all comparison regions (E_i/E).

(3) identify the smallest industry employment share for each industry

---

[1] Edward Ullman and Michael Dacey. 1960. The minimum requirements approach to the urban economic base. In: *Papers and Proceedings, Regional Science Association* 6, pp. 175 – 194.

[2] Tiebout, 1962, *The community economic base study*, p. 50.

i ($E_i^{\min} / E^{\min}$) among all regions, including the study region. The smallest industry employment share for each industry i ($E_i^{\min} / E^{\min}$) determines the level of non-basic employment (n_i) required to satisfy local demand for any of these regions.

(4) compute basic sector employment (b_i) for the study region by using each industry's minimum share ($E_i^{\min} / E^{\min}$) in the formula:

$$b_i = \left[\left(\frac{e_i}{e}\right) - \left(\frac{E_i^{\min}}{E^{\min}}\right)\right] \cdot e \qquad (4.60)$$

The similarity of the minimum requirement and the location quotient methods can be seen by writing the location quotient (LQ_i) using minimum employment shares ($E_i^{\min} / E^{\min}$) rather than national employment:

$$LQ_i^{MR} = \left(\frac{e_i}{e}\right) \Big/ \left(\frac{E_i^{\min}}{E^{\min}}\right) \qquad (4.61)$$

It is important to note that the employment ratio in the denominator ($E_i^{\min} / E^{\min}$) now refers to the region with the smallest employment share for that particular industry i and not to the nation or state as usually done in the location quotient approach. The identified "minimum shares" region produces just enough goods and services to meet local demand and as such does not export. In general, there are two possible outcomes:

(1) The study region is the "minimum employment shares region", such that:

$$\left(\frac{e_i}{e}\right) = \left(\frac{E_i^{\min}}{E^{\min}}\right)$$

Therefore, there is no basic employment (b_i) in industry sector i in the study region. Under these circumstances, the location quotient equals one ($LQ_i^{MR} = 1$), indicating that the study region is self-sufficient but has no excess production of i for export.

(2) The minimum employment shares region for industry i is identified as one of the selected comparison regions, or $\left(\frac{e_i}{e}\right) > \left(\frac{E_i^{\min}}{E^{\min}}\right)$.

Our study region will have some basic employment (b_i), and the location quotient (LQ_i^{MR}) will be greater than one.

Computationally, the minimum requirement method is easy to perform.

However, studies with large numbers of comparison regions create additional challenges. Imagine identifying dozens of comparison regions and collecting all the necessary employment data for each. For the purpose of demonstrating the minimum requirement approach, we compare Boone County with six selected counties in Kentucky, Indiana, and West Virginia. The selected counties are:

Campbell County, KY   Hardin County, KY
Daviess, County, KY   Clark County, IN
Warren, County, KY   Cabell County, WV

As indicated in Table 4.14, all comparison region counties meet the above selection criteria—they are of similar population size, are part of a metropolitan statistical area, and are located in the Midwest United States. Table 4.14 further contains all employment data used for calculating the minimum employment shares. Unfortunately, in some counties employment figures are not disclosed for reasons of confidentiality (indicated as "D"), but are included in total county employment numbers.

Having identified counties for comparison, in the next step, we calculate the employment shares for all industries: for Boone County (e_i / e) and for all comparison counties (E_i / E). Employment shares are simply the ratio of industry employment (e_i and E_i) over total employment (e and E) in a county. All employment shares are listed in Table 4.15. For instance, Clark County's information sector's (NAICS 51) employment share is calculated as:

$$\frac{E_i}{E} = \frac{85}{15,190} = 0.0056$$

Next, for each industry i, we identify the smallest industry employment share (E_i^{min} / E^{min}), or the smallest number in a row. All minimum employment shares are highlighted in Table 4.15. For instance, the minimum employment share for retail trade belongs to Clark County at 0.1223 (1,857/15,190). We can interpret this minimum employment share as follows: for any of the counties listed in Table 4.15, a minimum of 12.23 percent of all employees are required to work in retail trade to meet local demand in any of these counties. Employees beyond this minimum employment share are assumed to serve non-regional customers and are therefore classified as basic employment. For Boone County, where 12.46 percent of the workforce is employed by retail trade, 12.23 percent are therefore assumed to be required for regional (non-basic) customers, while the remaining 0.23 percent serve non-regional (basic) customers.

The minimum employment shares for each industry i (E_i^{min} / E^{min}) are listed in Table 4.16. They allow us to calculate the level of basic employment (b_i) for the study region. For the calculation of basic employment in Boone County we

Table 4.14   Employment by major industries—Boone County and comparison regions, 2002[1]

County		Boone	Campbell	Hardin	Daviess	Warren	Clark	Cabell
MSA,state		Cincinnati, OH-KY-IN	Cincinnati, OH-KY-IN	Elizabeth-town, KY	Owensboro, KY	Bowling Greene, KY	Louisville, KY-IN	Huntington-Ashland, WV-KY-OH
July 1, 2002 Pop Estimate		93,290	88,604	95,724	91,694	94,730	98,198	95,266
NAICS Code	Industry Sector							
11	Agriculture, Forestry, Fishing and Hunting	79	(D)	(D)	114	64	(D)	22
21	Mining	35	(D)	(D)	131	171	(D)	48
22	Utilities	481	(D)	(D)	(D)	(D)	41	305
23	Construction	2,230	1,376	1,557	2,743	2,559	1,817	2,099
31 – 33	Manufacturing	10,360	2,975	6,258	6,159	8,619	2,007	5,046
42	Wholesale Trade	5,166	888	910	1,812	1,749	769	2,163
44 – 45	Retail Trade	8,724	3,727	5,399	5,639	6,829	1,857	6,975
48 – 49	Transportation and Warehousing	12,855	(D)	(D)	(D)	(D)	911	636
51	Information	1,657	261	749	552	619	85	910
52	Finance and Insurance	4,506	458	1,229	1,574	1,446	328	2,214
53	Real Estate and Rental and Leasing	934	507	440	430	540	154	667
54	Professional, Scientific, and Technical Services	1,341	955	983	(D)	1,191	409	1,931
55	Management of Companies and Enterprises	995	249	121	(D)	1,320	18	154
56	Administrative and Support and Waste Mgm.	4,233	988	1,557	1,743	2,301	889	3,491
61	Educational Services	267	94	98	401	130	22	196
62	Health Care and Social Assistance	2,897	3,380	3,311	3,771	5,812	1,208	9,540
71	Arts, Entertainment, and Recreation	489	365	160	316	300	238	281
72	Accommodation and Food Services	5,821	3,485	3,247	3,379	4,653	1,294	4,918
81	Other Services (except Public Administration)	1,733	906	1,116	1,292	1,099	411	1,722
92	Public Administration Total	5,107	5,166	10,620	7,999	8,122	2,476	7,083
92	Federal Government	1,161	308	4,534	301	789	102	1,118
92	State Government	273	2,017	1,123	1,062	3,537	70	2,629
92	Local Government	3,673	2,841	4,963	6,636	3,796	2,304	3,336
99	Unclassified	97	27	19	12	16	5	10
Total Employment		70,007	26,371	38,814	40,937	49,166	15,190	50,411

(1) Data: Bureau of Labor Statistics, Quarterly Census of Employment and Wages (QCEW).

Table 4.15 Employment shares by major industries – Boone County and comparison regions, 2002

NAICS Code	Industry Sector	Boone Cincinnati, OH-KY-IN	Campbell Cincinnati, OH-KY-IN	Hardin Elizabeth-town, KY	Daviess Owensboro, KY	Warren Bowling Greene, KY	Clark Louisville, KY-IN	Cabell Huntington-Ashland, WV-KY-OH
11	Agriculture, Forestry, Fishing and Hunting	0.0011	(D)	(D)	0.0028	0.0013	(D)	0.0004
21	Mining	0.0005	(D)	(D)	0.0032	0.0035	(D)	0.0010
22	Utilities	0.0069	(D)	(D)	(D)	(D)	0.0027	0.0061
23	Construction	0.0319	0.0522	0.0401	0.0670	0.0520	0.1196	0.0416
31 – 33	Manufacturing	0.1480	0.1128	0.1612	0.1505	0.1753	0.1321	0.1001
42	Wholesale Trade	0.0738	0.0337	0.0234	0.0443	0.0356	0.0506	0.0429
44 – 45	Retail Trade	0.1246	0.1413	0.1391	0.1377	0.1389	0.1223	0.1384
48 – 49	Transportation and Warehousing	0.1836	(D)	(D)	(D)	(D)	0.0600	0.0126
51	Information	0.0237	0.0099	0.0193	0.0135	0.0126	0.0056	0.0181
52	Finance and Insurance	0.0644	0.0174	0.0317	0.0384	0.0294	0.0216	0.0439
53	Real Estate and Rental and Leasing	0.0133	0.0192	0.0113	0.0105	0.0110	0.0101	0.0132
54	Professional, Scientific, and Technical Services	0.0192	0.0362	0.0253	(D)	0.0242	0.0269	0.0383
55	Management of Companies and Enterprises	0.0142	0.0094	0.0031	(D)	0.0268	0.0012	0.0031
56	Administrative and Support and Waste Mgm.	0.0605	0.0375	0.0401	0.0426	0.0468	0.0585	0.0693
61	Educational Services	0.0038	0.0036	0.0025	0.0098	0.0026	0.0014	0.0039
62	Health Care and Social Assistance	0.0414	0.1282	0.0853	0.0921	0.1182	0.0795	0.1892
71	Arts, Entertainment, and Recreation	0.0070	0.0138	0.0041	0.0077	0.0061	0.0157	0.0056
72	Accommodation and Food Services	0.0831	0.1322	0.0837	0.0825	0.0946	0.0852	0.0976
81	Other Services (except Public Administration)	0.0248	0.0344	0.0288	0.0316	0.0224	0.0271	0.0342
92	Public Administration Total	0.0729	0.1959	0.2736	0.1954	0.1652	0.1630	0.1405
92	Federal Government	0.0166	0.0117	0.1168	0.0074	0.0160	0.0067	0.0222
92	State Government	0.0039	0.0765	0.0289	0.0259	0.0719	0.0046	0.0522
92	Local Government	0.0525	0.1077	0.1279	0.1621	0.0772	0.1517	0.0662
99	Unclassified	0.0014	0.0010	0.0005	0.0003	0.0003	0.0003	0.0002
	Total	1.0000	1.0000	1.0000	1.0000	1.0000	1.0000	1.0000

Table 4.16   Basic employment calculation—Boone County, KY, 2002

Boone County, KY, 2002 NAICS Code	Industry Sector	Regional Employment Share (e_i/e)	Minimum Employment Share (E_i^{min}/E^{min})	Total Employment (e_i)	Basic Employment (b_i)	Nonbasic Employment (n_i)
11	Agriculture, Forestry, Fishing and Hunting	0.0011	0.0004	79	49	30
21	Mining	0.0005	0.0005	35	0	35
22	Utilities	0.0069	0.0027	481	294	187
23	Construction	0.0319	0.0319	2,230	0	2,230
31 – 33	Manufacturing	0.1480	0.1001	10,360	3,353	7,007
42	Wholesale Trade	0.0738	0.0234	5,166	3,528	1,638
44 – 45	Retail Trade	0.1246	0.1223	8,724	161	8,563
48 – 49	Transportation and Warehousing	0.1836	0.0126	12,855	11,971	884
51	Information	0.0237	0.0056	1,657	1,267	390
52	Finance and Insurance	0.0644	0.0174	4,506	3,290	1,216
53	Real Estate and Rental and Leasing	0.0133	0.0101	934	224	710
54	Professional, Scientific, and Technical Services	0.0192	0.0192	1,341	0	1,341
55	Management of Companies and Enterprises	0.0142	0.0012	995	910	85
56	Administrative and Support and Waste Mgm.	0.0605	0.0375	4,233	1,610	2,623
61	Educational Services	0.0038	0.0014	267	168	99
62	Health Care and Social Assistance	0.0414	0.0414	2,897	0	2,897
71	Arts, Entertainment, and Recreation	0.0070	0.0041	489	203	286
72	Accommodation and Food Services	0.0831	0.0825	5,821	42	5,779
81	Other Services (except Public Administration)	0.0248	0.0224	1,733	168	1,565
92	Public Administration Total	0.0729	0.0729	5,107	1,434	3,673
92	Federal Government	0.0166	0.0067	1,161	1,161	0
92	State Government	0.0039	0.0039	273	273	0
92	Local Government	0.0525	0.0525	3,673	0	3,673
99	Unclassified	0.0014	0.0002	97	84	13
Total				70,007	28,758	41,249

apply the formula:

$$b_i = \left[\left(\frac{e_i}{e} \right) - \left(\frac{E_i^{\min}}{E^{\min}} \right) \right] \cdot e \tag{4.60}$$

For example, basic employment in manufacturing (b_{mfg} —NAICS 31 – 33) for Boone County is calculated as:

$$b_{\mathrm{mfg}} = (0.1480 - 0.1001) \times 70{,}007 = 3{,}353$$

All calculations can easily be carried out using spreadsheet software. However, attention must be paid to those sectors that are clearly (intuitively) either basic or non-basic. For Boone County, we classify federal and state governments as entirely basic, while local government is deemed an entirely non-basic activity. Understanding the region's economy prior to classifying what industry sectors might be either completely basic or non-basic helps to avoid incorrect assumptions. Altogether, based on the minimum requirement method, 28,758 employees of the total workforce of 70,007 employees in Boone County are classified as basic, while the remaining 41,249 employees serve in non-basic activites.

Like other methods described under the economic base analysis umbrella, the minimum requirement method has its shortcomings. The first and probably most significant criticism of the minimum requirement method is the absence of imports. Calculating basic employment (b_i) for industry i as:

$$b_i = \left[\left(\frac{e_i}{e} \right) - \left(\frac{E_i^{\min}}{E^{\min}} \right) \right] \cdot e \tag{4.60}$$

assumes that the study region never falls short of meeting local demand. In other words, the study region must never import goods and services. The minimum requirement approach allows only for two possible scenarios:

(1) $\left(\dfrac{e_i}{e} \right) = \left(\dfrac{E_i^{\min}}{E^{\min}} \right)$, which implies a location quotient (LQ_i) of exactly 1.0.

The study region is just self-sufficient and neither exports nor imports.

(2) $\left(\dfrac{e_i}{e} \right) > \left(\dfrac{E_i^{\min}}{E^{\min}} \right)$, which results in a location quotient greater than 1.0.

The study region therefore exports its excess production.

Technically, the minimum requirement method does not account for the possibility of a location quotient (LQ_i) of less than 1.0, the only scenario under which the study region must import to meet local demand.

Second, increasing the number of comparison regions and/or choosing a higher level of sector disaggregation inevitably decreases the magnitude of the minimum shares, thereby increasing the level of exports or basic activities. The more regions are included among the comparison regions, the greater the possibility of including regions with almost no needs in certain industries. Without excluding the aberrant region's minimum shares from the analysis, we basically reduce local needs for that industry to almost zero and overemphasize other regions' export activities in that sector. Tiebout (1962), for instance, recommended excluding the lowest minimum share values from the analysis to avoid the fallacy resulting from regions with unusually low local demand for certain products.

Third, the minimum requirement method should not be done in isolation from other economic base methods. Combining it with the assumption method helps to avoid calculating basic employment for sectors that are clearly oriented towards local markets only (e.g., local government) and vice versa.

4.6   Evaluating Regional Economies Using the Economic Base Multiplier and Shift-Share Analysis

The last section of this chapter on economic base theory deals with its applicability for evaluating economic impacts and decomposition of economic changes. **Economic impact studies** usually assess regional economy changes in selected key variable, such as employment, income, or output, following an initial exogenous change. An example of an initial exogenous change, also referred to as an injection, exogenous inflow, or increase in basic activities, can be a local manufacturer receiving a lucrative contract that will significantly increase its export sales. The question in which economic developers are interested is how to estimate the total impact on, for instance, regional employment following a change in basic employment. The total impact on a region's employment exceeds the original impact—the change in basic employment. This effect—also referred to as **ripple-effect**—can be explained by the fact that an increase in export demand for a region's goods and services will create additional economic activities beyond the initial exogenous inflow of spending. For instance, for an industry i to increase its output it also requires an increase of its own inputs. And part of these new inputs will come from non-basic sectors, which support basic activities. Technically, the economic base multiplier is a ratio measuring the stimulus and the cumulative multiplier effect following the initial stimulus. In the case of employment, the employment multiplier measures the expected total employment change in the region following a change in basic employment. The multiplier thus accounts for two effects: the initial stimulus, or direct effect, and the multiplier, or indirect effect.[1]

---

[1] For the time being we use a more simplistic approach by dividing the total effect into direct and indirect effects. In the following chapter on input-output analyses we will revise this statement and account for as many as three effects, namely the direct, indirect, and induced effect.

4.6.1 The Economic Base Multiplier

The economic base model builds on the notion of an economic dichotomy. Every economy can be divided into two sectors: a basic sector which depends largely on conditions external to a study region and a non-basic sector which depends widely on conditions within the region. In a hypothetical framework consisting only of a basic sector and a non-basic sector, we assume that the basic sector is the driving force of the regional economy. Thus, increases in export activities will lead to economic development. From that, we can directly infer that the increases in basic activities ultimately lead to increases in non-basic activities and, therefore, to an overall increase of the region's economic activities.

For instance, an increase in export sales generates additional income—inflow of money—for the region. In return, part of this additional income is spent on regionally produced goods and services while the other part is spent on imports (e.g., leakages). The part of additional income spent locally, therefore, increases the level of regional economic activities, which in return generates new additional income, of which a part is again spent on regional goods and services and a part is spent on imports, and so on. This chain reaction of economic activities, the ripple-effect, following an exogenous injection is captured in its entity by the economic base multiplier. In this sense, the economic base multiplier is a measure of the entire level of economic activities following a stimulus in the regional basic sector. Whereby the magnitude of the economic base multiplier depends largely on the part of the (additional) income spent that remains within the region, which in return also depends directly on the leakage, i.e., the money leaving the region.

Using economic base multipliers is thus one way of estimating economy-wide impacts following an exogenous injection. In this section, we will in particular discuss the two most commonly used economic base multipliers: the employment multiplier and the income multiplier.

4.6.1.1 The Employment Multiplier

The employment multiplier (EM) is defined as the ratio of total employment (e) over basic employment (b) for a study region:

$$\mathrm{EM} = \frac{e}{b} = \frac{\text{total employment}}{\text{basic employment}} \qquad (4.62)$$

where,

$$e = \sum_i e_i \text{ and } b = \sum_i b_i$$

All it requires to calculate the employment multiplier is to estimate aggregate basic employment (b). This can be done using the assumption, location quotient, or minimum requirement method. For Boone County, Kentucky, using the location quotient method we have estimated total basic employment (b) as 24,478 (see Table 4.8). The employment multiplier (EM) for Boone County for the year 2002 can be calculated as:

$$\text{EM} = \frac{e}{b} = \frac{70,007}{24,478} = 2.86$$

We can read the multiplier as follows: an increase in basic employment due to an increase in export activities of 1 person will lead to a total increase in regional employment of 2.86 persons.

Although the multiplier is a single number, e.g., 2.86, it must be understood that it represents the ratio of total over basic employment. The multiplier is thus usable as a predictive tool for answering questions of the type: "**If... then...**". For example, what happens to total regional employment if basic employment in retail trade increases because of an expansion of the Florence shopping mall?

Based on the simple fact that total area employment (e) is the sum of basic (b) and non-basic employment (n), or:

$$e = b + n \tag{4.63}$$

we can rearrange and rewrite the multiplier notation using simple algebra. In return this will provide us with more ways to interpret the multiplier result. One alternative way of rearranging the multiplier notation is:

$$\text{EM} = \frac{e}{b} = \frac{b+n}{b} = 1 + \frac{n}{b} = 1 + 1.86 \tag{4.64}$$

The emphasis here is now on the distinction between direct and indirect effects. Clearly, the direct effect, or the initial change in basic employment, is represented by the ratio n/b, which equals one. This is not surprising, considering how we have defined the initial change in basic employment. If ten more retailers open stores at the Florence mall and create a total of 80 new jobs, all of which serve nonresidents, these 80 new jobs would thus represent the direct effect.

Therefore, after subtracting the direct effect from the total multiplier value, what remains must be the indirect effect, or the multiplier effect. It is expressed as the ratio of non-basic employment (n) over basic employment (b), or n/b. It accounts for all of additional employment that will be created in the region following the initial increase of basic employment. The magnitude of the multiplier effects, thus, clearly depends upon the ratio of non-basic over basic employment. For the example of the 80 new basic retail jobs in the Florence mall it would imply that an additional 149 jobs would be created (e.g., $80 \times 1.86 = 149$).

Tiebout showed how the ratio of non-basic over total area employment (n/e)—which in the Keynesian framework refers to the marginal propensity to consume (mpc) —can be used to express the economic base multiplier. In the case of Boone County's 2002 employment multiplier, we can rearrange the multiplier definition using employment as

$$\text{EM} = \frac{e}{b} = \frac{1}{b/e} = \frac{1}{\dfrac{e-n}{e}} = \frac{1}{1-\dfrac{n}{e}} = \frac{1}{1-\text{mpc}} = \frac{1}{1-0.65} = 2.86 \qquad (4.65)$$

Here, the ratio of non-basic employment to total employment (n/e) is the equivalent to the marginal propensity to consume locally produced goods (mpp), the economic base equivalent of the Keynesian marginal propensity to consume (mpc). Considering that the consumption of locally produced commodities is a non-basic activity, the ratio of non-basic over basic employment can be used as a proxy for the marginal propensity to consume locally produced goods (mpp). The outcome must, however, be the same as before. And in the case of Boone County, the employment multiplier indeed equals 2.86.

Multipliers may change from year to year. We used data from one single year, namely 2002 in the calculation, therefore the multiplier refers to that particular point in time. For past and present years where data are readily available, we must recalculate basic multipliers for each year. The more challenging task, however, is to answer so-called "if ... then ..." questions, which often involves future projections.

So far, we have repeatedly stated that the employment multiplier is the ratio of total over basic employment. Knowing the employment multiplier therefore means having, to some extent, knowledge of the regional economic structure, namely, how much employment is dependent on export demand versus how much employment serves local consumption. Consequently, projecting future employment using economic base multipliers calculated from historic employment data explicitly assumes that the future economic structure of an area's economy remains unchanged. For short-term projections this assumption is quite reasonable as it takes usually several years for the whole economic structure to respond a change. For example, increasing basic retail employment in the Florence mall by 80 employees will not lead to a total employment increase of 229 jobs in the county within a few months. It will take time for the newly generated income to be re-spent locally and, in return, increase the need for more employment. Evaluating changes in total employment (Δe) following changes in basic employment (Δb) is thus one possible practical application of the employment multiplier.[1] Alternatively and in particular for regions demonstrating fast economic changes—for instance, fast employment growth—simple regression

---

[1] Klosterman (1990) also demonstrates how to estimate basic employment for long-term total employment projections using the constant-share method and an invariant historical multiplier (p. 189).

analysis provides the means to project the employment multiplier into the near future based on a series of historic employment multipliers.[1] Either way, we make assumptions about the future structure of the region under study as we choose an invariant employment multiplier or historic employment multipliers.

Having referred to the problem of time in economic base analysis, we want to conclude this discussion by emphasizing that the employment multiplier notation used in this section does not include a time reference for two simple reasons: first, it keeps the notations simpler, and second we explicitly stated that the multiplier refers only to the year for which it is been calculated.[2] For instance, the Boone County employment multiplier is for the year 2002 as we have used 2002 employment data to calculate it. The explicit conclusion from that is that the multiplier reflects the economic conditions for only this particular year.

Referring once again to the hypothetical example of the 80 new basic retail jobs in the Florence mall, the economic base projection model using 2002 Boone County employment multiplier (EM) can be written as:

$$\Delta e = \Delta b \cdot \text{EM} \tag{4.66}$$

where, the symbol Δ refers to changes. Note that we are answering the so-called "If... then..." question. **If** basic retail employment in Florence mall increases by 80 employees due to more people from outside using the mall as a shopping destination, **then** the economic base theory tells us that the total employment (e) in the area will increase by 229 jobs following this increase in basic employment, or:

$$\Delta e = \Delta b \cdot \text{EM} = 80 \times 2.86 = 229$$

Whereby for this particular case, the direct effect is the initial stimulus— or the 80 new basic retail jobs—and the indirect effect is the multiplier effect— or the 149 additional jobs created in the region resulting from the initial stimulus. And of course, total effect is the sum of direct and indirect effect. Last we want to reemphasize that the initial employment change must occur in the basic sector which means that these 80 newly created jobs will serve people from outside the county using the mall as shopping destination.

Although employment data are most widely used for calculating economic base multipliers, other economic data, such as wages, earnings, or income also may be suitable for estimating the basic activity level of a study region. Conceptually there is no difference to the basic multiplier using employment. For instance, the basic multiplier (BM) using wages can be expressed as:

---

[1] Schaffer (1999) recommends regression analysis for calculating marginal multipliers (p. 9).

[2] Alternatively, the employment multiplier could be expressed as: EM^t where t refers to the year the data were collected.

$$BM = \frac{w}{bw} = \frac{\text{total regional wages}}{\text{total wages in the basic sector}} \qquad (4.67)$$

4.6.1.2 The Income Multiplier (IM)[1]

In a simplified world without governments, major regional spending is attributable to local consumption, local investment, and exports. The spending in these three sectors in return leads to income for local residents. The main assumption for deriving an income multiplier IM is that both exports (X) and local investment (I) depend on forces outside the region. We already stated earlier that exports clearly depend on external market demand and, as such, on economic conditions outside the study region. Local investment, at least in the short-term, also reflects outside forces, such as interest rates and outside investment opportunities. As a result, both exports and local investments are considered exogenous and, therefore, are not explained by the economic base model.

Referring back to Fig. 4.1—the circular flow of income and expenditures—there is a direct positive relationship between household income and local consumption. Generally, the higher people's income is, the more they can spend either locally—on regional consumption—or non-locally—on imports or leakages. And, the higher the marginal propensity to purchase regionally produced products (mpp), the more they consume locally and, therefore, the higher the multiplier effect. Comparing the economic base multiplier to the Keynesian multiplier, we also made a cross-reference between the marginal propensity to purchase regional products (mpp) in the economic base model and the marginal propensity to consume (mpc) in the Keynesian model. While this is conceptually straight forwards, in the context of local income generation, we must refine the term marginal propensity to purchase regionally produced products (mpp).

Zooming in on how income is generated in a regional economy we will find that the regional income level actually depends on two factors:

(1) pcl: the propensity to consume locally captures how much of their income residents spend locally. Let us say for example residents in Boone County spend 80 percent of their income locally; pcl = 0.80. The remaining 20 percent must be spent on imports.

(2) ipls: the income propensity of the local sales dollar. Local firms and businesses can employ nonresidents or buy inputs from outside the region. Both cases represent a leakage where money is leaving the region. For example, an employee commuting from neighboring Hamilton County to Boone County for work increases the leakage as she will take her income back home. To complete the example of Boone County, we assume the ipls to be 0.8125.

---

[1] This section follows closely Charles Tiebout (1962), pp.58 – 61.

The income multiplier can then be defined as:

$$IM = \frac{1}{1-(pcl \cdot ipls)} \tag{4.68}$$

where IM is the income multiplier. The product of pcl times ipls resembles the formerly determined marginal propensity to purchase regional products (mpp). For Boone County the income multiplier thus is calculates as:

$$IM = \frac{1}{1-(0.8 \times 0.815)} = 2.86$$

Tiebout (1962) in the 1960's referred to the income multiplier as the simpler approach compared to the economic base multiplier. However, considering the Internet and today's computing power, Tiebout's statement might no longer hold. The ease of downloading employment, income, and earnings data from the Internet and the simplicity of deriving basic activities and economic base multipliers using spreadsheet software make the economic base multiplier a practicable tool for assessing economic impacts.

4.6.1.3   Critics of the Economic Base Multiplier

Every economic model is based on a set of assumptions. The big advantage of the economic base multiplier analysis are:

(1) it builds on a conceptually simple economic framework,

(2) it does not require a lot of training, time, or money to be carried out using a spreadsheet software,

(3) it helps make more informed decisions about pursuing new economic development projects,

(4) it emphasizes economic interdependencies, and

(5) the availability of necessary data makes it an applied method that should be included in the tool box of every economic development planner.

However, it also comes with shortcomings that one must keep in mind when using economic base multipliers:

(1) First, for calculating employment multipliers we need to estimate total basic employment. Therefore, employment multipliers depend highly on the accuracy of the preceding basic employment estimation and inherit all assumptions built into the method used to estimate basic employment. For instance, the magnitude of the employment multiplier depends to a large extent to the choice of the benchmark region and the level of industrial detail.

(2) The size of the regional economy itself is also crucial for the magnitude of the economic base multiplier. Generally, increasing sizes of regional economies lead to larger multipliers as the ratio of non-basic to basic activities (n/b) increases. Larger diversified metropolitan regions offer most commodities locally and, therefore, only rely to a small extent on exports. Outcomes are large economic

base multipliers, often in a magnitude beyond the point of plausibility. Contrarily, smaller and more specialized regions have smaller multipliers as they depend to a larger extent on exports.

(3) Time plays a role as it takes years for the total multiplier effect to take place.

(4) Multiplier analysis assumes the absence of supply constraints, which means that any increase in demand can be met through local production. Further, there are no changes in prices or the economic structure which could lead to a change in the ratio of non-basic to basic activities (n/b).

4.6.2   Shift-Share Analysis

So far, the economic base analysis has primarily employed single year data. We have compiled a regional economic profile, have calculated basic economic activities, and have used this information in the economic base projection model to answer how total economic activities in the region are expected to change as a result of an exogenous stimulus in the basic sector. Contrary to this rather **static** evaluation, **shift-share analysis** compares regional economic changes (e.g., growth or decline) for a selected time period to economic changes of a selected benchmark region. Shift-share analysis is a widely used economic base approach that assesses past observed growth or decline of an industry i between two points in time (e.g., $t \rightarrow t+n$). It is a more **dynamic** approach as it uses data for two points in time. Generally, shift- share analysis can be done for any two points in time data are available. But unless the study focuses on understanding historic economic trends, more recent data should be used. Time periods of five to ten years are commonly used for most analyses. Important to note is that the outcome of the shift-share analysis can vary substantially by using a five-year period versus a ten-year period. The underlying idea here is that regional industry growth or decline may have several causes; some may be purely regional and some may reflect to a large extent state-or national economic trends. More specifically, shift-share analysis breaks down a regional industry sector's change (e.g., growth or decline) into three individual components: national growth share (ns_i), industry mix share (im_i), and regional growth share (rs_i), and use this information to shed light into what made the regional economy grow differently from the reference region.

The first component compares regional economic growth in industry i to the general economic growth of the benchmark region—the **national growth share** (ng_i). The assumption is that overall observed economic growth in a benchmark region will inevitably be reflected in regional economic growth. For instance, given that Boone County is located in Kentucky an overall employment increase in Kentucky for all industries combined is likely to positively influence employment growth in Boone County. In the case of using employment, the national growth share (ng_i) calculates the expected employment growth that would have occurred in Boone County's industry i if this industry sector's employment would have grown at exactly the same rate as combined employment in Kentucky. More formal, this can be written as:

$$\mathrm{ng}_i = e_i^t \cdot G^{t \to t+n} \tag{4.69}$$

where,

ng_i — the national growth share in industry i;

e_i^t — regional employment in industry i in the year t;

$G^{t \to t+n}$ — average growth rate for employment in the benchmark region for the time interval $t \to t+n$;

t — beginning year of the time period;

n — number of years included in the time interval.

A second component captures economic change attributable directly to the so-called **regional industry mix** (im_i). The aim of this component is to assess whether or not certain industries in the reference region grew faster or slower compared to overall regional growth of the reference region and to translate this observed difference in (employment) growth onto the corresponding industry sector in the study region. Outcome of this decomposition is to identify whether or not the study region specializes in industries that experience faster or slower than average growth in the reference region. For Boone County, industries with positive mix components thus will indicate regional specialization in industries that are growing at a faster rate than overall economic growth in Kentucky and vice versa. This observation is of importance as you might expect that a regional industry mix of state-wide fast growing industries will attribute more to regional growth than a regional industry mix of slow growing industries. The regional industry mix can be expressed as:

$$\mathrm{im}_i = e_i^t \cdot (G_i^{t \to t+n} - G^{t \to t+n}) \tag{4.70}$$

where,

im_i — the regional industry mix share in industry i;

$G_i^{t \to t+n}$ — growth rate for employment in industry i in the benchmark region for the time interval $t \to t+n$.

The third component accounts for the difference in growth between the study and the reference regions that can be credited solely to regional factors— **regional growth share** (rg_i). Some industries grow faster/slower in the study region than those in the benchmark region. In any case the regional growth share attributes the regional growth or decline to purely regional factors and as such indicates regional economic strengths or weaknesses. The regional growth share evaluates a regional industry's competitive situation within the larger economy of the reference region due to regional comparative advantages such as industrial clustering, infrastructure and resource availability, or non-unionized labor markets. The formal definition of the regional growth share is:

$$rg_i = e_i^t \cdot (g_i^{t \to t+n} - G_i^{t \to t+n}) \qquad (4.71)$$

where,

rg_i — the regional growth share in industry i;

$g_i^{t \to t+n}$ — growth rate for employment in industry i in the study region for the time interval $t \to t + n$.

The outcome of adding these three components of growth together, see below, is the **total growth** (tg_i), which in turn is equivalent to the actual growth or decline of industry i in the study region, e.g., $g_i^{t \to t+n}$.

$$
\begin{aligned}
tg_i &= ng_i + im_i + rg_i \\
&= e_i^t \cdot (G^{t \to t+n}) + e_i^t \cdot (G_i^{t \to t+n} - G^{t \to t+n}) + e_i^t \cdot (g_i^{t \to t+n} - G_i^{t \to t+n}) \\
&= e_i^t \cdot (G^{t \to t+n} + G_i^{t \to t+n} - G^{t \to t+n} + g_i^{t \to t+n} - G_i^{t \to t+n}) \\
&= e_i^t \cdot g_i^{t \to t+n}
\end{aligned} \qquad (4.72)
$$

The choice of the benchmark region for a shift-share analysis is of major importance for the outcome of the analysis. Generally a larger benchmark region is chosen of which the local region is a part. The state or the nation is a common choice. Alternatively, a larger metropolitan region might be chosen if compatible with the motivation for the study. We choose Kentucky as benchmark region for the study for the following reasons:

(1) Boone County lies in Kentucky;

(2) Both the county and the state are very rural in character;

(3) Many decisions influencing economic competitiveness follow political rather than regional boundaries.

For instance, tax incentives and the provision of utilities and infrastructure follow political boundaries closely rather than regional boundaries across states. We could also use the nation as the reference region, particularly for industries underlying more national trends. One may argue that national trends are more influential for the economic performance than state or regional trends for industry sectors like transportation, biomedical research, telecommunication, and information services.

The reminder of this section describes in detail how to break down total growth into three individual growth components for manufacturing industries in Boone County. Employment data for 1997 were converted from SIC to the

NAICS subject to data availability. However, no exact match is possible, particularly at the three-digit level; some data were not disclosed for reasons of confidentiality. Further, three-digit SIC sectors often split into two or more three-digit NAICS sectors. Consequently, the employment data in Table 4.17 must be considered an approximation rather than a reflection of true employment trends.

Table 4.17   Manufacturing employment data for Boone County and Kentucky[1]

		Boone County Employment		Kentucky Employment	
		2002 (e_i^{t+n})	1997 (e_i^t)	2002 (E_i^{t+n})	1997 (E_i^t)
31 – 33	Total Manufacturing	10,360	12,332	275,466	314,528
311	Food Manufacturing	1,498	1,265	23,551	23,613
314	Textile Product Mills	365	295	2,714	9,593
322	Paper Manufacturing	708	1,279	11,015	13,743
323	Printing and Related Support Activities	935	1,488	13,554	16,614
325	Chemical Manufacturing	686	778	13,958	18,530
326	Plastics and Rubber Products Mfg.	1,770	2,046	17,542	19,849
333	Machinery Manufacturing	1,545	2,359	21,010	36,702
336	Transportation Equipment Mfg.	1,317	923	56,932	57,359
N/A	Other Manufacturing	1,536	1,899	115,190	118,525
Total area employment		70,007	59,540	1,717,978	1,657,494

(1) Source: Bureau of Labor Statistics, Quarterly Census of Employment and Wages.

Employment data for Boone County and Kentucky were chosen for 1997 and 2002. Total manufacturing employment is broken down into three-digit NAICS sub-sectors. The most significant sub-sectors are listed explicitly while all remaining sectors are lumped into **Other Manufacturing**. The first analytical step is to calculate absolute and percent employment changes for Boone County and Kentucky for the five-year period between 1997 and 2002.

The growth rates listed in Table 4.18 basically provide all the information necessary for breaking down total growth (tg_i) into its three components. Absolute changes are calculated by subtracting employment in the later year from employment in the earlier year, or:

$$\Delta e_i^{t \to t+n} = e_i^{t+n} - e_i^t \qquad (4.73)$$

where,

$\Delta e_i^{t \to t+n}$ — absolute change in regional employment in industry i from $t \to t + n$;

e_i^t — regional employment in industry i in year t;

e_i^{t+n} — regional employment in industry i in year $t + n$.

Table 4.18 Absolute and percent employment changes in Boone County and Kentucky

	Boone County		Kentucky	
	Absolute Change in Employment $(\Delta e_i^{t \to t+n})$	Growth Rate $(g_i^{t \to t+n})/\%$	Absolute Change in Employment $(\Delta E_i^{t \to t+n})$	Growth Rate $(G_i^{t \to t+n})/\%$
31 – 33 Total Manufacturing	– 1,972	– 15.99	– 39,062	– 12.42
311 Food Manufacturing	233	18.42	– 62	– 0.26
314 Textile Product Mills	70	23.73	– 6,879	– 71.71
322 Paper Manufacturing	– 571	– 44.64	– 2,728	– 19.85
323 Printing and Related Support Activities	– 553	– 37.16	– 3,060	– 18.42
325 Chemical Manufacturing	– 92	– 11.83	– 4,572	– 24.67
326 Plastics and Rubber Products Mfg.	– 276	– 13.49	– 2,307	– 11.62
333 Machinery Manufacturing	– 814	– 34.51	– 15,692	– 42.76
336 Transportation Equipment Mfg.	394	42.69	– 427	– 0.74
N/A Other Manufacturing	– 363	– 19.12	– 3,335	– 2.81
Total Area Employment	10,467	17.58	60,484	3.65

Analogously, state-wide absolute employment changes are derived as:

$$\Delta E_i^{t \to t+n} = E_i^{t+n} - E_i^t \qquad (4.74)$$

where,

ΔE_i^t — absolute change in state employment in industry i from $t \to t + n$;

E_i^t — state employment in industry i in the earlier year t;

E_i^{t+n} — state employment in industry i in the later year $t + n$.

For instance, the absolute employment change of 233 persons in food manufacturing (NAICS 311) in Boone County is calculated as:

$$\Delta e_i^{1997 \to 2002} = e_i^{2002} - e_i^{1997} = 1,498 - 1,265 = 233$$

Employment growth rates are calculated as:

$$\text{growth rate} = \frac{\text{employment in later year } t+n - \text{employment in earlier year } t}{\text{employment in earlier year } t}$$

(4.75)

In particular, we need three individual growth rates:
(1) the overall growth rate $(G^{t\to t+n})$ for employment in the benchmark region:

$$G^{t\to t+n} = \frac{E^{t+n} - E^t}{E^t},$$

(4.76)

(2) the growth rate $(G_i^{t\to t+n})$ for employment in the benchmark region by industry i:

$$G_i^{t\to t+n} = \frac{E_i^{t+n} - E_i^t}{E_i^t},$$

(4.77)

(3) and the growth rate $(g_i^{t\to t+n})$ for employment in the study region by industry i:

$$g_i^{t\to t+n} = \frac{e_i^{t+n} - e_i^t}{e_i^t}$$

(4.78)

where,

e_i^t — regional employment in industry i in year t;

e_i^{t+n} — regional employment in industry i in year $t+n$;

E_i^t — state employment in industry i at time t;

E_i^{t+n} — state employment in industry i at time $t+n$;

E^t — aggregated state employment at time t;

E^{t+n} — aggregated state employment at time $t+n$.

Using these growth rate formulas, we define the necessary growth rates for Boone County as follows:
(1) the average growth rate $(G^{t\to t+n})$ for employment in Kentucky is

$$G^{1997\to 2002} = \frac{1,717,978 - 1,657,494}{1,657,494} = 0.0365 = 3.65\%$$

indicating that total employment in Kentucky grew by 3.65% between 1997 and 2002.
(2) the growth rate $(G_i^{t\to t+n})$ for employment in Kentucky in food manufacturing:

$$G_{\text{food}}^{1997-2002} = \frac{23,551-23,613}{23,613} = -0.0026 = -0.26\%$$

meaning that employment in food processing establishments in Kentucky declined by 0.26% for the five year period.

(3) and the growth rate $(g_i^{t \to t+n})$ for employment in Boone County in food manufacturing:

$$g_{\text{food}}^{1997-2002} = \frac{1,498-1,265}{1,265} = 0.1842 = 18.42\%$$

showing that Boone County's employment in food processing establishments grew by 18.42%.

The decomposition of total growth (tg_i) into its three components, namely national growth share (ng_i), regional industry mix (im_i), and regional growth share (rg_i), is demonstrated below as a three-step procedure. While this task can easily be performed in one single table using spreadsheet software, for demonstration purposes we show each individual component calculation individually in a separate table.

4.6.2.1   National Growth Share Calculations

What portion of change—either growth or decline—in regional employment in industry $I(tg_i)$ can be explained through the observed trend in overall growth (or decline) of the benchmark region? In the case of Boone County it explains how much each industry sector might have grown (or declined) over the observed time span because of an observable positive or negative growth trend in Kentucky. More specifically, overall employment in Kentucky grew from 1997 to 2002 by 3.65%. From this we might expect a positive spill-over on employment growth by industry in Boone County for this specific time period. The national growth shares (ng_i) are calculated by multiplying regional employment in industry i by the overall growth rate for the benchmark region, or:

$$ng_i = e_i^t \cdot G^{t \to t+n} \tag{4.69}$$

For example, the national growth share for food manufacturing (ng_{food}) is calculated as:

$$ng_{\text{food}} = 1,265 \times 0.0365 = 46$$

Food manufacturing employment in Boone County would have increased by 46 persons for the time period from 1997 to 2002 if it would have followed the overall employment growth in Kentucky of 3.65% for this five-year period. As

Table 4.19 clearly shows, all national growth shares must be positive as Kentucky employment increased by 3.65%.

Table 4.19 National growth share calculations, manufacturing industries, Boone County

		National Growth Share (ng_i)	Boone County Employment 1997 (e_i')	Average Employment Growth Rate in Kentucky $(G^{t \to t+n})$
311	Food Manufacturing	46	1,265	0.0365
314	Textile Product Mills	11	295	0.0365
322	Paper Manufacturing	47	1,279	0.0365
323	Printing and Related Support Activities	54	1,488	0.0365
325	Chemical Manufacturing	28 =	778 ×	0.0365
326	Plastics and Rubber Products Mfg.	75	2,046	0.0365
333	Machinery Manufacturing	86	2,359	0.0365
336	Transportation Equipment Mfg.	34	923	0.0365
N/A	Other Manufacturing	69	1,899	0.0365
31 – 33	Total Mfg. National Growth Share	450		

4.6.2.2 Industrial Mix Share Calculations

What portion of change—either growth or decline—in regional employment in industry i (tg_i) can be attributed to the fact that industries in the benchmark region might grow faster or slower than the observed trend in overall growth (or decline) of the benchmark region? As a matter of fact, the average growth rate for employment in the benchmark region $(G^{t \to t+n})$ is only a summary measure. Individual industries usually do not exactly mirror this overall growth rate. Some industries grow faster, some grow slower, and others even show opposite trends, e.g., decline while total employment in the benchmark region increases. For the food manufacturing industry in Kentucky, we have observed a marginal decrease of 0.26% (e.g., 62 jobs) for the period from 1997 to 2002. With an overall employment growth in Kentucky of 3.65% this means that food manufacturing industries did not follow the overall economic growth. How does this difference in growth of 3.91% (e.g., $-0.26\% - 3.65\%$) translate onto the food manufacturing industry in Boone County? The industrial mix component (im_{food}) is calculated by multiplying the study region employment by the difference in growth:

$$im_i = e_i^t \cdot (G_i^{t \to t+n} - G^{t \to t+n}) \qquad (4.70)$$

For food manufacturing in Boone County, the industry mix share is

$$\text{im}_{\text{food}} = 1,265 \times (-0.0026 - 0.0365) = -49$$

Assuming an identical industry mix in Boone County to that in Kentucky, food manufacturing would have lost 49 jobs for the five-year period from 1997 to 2002. As Table 4.20 indicates, all industrial mix shares are negative. We further see that Boone County's manufacturing industries $(31-33)$ would have lost a total of 2,691 jobs if there were no structural difference between the county and the state.

Table 4.20   Industry mix share calculations, manufacturing industries, Boone County

		Regional Industry Mix Share (im_i)		Boone County Employment 1997 (e_i')		Employment Growth Rate by Industry $(G_i^{t \to t+n})$	Average Employment Growth Rate in Kentucky $(G^{t \to t+n})$
311	Food Manufacturing	-49		$1,265$		-0.0026	-0.0365
314	Textile Product Mills	-222		295		-0.7171	-0.0365
322	Paper Manufacturing	-301		$1,279$		-0.1985	-0.0365
323	Printing and Related Support Activities	-328		$1,488$		-0.1842	-0.0365
325	Chemical Manufacturing	-220	$=$	778	$\times$	-0.2467	-0.0365
326	Plastics and Rubber Products Mfg.	-312		$2,046$		-0.1162	-0.0365
333	Machinery Manufacturing	$-1,095$		$2,359$		-0.4276	-0.0365
336	Transportation Equipment Mfg.	-41		923		-0.0074	-0.0365
N/A	Other Manufacturing	-123		$1,899$		-0.0281	-0.0365
31–33	Total Mfg. Regional Industry Mix Share	$-2,691$					

4.6.2.3   Regional Growth Share Calculations

What portion of the change—either the growth or decline—in regional employment (tg_i) can be attributed directly to local factors and, as such, reflect the region's competitive position in a particular industry i? This share component measures to what extent the growth/decline of a specific industry i different from its state-wide counterpart. Employment in the food manufacturing industry in Boone County grew by 18.42%. The difference in growth in food manufacturing employment between the county and the state is translated directly into the regional growth share component using the formula:

$$\text{rg}_{\text{food}} = e_{\text{food}}^{1997} \cdot (g_{\text{food}}^{1997 \to 2002} - G_{\text{food}}^{1997 \to 2002}) \qquad (4.79)$$

and results in:

$$rg_{food} = 1,265 \times [0.1842 - (-0.0026)] = 236$$

While food manufacturing industries lost statewide employment, Boone County on the other hand shows a strong competitive position as indicated by a large positive regional growth share component of 236 jobs. Manufacturing-wide, Table 4.21 indicates that Boone County is very competitive in food manufacturing, textile product mills, chemical manufacturing, machinery manufacturing, and transportation equipment manufacturing.

Table 4.21   National growth share calculations, manufacturing industries, Boone County

		Regional Growth Share (rg_i)	Boone County Employment 1997 (e'_i)	Employment Growth Rate by Industry in Boone County $(g_i^{t \to t+n})$	Employment Growth Rate by Industry in Kentucky $(G_i^{t \to t+n})$
311	Food Manufacturing	236	1,265	0.1842 –	−0.0026
314	Textile Product Mills	282	295	0.2373 –	−0.7171
322	Paper Manufacturing	−317	1,279	−0.4464 –	−0.1985
323	Printing and Related Support Activities	−279	1,488	−0.3716 –	−0.1842
325	Chemical Manufacturing	100 =	778 ×	−0.1183 –	−0.2467
326	Plastics and Rubber Products Mfg.	−38	2,046	−0.1349 –	−0.1162
333	Machinery Manufacturing	195	2,359	−0.3451 –	−0.4276
336	Transportation Equipment Mfg.	401	923	0.4269 –	−0.0074
N/A	Other Manufacturing	−310	1,899	−0.1912 –	−0.0281
31–33	Total Mfg. Regional Growth Share	269			

Adding the three components of growth together then results in total growth (tg_i) as indicated in Table 4.22. For food manufacturing, total employment change is calculated as:

$$tg_{food} = ng_{food} + im_{food} + rg_{food}$$
$$= 49 - 49 + 236$$
$$= 236$$

Breaking down employment data into three individual components helps to shed light on the reasons why some industries grew and while others declined between 1997 and 2002. For instance, machinery manufacturing is the biggest loser of manufacturing employment in Boone County with 814 jobs. The main reason for this tremendous job loss lies in the industry mix share component

Table 4.22 Total growth calculations, manufacturing industries, Boone County

		Boone County Employment 1997	National Growth Share	Regional Industry Mix Share	Regional Growth Share	Total Employment Change	Boone County Employment 2002
31 – 33	Total Manufacturing	12,332	450	– 2,691	269	– 1,972	10,360
311	Food Manufacturing	1,265	46	– 49	236	233	1,498
314	Textile Product Mills	295	11	– 222	282	70	365
322	Paper Manufacturing	1,279	47	– 301	– 317	– 571	708
323	Printing and Related Support Activities	1,488	54	– 328	– 279	– 553	935
325	Chemical Manufacturing	778	28	– 220	100	– 92	686
326	Plastics and Rubber Products Mfg.	2,046	75	– 312	– 38	– 276	1,770
333	Machinery Manufacturing	2,359	86	– 1,095	195	– 814	1,545
336	Transportation Equipment Mfg.	923	34	– 41	401	394	1,317
N/A	Other Manufacturing	1,899	69	– 123	– 310	– 363	1,536

(e.g., 1,095) or that statewide machinery manufacturing declined relatively by 46.40% (e.g., – 42.76% – 3.65%) when compared to the total economy in Kentucky. Machinery manufacturing in Boone County increased its performance when compared with Kentucky as indicated by a positive regional share component of 195 jobs. In general, Boone County's manufacturing industries gained in competitiveness (e.g., regional growth share of 269), took advantage of an overall aggregate employment change in Kentucky (e.g., national growth share of 450), but was not spared by a state-wide employment drop in manufacturing industries (e.g., industry mix component of 2,691). The overall county-wide employment loss in manufacturing amounts to 1,972 jobs.

4.6.2.4 Summary

While shift-share analysis is a relative straight forward method of analyzing changes in economic performance by comparing economic change in a study region to that of a larger reference region, it also relies on a set of assumptions.

First, the choice of the benchmark region has a major impact on the outcome of the shift-share analysis. Industrial clustering and different comparative advantages of regions inevitably lead to differences in economic growth in general and for individual industries. For example, while employment grew in Kentucky by 3.65% between 1997 and 2002, at the national level employment grew by 5.94% for the same time period. Thus using the nation as benchmark region will lead to different results and conclusions.

Second, the choice of the time period is rather arbitrary and often heavily influenced by data availability. Going too far back in time may raise the question whether observed trends are still relevant in present contexts. On the other hand, shorter time periods are more likely influenced by unusual short-term economic fluctuations. As a general rule, time periods of five to ten years seem appropriate for most analyses. Change of industrial classification system, such as the replacement of SIC system by the NAICS in the United States, complicates shift-share analysis for the periods when data conversion from one to the other system is necessary.

Third, like any other technique in economic base analysis it does not answer the question of why. The shift-share analysis helps to understand **what** happened and **where** it happened. It helps to identify strengths and weaknesses of local economies in comparison to larger benchmark regions. Unfortunately, it does not answer the question of **why** a regional economy has a comparative (dis)advantage over the benchmark region and what could be done to improve regional competitiveness and make a region more attractive for firms to choose it as their business location.

Finally, the level of industrial aggregation will alter the outcome of the shift-share approach. In general, using more detailed levels of aggregation (e.g., 3-digit or 4-digit NAICS) will provide more exhaustive results for understanding regional economic changes. Deciding for a less detailed level of industrial aggregation (e.g., 2-digit NAICS) runs the risk that valuable and important information on specific industry sectors is lumped together with other industries and as such lost for the analyst.

Review Questions

1. In order to make economic development policy recommendations, it is important to understand the regional economy, its markets and who the essential actors are. Describe the working mechanism of a local/regional economy as discussed in the chapter. Include all actors and markets.

2. What is the theoretical foundation of the economic base theory? More specifically, how can the economic base theory be used as a conceptual framework for explaining regional economic growth?

3. Explain in detail the importance of the benchmark (i.e., comparison) region for location quotients and shift-share calculations. What benchmark region would you choose for calculating location quotients and shift-share analysis for a county in California? Explain your answers.

4. The North American Industry Classification System (NAICS) was introduced in 1997. What are the major improvements of the NAICS over the 1987 U.S. Standard Industrial Classification (SIC) system?

5. What exactly does a location quotient identify? In other words, what would you use the LQ method for? Explain the assumptions and limitations of the location quotient method.

6. Which should be larger, the location quotient of a small town or a large metropolitan area? Explain your answer.

7. Name five typical basic businesses and five typical non-basic businesses.

8. Briefly explain how the minimum requirement approach works.

9. The employment multiplier is one way to predict economy-wide changes in employment following an increase in export demand. Briefly explain how you derive the employment multiplier and how it can be used. And more specifically, what is meant when referring to direct and indirect effects in multiplier analysis?

10. Shift-share analysis breaks down economic growth/decline into three individual components. Identify and describe these three components of economic growth/decline.

Exercises

Table 4.23 contains data on average annual employment for Metropolis, a hypothetical urbanized area for the years 1994 and 2004. In addition, Table 4.24 shows employment data for a benchmark region, again for 1994 and 2004. The employment data are grouped according to the 2-digit 2002 North American Industry Classification System (NAICS) identifying a total of 20 industry sectors.

Table 4.23 Annual average employment, Metropolis, 1994 and 2004

2002 NAICS Code	2002 NAICS Title	Metropolis Employment 1994	Metropolis Employment 2004
11	Agriculture, Forestry, Fishing and Hunting	20	30
21	Mining	40	30
22	Utilities	450	350
23	Construction	2,350	2,900
31 – 33	Manufacturing	6,000	4,700
42	Wholesale Trade	2,750	3,100
44 – 45	Retail Trade	8,400	8,300
48 – 49	Transportation and Warehousing	1,850	3,300
51	Information	1,800	2,050
52	Finance and Insurance	4,300	5,050

Continued

2002 NAICS Code	2002 NAICS Title	Metropolis Employment 1994	Metropolis Employment 2004
53	Real Estate and Rental and Leasing	900	1,300
54	Professional, Scientific, and Technical Services	2,900	4,100
55	Management of Companies and Enterprises	350	1,500
56	Administrative and Support and Waste Mgm.	3,500	5,200
61	Educational Services	2,800	3,850
62	Health Care and Social Assistance	5,050	7,200
71	Arts, Entertainment, and Recreation	2,500	900
72	Accommodation and Food Services	2,750	5,650
81	Other Services (except Public Administration)	1,800	2,350
92	Public Administration	3,800	4,100
Total		54,310	65,960

Table 4.24   Annual average employment, Benchmark Region, 1994 and 2004

2002 NAICS Code	2002 NAICS Title	Benchmark Region Employment 1994	Benchmark Region Employment 2004
11	Agriculture, Forestry, Fishing and Hunting	13,000	15,000
21	Mining	18,000	12,000
22	Utilities	48,000	35,000
23	Construction	203,000	254,000
31 – 33	Manufacturing	1,081,000	1,023,000
42	Wholesale Trade	223,000	248,000
44 – 45	Retail Trade	616,000	673,000
48 – 49	Transportation and Warehousing	140,000	200,000
51	Information	114,000	129,000
52	Finance and Insurance	198,000	225,000
53	Real Estate and Rental and Leasing	62,000	73,000
54	Professional, Scientific, and Technical Services	166,000	241,000
55	Management of Companies and Enterprises	11,000	82,000
56	Administrative and Support and Waste Mgm.	203,000	333,000
61	Educational Services	358,000	414,000
62	Health Care and Social Assistance	525,000	654,000
71	Arts, Entertainment, and Recreation	163,000	70,000
72	Accommodation and Food Services	249,000	415,000
81	Other Services (except Public Administration)	148,000	179,000
92	Public Administration	211,000	225,000
Total		4,750,000	5,500,000

Using the data provided in these two tables, compile an economic profile for Metropolis showing the city's economic specializations and identify growth patterns of its industry sectors.

1. Use graphs to identify regional specialization by comparing Metropolis's employment shares by industry with the employment shares of the benchmark region. In addition, make a graph that shows the employment growth or decline by industry sector.

2. Calculate the location quotients (LQ) for all industry sectors. Based on the magnitude of calculated location quotients, identify the industry sectors in which Metropolis appears to be specialized. Do the identified industry sectors of specialization match the ones identified graphically?

3. Using the location quotient method, identify basic employment for each industry sector and calculate the economic base multiplier.

4. Assuming an increase in employment in transportation and warehousing by 250 new jobs, what is the projected increase in total employment in Metropolis?

5. Do a complete shift-share analysis including calculations of national growth share, industrial mix share, and regional growth share. How much of total observed employment growth can be attributed to the local competitiveness of Metropolis?

References

Bendavid-Val, Avrom. 1991. *Regional and Local Economic Analysis for Practitioners*, 4th ed. Westport, CT: Praeger Publishers.

Blair, J. and R. 2000. *Economic Analysis in Practice of Local Government Planning*. Washington DC: International City Managers Association.

Blakely, Edward J. 1994. *Planning Local Economic Development*. Thousand Oaks, CA: Sage Publications.

Casler, S.D. 1989. A theoretical context for shift and share analysis. *Journal of Regional Science*, 18: 463 – 469.

Cortright, Joseph and Andrew Reamer. 1998. *Socioeconomic Data for Understanding your Regional Economy*. Washington, DC: Economic Development Administration, U.S. Department of Commerce.

De la Court, Pieter. 1659. *'t Welvaren der Stadt Leiden*. Available online at: http://www.childandfamilystudies.leidenuniv.nl/index.php3?c = 268.

Deller, S. and M. Shields. 1998. Economic impact modeling as a tool for community economic development. Paper prepared for presentation at the Presidential Symposium, Mid-Continent Regional Science Association Meetings, Rockford, IL (June 4 – 6).

Farness, Donald. 1989. Detecting the economic base: new challenges. *International Regional Science Review*, 12(3): 319 – 328.

Fothergill, S. and G. Gudgin. 1979. In defense of shift-share analysis. *Regional and Urban Economics*, 12: 249 – 255.

Gibson, Lay James. 1997. Using economic base analysis to solve development planning problems. *Applied Geographic Studies*. 1(3): 169 – 186.

Hoyt, Homer and Arthur M. Weimer. 1948. *Principles of Urban Real Estate*. New York: The Ronald Press Company.

Isard, Walter. 1960. *Methods of Regional Analysis; an Introduction to Regional Science*. Cambridge, MA: MIT Press.

Isard, W. and S. Czamanski. 1965. Techniques for estimating local and regional multiplier effects of changes in the level of major government programs. Papers (Peace Research Society International), III: 19 – 45.

Isserman, A. M. 2000. *Economic Base Studies for Urban and Regional Planning in the Profession of City Planning: Changes, Images, and Challenges, 1950 – 2000*. New Brunswick, NJ: Center for Urban Policy Research.

Keynes, John M. 1936. The General Theory of Employment, Interest and Money. Macmillan: Cambridge University Press. For Royal Economics Society.

Klosterman, Richard E. 1990. *Community Analysis and Planning Techniques*. Savage, MD: Rowman & Littlefield Publishers, Inc.

Koven, Steven G. and Thomas S. Lyons. 2003. *Economic Development: Strategies for State and Local Practice*. Washington, DC: International City/County Management Association (ICMA).

Krikelas, Andrew C. 1992. Why regions grow: a review of research on the economic base model. *Federal Reserve Bank of Atlanta Economic Review*, 77(4): 16 – 29.

Krumme, Guenther. 1968. Werner Sombart and the economic base concept. *Land Economics*, 44(1): 112 – 116.

Krumme, Guenther. 2001. Website on economic base theory and analysis. Available online at http://faculty.washington.edu/krumme/350/econbase.html.

Lichty, R. and K. Knudsen. 1999. Measuring regional economic base. *Economic Development Review*, 47 – 52.

Maki, Wilbur R. and Richard W. Lichty. 2000. *Urban Regional Economics: Concepts, Tools, Applications*. Ames, IA: Iowa State University Press.

Mayers, Dowell 1992. *Analysis with Local Census Data—Portraits of Change*. San Diego, CA: Academic Press Inc.

McClean, Mary L. and Kenneth P. Voytek. 1992. *Understanding Your Economy: Using Analysis to Guide Local Strategic Planning*. Chicago, MI: Planners Press.

Nussbaum, Frederick L. 1933. *A History of the Economic Institutions of Modern Europe*. New York, NY: F.S. Crofts & Co.. 2002/2001 reprint available from Beard Books.

Reed, Christine M., B.J. Reed and Jeffrey S. Luke. 1987. Assessing readiness for economic development strategic planning, *Journal of the American Planning Association*, 53(4): 521 – 530.

Richardson, Harry W. 1985. Input-output and economic base multipliers: looking backward and forward. *Journal of Regional Science*, 25(4): 607 – 661.

Schaffer, William A. 1999. Regional impact models. In: The Web Book of Regional Science. Available online at http://www.rri.wvu.edu/WebBook/Schaffer/index.html.

Sombart, Werner. 1927. *Der Moderne Kapitalismus*. 3 Volumes, Verlag von Duncker & Humblot München, Germany.

Tiebout, Charles. 1962. *The Community Economic Base Study*. Supplementary Paper No. 16, New York, NY: The Committee for Economic Development.

Ullman, Edward and Michael Dacey. 1960. The Minimum Requirements Approach to the Urban Economic Base, Papers and Proceedings, *Regional Science Association* 6: 175 – 194.

Chapter 5   Input-Output Analysis for Planning Purposes

5.1   Introduction to Input-Output Analysis

The goal of this chapter is to introduce the fundamentals of input-output (I-O) analysis and its use in economic impact analysis and economic development planning. Input-output analysis has been around for decades in various disciplines of economics and is widely used by researchers, policy analysts, and practitioners. Applications of input-output analysis can be found in such economic sub-disciplines as agricultural, resource, environmental, transportation, energy, education, and tourism economics. More recently, input-output analysis has become a strong force in the field of planning and economic geography, reinforced by readily available commercial software and data packages.

   The first attempt at an accounting system, which led to today's input-output tables, was undertaken by the French economist François Quesnay. In 1758, Quesnay published his "Tableau Économique" to explain the interrelationship of production, distribution and use of national wealth by means of tracing expenditures in a circular economic system—the "Tableau Économique". Many scholars picked up on this idea of an accounting framework, including Adam Smith, David Ricardo, Karl Marx, and Leon Walrus, but it was Wassily Leontief who developed the input-output framework as we know it today. In his 1928 manuscript entitled "Die Wirtschaft als Kreislauf" Leontief presented the economy as a circular framework and referred explicitly to **cost items**—the inputs—and **return items**—the outputs. Research in the 1930s then led to his 1936 and 1941 publications, *Quantitative input and output relations in the economic system of the United States* and *The structure of American economy, 1919 – 1929*, in which he introduced the analytical input-output framework and for which he was awarded the Nobel Memorial Prize in Economic Science in 1973.[1] Seventy years later, the principle idea of Leontief's input-output framework remains the same.

   While there is much written on the input-output framework per say, textbooks

---

[1] More on the evolution of input-output analysis can be found in: (1) Polenske and Skolka (1974), *Introduction in Advances in Input-Output Analysis.* (2) Stone (1986) in Readings in Input-Output Analysis: *Theory and Applications*, edited by Ira Sohn. (3) Kurz, Dietzenbacher, and Lager (1998), *Introduction to Part I: Foundations of Input-Output Analysis.* (4) Both of Leontief 's 1928 and 1936 manuscript are included in Kurz, Dietzenbacher, and Lager (1998), Vol. I.

pay little attention to how input-output analysis relates to economic base analysis and national economic accounting systems. In Chapter 4, we described the economic base framework as a simplification of the circular flow of income and expenditure framework which is widely used to describe an economy (Fig. 4.2). In particular, we saw that the economic base framework simplifies the portrayal of the economy on the final demand side (e.g., the right-hand side in the income flow diagram in Fig. 5.1 by distinguishing only between basic and non-basic activities).

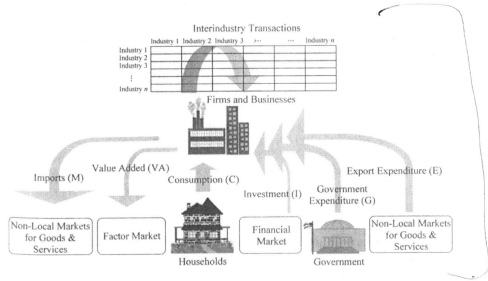

Figure 5.1   Flow of income and expenditure in an input-output framework

To explain the input-output framework we begin, once again, with the circular flow of the income and expenditure diagram, focusing now on the firms and businesses or "industries". As indicated in Fig. 5.1, the input-output framework takes a close look at the industries—their sources of income and how they spend it. In particular, the input-output framework records financial transactions of industries with respect to final demand consumption (e.g., household, investment, government, and export expenditures), their contribution to value added (e.g., wages, interest, rent, and profit), and their imports. The centerpiece of input-output tables, which makes them different from the national industry and products accounts (NIPA), is the explicit treatment of inter-industry transactions—also referred to as intermediate inputs. While intermediate inputs are not counted towards the region's gross regional product (GRP) (to avoid double-counting), the level of inter-industry transactions plays a main role in input-output analysis.

The starting point for deriving input-output tables is the economic accounts of firms and businesses. The United Nations (UN) Statistics Division maintains a system of national accounts (SNA) including data for more than 200 countries. Following internationally used concepts and accounting rules, this system of national accounts presents a comprehensive accounting system consisting of a coherent, consistent and integrated set of macroeconomic accounts, balance sheets, and tables.[1] Governments, including the United States, have well established national accounting systems to provide a coherent and comprehensive snapshot of the Nation's economy. In the United States, the national economic accounting system has three major branches: (1) the **national industry and products accounts**, which focus on the value and composition of national output and the distribution of income generated in its production; (2) the **capital finance accounts** (e.g., flow of funds accounts), which display the role of financial institutions in the transformation of savings into investment (e.g., changes in assets and liabilities); and (3) the **input-output account**, emphasizing the flow of goods and services among the producing sectors of the economy, the value added of each business, and the composition of final demand sales. The building blocks of each of these three branches of the national economic accounting system are the economic accounts of firms and businesses, namely: (1) the balance sheet, which shows the firm at one point in time; (2) the statement of income and retained earnings, focusing on net income for the period between balance sheets; and (3) the statement of change in financial position indicating the firm's change in working capital. With this information at hand, production accounts can be derived, which must be balanced according to accounting principles.[2]

As an example, the production account in Table 5.1 is set up for the industry sector transportation and warehousing, NAICS 48 – 49, based on information from business economic accounts. For simplicity, we will refer to it as transportation. All firms and businesses engaged in the production of transportation services are lumped together into one industry sector, namely transportation. As stated in previous chapters, Boone County is the home of the Cincinnati/Northern Kentucky International Airport, the main airport for the entire metropolitan region. According to airport administration, the airport served 22.5 million passengers in 2000, employs currently more than 15,000 people, and annually pumps an estimated 3.9 billion dollar into the regional economy.[3]

The production account identifies six industries—extraction, utilities, construction, manufacturing, transportation, and services. Each industry sector produces a unique commodity, labeled accordingly. Industries producing more than one commodity are labeled according to their main activity. Hence,

---

[1] United Nations Statistics Division: http://unstats.un.org/unsd/nationalaccount/default.htm.

[2] According to the United Nations Statistics Division, the production account "records the activity of producing goods and services as defined within the SNA. Its balancing item, gross value added, is defined as the value of output less the value of intermediate consumption and is a measure of the contribution to GDP made by an individual producer, industry or sector. Gross value added is the source from which the primary incomes of the System are generated and is therefore carried forward into the primary distribution of income account." Source: http://unstats.un.org/unsd/sna1993/glossary.asp.

[3] Source: http://www.cvgairport.com/airport/econimp.shtml

Table 5.1   Production account for transportation and warehousing, Boone County, KY, 2001

million $

Uses		Sources	
Purchases from:		Sales to:	
Extraction	0.01	Extraction	0.13
Utilities	8.29	Utilities	3.93
Construction	7.18	Construction	2.28
Manufacturing	112.95	Manufacturing	21.32
Transport	79.00	Transport	79.00
Services	356.21	Services	19.27
Value Added		Final Demand Sales	
Payments to households	583.64	Households	16.47
Other payments	252.68	Governments	− 1.23
		Investment	8.01
Imports	797.99	Exports	2,048.77
Chargesagainst Gross Output	2,197.94	Gross Output	2,197.94

financial services provided by manufacturing industries appear under manufacturing rather than under services. Another important feature is the treatment of investment spending in the production account. Investment, which also includes inventory adjustments, represents the purchase of domestic capital goods and appears in the input-output framework under final demand rather than as an intermediate demand transaction. For instance, a manufacturing plant's purchases of equipment would be treated as a final demand activity even though the plant purchases the equipment from another firm.

For simplicity, we limited our snapshot of the Boone County economy to six industry sectors. Six production accounts, one for each industry, are needed to get a complete picture of the entire local economy. Taking a closer look at the production account for transportation, we can identify three different charges against output (e.g., uses): (1) the consumption of transportation services from other industries or intermediate inputs; (2) value added payment to households and other sources (e.g., wages and salaries, rent, interest and profits); and (3) imports. Sales by transportation are listed on the right-hand side and include: (1) sales to other industries; (2) final demand sales to households, governments, and investment; and (3) export sales. Following accounting principles, the industry product account for manufacturing must be balanced. In other words, charges against output must equal output.

In an economy consisting of only six industries, the input-output table can be derived directly from the six production accounts by combining the six production accounts into one single table—the input-output table. A highly disaggregated input-output table for Boone County is shown in Table 5.2. All data reported in the production account for transportation and warehousing, Table 5.1, appear in

Table 5.2   Simplified input-output table for Boone County, KY, 2001

million $

Purchases by / Sales by	Intermediate Users-Buying Industries						Final Demand (Y)				Total Output (X)
	Extraction	Utilities	Construction	Manufacturing	Transportation	Services	Households (C)	Government (G)	Investment (I)	Exports (E)	
Producing Industries											
Extraction	0.63	0.02	0.08	12.43	0.01	0.80	1.75	0.07	0.01	5.52	21.32
Utilities	0.22	0.17	1.11	28.03	8.29	29.42	39.32	10.16	-0.05	99.11	215.78
Construction	0.07	2.68	0.40	5.06	7.18	21.04	0.00	6.00	298.31	11.24	351.98
Manufacturing	1.41	2.85	44.65	378.25	112.95	106.77	156.06	30.69	96.36	1,562.63	2,492.60
Transportation	0.13	3.93	2.28	21.32	79.00	19.27	16.47	-1.23	8.01	2,048.77	2,197.94
Services	2.15	6.62	65.88	325.70	356.21	519.31	1,075.71	242.61	52.47	1,264.90	3,911.55
Payments											
Households (H)	5.13	59.72	100.77	465.45	583.64	1,383.58	134.64	352.52	0.03	0.09	3,085.54
Other Payments (P)	2.54	59.13	12.31	207.38	252.68	760.45	1,005.42	571.59	53.55	41.74	2,966.80
Imports (M)	9.04	80.67	124.51	1,049.00	797.99	1,070.92	685.09	127.24	1,089.56	0.00	5,034.00
Total Input (X)	21.32	215.78	351.98	2,492.60	2,197.94	3,911.55	3,114.45	1,339.65	1,598.25	5,034.00	20,277.52

the input-output table. What is reported in the production account on the left-hand side under uses now appears in the column labeled transportation. Analogously, the right-hand side of the production account appears unchanged in the row of the transportation industry.

But rather than using production accounts for deriving the Boone County input-output table, we used a commercially available software and data package made available through the Minnesota IMPLAN Group, Inc (MIG, Inc), the developer of the IMPLAN® economic impact modeling system.[1] The Minnesota IMPLAN Group makes data available at the national, state, county, and ZIP code level, which makes input-output analysis a widely used economic impact analysis tool. Beginning with 2001, available input-output tables are NAICS based and contain as many as 509 individual industry sectors. Of course, for many smaller and more specialized local economies, all of the 509 industries might not be available.

For Boone County, for instance, the data filed included 229 industries. In addition to the detailed inter-industry transactions, value added, and final demand components, IMPLAN^Pro data files contain inter-institutional transfers, which allow expansion of input-output tables to social accounting matrices.

5.2   The Input-Output Table

Input-output tables derived from industry production accounts are the building block for a wide variety of planning and analysis purposes. Among others, their versatility is based on the fact that input-output tables are nowadays available for national, state, metropolitan, multi-county, and county-level economies in the United States. They can be constructed for single regions or to emphasize flows between regions as multi-region input-output tables. All input-output tables are similar in that they map the economy of interest at one point in time. The main focus of input-output tables is the interdependencies of industries—the **inter-industry transactions**. Depending on the purpose they serve, input-output tables vary with respect to industry aggregation. Subject to data availability and the focus of the research, input-output tables may show various degrees of sector aggregation. In common, they represent a complete snapshot of the regional economy and include all industry transaction.

Input-output tables can be described as a very inclusive set of industry accounts. They show all sales and purchases made by industries in one particular year. Reading across the rows identifies sales made by industries— the **output**—

---

[1] A detailed description of the IMPLAN Professional® Software and IMPLAN Data is available in the documentation "The IMPLAN Input-Output System" provided by the Minnesota IMPLAN Group, Inc. at: www.implan.com.

and reading down the columns shows purchases made by industries—the **inputs**. The left-hand side of the table shows the buying industries; the right-hand side of the table identifies final demand (Y) from households (C), governments (G), investment (I), and exports (E). Horizontally, the input-output table distinguishes between processing industries in the upper part and industry payments in the lower part. Thus, conceptually, we can now divide the input-output table into four distinct quadrants. We use Table 5.2 to describe these four quadrants in more detail:

Inter-industry transactions (upper left-hand quadrant). Industries sell goods and services to other industries—indicated by reading across the rows. Reading along the row, transportation sells goods and services worth $0.13 million, $3.93 million, $2.28 million, $21.32 million, $79.00 million, and $19.27 million to extraction, utilities, construction, manufacturing, transportation, and services respectively. Reading down the column shows industries buying from other industries. Putting it differently, reading down the column of industry sectors shows the use of intermediate inputs into the production process. Reading down the transportation column we see that transportation buys inputs worth $0.01 million form extraction firms, $8.29 million from utilities, $7.18 million from construction, $112.95 million from manufacturing, $79.00 million from transportation, and finally $356.21 million from services. The inter-industry transaction quadrant is the most important part of the input-output table and can contain as many as several hundred individual industry sectors.

Final demand consumption (upper right-hand quadrant). Households, governments, investment, and exports are consumers of final products. This subsection of the input-output table focuses on local consumption pattern. In addition, it shows how much of the regional products are exported outside the region. For Boone County, most of the output of manufacturing and transportation, for instance, is exported with $1.56 billion and $2.05 billion, respectively. Construction is consumed primarily locally in the county by the investment sector ($298 million). The row totals show **total output** (X) for each industry. It is also referred to as total receipts or total demand.

Payments to the factors of production and foreign imports (lower left-hand quadrant). Payments to the factors of production—the value added—in the IMPLAN^{Pro} framework consists of employee compensation, proprietary income, other property income, and indirect businesses taxes. Note that there are many ways in which value added payments can be reported. Some studies break value added down into wages, rent, interest, and profits. Other studies distinguish between labor, capital, and land. We decided to distinguish according to the ownership of the factors of production; namely households and other payments (e.g., governments and savings/investment). For instance, households receive payments from transportation services for the ownership of the factors of production worth $583.64 million. Other value added payments by transportation total $252.68 million. Finally, imports used by transportation amount to $797.99 million. Income earned in Boone County by nonresidents is included in imports and, as such, is excluded from factor payments. Explicitly accounting for net factor income to the rest-of-the-world means that the IMPLAN-based input-output table is based on GNP totals and not on GDP totals.[①] The column totals indicate **total inputs** (X) for each industry. Therefore, it is also called "total outlays" per industry or "total supplies". In an economic framework built on accounting principles, total inputs must equal total supplies. This means that the row and column totals are identical.

Inter-institutional transfers (lower right-hand quadrant). Inter-institutional transfers are an optional sub-matrix which includes all non-market transactions. Among others, this sub-matrix contains information of inter-governmental transfers, government transfers to households (e.g., social security payments), household tax payments, payments among households (e.g., payments for babysitters), and payments made by households and governments for commodities purchased outside the region. For instance, households in Boone County spent $685.09 million on products from outside the county and $1.00 billion on other payments, mainly tax payments and household savings. However, non-market transactions are not the centerpiece of input-output analysis; and therefore, many input-output tables neglect inter- institutional transfers from their tables. Further, you may have already noticed that, while industry input equals industry output for each industry, the totals of payment rows do not match the totals of final demand columns. This is simply due to the fact that payments rows do not have matching columns and final demand column does not have matching rows (Table 5.2). There are only three payment sectors (e.g., households, other payments, and imports) while there are four final demand sectors (e.g., households, governments, investment, and exports).

So far we have described the individual components of an input-output table. The input-output table contains information on each industry sector's transactions in monetary units. In the example, all entries represent millions of 2001 dollars. With this information, we can trace how money flows through the economy. In particular, rows contain sales made by industries to other industries and final demand consumers, or income received by industries. Columns on the other hand show how industries spend their money—thus outlays—on intermediate inputs purchased form other industries and on payments to the factors of production and imports. The fact that the input-output framework reports value added and final demand consumption allows us to measure gross regional product in two different ways.

---

① Gross domestic product (GDP) is a common measure of economic activity in a country. It is usually derived as: (1) the sum of household consumption, government expenditure, investment, and net exports (exports—imports). It refers to the level of economic activity within one country's boundaries. (2) Gross national product (GNP), a second commonly used measure of economic activity, is derived by adding income to GDP earned by residents from abroad minus income earned by (non)residents leaving the country.

First, we can measure gross regional product using the income approach or payments made by industries to the factors of production. Total income earned by the factors of production includes employee compensation, proprietary income, other property income, and indirect businesses taxes. In the Boone County input-output table, this is lumped together into the two sectors labeled "Households (H)" and "Other Payments (P)" in the lower left-hand quadrant of the table. This can be expressed as:

$$\text{value added GRP} = H + P = \$3,892.77\text{million} \qquad (5.1)$$

where,

H — value added payments received by households in form of employee compensation, proprietary income, and other property income;

P — value added payments received by other payments, i.e., government and investment, in form of employee compensation, proprietary income, other property income, and indirect business taxes.

Thus, total gross regional product is the sum of all payments made by industries towards households (H) and other payments (P) and equals \$3,892.77 million.

Second, we can derive gross regional product using expenditures made by households (C), governments (G), investment (I), and net exports $(E - M)$. It is important to use net exports—by subtracting imports (M) from exports (E)—to avoid overestimating the gross regional product. Remember, this is done because importing means purchasing commodities outside the region and, as such, money leaves the region and does not contribute towards the productive output of the region's economy. This can be summarized as:

$$\text{real GRP} = C + G + I + (E - M) = \$3,892.77 \text{ million} \qquad (5.2)$$

where,

C — household consumption;
G — government expenditures;
I — investment expenditure;
E — exports;
M — imports.

Total gross regional product calculated on the expenditure side of the economy equals \$3,892.77 million. For a balanced input-output table, the calculation of gross regional product, either on the income side or the expenditure side of the economy, must result in the same outcome, or value added GRP = real GRP.

The level of total economic transactions indicated in the lower left-hand corner of the input-output table amounts to \$20,277.52 million. The difference to the gross regional product (GRP) of \$3,892.77 million can be explained in that: (1) intermediate demand (\$2,166.29 million) and inter-institutional transfers (\$4,061.46 million) do not count towards GRP and (2) GRP is measured twice in the input-output table: once, using the income approach, and second, using the expenditure approach. Another important observation is that due to the small size of the region, imports and exports play a comparatively large role in the region's economic activity with $5,034.00 million. With the increasing size of the region, the importance of exports and imports is expected to decrease as more and more transactions will occur within the region.

5.3 Deriving Input-Output Multipliers—The Economic Model

Up to now we have used the input-output table as a descriptive framework for describing the state of Boone County's economy. We have seen that all table entries represent dollar values referring to transactions between and among industries, factors of production, and final demand consumers. While this sheds light onto inter-industry interactions, the use of factors by industries, and final consumption patterns, it does not answer questions of how changes in exogenous final demand (ΔY) impact economic activities in the region. For this reason, we will use the descriptive input-output framework to develop a predictive model for economic impact analysis. Economic impact analysis is one way of measuring economy-wide changes in, for instance, output, employment, and income following an exogenous stimulus through the final demand sector. This change can be measured by the increase in final demand for an industry's products due to a new construction project or due to increases in exports. The fact that the input-output table presents the economy at one point in time is important for economic impact analysis. In this sense, economic impact analysis assesses how the economy as of today, will respond to changes in exogenous final demand. For instance, **how** will total output, employment, and income change, **if** final demand for a local business's products increases by $1.5 million? In this section we will explore in more detail how to use multipliers derived from the input-output framework as a tool for economic impact analysis.

The idea of the input output-multiplier is similar to that of the economic base multiplier. An increase in final demand consumption, let us say exports, would lead to an even larger increase of all economic activities due to the multiplying effect of the initial exogenous impact. More specifically, an input-output multiplier is a single number for each sector, which measures the total economic impact following a change in exogenous final demand on all endogenous sectors of the economy. It captures the **ripple-effect** or **round-by-round effect** initiated by the initial stimulus. The round-by-round effect describes the fact that an initial change in final demand will initiate subsequent rounds of income generation, spending, and re-spending in the economy. Ultimately, expected changes in all subsequent economic transactions—or the total effect in economic activities—are therefore expected to be larger than changes from the initial stimulus alone. In the case of input-output models, final demand drives the economy.

Before we derive different multipliers based on the input-output table, we need to specify some commonly used input-output terminology:

Endogenous versus exogenous accounts: By default, all inter-industry transactions depend on regional economic conditions. Industries make their decisions in accordance with the economic environment of which they are part. Therefore, all industries are treated endogenously. Contrarily, government and investment decisions, at least in the short-run, are considered to be largely independent of local economic conditions and are therefore treated exogenously. In the same manner, exports are treated exogenously. As you will see later, it is common practice to lump all exogenous sectors together and label it **final demand**. For economic impact analyses, the important distinction is that as long as the initial stimulus originates from an exogenous activity, whether government, investment, or export sector, it would lead to the same result.

Closing with respect to households: Households have an exceptional position in input-output analysis. On one hand, they clearly take the position of final demand consumers. On the other hand, households' buying decisions clearly depend on their income earned, which in return directly relates to the level of regional industry activity. Thus, an initial stimulus which leads to an increase in industry output, at the same time results in an increase in household income. Given that part of the additional household income is spent locally, further increases in industry activities must result, and so on. Therefore, households are often treated endogenously like industry sectors. In input-output terminology, **the model is closed with respect to households**.

Direct effect: measures only the initial immediate effects in output, employment, or income following an exogenous stimulus. For instance, export demand for manufacturing goods increases by $2 million. As an immediate result, output in the manufacturing sector will increase by $2 million to meet this change in final demand which is expressed as the direct effect.

Indirect effect: measures changes in output, employment, and income, which subsequently follow the direct effect, and as thus are attributable to the round-by-round effect. It accounts for the fact that industries, in order to meet new final demand themselves, have additional outlays towards intermediate inputs and the factors of production (capital and labor payments) and require additional employment. In the example, the manufacturing sector has to buy additional inputs from other industries, pay additional salaries to households, or import additional goods in order to be able to produce the additional output worth $2 million.

Induced effect: measures the portion of the total effect, which is attributable to the fact that households are endogenous to the system. The induced effect results directly from the fact that household income and spending increases due to the direct and indirect effects.

Total effect: sum of direct, indirect, and if applicable induced effects.

Type I multipliers: derived from a conceptual framework which is *open with respect to households*—where households are treated exogenously. It accounts only for direct and indirect effects.

Type II multipliers: derived from a conceptual framework, which is closed with respect to households. It includes direct, indirect, and induced effects.

SAM multipliers: derived from a social accounting matrix which includes industries, factors of production, and institutions.

5.3.1   The Open Model—Calculating Type I Output Multipliers[①]

Four factors in constructing the present input-output table are important to note. First, the input-output table is complete in that no transactions are missing, an important characteristic for building a predictive model for economic impact analysis. In addition, row and column totals must be balanced for all industry sectors. This implies that the regional economy is in a state of equilibrium where supply equals demand. Third, a decision has to be made whether households should be treated endogenously in a fashion similar to industries or remain exogenous as part of the final demand. In the algebraic example below of deriving output multipliers we treat households as exogenous which refers to type I multipliers; or the model is open with respect to households. Finally, we have revised the input-output table and combined all four final demand sectors into one aggregate sector labeled **final demand**. Table 5.3 below shows the revised input-output table used for setting up the economic impact model.

The highlighted part of the industry transaction table indicates the endogenous account—the industries. Final demand is exogenous consisting of households, governments, investment, and exports. To obtain a general solution for the input-output model, we substitute data entries with algebraic variable notations as indicated in Table 5.4. The subscripts refer to the position in the table. Notational conventions in input-output analysis are usually easy to follow. Interindustry transactions are denoted as t_{ij}, where i identifies the origin (from) and j the destination (to) of the output. For instance, t_{63} indicates a transaction between the service sector (6) as selling industry and the construction sector (3) as buying industry. The first subscript (i) denotes the row and (j), the column.

---

① For convenience we widely follow the IMPLAN[Pro] definition of type I , type II multipliers throughout the remainder of this chapter. Note that the IMPLAN[Pro] type II multipliers are derived using complete household outlays. Contrary, many textbooks derive type II multipliers without accounting for household inter-institutional transfer payments. Therefore, household outlays are only partially accounted for. For the interested reader, Schaffer (1999) provides a review on multiplier concepts, names, and interpretations, p. 43 – 48.

Table 5.3 Revised industry transaction table for Boone County, 2001

million $

Purchases by / Sales by	Endogenous						Exogenous	
	Extraction	Utilities	Construction	Manufacturing	Transportation	Services	Final Demand (Y)	Total Demand (X)
Extraction	0.63	0.02	0.08	12.43	0.01	0.80	7.35	21.32
Utilities	0.22	0.17	1.11	28.03	8.29	29.42	148.53	215.78
Construction	0.07	2.68	0.40	5.06	7.18	21.04	315.55	351.98
Manufacturing	1.41	2.85	44.65	378.25	112.95	106.77	1,845.74	2,492.60
Transportation	0.13	3.93	2.28	21.32	79.00	19.27	2,072.02	2,197.94
Services	2.15	6.62	65.88	325.70	356.21	519.31	2,635.69	3,911.55
Households (H)	5.13	59.72	100.77	465.45	583.64	1,383.58	487.27	3,085.54
Other Payments (P)	2.54	59.13	12.31	207.38	252.68	760.45	1,672.31	2,966.80
Imports (M)	9.04	80.67	124.51	1,049.00	797.99	1,070.92	1,901.89	5,034.00
Total Input (X)	21.32	215.78	351.98	2,492.60	2,197.94	3,911.55	7,024.88	20,277.52

Table 5.4 The algebraic transaction table

Purchases by / Sales by	Endogenous						Exogenous	
	Extraction	Utilities	Construction	Manufacturing	Transportation	Services	Final Demand (Y)	Total Demand (X)
Extraction	t_{11}	t_{12}	t_{13}	t_{14}	t_{15}	t_{16}	Y_1	X_1
Utilities	t_{21}	t_{22}	t_{23}	t_{24}	t_{25}	t_{26}	Y_2	X_2
Construction	t_{31}	t_{32}	t_{33}	t_{34}	t_{35}	t_{36}	Y_3	X_3
Manufacturing	t_{41}	t_{42}	t_{43}	t_{44}	t_{45}	t_{46}	Y_4	X_4
Transportation	t_{51}	t_{52}	t_{53}	t_{54}	t_{55}	t_{56}	Y_5	X_5
Services	t_{61}	t_{62}	t_{63}	t_{64}	t_{65}	t_{66}	Y_6	X_6
Households (H)	H_1	H_2	H_3	H_4	H_5	H_6	H_Y	H
Other Payments (P)	P_1	P_2	P_3	P_4	P_5	P_6	P_Y	P
Imports (M)	M_1	M_2	M_3	M_4	M_5	M_6	M_Y	M
Total Input (X)	X_1	X_2	X_3	X_4	X_5	X_6	Y	X

Total output is denoted as X_i with i identifying the selling industry i. X_j denotes total inputs bought by industry j—the column total. Next is Y_i, which identifies final demand by households, governments, investment, and the exports sectors. H_j, P_j, M_j denote payments by industry j towards households, other payment sector, and imports respectively.

Based on the information of the algebraic industry transaction table we can now define each industry's output as the sum of all intermediate and final demand sales, which can be expressed as a set of linear functions, or:

$$\left.\begin{array}{l} X_1 = t_{11} + t_{12} + t_{13} + t_{14} + t_{15} + t_{16} + Y_1 \\ X_2 = t_{21} + t_{22} + t_{23} + t_{24} + t_{25} + t_{26} + Y_2 \\ X_3 = t_{31} + t_{32} + t_{33} + t_{34} + t_{35} + t_{36} + Y_3 \\ X_4 = t_{41} + t_{42} + t_{43} + t_{44} + t_{45} + t_{46} + Y_4 \\ X_5 = t_{51} + t_{52} + t_{53} + t_{54} + t_{55} + t_{56} + Y_5 \\ X_6 = t_{61} + t_{62} + t_{63} + t_{64} + t_{65} + t_{66} + Y_6 \end{array}\right\} \tag{5.3}$$

For instance, total output by transportation (X_5) is the sum of intermediate demand $(t_{51} + \cdots + t_{56})$ and final demand (Y_5). In a second step we incorporate the industry sector's production technology into the equation system. We already know that a sector's total output (X_i) equals its total input (X_j). In addition we know that reading down an industry's column identifies all inputs necessary to produce an industry's output. Putting it differently, reading down the column identifies an industry's production function, consisting of intermediate purchases, payments to the factors of production (households and other payments), and imports. The general form of the Leontief production function can be expressed as:

$$X_j = f(t_{1j}, t_{2j}, \cdots, x_{nj}, H_j, P_j, M_j) \tag{5.4}$$

where n refers to number of total industries in the transaction table, six in this example. Using this information we now establish a fixed relationship between a sector's input demand and its output. This is achieved through technical coefficients (a_{ij}), which are expressed as the ratio of an inter-industry transaction (t_{ij}) over the corresponding column total (X_j), or:

$$a_{ij} = \frac{t_{ij}}{X_j} \tag{5.5}$$

These technical coefficients define the proportion of input requirements for an industry j with i denoting the selling industry. The calculation of these technical coefficients is rather trivial but has far-reaching implications. Technical coefficients in input-output analysis are fixed coefficients indicating that an industry's input requirements change proportionally with a change in final demand for that industry. For example, an industry that increases its output by 20% will also increase all its inputs proportionally by 20%. The technical coefficients for the example with six industries are calculated as:

$$
\left.
\begin{aligned}
a_{11} &= \frac{t_{11}}{X_1}; a_{12} = \frac{t_{12}}{X_2}; \ldots; a_{16} = \frac{t_{16}}{X_6} \\
a_{21} &= \frac{t_{21}}{X_1}; a_{22} = \frac{t_{22}}{X_2}; \ldots; a_{26} = \frac{t_{26}}{X_6} \\
&\vdots \\
a_{61} &= \frac{t_{61}}{X_1}; a_{62} = \frac{t_{62}}{X_2}; \ldots; a_{66} = \frac{t_{66}}{X_6}
\end{aligned}
\right\}
\tag{5.6}
$$

Once the fixed relationship between outputs and input requirements is established, we use this information and replace each t_{ij} in the set of linear Eq. (5.3) by the corresponding $(a_{ij} \cdot X_j)$. For example, t_{11} can be expressed as $(a_{11} \cdot X_1)$ and so on. This step is necessary to reduce the number of variables in the linear set of equations. The original linear system in Eq. (5.3) consists of 48 individual variables. Using fixed technical coefficients reduces the number of variables by 36, leaving us with six exogenous variables—the policy variables—and six endogenous variables—the total outputs.

$$
\left.
\begin{aligned}
X_1 &= a_{11} \cdot X_1 + a_{12} \cdot X_2 + a_{13} \cdot X_3 + a_{14} \cdot X_4 + a_{15} \cdot X_5 + a_{16} \cdot X_6 + Y_1 \\
X_2 &= a_{21} \cdot X_1 + a_{22} \cdot X_2 + a_{23} \cdot X_3 + a_{24} \cdot X_4 + a_{25} \cdot X_5 + a_{26} \cdot X_6 + Y_2 \\
X_3 &= a_{31} \cdot X_1 + a_{32} \cdot X_2 + a_{33} \cdot X_3 + a_{34} \cdot X_4 + a_{35} \cdot X_5 + a_{36} \cdot X_6 + Y_3 \\
X_4 &= a_{41} \cdot X_1 + a_{42} \cdot X_2 + a_{43} \cdot X_3 + a_{44} \cdot X_4 + a_{45} \cdot X_5 + a_{46} \cdot X_6 + Y_4 \\
X_5 &= a_{51} \cdot X_1 + a_{52} \cdot X_2 + a_{53} \cdot X_3 + a_{54} \cdot X_4 + a_{55} \cdot X_5 + a_{56} \cdot X_6 + Y_5 \\
X_6 &= a_{61} \cdot X_1 + a_{62} \cdot X_2 + a_{63} \cdot X_3 + a_{64} \cdot X_4 + a_{65} \cdot X_5 + a_{66} \cdot X_6 + Y_6
\end{aligned}
\right\}
\tag{5.7}
$$

The next step is bringing all X's over to the left-hand side. The result is Eq. (5.8), a linear system in which the exogenous terms—the Y's—remain on the right-hand side, and the endogenous terms—the X's—are all on the left-hand side.

$$
\left.
\begin{aligned}
X_1 - a_{11} \cdot X_1 - a_{12} \cdot X_2 - a_{13} \cdot X_3 - a_{14} \cdot X_4 - a_{15} \cdot X_5 - a_{16} \cdot X_6 &= Y_1 \\
X_2 - a_{21} \cdot X_1 - a_{22} \cdot X_2 - a_{23} \cdot X_3 - a_{24} \cdot X_4 - a_{25} \cdot X_5 - a_{26} \cdot X_6 &= Y_2 \\
X_3 - a_{31} \cdot X_1 - a_{32} \cdot X_2 - a_{33} \cdot X_3 - a_{34} \cdot X_4 - a_{35} \cdot X_5 - a_{36} \cdot X_6 &= Y_3 \\
X_4 - a_{41} \cdot X_1 - a_{42} \cdot X_2 - a_{43} \cdot X_3 - a_{44} \cdot X_4 - a_{45} \cdot X_5 - a_{46} \cdot X_6 &= Y_4 \\
X_5 - a_{51} \cdot X_1 - a_{52} \cdot X_2 - a_{53} \cdot X_3 - a_{54} \cdot X_4 - a_{55} \cdot X_5 - a_{56} \cdot X_6 &= Y_5 \\
X_6 - a_{61} \cdot X_1 - a_{62} \cdot X_2 - a_{63} \cdot X_3 - a_{64} \cdot X_4 - a_{65} \cdot X_5 - a_{66} \cdot X_6 &= Y_6
\end{aligned}
\right\}
\tag{5.8}
$$

Applying basic rules of matrix algebra allows further simplifications of the linear system of six equations into one matrix and two column vectors:

$$\begin{pmatrix} (1-a_{11}) & -a_{12} & -a_{13} & -a_{14} & -a_{15} & -a_{16} \\ -a_{21} & (1-a_{22}) & -a_{23} & -a_{24} & -a_{25} & -a_{26} \\ -a_{31} & -a_{32} & (1-a_{33}) & -a_{34} & -a_{35} & -a_{36} \\ -a_{41} & -a_{42} & -a_{43} & (1-a_{44}) & -a_{45} & -a_{46} \\ -a_{51} & -a_{52} & -a_{53} & -a_{54} & (1-a_{55}) & -a_{56} \\ -a_{61} & -a_{62} & -a_{63} & -a_{64} & -a_{65} & (1-a_{66}) \end{pmatrix} \cdot \begin{pmatrix} X_1 \\ X_2 \\ X_3 \\ X_4 \\ X_5 \\ X_6 \end{pmatrix} = \begin{pmatrix} Y_1 \\ Y_2 \\ Y_3 \\ Y_4 \\ Y_5 \\ Y_6 \end{pmatrix}$$

(5.9)

The first term on the left-hand side, the square matrix, collects all the technical coefficients. The dimension of the square matrix is six by six, referring to six rows and six columns, written as (6×6). The second term on the left-hand side is a column vector containing total outputs for each industry. Final demand is to the right of the equal sign, also in form of a single column vector.

The square matrix can further be simplified by splitting it into two matrices of the same size. The matrix containing ones on the main diagonal and zeros elsewhere is the identity matrix, I. It is a multiplicative identity for matrices, in the same way as the number one is for real numbers. The second matrix is now the technical coefficient matrix containing the technical coefficients as defined in Eq. (5.5). The two column vectors with total output and final demand have remained unchanged.

$$\left[\begin{pmatrix} 1 & 0 & 0 & 0 & 0 & 0 \\ 0 & 1 & 0 & 0 & 0 & 0 \\ 0 & 0 & 1 & 0 & 0 & 0 \\ 0 & 0 & 0 & 1 & 0 & 0 \\ 0 & 0 & 0 & 0 & 1 & 0 \\ 0 & 0 & 0 & 0 & 0 & 1 \end{pmatrix} - \begin{pmatrix} a_{11} & a_{12} & a_{13} & a_{14} & a_{15} & a_{16} \\ a_{21} & a_{22} & a_{23} & a_{24} & a_{25} & a_{26} \\ a_{31} & a_{32} & a_{33} & a_{34} & a_{35} & a_{36} \\ a_{41} & a_{42} & a_{43} & a_{44} & a_{45} & a_{46} \\ a_{51} & a_{52} & a_{53} & a_{54} & a_{55} & a_{56} \\ a_{61} & a_{62} & a_{63} & a_{64} & a_{65} & a_{66} \end{pmatrix} \right] \cdot \begin{pmatrix} X_1 \\ X_2 \\ X_3 \\ X_4 \\ X_5 \\ X_6 \end{pmatrix} = \begin{pmatrix} Y_1 \\ Y_2 \\ Y_3 \\ Y_4 \\ Y_5 \\ Y_6 \end{pmatrix}$$

(5.10)

Some basic matrix algebra

Matrix algebra is preferred whenever we deal with a larger system of linear equations. A matrix is a rectangular array of numbers. A matrix with m rows and n columns has the dimension $m \times n$ and is called an $m \times n$ matrix. The number in row i and column j of the $m \times n$ matrix is the (i, j)th element in the matrix. A matrix is square if $m = n$ and rectangular if $m \neq n$. The general form of a matrix, A, with m rows and n columns is:

$$A = \begin{pmatrix} a_{11} & \cdots & a_{1n} \\ \cdots & a_{ij} & \cdots \\ a_{m1} & \cdots & a_{mn} \end{pmatrix}$$

An $m \times 1$ matrix is a column vector and a $1 \times n$ matrix is a row vector:

$$m \times 1 \text{ column vector: } \begin{pmatrix} c_1 \\ c_2 \\ \vdots \\ c_m \end{pmatrix}; \quad 1 \times n \text{ row vector: } (r_1 \ r_2 \cdots r_n)$$

Addition

One can add two matrices A and B of the same size by adding the (i, j)th element in matrix A to the (i, j)-th element in matrix B:

$$A + B = \begin{pmatrix} a_{11} & a_{12} \\ a_{21} & a_{22} \end{pmatrix} + \begin{pmatrix} b_{11} & b_{12} \\ b_{21} & b_{22} \end{pmatrix} = \begin{pmatrix} a_{11} + b_{11} & a_{12} + b_{12} \\ a_{21} + b_{21} & a_{22} + b_{22} \end{pmatrix}$$

Subtraction

Matrix B is subtracted from matrix A by subtracting the (i, j)th element in matrix B from the (i, j)th element in matrix A:

$$A - B = \begin{pmatrix} a_{11} & a_{12} \\ a_{21} & a_{22} \end{pmatrix} - \begin{pmatrix} b_{11} & b_{12} \\ b_{21} & b_{22} \end{pmatrix} = \begin{pmatrix} a_{11} - b_{11} & a_{12} - b_{12} \\ a_{21} - b_{21} & a_{22} - b_{22} \end{pmatrix}$$

Subtracting matrix A from the identity matrix I:

$$I - A = \begin{pmatrix} 1 & 0 \\ 0 & 1 \end{pmatrix} - \begin{pmatrix} a_{11} & a_{12} \\ a_{21} & a_{22} \end{pmatrix} = \begin{pmatrix} 1 - a_{11} & -a_{12} \\ -a_{21} & 1 - a_{22} \end{pmatrix}$$

Multiplication

Scalar multiplication—multiplying the matrix A by a scalar s—means multiplying each number in the matrix by s:

$$sA = s \cdot \begin{pmatrix} a_{11} & a_{12} \\ a_{21} & a_{22} \end{pmatrix} = \begin{pmatrix} sa_{11} & sa_{12} \\ sa_{21} & sa_{22} \end{pmatrix}$$

Matrix A can be multiplied by matrix B only if:

the number of columns in matrix $A(m)$ = the number of rows in matrix $B(m)$

The dimensions of the matrices must satisfy: $(n \times m)\,(m \times p) = (n \times p)$

$$A \cdot B = \begin{pmatrix} a_{11} & a_{12} \\ a_{21} & a_{22} \end{pmatrix} \cdot \begin{pmatrix} b_{11} & b_{12} \\ b_{21} & b_{22} \end{pmatrix} = \begin{pmatrix} a_{11} \cdot b_{11} + a_{12} \cdot b_{21} & a_{11} \cdot b_{12} + a_{12} \cdot b_{22} \\ a_{21} \cdot b_{11} + a_{22} \cdot b_{21} & a_{21} \cdot b_{12} + a_{22} \cdot b_{22} \end{pmatrix}$$

Analogously, a matrix A can be multiplied by a column vector X:

$$A \cdot X = \begin{pmatrix} a_{11} & a_{12} \\ a_{21} & a_{22} \end{pmatrix} \cdot \begin{pmatrix} x_1 \\ x_2 \end{pmatrix} = \begin{pmatrix} a_{11} \cdot x_1 + a_{12} \cdot x_2 \\ a_{21} \cdot x_1 + a_{22} \cdot x_2 \end{pmatrix}$$

or, by a row vector Z:

$$Z \cdot A = (z_1 \quad z_2) \cdot \begin{pmatrix} a_{11} & a_{12} \\ a_{21} & a_{22} \end{pmatrix} = (z_1 \cdot a_{11} + z_2 \cdot a_{21} \quad z_1 \cdot a_{12} + z_2 \cdot a_{22})$$

Multiplying a matrix A by an identity matrix I replicates matrix A:

$$I \cdot A = \begin{pmatrix} 1 & 0 \\ 0 & 1 \end{pmatrix} \cdot \begin{pmatrix} a_{11} & a_{12} \\ a_{21} & a_{22} \end{pmatrix} = \begin{pmatrix} a_{11} & a_{12} \\ a_{21} & a_{22} \end{pmatrix}$$

Inversion
Division in matrix algebra is defined as "*multiplication by the reciprocal matrix*" or matrix inversion. Multiplying a scalar by its reciprocal is one. This is analogous to multiplying a number by its reciprocal, for instance, $8 \times \frac{1}{8} = 1$. The same must hold for matrices and we can define the inverse as:

$$A \cdot A^{-1} = I$$

Applying the rule of matrix inversion allows solving linear equation systems like the input-output system as:

$$B \cdot X = Y \Rightarrow B^{-1} \cdot B \cdot X = B^{-1} \cdot Y \Rightarrow I \cdot X = B^{-1} \cdot Y \Rightarrow X = B^{-1} \cdot Y$$

where:
B is a $(m \times m)$ matrix and X and Y are two column vectors.

Using matrix notation, the linear system of six equations can be expressed in a more simple form as

$$(I - A) \cdot X = Y \tag{5.11}$$

where, I is a (6×6) identity matrix, A is a (6×6) technical coefficient matrix, X denotes the total output vector, and Y is the final demand vector. A last step solves the system of linear equations for X. Using this economic model for measuring changes in total output (ΔX) following a change in final demand (ΔY) requires solving the system in terms of X, or:

$$X = (I - A)^{-1} \cdot Y \tag{5.12}$$

Honoring Wassily Leontief for his contribution to input-output analysis, $(I - A)^{-1}$ is also referred to as the **Leontief inverse**. Alternatively, this inverse matrix is called **output multiplier table** or **total requirements table**; and as the example will show, it is the table with all input requirements necessary for each industry in the regional economy in order to meet any change in final demand.

Now let us consider an arithmetic example using the Boone County input-output table. Today's spreadsheet software packages provide all means for solving large linear equation systems. The starting point is the revised industry transaction table for Boone County, 2001, with six endogenous industry sectors and one exogenous final demand vector. From the revised industry transaction table for Boone County—Table 5.3—the first step is to calculate the technical coefficients by dividing each cell entry in the endogenous account of the table by its corresponding column total. The results are shown in Table 5.5, the technical coefficient table.

Table 5.5   Technical coefficient table, Boone County, 2001

	Extrac-tion	Utili-ties	Construc-tion	Manufac-turing	Trans-portation	Servi-ces
Extraction	0.030	0.000	0.000	0.005	0.000	0.000
Utilities	0.010	0.001	0.003	0.011	0.004	0.008
Construction	0.003	0.012	0.001	0.002	0.003	0.005
Manufacturing	0.066	0.013	0.127	0.152	0.051	0.027
Transport	0.006	0.018	0.006	0.009	0.036	0.005
Services	0.101	0.031	0.187	0.131	0.162	0.133
Households (H)	0.240	0.277	0.286	0.187	0.266	0.354
Other Payments (P)	0.119	0.274	0.035	0.083	0.115	0.194
Imports (M)	0.424	0.374	0.354	0.421	0.363	0.274
Total Input (X)	1.000	1.000	1.000	1.000	1.000	1.000

For instance, $a_{41} = 0.066$ and is calculated as: $(1.41/21.32)$. We can read the information in the technical coefficients table as follows: for manufacturing (column 4) to produce one dollar worth of output, it needs to buy intermediate inputs worth 0.5 cents from extraction, 1.1 cents from utilities, 0.2 cents from construction, 15.2 cents from manufacturing, 0.9 cents from transportation, and 13.1 cents from services. All together, manufacturing spends 30.9 cents on buying intermediate goods and services from other industries for every dollar worth of its output. An additional 18.7 cents is paid towards households, 8.3 cent towards other payments, and the largest outlay goes for imports, namely 42.1 cents. If you did your calculations correctly, total inputs equal one dollar.

In the second step, we zoom in on the highlighted section of the technical coefficient table—the A matrix. We are now going to derive the $(I - A)$ matrix. To do so, we simply set up an identity matrix (ones on the main diagonal and zeros in all other cells) and subtract the A matrix from it. The result, the Leontief or $(I - A)$ matrix, is shown in Table 5.6.

Table 5.6   Leontief or $(I - A)$ matrix, Boone County, 2001

	Extraction	Utilities	Construction	Manufacturing	Transportation	Services
Extraction	0.970	0.000	0.000	− 0.005	0.000	0.000
Utilities	− 0.010	0.999	− 0.003	− 0.011	− 0.004	− 0.008
Construction	− 0.003	− 0.012	0.999	− 0.002	− 0.003	− 0.005
Manufacturing	− 0.066	− 0.013	− 0.127	0.848	− 0.051	− 0.027
Transportation	− 0.006	− 0.018	− 0.006	− 0.009	0.964	− 0.005
Services	− 0.101	− 0.031	− 0.187	− 0.131	− 0.162	0.867

All cell entries, except the ones on the main diagonal, reappear from the A matrix but now with a negative sign. Only the values on the main diagonal are positive. The first value, for example, is calculated by subtracting the technical coefficient (a_{11}) from one, or: $0.970 = 1 - 0.030$.

The last step is the inversion of the $(I - A)$ matrix. While smaller matrices— 2×2 or 3×3 matrices—can still be inverted by hand, for large input-output tables spreadsheet software packages provide the means for matrix calculations.[1] The outcome of the inverting the Boone County $(I - A)$ matrix is shown in Table 5.7. The $(I - A)^{-1}$ matrix, or the type I output multiplier table, shows the 36 (e.g., 6×6) partial multipliers. The column totals report the type I output multipliers (OM_j) which in the example range from 1.099 to 1.421.

What do output multipliers now tell us? An output multiplier for industry j measures the total value of output in all industries required in order to meet a change in final demand (ΔY) in industry j of exactly one dollar. For instance, for construction to increase its output by one dollar, it requires extraction to increase its output by 0.1 cents, utilities by 0.7 cents, construction by 100.3 cents, manufacturing by 15.9 cents, transportation by 1.0 cents, and services by 24.2 cents. The cell entries in the $(I - A)^{-1}$ matrix can be interpreted as partial multipliers. Partial because they only measure the change in output for one specific industry; e.g., services by 24.2 cents. The column total then refers to the type I output multiplier; e.g., 1.421 for construction. Thus, in the case of construction, the total output in the region would increase by $1.42 in order to meet construction's increase in output by an initial $1.00. The total effect of a change in final demand in construction worth $1.00 exceeds the initial stimulus by 42.1 percent. The initial change in final demand of $1.00 from the exogenous sector is captured by the direct effect. The indirect effect then measures the

---

[1]   We used Microsoft Excel: the matrix inversion feature is included in **Lotus 1-2-3 help** which can be found in the MS excel help menu. In **Lotus 1-2-3 help**, double-click first on **data** and second on **matrix**. You should then get the choice of matrix **inversion** or **multiplication**, either of which will be used frequently in input-output analysis. The use of the **Lotus 1-2-3 help** function is self-explanatory.

additional economic activities worth 42 cents as a direct result of the initial change in final demand. The multiplier then can be defined as:

$$\text{type I output multiplier } (OM_j) = \frac{\text{direct effect} + \text{indirect effect}}{\text{initial stimulus}},$$

or

$$OM_j = \sum_{i=1}^{n} \text{mult}_{ij} \qquad (5.13)$$

where,

OM_j — type I output multiplier, e.g., the total in column j in Table 5.7;

mult_{ij} — partial multiplier in row i and column j;

n — number of industries; e.g., six in the presented example.

Table 5.7 Total requirement table, $(I - A)^{-1}$ matrix, Boone County, 2001

	Extraction	Utilities	Construction	Manufacturing	Transportation	Services
Extraction	1.031	0.000	0.001	0.006	0.000	0.000
Utilities	0.013	1.001	0.007	0.015	0.006	0.009
Construction	0.005	0.013	1.003	0.004	0.005	0.006
Manufacturing	0.086	0.020	0.159	1.187	0.070	0.039
Transportation	0.008	0.019	0.010	0.012	1.039	0.007
Services	0.136	0.045	0.242	0.183	0.206	1.162
Type I Multiplier (OM_j)	1.279	1.099	1.421	1.406	1.327	1.224

As mentioned earlier, the fact that the total effect outnumbers the initial stimulus is commonly referred to as the round-by-round effect or ripple effect. The rationale behind the round-by-round effect is that the initial stimulus, which originates in final demand, leads to a chain reaction of economic activities. With final demand for one or more industry's output increasing, these industries in return need to increase intermediate inputs, factors of production (e.g., household and other payments), and imports to be able to meet this new final demand. For instance, if the demand for manufacturing products increases, manufacturing in return needs to buy more intermediate inputs from all other industries. Next, all these industries require more intermediate inputs, factors of production, and imports to be able to deliver the extra demand coming from manufacturing. The idea here is that although the initial change in final demand occurs, as in the demonstration, in manufacturing only, the interconnectivity of industries amplifies the initial change in final demand. The bottom line is that the gross output requirements exceed the initial stimulus expressed by the output multiplier.

One efficient way of demonstrating the round-by-round effect is by using the power series approximation of the Leontief inverse or the $(I - A)^{-1}$ matrix. Before computing power allowed the inversion of large matrices, the power series approximation enabled analysts to approximate the $(I - A)^{-1}$ matrix without matrix inversion. From algebra we know that:

$$\frac{1}{1-a} = 1 + a + a^2 + a^3 + a^4 + a^5 + \cdots; \text{ for } |a| < 1 \tag{5.14}$$

Using the principle of the power series approximation, we thus can invert the Leontief or $(I - A)$ matrix through a series of additions, or:

$$(I-A)^{-1} = I + A + A^2 + A^3 + A^4 + A^5 + \cdots; \text{ for } |I - A| \neq 0 \tag{5.15}$$

The matrix can be inverted if the determined of the matrix $|I - A| \neq 0$. And the linear system of six Eq. (5.12) can be approximated as:

$$X = (I + A + A^2 + A^3 + A^4 + A^5 + \cdots) \cdot Y \tag{5.16}$$

Multiplying the final demand vector, Y, by the first term in the parenthesis, the identity matrix, I, accounts for the direct effect. Note that $I \cdot Y = Y$ simply reproduces the initial change in final demand—the direct effect. The consecutive terms in parenthesis signify the round-by-round effects following the initial stimulus—the indirect effect.

To demonstrate the round-by-round effects, we simulate a construction project worth $1.0 billion in Boone County. That is, final demand for the construction industry increases by exactly that amount. Our type I output multiplier for construction of 1.421 indicates that total economic activities in Boone County will amount to as much as $1.421 billion, or

$$\Delta X = OM_{Const} \cdot \Delta Y = 1.421 \cdot \$1.00 \text{ billion} = \$1,421 \text{ billion} \tag{5.17}$$

where,

ΔX — change in output;

ΔY — change in final demand;

OM_{Const} — construction type I output multiplier.

Using the power series approximation, we have calculated the initial stimulus plus the first five rounds. The results are listed in Table 5.8. For instance, the initial impact is calculated as $X = I \cdot Y$, the first round is calculated as $X = A \cdot Y$, and so on. Generally, with each round the indirect effects decrease, as can be seen by the magnitude of the results in the output vectors (X). For better comparison we additionally put the results in changes in output per round in a summary table—Table 5.9.

From Table 5.9 we see that change in output decreases significantly with each round from $324.99 million in the first round to a mere $0.82 million in the fifth round. After accounting for five rounds, the total change in output amounts already to the $1.421 billion as estimated in Eq. (5.17) using the type I

Table 5.8 Round-by-round effect calculation, Boone County, 2001

$$
\begin{array}{ccc}
X & L\text{ Matrix} & Y
\end{array}
$$

$$
\begin{pmatrix} 0.00 \\ 0.00 \\ 1000.00 \\ 0.00 \\ 0.00 \\ 0.00 \end{pmatrix}
=
\begin{pmatrix}
1 & 0 & 0 & 0 & 0 & 0 \\
0 & 1 & 0 & 0 & 0 & 0 \\
0 & 0 & 1 & 0 & 0 & 0 \\
0 & 0 & 0 & 1 & 0 & 0 \\
0 & 0 & 0 & 0 & 1 & 0 \\
0 & 0 & 0 & 0 & 0 & 1
\end{pmatrix}
\times
\begin{pmatrix} 0 \\ 0 \\ 1{,}000 \\ 0 \\ 0 \\ 0 \end{pmatrix}
$$

$$
\begin{array}{ccc}
X & A\text{ Matrix} & Y
\end{array}
$$

$$
\begin{pmatrix} 0.23 \\ 3.14 \\ 1.13 \\ 126.85 \\ 6.46 \\ 187.18 \end{pmatrix}
=
\begin{pmatrix}
0.02969 & 0.00007 & 0.00023 & 0.00499 & 0.00001 & 0.00020 \\
0.01037 & 0.00080 & 0.00314 & 0.01124 & 0.00377 & 0.00752 \\
0.00333 & 0.01244 & 0.00113 & 0.00203 & 0.00327 & 0.00538 \\
0.06614 & 0.01318 & 0.12685 & 0.15175 & 0.05139 & 0.02730 \\
0.00624 & 0.01820 & 0.00646 & 0.00855 & 0.03594 & 0.00493 \\
0.10067 & 0.03068 & 0.18718 & 0.13067 & 0.16206 & 0.13276
\end{pmatrix}
\times
\begin{pmatrix} 0 \\ 0 \\ 1{,}000 \\ 0 \\ 0 \\ 0 \end{pmatrix}
$$

$$
\begin{array}{ccc}
X & A^2\text{ Matrix} & Y
\end{array}
$$

$$
\begin{pmatrix} 0.68 \\ 2.87 \\ 1.33 \\ 24.89 \\ 2.31 \\ 42.80 \end{pmatrix}
=
\begin{pmatrix}
0.00123 & 0.00008 & 0.00068 & 0.00093 & 0.00029 & 0.00017 \\
0.00185 & 0.00049 & 0.00287 & 0.00279 & 0.00195 & 0.00135 \\
0.00093 & 0.00028 & 0.00133 & 0.00120 & 0.00114 & 0.00089 \\
0.01563 & 0.00537 & 0.02489 & 0.02777 & 0.01453 & 0.00881 \\
0.00168 & 0.00101 & 0.00231 & 0.00250 & 0.00262 & 0.00124 \\
0.02695 & 0.01111 & 0.04280 & 0.03979 & 0.03478 & 0.02325
\end{pmatrix}
\times
\begin{pmatrix} 0 \\ 0 \\ 1{,}000 \\ 0 \\ 0 \\ 0 \end{pmatrix}
$$

$$
\begin{array}{ccc}
X & A^3\text{ Matrix} & Y
\end{array}
$$

$$
\begin{pmatrix} 0.15 \\ 0.62 \\ 0.33 \\ 5.31 \\ 0.57 \\ 9.71 \end{pmatrix}
=
\begin{pmatrix}
0.00012 & 0.00003 & 0.00015 & 0.00017 & 0.00009 & 0.00005 \\
0.00040 & 0.00015 & 0.00062 & 0.00064 & 0.00044 & 0.00028 \\
0.00021 & 0.00008 & 0.00033 & 0.00032 & 0.00025 & 0.00017 \\
0.00342 & 0.00122 & 0.00531 & 0.00568 & 0.00348 & 0.00218 \\
0.00037 & 0.00015 & 0.00057 & 0.00059 & 0.00043 & 0.00027 \\
0.00625 & 0.00241 & 0.00971 & 0.00972 & 0.00724 & 0.00466
\end{pmatrix}
\times
\begin{pmatrix} 0 \\ 0 \\ 1{,}000 \\ 0 \\ 0 \\ 0 \end{pmatrix}
$$

$$
\begin{array}{ccc}
X & A^4\text{ Matrix} & Y
\end{array}
$$

$$
\begin{pmatrix} 0.03 \\ 0.14 \\ 0.07 \\ 1.16 \\ 0.13 \\ 2.17 \end{pmatrix}
=
\begin{pmatrix}
0.00002 & 0.00001 & 0.00003 & 0.00004 & 0.00002 & 0.00001 \\
0.00009 & 0.00003 & 0.00014 & 0.00014 & 0.00010 & 0.00006 \\
0.00005 & 0.00002 & 0.00007 & 0.00007 & 0.00005 & 0.00003 \\
0.00075 & 0.00027 & 0.00116 & 0.00122 & 0.00079 & 0.00050 \\
0.00008 & 0.00003 & 0.00013 & 0.00013 & 0.00009 & 0.00006 \\
0.00140 & 0.00053 & 0.00217 & 0.00222 & 0.00156 & 0.00099
\end{pmatrix}
\times
\begin{pmatrix} 0 \\ 0 \\ 1{,}000 \\ 0 \\ 0 \\ 0 \end{pmatrix}
$$

Continued

X	A^5 Matrix						Y

$$\begin{pmatrix} 0.01 \\ 0.03 \\ 0.02 \\ 0.26 \\ 0.03 \\ 0.48 \end{pmatrix} = \begin{pmatrix} 0.00000 & 0.00000 & 0.00001 & 0.00001 & 0.00000 & 0.00000 \\ 0.00002 & 0.00001 & 0.00003 & 0.00003 & 0.00002 & 0.00001 \\ 0.00001 & 0.00000 & 0.00002 & 0.00002 & 0.00001 & 0.00001 \\ 0.00016 & 0.00006 & 0.00026 & 0.00027 & 0.00018 & 0.00011 \\ 0.00002 & 0.00001 & 0.00003 & 0.00003 & 0.00002 & 0.00001 \\ 0.00031 & 0.00012 & 0.00048 & 0.00050 & 0.00034 & 0.00022 \end{pmatrix} \times \begin{pmatrix} 0 \\ 0 \\ 1{,}000 \\ 0 \\ 0 \\ 0 \end{pmatrix}$$

Table 5.9   Comparison of round-by-round effects, Boone County, 2001

Industry	Initial Stimulus	Round 1	Round 2	Round 3	Round 4	Round 5	⋯ Total
Extraction	0	0.23	0.68	0.15	0.03	0.01	1.10
Utilities	0	3.14	2.87	0.62	0.14	0.03	6.80
Construction	1,000	1.13	1.33	0.33	0.07	0.02	1,002.87
Manufacturing	0	126.85	24.89	5.31	1.16	0.26	158.47
Transportation	0	6.46	2.31	0.57	0.13	0.03	9.50
Services	0	187.18	42.80	9.71	2.17	0.48	242.35
Total Output	1,000.00	324.99	74.87	16.70	3.71	0.82	1,421.10

construction output multiplier. But additionally we see that besides construction itself, other main beneficiaries of the construction project would be services and manufacturing with increases in output of $242.35 million and $158.47 million. A final demonstration of the round-by-round effects is shown in Fig. 5.2, which shows how change in output levels off with increasing rounds.

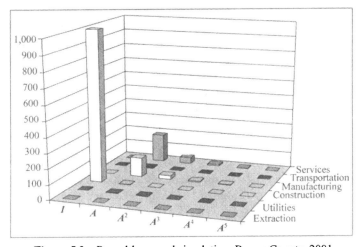

Figure 5.2   Round-by-round simulation, Boone County, 2001

The goal here is to derive a multiplier model usable for economic impact analysis. The solution is found in Eq. (5.12), which stated:

$$X = (I - A)^{-1} \cdot Y \tag{5.12}$$

We can replicate the total output column (X) with the final demand for Boone County from the revised industry transaction table for Boone County, 2001, Table 5.3. Multiplying the $(I - A)^{-1}$ matrix by the final demand column (Y) from Table 5.3 must reproduce the total output column (X). While this appears at first to be trivial, it nevertheless provides the means to double-check your calculations and matrix manipulations. For Boone County, we were able to replicate total output for each industry as indicated in Eq. (5.18). Meaning that the derived $(I - A)^{-1}$ matrix is the correct solution to the system of equations and, as such, can be used for economic impact analysis.

$$
\begin{pmatrix}
1.031 & 0.000 & 0.001 & 0.006 & 0.000 & 0.000 \\
0.013 & 1.001 & 0.007 & 0.015 & 0.006 & 0.009 \\
0.005 & 0.013 & 1.003 & 0.004 & 0.005 & 0.006 \\
0.086 & 0.020 & 0.159 & 1.187 & 0.070 & 0.039 \\
0.008 & 0.019 & 0.010 & 0.012 & 1.039 & 0.007 \\
0.136 & 0.045 & 0.242 & 0.183 & 0.206 & 1.162
\end{pmatrix}
\times
\begin{pmatrix}
7.35 \\
148.53 \\
315.55 \\
1,845.74 \\
2,072.02 \\
2,635.69
\end{pmatrix}
=
\begin{pmatrix}
21.32 \\
215.78 \\
351.98 \\
2,492.60 \\
2,197.94 \\
3,911.55
\end{pmatrix}
\tag{5.18}
$$

5.3.2 The Closed Model—Calculating Type II Output Multipliers

One of the important decisions in deriving the multiplier model for measuring economic impacts is whether or not to consider households as part of the endogenous account. Households, which own most of the factors of production, receive income from the industries in form of wages and salaries, self-employed income, rent, and dividends. In return, households spend a large share of their income on regional goods and services. Although household consumption is clearly a final demand activity, household buying decisions depend largely on their generated income, which is closely related to the level of economic activities in the region. For this reason, households are often included in the endogenous account and treated in the same manner as the industries.

Calculating type II output multipliers starts with including households in the endogenous account. This is done in the revised industry transaction table for Boone County in Table 5.10. Comparing the industry transaction table with households as endogenous (Table 5.10) to the industry transaction table with households as exogenous (Table 5.3) shows the inclusion of the household row (H) and household column (C) into the endogenous account. Before, final demand by households (C) was part of the final demand column (Y). The sub-matrix used for

Table 5.10 Industry transaction table with households endogenous, Boone County, 2001

in million $

Purchases by / Sales by	Endogenous							Exogenous	Total
	Extraction	Utilities	Construction	Manufacturing	Transportation	Services	Households (C)	FinalDemand (Y)	Demand (X)
Extraction	0.63	0.02	0.08	12.43	0.01	0.80	1.75	5.60	21.32
Utilities	0.22	0.17	1.11	28.03	8.29	29.42	39.32	109.22	215.78
Construction	0.07	2.68	0.40	5.06	7.18	21.04	0.00	315.56	351.98
Manufacturing	1.41	2.85	44.65	378.25	112.95	106.77	156.06	1,689.68	2,492.60
Transportation	0.13	3.93	2.28	21.32	79.00	19.27	16.47	2,055.55	2,197.94
Services	2.15	6.62	65.88	325.70	356.21	519.31	1,075.71	1,559.98	3,911.55
Households (H)	5.13	59.72	100.77	465.45	583.64	1,383.58	134.64	352.63	3,085.54
Other Payments (P)	2.54	59.13	12.31	207.38	252.68	760.45	1,005.42	666.89	2,966.80
Imports (M)	9.04	80.67	124.51	1,049.00	797.99	1,070.92	685.09	1,216.80	5,034.00
Total Input (X)	21.32	215.78	351.98	2,492.60	2,197.94	3,911.55	3,114.45	5,735.58	20,277.52

calculating the output multipliers extended by one row and one column to the dimension of 7×7—closing the model with respect to households.

The multiplier derivation does not differ from the one demonstrated for the open model with households as part of the exogenous account. The only difference is that the linear system of equations now has seven instead of six individual equations. At this point we strongly recommend that you attempt to use the industry transaction table with households endogenous for Boone County (Table 5.10) and derive the 7×7 Leontief inverse or $(I - \overline{A})^{-1}$ matrix. If your calculations are correct, you should get the result as shown in Table 5.11.

Table 5.11 Type II output multipliers (OM2$_j$)—total requirement matrix, Boone County

	Extraction	Utilities	Construction	Manufacturing	Transportation	Services	Households(C)
Extraction	1.031	0.001	0.002	0.007	0.001	0.001	0.001
Utilities	0.019	1.008	0.015	0.021	0.014	0.018	0.021
Construction	0.006	0.014	1.004	0.005	0.006	0.008	0.003
Manufacturing	0.116	0.049	0.197	1.214	0.104	0.079	0.093
Transportation	0.012	0.023	0.014	0.015	1.043	0.011	0.011
Services	0.302	0.205	0.455	0.338	0.397	1.384	0.522
Households (H)	0.404	0.387	0.516	0.375	0.463	0.538	1.267
Type II Output Multiplier (OM2$_j$)	1.487	1.298	1.687	1.599	1.565	1.500	0.652
Sum of Marginal Multipliers	1.891	1.685	2.203	1.974	2.028	2.038	1.919

Although households are treated in the same way as industries during the arithmetical derivation of the total requirement table, special attention is required to interpret the results from the closed model. In particular, the marginal multipliers in the household (H) row do not count towards the type II output multipliers (OM2$_j$). The type II output multipliers (OM2$_j$) are represented as the column totals by summing only across the industry rows, or:

$$OM2_j = \sum_{i=1}^{n} \overline{\text{mult}}_{ij} \qquad (5.19)$$

where,

OM2$_j$ — type II output multipliers, e.g., the industry total in column j in table 5.11;

$\overline{\text{mult}}_{ij}$ — partial multipliers from the $(I - \overline{A})^{-1}$ matrix;

$\overline{A}$ — 7×7 technical coefficient matrix with households endogenous;

n — number of industries; e.g., six in the example.

To differentiate between the open model and the closed model, we use a bar over the variable notation (e.g., $\overline{A}$, $\overline{mult}_{ij}$) whenever we derive type II multipliers from the closed model. By including households into the endogenous account of the transaction table one would clearly expect the magnitude of the output multipliers to go up due to a reduction of leakages. Part of the additional household income will be spent in the region and increase the volume of economic activities leading to larger type II output multipliers compared with type I output multipliers. Table 5.12 shows a direct comparison between these two types of common output multipliers and the breakdown into their individual components.

Table 5.12   Type I and type II output multiplier comparison

Industry	Type I Output Multipliers (OM_j)	Type II Output Multipliers ($OM2_j$)	Direct Effect	Indirect Effect	Induced Effect
Extraction	1.279	1.487	1.0	0.279	0.208
Utilities	1.099	1.298	1.0	0.099	0.199
Construction	1.421	1.687	1.0	0.421	0.265
Manufacturing	1.406	1.599	1.0	0.406	0.193
Transportation	1.327	1.565	1.0	0.327	0.238
Services	1.224	1.500	1.0	0.224	0.277

(1) Type I output multipliers are the sum of direct and indirect effects over the initial stimulus. For instance, the construction type I output multiplier (OM_{Const}) is the sum of the direct effect of 1.0 and the indirect effect of 0.421.

(2) Type II output multipliers increase marginally in magnitude due to the inclusion of households in the endogenous account, referred to as **induced effect**. Type II output multipliers can alternatively be defined as:

$$\text{type II output multiplier } (OM2_j)$$
$$= \frac{\text{direct effect+indirect effect+induced effect}}{\text{initial stimulus}}$$

The type II output multiplier for construction ($OM2_{Const}$) of 1.687 is therefore the sum of the direct effect of 1.0, the indirect effect of 0.421, and the induced effect of 0.265.

We conclude this section on type II output multipliers with a final remark on the column total of the total requirement table—the sum of all seven marginal multipliers—which in itself has no specific economic meaning. For instance, the column total reported for construction is 2.203. The difference from the type II construction output multiplier of 1.687 stems from the fact that the marginal multipliers for the households (H) are not added to the type II output multipliers ($OM2_j$). In the successive section we will define the marginal multiplier in the household row as a type II household income multiplier. It is important to recognize that the column sums of marginal multipliers have no significance in input-output analysis.

5.3.3 Household Income Multipliers

While much attention is paid in economic development to firms and businesses, households and household income are equally important. In the input-output framework, household income multipliers are one effective way of translating the change in final demand (ΔY) into new income received by households. The idea is the same as with output multipliers: how much will income received by households increase if, for instance, final demand for an industry's output increases? Like output multipliers, household income multipliers can be broken down into direct, indirect, and induced effects. Analogous to the multiplier definition used for output, we define type I household income multipliers (HM$_j$) as based on direct and indirect output effects, while type II household income multipliers (HM2$_j$) include direct, indirect, and induced effects. The idea is that changes in final demand (ΔY) are followed by changes in output (ΔX) which in return lead to changes in household income. Therefore, as you will see below, household income multipliers are also derived using the Leontief inverse matrix. For calculating type I household income multipliers (HM$_j$) we will use the $(I - A)^{-1}$ matrix from the open model with households exogenous; for calculating type II household income multipliers (HM2$_j$), we then use the $(I - \overline{A})^{-1}$ matrix from the closed model with households endogenous.

Now, let us take a closer look at the idea of how a change in final demand transforms into additional household income. The origin of any economic impacts is the exogenous account, or the final demand sector (Y). Let us assume, for example, that investment demand—which is exogenous in the input-output framework—towards manufacturing products increases by $1,000. Of course, manufacturing responds to this increase in final demand (ΔY) and sells the demanded products. In other words, manufacturing immediately increases its output by $1,000—indicated by the direct effect. This change in output of $1,000 is the trigger to a chain reaction of inter-industry transactions. But how does this initial stimulus finally translate into household income that can further be broken down into direct, indirect, and, if applicable, induced effects? We simply follow the chain of economic transactions. For manufacturing to increase immediate output by $1,000, it requires, in return, the purchase of additional inputs worth also $1,000. And, by looking at the technical coefficient table (Table 5.5), we can identify that the payments to households that would therefore increase by exactly

$187. This $187 increase represents the direct effect in household payments following the initial change in output of $1,000. It is important to understand that the initial stimulus (ΔY) is the same for calculating output and household income multipliers. What differs is that the direct effect in the case of household income multipliers is expressed only by the household (H) row in the technical coefficient matrix. Table 5.13 shows the direct effects on household income for all six industries in the Boone County example.

Table 5.13   Type I and type II household income multipliers

Industry	Type I Household Income Multipliers (HM$_j$)	Type II Household Income Multipliers (HM2$_j$)	Direct Effect	Indirect Effect	Induced Effect
Extraction	0.319	0.404	0.240	0.079	0.085
Utilities	0.306	0.387	0.277	0.029	0.082
Construction	0.407	0.516	0.286	0.121	0.109
Manufacturing	0.296	0.375	0.187	0.109	0.079
Transportation	0.365	0.463	0.266	0.100	0.097
Services	0.425	0.538	0.354	0.071	0.113

The calculations of type I and type II household income multipliers (HM$_j$, HM2$_j$) are straightforward and based on the corresponding Leontief inverse matrices $(I-A)^{-1}$ or $(I-\bar{A})^{-1}$, with the partial multipliers mult$_{ij}$ or $\overline{mult}_{ij}$ respectively.

Type I household income multipliers (HM$_j$) are calculated as:

$$HM_j = \sum_{i=1}^{n} h_i \cdot mult_{ij}; \text{ where } h_i = \frac{H_i}{X_i} \qquad (5.20)$$

where,

HM$_j$ — type I household income multipliers;

h_i — technical coefficients from the A matrix for households, e.g., row 7[1];

mult$_{ij}$ — partial multipliers in row i and column j from the $(I-A)^{-1}$ matrix;

H_i — household payments by industry i from the industry transaction table;

X_i — output by industry i;

n — number of industries; e.g., six in the open model.

---

[1] Another common variable notation for the technical coefficients in the household row is $a_{n+1,i}$. In a matrix with n industries, it denotes the succeeding row, in this example, the household row.

Type I household income multipliers for Boone County, with six industries and households as exogenous, are calculated as:

$$\text{HM}_j = \sum_i^n h_i \cdot \text{mult}_{ij} = (0.240\ 0.277\ 0.286\ 0.187\ 0.266\ 0.354\ )$$

$$\times \begin{pmatrix} 1.031 & 0.000 & 0.001 & 0.006 & 0.000 & 0.000 \\ 0.013 & 1.001 & 0.007 & 0.015 & 0.006 & 0.009 \\ 0.005 & 0.013 & 1.003 & 0.004 & 0.005 & 0.006 \\ 0.086 & 0.020 & 0.159 & 1.187 & 0.070 & 0.039 \\ 0.008 & 0.019 & 0.010 & 0.012 & 1.039 & 0.007 \\ 0.136 & 0.045 & 0.242 & 0.183 & 0.206 & 1.162 \end{pmatrix}$$

$$= (0.319\ 0.306\ 0.407\ 0.296\ 0.365\ 0.425) \tag{5.21}$$

Multiplying the row vector containing the technical coefficients for households with each column of the $(I-A)^{-1}$ matrix results in a row vector containing all six household income multipliers. The manufacturing household income multiplier (HM_{mfg}), for instance, is calculated as

$$\begin{aligned}\text{HM}_{\text{mfg}} &= (0.240\times0.006)+(0.277\times0.015)+(0.286\times0.004)\\ &\quad +(0.187\times1.187)+(0.266\times0.012)+(0.354\times0.183)\\ &= 0.296\end{aligned} \tag{5.22}$$

Following an increase in final demand for manufacturing industries (ΔY_{mfg}) in value of one dollar and as a result of direct and indirect effects, household income is expected to increase by 29.6 cent. Using an initial stimulus of a $1,000 increase in demand for manufacturing products, would translate into a total additional household income of $296.

Type II household income multipliers (HM2_j) are calculated using the same logic. But now to account for households endogenously, we use the $(I-\bar{A})^{-1}$ matrix derived from the closed model. Mathematically, the type II household income multipliers (HM2_j) are expressed as

$$\text{HM2}_j = \sum_{i=1}^{n+1} h_i \cdot \text{mult}_{ij}; \quad \text{where } h_i = \frac{H_i}{X_i} \tag{5.23}$$

where,

HM2_j — type II household income multipliers;

h_i — technical coefficients from the $\bar{A}$ matrix for households;

mult_{ij} — partial multipliers from the $(I-\bar{A})^{-1}$ matrix;

H_i— household payments by industry i from the transaction table;

X_i— output by industry i;

n — number of industries; e.g., six in the example;

$n+1$ — household (H) row; e.g., row seven in the example.

In the case of Boone County, the type II household income multipliers are calculated using a 7×7 matrix with six industries augmented by a household row and column:

$$\text{HM2}_j = \sum_{i=1}^{n+1} h_i \cdot \text{mult}_{ij} = (0.240\ 0.277\ 0.286\ 0.187\ 0.266\ 0.354\ 0.043)$$

$$\times \begin{pmatrix} 1.031 & 0.001 & 0.002 & 0.007 & 0.001 & 0.001 & 0.001 \\ 0.019 & 1.008 & 0.015 & 0.021 & 0.014 & 0.018 & 0.021 \\ 0.006 & 0.014 & 1.004 & 0.005 & 0.006 & 0.008 & 0.003 \\ 0.116 & 0.049 & 0.197 & 1.214 & 0.104 & 0.079 & 0.093 \\ 0.012 & 0.023 & 0.014 & 0.015 & 1.043 & 0.011 & 0.011 \\ 0.302 & 0.205 & 0.455 & 0.338 & 0.397 & 1.384 & 0.522 \\ 0.404 & 0.387 & 0.516 & 0.375 & 0.463 & 0.538 & 1.267 \end{pmatrix}$$

$$= (0.404\ 0.387\ 0.516\ 0.375\ 0.463\ 0.538\ 0.267) \tag{5.24}$$

Again, multiplying each element of the household (H) row vector from the technical coefficient table by each column of the $(I - \bar{A})^{-1}$ matrix results in this particular industry's type II household income multipliers. For instance, manufacturing's Type II household income multiplier is 0.375. Thus, with households endogenous, an increase in final demand in manufacturing (ΔY_{mfg}) of one dollar would increase household income by 37.5 cents. Thus, an increase in final demand for manufacturing products, as in the example, of $1,000, would lead to total additional household income of $375.

Table 5.13 summarizes all type I and type II household income multipliers and breaks down the multipliers into their individual effects, namely direct, indirect, and induced effects. From this comparison we conclude that changes in final demand for services have the largest impact on household income, while contrarily changes in final demand for manufacturing output has the smallest impact on household income. Another observation is that the calculated type II household income multipliers (HM2_j) are identical to the industry entries in the household (H) row in the type II output multipliers (OM2_j) matrix, Table 5.11. In practice this means that there is no need to calculate type II household income multipliers (HM2_j). For economic impact analysis, type II multipliers, both output and household income, can always be taken directly from the Leontief inverse, the $(I - \bar{A})^{-1}$ matrix.

5.3.4   More on Input-Output Multipliers

So far we have focused on two multipliers that can be derived from the input-output framework and used for economic impact analysis. Using these multipliers, we can answer questions on how total output for each industry is expected to change following an initial change in final demand. Additionally, household income multipliers measure how additional final demand would transform into additional household income. It is important to recognize that a change in final demand leads to an increase in industry output, which in return translates into additional income for households. After all, industries must increase their inputs to be able to meet the increase in final demand.

Up to now we have considered cases where the economic stimulus originated in final demand. But this is not always the case. Imagine a scenario in which an existing firm announces that it expects its economic activities to increase significantly in the next year. In return this increase in economic activity will lead to additional payments of wages and salaries to households. Let us take an example of $1.0 million. Here, the initial stimulus will take place via the payroll rather than through final demand. The question one may ask is now: how does this expected change in the payroll stimulate the regional economy? The answer to this question can be found by using income multipliers.

5.3.4.1   Income Multipliers

Like household income multipliers, income multipliers (IM_j and $IM2_j$) measure additional industry payments to households following an exogenous injection. Household income multipliers translate changes in final demand into new household income via output. In contrast, income multipliers measure total change in household income through initial stimuli taking place in income that households receive. To be more specific, this estimated additional $1.0 million in household income will inevitably increase regional household consumption. In return, an increase in final demand by household translates into increases in industry output. Industries require more intermediate inputs, which lead to added inter-industry transactions, more household payments, and so on. Again, we have a chain reaction of economic activities; but with income multipliers, the starting point of the round-by-round effects is the initial estimated $1.0 million change in household income payments.

Like output or household income multipliers, we have the choice of using an economic model which is open with respect to households—type I—or which is closed with respect to households—type II. The type I income multipliers (IM_j) are defined as:

$$IM_j = \sum_{i=1}^{n} \frac{(h_i \cdot mult_{ij})}{h_j} = \frac{HM_j}{h_j} \qquad (5.25)$$

where,

IM_j — type I income multipliers;

h_j — technical coefficients from the A matrix for households;

$mult_{ij}$ — partial multipliers from the $(I - A)^{-1}$ matrix;

HM_j — household income multipliers;

n — number of industries; e.g., six in the example.

Analogously, the type II income multipliers are defined as:

$$IM2_j = \sum_{i=1}^{n+1} \frac{(h_i \cdot mult_{ij})}{h_j} = \frac{HM2_j}{h_j} \qquad (5.26)$$

where,

$IM2_j$ — type II income multipliers;

$mult_{ij}$ — partial multipliers from the $(I - \bar{A})^{-1}$ matrix;

$HM2_j$ — type II household income multipliers.

Thus, in the Boone County example, we can calculate the type I income multiplier for manufacturing as:

$$IM_{mfg} = \frac{HM_{mfg}}{h_{mfg}} = \frac{0.296}{0.187} = 1.586^{[1]} \qquad (5.27)$$

Continuing with the Boone County example, the type II income multiplier for manufacturing is calculates as:

$$IM2_{mfg} = \frac{HM2_{mfg}}{h_{mfg}} = \frac{0.375}{0.187} = 2.009 \qquad (5.28)$$

Once again, and in accordance with other multipliers, we can break down the total multiplier effects into their individual components, namely direct, indirect, and, if applicable, induced effects. All income multipliers for Boone County are listed for comparison in Table 5.14. Note that, in the case of income multipliers, the direct effect of 1.00 accounts now for the fact that the initial stimulus leading to the round-by-round effect stems from an expected increase in household payments (ΔH).

---

[1] Please note that all calculations were done in a spreadsheet. Recalculating individual multipliers might show some deviations from the results listed due to rounding.

Table 5.14 Type I and type II income multipliers

Industry	Type I Income Multipliers (IM_j)	Type II Income Multipliers $(IM2_j)$	Direct Effect	Indirect Effect	Induced Effect
Extraction	1.327	1.681	1.00	0.327	0.354
Utilities	1.104	1.399	1.00	0.104	0.295
Construction	1.422	1.802	1.00	0.422	0.380
Manufacturing	1.586	2.009	1.00	0.586	0.423
Transportation	1.375	1.742	1.00	0.375	0.367
Services	1.200	1.520	1.00	0.200	0.320

In the case of an estimated payroll increase of a manufacturing firm in Boone County of $1.0 million, total household income is expected to increase by $1.586 million when accounting for direct and indirect effects. The additional inclusion of households into the model augments the multiplier through the induced effects. For Boone County, this means that total household income increases to $2.009 million when using the economic model, which is closed with respect to households.

5.3.4.2 Household Employment Multipliers

Employment is another economic key variable that is given much attention in economic analysis. So far, all data, such as inter-industry transactions, output, or final demand, have been expressed in monetary values. The key for integrating employment, which is measured by the number of jobs per industry, is establishing a connection between jobs and output per industry. This is usually done by computing employment/output ratios, or:

$$e_i = \frac{E_i}{X_i} \tag{5.29}$$

where,

e_i — employment/output ratio for industry i;

E_i — employment for industry i;

X_i — output for industry i.

The employment/output ratio e_i measures the number of employees per monetary unit worth of output. Using the employment (E_i) data for Boone County together with the output data reported in the county's input-output table (e.g., Table 5.2) we can calculate the employment/output ratios (e_i) as demonstrated in Table 5.15 below.

Table 5.15   Employment/output ratios (e_i), Boone County[1]

Industry	Employment (E_i)	Output (X_i) [1]	Employment/Output Ratio (e_i)
Extraction	852	21.32	39.97
Utilities	313	215.78	1.45
Construction	4,072	351.98	11.57
Manufacturing	12,151	2,492.60	4.87
Transportation	14,319	2,197.94	6.51
Services	53,954	3,911.55	13.79
Households	217	3,085.54	0.07

(1) Output is reported in million dollars.

For instance, the transportation employment/output ratio (e_i) of 6.51 indicates that for every one million dollars worth of output, the transportation service industry employs 6.51 people. Output in this example is reported in million dollars. The 217 people reported under households refer to personal and home care aides only. The data on household employment are supplemented by data from the Bureau of Labor Statistics. Total output for households, as reported in table 5.15, refers to the sum of household income from industries, payments among households, government transfer, and dividends. In this sense, the employment/output ratio for households is the ratio of personal and home care aides over total income earned by households.

Again, we first evaluate the expected change in employment following a change in output—stimulated by a change in final demand—as expressed by the type I and II household employment multipliers $(LM_j$ and $LM2_j)$.

Type I household employment multipliers (LM_j) are defined as:

$$LM_j = \sum_{i=1}^{n} e_i \cdot mult_{ij}; \quad where \ e_i = \frac{E_i}{X_i} \tag{5.30}$$

where,

LM_j — type I household employment multipliers;

e_i — employment/output ratio by industry i;

$mult_{ij}$ — partial multipliers in row i and column j from the $(I-A)^{-1}$ matrix;

E_i — employment by industry i;

X_i — output by industry i;

n — number of industries; e.g., six in the example.

The type I household employment multipliers for Boone County using the open model are calculated as:

$$LM_j = \sum_i^n e_i \cdot \text{mult}_{ij} = (39.97 \; 1.45 \; 11.57 \; 4.87 \; 6.51 \; 13.79)$$

$$\times \begin{pmatrix} 1.031 & 0.000 & 0.001 & 0.006 & 0.000 & 0.000 \\ 0.013 & 1.001 & 0.007 & 0.015 & 0.006 & 0.009 \\ 0.005 & 0.013 & 1.003 & 0.004 & 0.005 & 0.006 \\ 0.086 & 0.020 & 0.159 & 1.187 & 0.070 & 0.039 \\ 0.008 & 0.019 & 0.010 & 0.012 & 1.039 & 0.007 \\ 0.136 & 0.045 & 0.242 & 0.183 & 0.206 & 1.162 \end{pmatrix}$$

$$= (43.62 \; 2.45 \; 15.84 \; 8.70 \; 10.04 \; 16.37) \tag{5.31}$$

A hypothetical increase in demand for transportation services of one million dollars would, based on direct and indirect effects, lead to a total of 10 new jobs in the economy.

Type II household employment multipliers ($LM2_j$) are calculated with households being endogenous using the $(I - \bar{A})^{-1}$ matrix. They are expressed as follows:

$$LM2_j = \sum_{i=1}^{n+1} e_i \cdot \text{mult}_{ij}; \quad \text{where } e_i = \frac{E_i}{X_i} \tag{5.32}$$

where,

$LM2_j$ — type II household employment multipliers;

e_i — employment/output ratio by industry i;

mult_{ij} — partial multipliers from the $(I - \bar{A})^{-1}$ matrix;

E_i — employment by industry i;

X_i — output by industry i;

n — number of industries; e.g., six in the example;

$n+1$ — household (H) row; e.g., row seven in the example.

For Boone County, using a model closed with respect to households, the type II household employment multipliers are calculated as:

$$LM2_j = \sum_{i=1}^{n+1} e_i \cdot \text{mult}_{ij} = (39.97 \; 1.45 \; 11.57 \; 4.87 \; 6.51 \; 13.79 \; 0.07)$$

$$\times \begin{pmatrix} 1.031 & 0.001 & 0.002 & 0.007 & 0.001 & 0.001 & 0.001 \\ 0.019 & 1.008 & 0.015 & 0.021 & 0.014 & 0.018 & 0.021 \\ 0.006 & 0.014 & 1.004 & 0.005 & 0.006 & 0.008 & 0.003 \\ 0.116 & 0.049 & 0.197 & 1.214 & 0.104 & 0.079 & 0.093 \\ 0.012 & 0.023 & 0.014 & 0.015 & 1.043 & 0.011 & 0.011 \\ 0.302 & 0.205 & 0.455 & 0.338 & 0.397 & 1.384 & 0.522 \\ 0.404 & 0.387 & 0.516 & 0.375 & 0.463 & 0.538 & 1.267 \end{pmatrix}$$

$$= (46.16 \; 4.88 \; 19.07 \; 11.05 \; 12.93 \; 19.74 \; 7.94) \tag{5.33}$$

Again, using the transportation industry as example, the employment multiplier now rises from 10.04 to 12.93 by additionally accounting for induced effects. Thus, an increase in demand for transportation of one million dollars would lead to an additional 13 jobs. For transportation, including inter-industry transactions would add 3.5 new jobs to the initial 6.5 new jobs. Including household transactions would add an extra 2.90 jobs per million dollar change in final demand. All type I and type II household employment multipliers are reported in Table 5.16 together with the direct, indirect, and induced effects.

Table 5.16   Type I and type II household employment multipliers

Industry	Type I Household Employment Multipliers (LM_j)	Type II Household Employment Multipliers $(LM2_j)$	Direct Effect	Indirect Effect	Induced Effect
Extraction	43.62	46.16	39.97	3.66	2.53
Utilities	2.45	4.88	1.45	1.00	2.43
Construction	15.84	19.07	11.57	4.27	3.23
Manufacturing	8.70	11.05	4.87	3.82	2.35
Transportation	10.04	12.93	6.51	3.52	2.90
Services	16.37	19.74	13.79	2.57	3.37

5.3.4.3   Employment Multipliers

Last in the long list of multipliers, employment multipliers evaluate how total employment would change if the initial stimulus does not come from a change in final demand for an industry's output, but rather from a change in employment itself. For instance, employment multipliers may be used to predict the total effect on employment including round-by-round effects from an increase in economic activities at the Cincinnati/Northern Kentucky International Airport that would bring 1,000 new jobs in the region. For all cases where the initial stimulus originates in employment itself, employment multipliers measure the expected change in total employment when accounting for additional inter-industry and household transactions.

Like output and income multipliers, type I employment multipliers (EM_j) account for direct and indirect effects and are defined as:

$$EM_j = \sum_{i=1}^{n} \frac{e_i \cdot mult_{ij}}{e_j} = \frac{LM_j}{e_j} \qquad (5.34)$$

where,

EM_j — type I employment multipliers;

e_i — employment/output ratio by industry i;

mult_{ij} — partial multipliers from the $(I - A)^{-1}$ matrix;

LM_j — household income multipliers;

n — number of industries; e.g., six in the example.

The corresponding type II employment multipliers $(EM2_j)$ are defined as:

$$EM2_j = \sum_{i=1}^{n+1} \frac{e_i \cdot \text{mult}_{ij}}{e_j} = \frac{HM2_j}{e_j} \tag{5.35}$$

where,

$EM2_j$ — type II income multipliers;

mult_{ij} — partial multipliers from the $(I - \overline{A})^{-1}$ matrix;

$EM2_j$ — type II household income multipliers.

The type I and type II employment multipliers for Boone County are listed together in Table 5.17 together with the direct, indirect, and induced effects. For cross-comparison with household employment multipliers listed in Table 5.16, the direct effect of 1.00 accounts for the fact that starting point for the round-by-round effect is an expected increase in employment (ΔE).

Table 5.17 Type I and type II employment multipliers

Industry	Type I Employment Multipliers (EM_j)	Type II Employment Multipliers $(EM2_j)$	Direct Effect	Indirect Effect	Induced Effect
Extraction	1.092	1.155	1.00	0.092	0.063
Utilities	1.690	3.363	1.00	0.690	1.673
Construction	1.369	1.648	1.00	0.369	0.279
Manufacturing	1.784	2.266	1.00	0.784	0.482
Transportation	1.540	1.985	1.00	0.540	0.445
Services	1.186	1.431	1.00	0.186	0.244

The type I and type II employment multipliers for transportation are calculated as:

$$EM_{transport} = \frac{LM_{transport}}{e_{transport}} = \frac{10.04}{6.51} = 1.540 \tag{5.36}$$

and

$$EM2_{transport} = \frac{LM2_{transport}}{e_{transport}} = \frac{12.93}{6.51} = 1.985 \tag{5.37}$$

respectively. For the example of an increase in airport transportation employment of 1,000, we would expect total employment in the county to increase by 1,540 when considering direct and indirect effects. The inclusion of induced effects increases the expectation to 1,985 new jobs.

In this section we have derived numerous multipliers using the simplified input-output table for Boone County. All of these multipliers allow us to assess **what** would happen **if**, for instance, changes in exogenous final demand were expected. Using the corresponding multipliers thus allows us to evaluate changes in output and employment necessary to meet this change in final demand. Further, we can make some statements about how household income is expected to change. As we have seen, exogenous changes can occur through final demand, which in return can be translated directly into changes in output, income, and employment. Alternatively, changes in the economy may be expressed in terms of income or employment changes, for which we also have derived the corresponding multipliers. Independent of the origin of these economic stimuli, we have learned how using multipliers allows us to assess the economic impacts on output, income, and employment following these exogenous changes. Additionally, we have derived two different economic models: an open model that considers only additional inter-industry transactions, and a closed model that incorporates household transactions in the round-by-round effects. For a better comparison, we have prepared a summary table (Table 5.18) including all multipliers covered in this section.

Table 5.18 Multiplier comparison and notational conventions

	Type I Multipliers: Model open with respect to households	Type II Multipliers: Model closed with respect to households
Leontief Inverse	$(I - A)^{-1}$	$(I - \overline{A})^{-1}$
Partial Multipliers	mult_{ij}	mult_{ij}
Output Multipliers	$OM_j = \sum_{i=1}^{n} \text{mult}_{ij}$	$OM2_j = \sum_{i=1}^{n} \overline{\text{mult}_{ij}}$
Household Income Multipliers	$HM_j = \sum_{i=1}^{n} \left(\dfrac{H_i}{X_i}\right) \cdot \text{mult}_{ij}$ $= \sum_{i=1}^{n} h_i \cdot \text{mult}_{ij}$ N/A	$HM2_j = \sum_{i=1}^{n+1} \left(\dfrac{H_i}{X_i}\right) \cdot \overline{\text{mult}_{ij}}$ $= \sum_{i=1}^{n+1} h_i \cdot \overline{\text{mult}_{ij}}$ $HM2_j = \overline{\text{mult}}_{n+1,j}$
Income Multipliers	$IM_j = \sum_{i=1}^{n} \dfrac{(h_i \cdot \text{mult}_{ij})}{h_j}$ $= \dfrac{HM_j}{h_j}$	$IM2_j = \sum_{i}^{n+1} \dfrac{(h_i \cdot \overline{\text{mult}_{ij}})}{h_j}$ $= \dfrac{HM2_j}{h_j}$

Continued

	Type I Multipliers: Model open with respect to households	Type II Multipliers: Model closed with respect to households
Household Employment Multipliers	$LM_j = \sum_{i=1}^{n}\left(\dfrac{E_i}{X_i}\right)\cdot mult_{ij}$ $= \sum_{i=1}^{n} e_i \cdot mult_{ij}$	$LM2_j = \sum_{i=1}^{n+1}\left(\dfrac{E_i}{X_i}\right)\cdot \overline{mult}_{ij}$ $= \sum_{i=1}^{n+1} e_i \cdot \overline{mult}_{ij}$
Employment Multipliers	$EM_j = \sum_{i=1}^{n}\dfrac{e_i \cdot mult_{ij}}{e_j}$ $= \dfrac{LM_j}{e_j}$	$EM2_j = \sum_{i=1}^{n+1}\dfrac{e_i \cdot \overline{mult}_{ij}}{e_j}$ $= \dfrac{LM2_j}{e_j}$

Several other multipliers can be derived from an input-output table. For instance, import requirements to meet a change in final demand can be estimated in a fashion similar to what has been done with income and employment. Import coefficients, defined as $m_i = M_i / X_i$, are the starting point here. Instead of using income or employment, we simply use imports to calculate the necessary coefficients. Likewise the next step would be to multiply the row vector with import coefficients by the $(I - A)^{-1}$ matrix for the open model with household as exogenous or by the $(I - \bar{A})^{-1}$ matrix for the closed model with households as endogenous. The same principle can be applied to assess additional revenues for federal, state, or local governments. In this case, using government revenue/output ratios would link government revenues to the economic model in order to evaluate how changes in output might affect government revenues.

5.4 Assumptions and Extensions of Input-Output Analysis

Like any other economic model, the application of input-output to economic impact analysis depends largely on what assumptions are applied. While little can be done to overcome these assumptions, misinterpretations can be avoided by understanding these assumptions and how they affect the results:

(1) Probably the most crucial assumption in traditional input-output analysis is that the **economy is totally demand-driven**. There exist no supply constraints for firms and businesses, meaning that each industry has enough excess production capacities to meet any increase in final demand. In particular, this assumption is likely to be unrealistic for evaluating larger economic impacts. Firms and businesses usually try to avoid larger unproductive capacities and, therefore, cannot meet any arbitrary increase in final demand.

(2) The **technical coefficients** (a_{ij}) **in the A-matrix are fixed**. The underlying production function is linear and exhibits constant returns to scale. Remember, reading down the column in the A-matrix shows an industry's production function, or the shares of intermediate inputs required. Fixed input coefficients imply that an industry's input requirements always change in proportion with an increase in output. The direct implication of fixed technical coefficients is the absence of substitutability between inputs of production. As a result, marginal input coefficients are equal to average input coefficients. In the short-run, the equality of marginal and average input coefficients may not be of much significance to the outcome of the analysis. But in the long run, technological changes, the possibility of increasing returns to scale, price changes, and the international trade pattern can substantially affect the input mix so that the equality of marginal and average input coefficients may no longer hold. Therefore, input-output technical coefficients need to be updated periodically over time and any long-term economic projections based on the input-output framework have to be done with precaution.

(3) **Prices are constant without** subject to change, making the input-output model a **fixed price** model. Again, for short-run analyses the assumption of fixed prices is tolerable, but questions the suitability of input-output models for long-run purposes and/or for analyzing large economic impacts. This is of importance as price changes influence buying decisions for final and intermediate demand.

(4) A last important shortcoming is that firms and businesses belonging to the same industry sector produce one **homogenous product**. As such, changes in the product mix of industries are not counted. For instance, many manufacturing firms maintain their own truck fleet. A manufacturing firm which uses its fleet to move its merchandise across the country is clearly providing a transportation service, but is accounted for under manufacturing.

Clearly, the input-output framework is built upon pillars of assumptions, which, depending on the economic impact scenario, might constrain its applicability. Especially for evaluating long-run projects or particularly large exogenous changes, one might consider alternative evaluation methods, which relax some of the assumptions described above. For short-run analysis, however, input-output analysis provides a convenient and easy to use tool for answering questions of the type: **what... if...**? But besides all its caveats, input-output analysis is a widely used method for assessing regional and industry-wide economic impacts.

Part of the popularity of input-output analysis is its versatility in extending the descriptive and multiplier framework to very specific topics. Each is covered in the relevant input-output literature. Here, we focus briefly on some of the fields where input-output tables provide the necessary platforms for extended and more sophisticated analyses.

Miller and Blair (1985) in their classical book—*Input-Output Analysis: Foundations and Extensions*—show how the input-output framework can be used to trace **energy uses** and account for **environmental pollution**. Here, transaction tables provide the means for expanding the original idea of the input-output framework by simply adding additional rows and columns to add additional information related to energy uses and pollutants. The Bureau of Economic Analysis (BEA), for instance, provides two satellite accounts, which are basically extended input-output accounts with focus on specific uses. The **environmental satellite account** adds an environmental dimension to the economic accounting system by linking the environment to production, income, consumption, and wealth.[1] In a similar fashion, the **transportation satellite account** tracks the various transportation mode ownership types. More specifically, in-house transportation captures all transportation activities by firms and businesses owning their own trucks while for-hire transportation accounts for all as transportation designated firms and businesses which are usually referred to in the input-output table as transportation industries.[2]

Other utilizations of the input-output framework include **inter-industry linkage analyses**. An idea that originated in the 1950s[3] is the use of input-output tables to show linkages between industries to measure how one industry may stimulate other industries. **Backward linkages** identify how one industry stimulates other industries through the purchase of their inputs. It is defined as the ratio of purchase of intermediate inputs to the total value of inputs, or:

$$BL_j = \frac{\sum_i t_{ij}}{X_j} = \sum_i a_{ij} \qquad (5.38)$$

where,

BL_j — backward linkage of industry j;

t_{ij} — inter-industry transactions between industry i and industry j;

X_j — total inputs (supply) by industry j;

a_{ij} — technical input-output coefficients.

We can see immediately that these total backward linkages are identical to the column sum of technical coefficients from the technical coefficients or A-matrix.

Forward linkages provide a measure of how an industry stimulates other industries by selling its output to other industries. It is defined as:

$$FL_j = \frac{\sum_j t_{ij}}{X_i} \qquad (5.39)$$

where,

---

[1] http://www.bea.gov/bea/articles/NATIONAL/NIPAREL/1994/0494od.pdf.

[2] http://www.bea.gov/bea/articles/NATIONAL/Inputout/1998/0498io.pdf.

[3] Rasmussen, 1956; Hirschman, 1958; Chenery and Watanabe, 1958.

FL_j — forward linkage of industry j;

X_i — total output (demand) by industry i.

Computationally, the derivation of total forward linkages for industries is very similar to calculating technical coefficients. But note the difference: instead of dividing the inter-industry transactions (t_{ij}) by the column total (X_j) and summing down the rows as we did to calculate technical coefficients, we divide the inter-industry transactions (t_{ij}) by the row total (X_i) and sum across the columns. Using row totals and summing across columns turns the input- output framework into a **supply-driven** economic model. The multipliers derived from this framework are referred to as **input** multipliers. While conceptually straightforward, it is questionable whether or not an economy can be presented conceptually as purely supply-driven.

Another widely used application of the input-output framework is the identification of **structural changes** in economies. Comparing input-output tables, technical coefficients, and linkages over time allows one to determine whether or not an economy has undergone structural changes. For instance, one may identify whether the region following the nationally observed trend of moving towards service delivery. Recent research by Guo and Planting (2000), for instance, has shown that the influence of manufacturing industries has gradually decreased and that this decrease in influence can partially be attributed to an increase in leakages from U.S. imports. In their study, the authors used six input-output tables for the period from 1972 to 1996. They found that while the importance of manufacturing declined, construction, real estate, and service gained importance in the U.S. economy.

So far, the discussion on economic impact analyses has centered on the input-output framework as originally introduced by Wassily Leontief. In the 1970s, pioneer work by Richard Stone and subsequent work by Pyatt, Round, and Thorbecke extended the input-output framework into a **social accounting framework (SAM)**.[1] While the input-output framework focuses mainly on interrelationships between the producing sectors, industry outlays to the factors of production and final demand consumption, the SAM extends this industry-focused framework by adding socioeconomic transactions. Depending on the level of disaggregation of households and the factors of production, social accounting matrices allow additional welfare and poverty analyses by tracing income generation, income distribution and consumption.

Conceptually, the SAM is also a square matrix that, for a period of time (usually one year), maps all economic transaction within a region. Like an input-output table, the rows depict inflows of money (e.g., income) and columns

---

① Thorbecke, 1998.

the outflows of money (e.g., expenditures). The major advantage of social accounting matrices over input-output tables is that the inclusion of socioeconomic transactions allows it to provide a more comprehensive snapshot of the economy. Table 5.19 provides a conceptual overview of the structure of a social accounting matrix which is broken down into four sub-accounts: production, factors of production, institutions, and trade.

The **production account** remains conceptually unchanged from the input-output table. Reading down the columns indicates inputs, such as intermediate demand, payments to the factors of production (e.g., labor and capital), indirect business tax payments, and imports. Across the rows we can identify sales to other industries; final demand consumption composed of household, government, and investment demand; and exports.

The main change from the input-output table is the inclusion of the **factors of production** as a separate account into the matrix. The input-output table already maps factor payments to capital and labor (in the Boone County input-output table, we have called it households and other payments). Reading down the factors of production columns, the SAM now traces exactly how these factor payments are distributed among the receiving institutions, namely households, governments, firms, and capital. The IMPLAN^Pro SAM, for instance, breaks down households into nine distinct household groups according to their annual income. In this way, one can identify income received by low-income households in the form of wages, salaries, rent and interest. Using SAM multipliers allows the evaluation of potential policies with respect to changes in income for selected household groups.

A third account covers **institutions**, which includes households, governments, firms, and capital. As in the input-output table these institutions map final demand consumption in the form of household, government, and investment final demand. The social accounting framework additionally maps inter-institutional transfers. The capital account row identifies, for example, savings from households, governments, and firms. Further, we can make out direct tax payments through households, transfer payments (like welfare and unemployment payments) and transfers between household groups.

A last account—**the trade account**—then denotes regional trade activities. Depending on the level of detail required, a break down is possible between domestic (e.g., with the rest of the U.S.) and foreign trade (e.g., with partners outside the U.S.). Here, the SAM adds information to the usual industry exports and imports by including net foreign investment and household and government commodity trade and transfers. For instance, these transfers include household remittances and foreign borrowing through the local government.

As with input-output tables there is no standard way of organizing the flow of income and expenditure within a social accounting framework. But regardless of how exactly incomes and expenditures are mapped or the level of disaggregation, the social accounting framework becomes a valuable policy tool when

Table 5.19   A simplified conceptual social accounting matrix

Incomes \ Expenditures	Endogenous Accounts			Exogenous Accounts					Totals Receipts
	Production (1)	Factors of Production Labor (2a)	Capital (2b)	Households (3a)	Governments (3b)	Firms (3c)	Capital Account (3d)	Trade Account (4)	
Production (1)	Intermediate Demand			Household Consumption	Government Consumption		Investment	Exports	Production Income
Factors of Production — Labor	Payments to Labor (wages)							Labor Incomes from Abroad	Factor Income
Factors of Production — Capital	Payments to Capital (rent)							Capital Incomes from Abroad	Factor Income
Households (3a)		Allocation of Labor Income to Households	Allocation of Capital Income to Households	Intrahousehold Transfers	Transfers i.e. Welfare & Unemployment Payments	Dividends		Transfers	Household Income
Government (3b)	Indirect Business Taxes	Social Security Tax	Taxes on Profits	Personal Taxes	Intragovernment Transfers	Dividends, Taxes		Transfers	Government Income
Firms (3c)			Nondistributed Profits		Transfers				Firms Income
Capital Account (3d)			Capital Consumption Allowance	Household Savings	Government Savings	Firm Savings			Total Savings
Trade Account (4)	Imports	Labor Payments Abroad	Capital Payments Abroad	Commodity Trade, Transfers	Commodity Trade, Transfers		Capital Purchases		Total Imports
Totals	Total Production Outlays	Factor Outlays		Household Expenditures	Government Expenditures	Firm Expenditures	Total Investment	Total Exports	

examining policies and planning measures that focus less on firms and business and more on the generation and distribution of income. Social accounting matrix multipliers prove to be useful for detailed evaluation of: (1) the generation of factorial income, (2) the distribution of these factor payments among the institutions, and (3) the inter-institutional transfers that follow exogenous changes. For instance, governments who often pay up front the cost of development projects can now evaluate how a specific project may stimulate the regional economy and how this stimulus can ultimately translate into additional tax revenues.

The derivation of the economic model derived from a social accounting matrix follows analogously the step-by-step procedure explained using input-output tables. Again, the starting point is the definition of what is included endogenously in the model and what remains exogenous. In the sample SAM above, we included households in the endogenous account while all other institutions and trade remain exogenous. A highly aggregated and partitioned SAM is shown in Table 5.20.

Table 5.20   The schematic algebraic social accounting matrix

Expenditures / Receipts	Endogenous Accounts			Exogenous Accounts	
	Production	Factors of Production	Households	Government, Firms, Capital, Exports	Totals Receipts
Production	T_{11}	0	T_{13}	Y_1	X_1
Factors of Production	T_{21}	0	0	Y_2	X_2
Households	0	T_{32}	T_{33}	Y_3	X_3
Government,Firms, Capital, Imports	O_1	O_2	O_3	R	X_4
Totals Expenditures	X_1	X_2	X_3	X_4	

Transactions within the endogenous sub-accounts are labeled T_{11} through T_{33}. Y_1, Y_2, Y_3 are column vectors of exogenous injections from combined government, firms, capital, and exports account towards production, factors of production, and households respectively. Leakages from industries, factors, and households are accordingly denoted by O_1, O_2, and O_3. Inter-institutional transactions among the exogenous accounts are labeled R and finally, X_1, X_2, X_3, and X_4 refer to both, total expenditures and total incomes.

The step-by-step approach to solving the system of linear equations represented by the schematic algebraic social accounting matrix follows exactly the solution algorithm for the input-output framework, Eq. (5.3) – (5.12). Accordingly, the final social accounting matrix multiplier model can be written in matrix notation as:

$$X = (I - A_n)^{-1} \cdot Y \tag{5.40}$$

where,

$$A_n = \begin{pmatrix} A_{11} & 0 & A_{13} \\ A_{21} & 0 & 0 \\ 0 & A_{32} & A_{33} \end{pmatrix},$$

is the partitioned matrix of technical coefficients following the division into endogenous and exogenous accounts mentioned earlier. Thus, using the SAM multiplier model in Eq. (5.39) allows us to evaluate changes in industry output (ΔX), payments to factors of production (e.g., labor and capital) and household income following an exogenous injection (ΔY). The $(I - A_n)^{-1}$ matrix is now referred to as the SAM multiplier matrix and the column totals represent the individual multipliers.

For Boone County, Table 5.21 lists a six-industry social accounting matrix for the year 2001. Please note that in the social accounting framework all corresponding row and column totals are equal, including those of the factor account and the institutions. In addition, Table 5.22 lists the final Boone County SAM multiplier matrix derived from the Boone County social accounting matrix in Table 5.21. Of course, the magnitude of SAM multipliers must increase compared to regular output multipliers as a result of including the factors of production and households in the multipliers calculation. Comparing the total requirement matrices for the open and closed input-output models, e.g., Table 5.7 and Table 5.11, respectively, we recognize that the multiplier matrix shown in Table 5.22 includes rows/columns with the individual factors of production—employee compensation (EC), proprietary income (PI), and other property income (OPI)—and a total of nine rows/columns with the households grouped by annual income.

Table 5.23 shows a comparison of type I and type II output multipliers with the corresponding SAM multipliers for the six industries example of Boone County. Accounting multipliers are consistently larger than output multipliers, ranging from 2.191 (Utilities) to 2.922 (Construction) in the six-industry economy. Further, SAM multipliers may increase by over 100 percent compared to type I output multipliers. For instance, the SAM multiplier for transportation of 2.692 represents an increase of 103 percent over the type I transportation output multiplier of 1.327. Compared to the type II transportation output multiplier of 1.565, it still shows an increase of 72 percent. We can conclude that expanding the input-output framework to a social accounting matrix also results in a significant magnification of the multipliers.

Table 5.21 The six-industry Boone County social accounting matrix, 2001

	Extract	Utilities	Construct	Mfg	Transport	Services	EC	PI	OPI	HHLT10	HH10–15	HH15–25
Extraction	0.63	0.02	0.08	12.43	0.01	0.80	–	–	–	0.04	0.04	0.11
Utilities	0.22	0.17	1.11	28.03	8.29	29.42	–	–	–	1.34	1.15	3.09
Construction	0.07	2.68	0.40	5.06	7.18	21.04	–	–	–	–	–	–
Manufacturing	1.41	2.85	44.65	378.25	112.95	106.77	–	–	–	3.90	3.39	9.09
Transportation	0.13	3.93	2.28	21.32	79.00	19.27	–	–	–	0.36	0.28	0.75
Services	2.15	6.63	65.88	325.70	356.21	519.31	–	–	–	24.93	21.04	56.42
Employee Compensation	3.51	48.21	117.66	537.03	808.03	1,517.77	–	–	–	–	–	–
Proprietary Income	1.41	2.81	33.61	13.48	15.67	177.52	–	–	–	–	–	–
Other Property Income	3.76	63.82	-13.12	272.47	140.70	615.45	–	–	–	–	–	–
Households LT10k	–	–	–	–	–	–	8.30	0.89	0.74	0.01	0.00	0.01
Households 10 – 15k	–	–	–	–	–	–	15.52	1.71	1.38	0.01	0.01	0.01
Households 15 – 25k	–	–	–	–	–	–	65.40	7.35	5.83	0.05	0.02	0.05
Households 25 – 35k	–	–	–	–	–	–	94.00	10.80	8.45	0.07	0.03	0.06
Households 35 – 50k	–	–	–	–	–	–	214.03	25.12	19.44	0.15	0.08	0.15
Households 50 – 75k	–	–	–	–	–	–	532.11	64.61	49.16	0.38	0.19	0.35
Households 75 – 100k	–	–	–	–	–	–	379.83	46.89	35.61	0.27	0.13	0.25
Households 100 – 150k	–	–	–	–	–	–	346.37	43.54	32.75	0.25	0.12	0.23
Households 150k +	–	–	–	–	–	–	258.50	31.65	24.00	0.18	0.09	0.17
Federal Government	0.10	6.74	0.80	5.59	25.88	81.52	351.91	11.96	– 0.51	0.46	0.87	3.72
State/Local Government	0.26	17.63	2.09	14.64	67.76	213.42	2.14	–	0.99	1.97	1.85	5.58
Enterprises (Corporations)	–	–	–	–	–	–	–	–	274.30	–	–	–
Public Investment	–	–	–	–	–	–	–	–	–	–	–	–
Private Investment	–	–	–	–	–	–	–	–	491.58	0.09	0.08	5.20
Inventory Additions/Deletions	–	–	–	–	–	–	–	–	–	0.09	0.08	0.20
Foreign Trade	0.67	1.76	6.80	67.50	30.89	19.58	–	–	3.69	0.71	0.63	1.92
Domestic Trade	7.00	58.55	89.75	811.11	545.38	589.69	764.09	–	135.67	15.68	13.44	36.04
Totals	21.32	215.78	351.98	2,492.60	2,197.94	3,911.55	3,032.21	244.50	1,083.07	50.91	43.53	123.40

Endogenous Account

Exogenous Account

Continued

	HH25–35	HH35–50	HH50–75	HH75–100	HH100–150	HH150+	FedGov	S/L Gov	Enterpr	Public Inv	Private Inv	Inventory	Foreign	Domes-tic	Total
Extraction	0.13	0.25	0.43	0.32	0.26	0.171	0.001	0.07	—	—	0.00	0.01	3.81	1.72	21.32
Utilities	3.16	5.80	10.06	6.28	5.11	3.328	0.381	9.78	—	0.00	0.00	−0.06	0.37	98.74	215.78
Construction	—	0.00	0.00	—	—	—	—	6.00	—	58.91	240.39	−0.98	0.04	11.20	351.98
Manufacturing	10.76	23.29	39.28	28.30	23.05	15.00	18.24	12.45	—	5.96	98.84	−8.43	361.11	1,201.52	2,492.60
Transportation	0.97	1.97	3.79	3.56	2.90	1.89	−0.01	−1.22	—	0.07	10.14	−2.20	290.40	1,758.37	2,197.94
Services	66.05	149.23	263.85	210.79	171.66	111.76	74.56	168.05	—	3.33	48.67	0.47	112.01	1,152.89	3,911.55
Employee Compensation	—	—	—	—	—	—	—	—	—	—	—	—	—	—	3,032.21
Proprietary Income	—	—	—	—	—	—	—	—	—	—	—	—	—	—	244.50
Other Property Income	—	—	—	—	—	—	—	—	—	—	—	—	—	—	1,083.07
Households LT10k	0.01	0.02	0.05	0.05	0.06	0.08	3.41	1.11	0.19	—	35.97	0.00	0.00	—	50.91
Households 10 – 15k	0.02	0.03	0.06	0.06	0.09	0.13	10.16	1.31	0.15	0.00	12.89	0.00	0.00	—	43.53
Households 15 – 25k	0.07	0.11	0.21	0.24	0.34	0.55	32.23	9.46	1.49	—	0.00	0.00	0.01	—	123.40
Households 25 – 35k	0.09	0.15	0.28	0.32	0.48	0.79	32.43	18.75	2.57	—	0.00	0.00	0.01	—	169.28
Households 35 – 50k	0.20	0.34	0.62	0.73	1.09	1.80	39.00	31.40	8.55	—	0.01	0.01	0.01	—	342.72
Households 50 – 75k	0.50	0.80	1.48	1.76	2.68	4.50	41.78	40.08	9.32	—	0.01	0.01	0.02	—	749.76
Households 75 – 100k	0.36	0.57	1.04	1.25	1.92	3.24	25.37	18.89	32.87	—	0.01	0.00	0.01	—	548.51
Households 100 – 150k	0.33	0.52	0.95	1.14	1.75	2.96	13.46	12.60	22.15	—	0.01	0.00	0.01	—	479.12
Households 150k+	0.24	0.38	0.69	0.83	1.28	2.16	15.09	5.98	11.69	—	0.00	0.00	0.01	—	352.93
Federal Government	5.42	20.76	68.79	49.51	53.55	39.56	0.01	0.02	69.03	—	—	—	0.01	0.03	795.72
State/Local Government	6.46	17.28	44.95	35.34	34.12	24.04	34.71	1.38	10.97	—	0.02	0.01	0.31	6.01	543.93
Enterprises (Corporations)	—	—	—	—	—	—	24.81	4.08	—	—	51.20	—	—	—	354.38
Public Investment	—	—	—	—	—	1.35		77.76	—	—	2.20	—	—	—	81.30
Private Investment	29.56	23.98	144.71	76.72	72.22	69.86	384.37	42.41	185.39	2.21	0.04	51.16	0.22	—	1,579.78
Inventory Additions/ Deletions	0.24	0.52	0.88	0.63	0.51	0.33	0.40	0.29	—	0.13	2.20	0.00	8.14	27.04	41.68
Foreign Trade	2.50	5.29	8.75	7.25	5.53	5.31	5.60	2.38	—	0.85	598.80	0.08	—	—	776.48
Domestic Trade	42.24	91.45	158.90	123.46	100.55	65.46	38.38	80.88	—	9.84	478.39	1.59	—	—	4,257.53
Totals	169.28	342.72	749.76	548.51	479.12	352.93	795.72	543.93	354.38	81.30	1,579.78	41.68	776.48	4,257.53	

Endogenous Account / Exogenous Account

Table 5.22 Boone County SAM multiplier matrix, $(I - A_n)^{-1}$

	Extract	Utilit-ies	Cons-truct	Mfg	Trans-portation	Servi-ces	EC	PI	OPI	HH LT10	HH10 -15	HH15 -25	HH25 -35	HH35 -50	HH50 -75	HH75 -100	HH100 -150	HH 150+
	1.03	0.00	0.00	0.01	0.00	0.00	0.00	0.00	0.00	0.00	0.00	0.00	0.00	0.00	0.00	0.00	0.00	0.00
	0.02	1.01	0.02	0.02	0.01	0.02	0.01	0.02	0.00	0.04	0.04	0.03	0.03	0.03	0.02	0.02	0.02	0.02
	0.01	0.01	1.00	0.00	0.01	0.01	0.00	0.00	0.00	0.00	0.00	0.00	0.00	0.00	0.00	0.00	0.00	0.00
	0.11	0.04	0.20	1.21	0.10	0.07	0.06	0.09	0.02	0.13	0.13	0.13	0.11	0.12	0.09	0.09	0.09	0.08
	0.01	0.02	0.01	0.01	1.04	0.01	0.01	0.01	0.00	0.01	0.01	0.01	0.01	0.01	0.01	0.01	0.01	0.01
	0.28	0.17	0.46	0.32	0.39	1.36	0.34	0.51	0.09	0.71	0.70	0.66	0.56	0.63	0.50	0.55	0.52	0.47
	0.31	0.31	0.56	0.40	0.56	0.56	1.15	0.23	0.04	0.32	0.32	0.30	0.25	0.28	0.23	0.24	0.23	0.21
	0.08	0.02	0.12	0.02	0.03	0.06	0.02	0.23	0.00	0.03	0.03	0.03	0.03	0.03	0.02	0.03	0.02	0.02
	0.24	0.33	0.06	0.19	0.14	0.23	0.06	0.10	1.02	0.14	0.14	0.13	0.11	0.12	0.10	0.10	0.10	0.09
	0.00	0.00	0.00	0.00	0.00	0.00	0.00	0.00	0.00	1.00	0.00	0.00	0.00	0.00	0.00	0.00	0.00	0.00
	0.00	0.00	0.00	0.00	0.00	0.00	0.01	0.01	0.00	0.00	1.00	0.00	0.00	0.00	0.00	0.00	0.00	0.00
	0.01	0.01	0.02	0.01	0.01	0.02	0.03	0.04	0.01	0.01	0.01	1.01	0.01	0.01	0.01	0.01	0.01	0.01
	0.02	0.01	0.02	0.02	0.02	0.02	0.04	0.05	0.01	0.01	0.01	0.01	1.01	0.01	0.01	0.01	0.01	0.01
	0.04	0.03	0.05	0.03	0.05	0.05	0.09	0.13	0.02	0.03	0.03	0.03	0.02	1.03	0.02	0.02	0.02	0.02
	0.09	0.08	0.14	0.09	0.11	0.13	0.21	0.32	0.06	0.08	0.08	0.07	0.06	0.07	1.05	0.06	0.06	0.06
	0.06	0.06	0.10	0.06	0.08	0.09	0.15	0.23	0.04	0.06	0.05	0.05	0.04	0.05	0.04	1.04	0.04	0.04
	0.06	0.05	0.09	0.06	0.07	0.08	0.14	0.21	0.04	0.05	0.05	0.05	0.04	0.04	0.03	0.04	1.04	0.04
	0.04	0.04	0.07	0.04	0.06	0.06	0.10	0.16	0.03	0.04	0.04	0.03	0.03	0.03	0.03	0.03	0.03	1.03
	2.41	2.19	2.92	2.49	2.69	2.78	2.42	3.13	1.37	2.69	2.65	2.55	2.32	2.45	2.17	2.27	2.20	2.13

Table 5.23   Output and SAM multiplier comparison, Boone County

Industry	Multipliers			Percent Increase versus	
	Type I Output	Type II Output	SAM	Type I Multiplier	Type II Multiplier
Extraction	1.279	1.487	2.413	88.70	62.30
Utilities	1.099	1.298	2.191	99.40	68.78
Construction	1.421	1.687	2.922	105.55	73.20
Manufacturing	1.406	1.599	2.495	77.41	56.00
Transportation	1.327	1.565	2.692	102.87	72.01
Services	1.224	1.500	2.779	127.12	85.22

This review of social accounting matrices and accounting multipliers is intended to briefly introduce further extensions of the input-output framework. While the derivation of SAM multipliers is analogous to the derivation of output multipliers, their interpretation and use for policy analyses requires training that goes beyond the understanding of input-output analysis. For the interested reader, we have listed some readings on social accounting matrices which should provide you with an entry point into the vast literature of the social accounting framework.

We want to conclude this chapter by reemphasizing the tremendous opportunities input-output analysis has to offer for planners in helping to understand the complexity of regional economies. Today, input-output is a valuable and readily available tool for economic impact analysis for answering questions of the type: **what... if... ?** In times of scarce resources, economic impact analysis using multipliers derived from input-output tables and social accounting matrices can provide the necessary means to make educated and informed decisions among different possible policy actions.

Review Questions

1. What is the significant improvement of the input-output framework with all its multipliers when comparing it to the economic base model and the economic base multiplier?

2. Explain the importance of production accounts, i.e., the interindustry transactions, for setting up an input-output table.

3. Describe in detail all individual components of a conceptual input-output table. Identify which of the sectors you would classify as endogenous and which as exogenous. What is the rational behind dividing the input-output table into an endogenous and an exogenous part?

4. What is the intuitive explanation for an output multiplier? Using your own words, specify what is exactly meant with direct, indirect, and induced effects.

5. Express the calculation of type II output multipliers using linear algebra (i.e., a system of linear equations).

6. What is the conceptual difference between household income multipliers and income multipliers?

7. Assume you have an input-output table that would include households (H) and a government sector within the payment section, explain how you could conceptually derive a government revenue multiplier using information from the government sector.

8. Explain in some detail what the expected outcome on the magnitude of the multipliers would be when you include "other payments" (P) into the endogenous part of the input-output table?

9. Discuss how input-output tables and social accounting matrices and their multipliers can be a powerful tool for economic development strategies.

10. Discuss the shortcomings of the input-output framework.

Exercises

You are given a hypothetical input-output table for a small urban region. Data entries in Table 5.24 are in million dollars. The input-output table identifies: five industry sectors, two consuming sectors, i.e., households (C) and final demand (FD), and industry outlays to households (H), other payments (P) and imports.

Table 5.24 Hypothetical input-output table

	Ind.1	Ind.2	Ind.3	Ind.4	Ind.5	House-holds (C)	Final Demand (FD)	Total Output
Industry 1	10	20	10	10	10	50	290	400
Industry 2	20	50	20	20	40	70	380	600
Industry 3	20	60	50	20	20	50	580	800
Industry 4	20	50	100	150	80	120	180	700
Industry 5	10	20	20	20	20	80	530	700
Households (H)	50	100	200	100	100	50	20	620
Other Payments (P)	100	100	200	100	200	50	100	850
Imports (M)	170	200	200	280	230	130	500	1,710
Total Input	400	600	800	700	700	600	2,580	

The use of a spreadsheet software program with matrix algebra functions will considerably help with these questions. In addition to calculating various types of multipliers, you will assess economic impacts following an exogenous stimulus. In particular, we are assuming that final demand (FD) for industry 2 will increase annually by as much as $20 million dollar, due to an increase in export activities of a local firm. Please answer the following questions:

1. Calculate the type I output multipliers. How would output for each industry sector change if final demand for industry 2 would increase by $20 million dollars?

2. Calculate the type II output multipliers. Again using this exogenous stimulus, how would industry output change when households are treated endogenously?

3. Derive the type II household income multipliers ($HM2_j$). How is household income expected to change following the $20 million dollar injection?

4. Calculate the type II household employment multipliers ($LM2_j$) and estimate total changes in employment following the exogenous stimulus?

5. Using "Other Payments" (P) as a proxy for government revenues in form of indirect business taxes, derive a type II government revenue multiplier and project potential future government revenues from the $20 million dollar increase in export activities in industry 2.

References

Chenery, Hollis and T. Watanabe. 1958. International comparisons of the structure of production. *Econometrica*, 26(4): 487 – 521.

Defourny, Jacques and Erik Thorbecke. 1984. Structural path analysis and multiplier decomposition within a social accounting matrix framework. *The Economic Journal*, 94: 111 – 136.

Hewings, Geoffrey J. D. and Rodney C. Jensen. 1995. Regional, interregional and multiregional input-output analysis. In: Peter Nijkamp (ed.). *Handbook of Regional and Urban Economics*, Volume 1. 2nd reprint. 2000 ed. New York, NY: Elsevier Science Publishing Co.

Hewings, Geoffrey J. D. 1982. The empirical identification of key sectors in an economy: a regional perspective. *The Developing Economies*, 20(2): 19 – 31.

Heinz D. Kurz, Erik Dietzenbacher, and Christian Lager. 1998. Input-output analysis. *The International Library of Critical Writings in Economics 92, Vol. I – III*. Cheltenham, UK: Edward Elgar Publishing Limited.

Hirschman, Albert. 1958. *The Strategy of Economic Development*. New Haven, CT: Yale University Press.

Miller, Ronald E. 1998. Regional and interregional input-output analysis. In: Walter Isard, Iwan Azis, Matthew P. Drennan, Ronald E. Miller, Sidney Saltzman and Erik Thorbecke (eds.) *Methods of Interregional and Regional Analysis*. Brookfield, VT: Ashgate Publisher.

Miller, Ronald E and Peter D. Blair. 1985. *Input-Output Analysis: Foundations and Extensions*. Englewood Cliffs: Prentice Hall, Inc.

Polenske, Karen R and Jiri V. Skolka. 1974. Advances in input-output analysis. In: *Proceedings of the Sixth International Conference on Input-Output Techniques*, Vienna, April 22 – 26, 1974, Cambridge: Ballinger Publishing Company.

Pyatt, Graham and Jeffrey I. Round. 1985. *Social Accounting Matrices: A Basis for Planning*. Washington, DC: The World Bank.

Rasmussen. 1956. *Studies in Intersectoral Relations*. Amsterdam: North Holland.

Reinert, Kenneth A. and David W. Roland-Holst. 1997. Social accounting matrices. In: Joseph F. Francois and Kenneth A. Reinert (eds.). *Applied Methods for Trade Policy Analysis: A Handbook*. Cambridge: Cambridge University Press.

Sonis, Michael, Geoffrey Hewings and J. Guo. 1996. Sources of structural change in input-output systems: A Field of Influence Approach. *Economic Systems Research*, 6(1): 15 – 32.

Schaffer, William A. 1999. Regional impact models. In: The Web Book of Regional Science. Available online at http: // www. rri. wvu.edu/Web Book/schaffer/index.html.

Stone, Richard. 1986. Where are we now? A short account of the development of input-output studies and their present trends. In: Ira Sohn (ed.). *Readings in Input-Output Analysis*. New York, NY: Oxford University Press.

Thorbecke. 1998. Social accounting matrices and social accounting Analysis. In: Isards et al. (eds.) *Methods of Interregional and Regional Analysis*. Brookfield, VT: Ashgate Publisher.

United Nations Statistics Division. *Handbooks and Manuals on National Accounting*. accessible online at http://unstats.un.org/unsd/sna1993/handbooks.asp.

U.S. Department of Commerce, Bureau of Economic Analysis. 1985. *An introduction to national economic accounting*. In: *Methodology Paper Series MP-1*, Washington DC, Government Printing Office.

William A. Schaffer. 1999. *Regional Impact Models*. Morgantown, WV: Regional Research Institute. West Virginia University.

Chapter 6   Land Use Analysis

As we discussed at the beginning of the book, the four planning analyses covered in this book answer questions related to "Who", "What to do", "Where" and "What connection." Land use analysis studies where and what types of human activities are taking place. Most human activities, such as employment, recreation, or residence, are linked to land. A land use study is one way of understanding those activities. A land use study may also focus on the land itself. Different activities may place different requirements on land and their impacts also vary. Through land use analysis, we can understand if a piece of land is suitable for a given activity. Also, we can understand the consequences of human activities and how they change the landscape.

At a conceptual level, land use refers to the human activities on land. Clawson and Steward (1965) realized the confusion of concepts about land and distinguished land data as:

(1) Location: All land is registered to a spatial coordinate system. Different data about a piece of land can be related to the land location, through which multiple data can be associated.

(2) Activity: This refers to the purpose, or use, of a piece of land.

(3) Natural qualities: The surface and subsurface characteristics and vegetative cover are examples of natural qualities.

(4) Improvements: This refers to the human modification of the land, such as leveling, filling drainage and building structures.

(5) Intensity of land use: The amount of activity per unit of area is measured as intensity.

(6) Land tenure: This refers to the ownership of a piece of land.

(7) Land price: This reflects the land market activity.

(8) Interrelations: This aspect recognizes that no piece of land stands alone. For example, the access to a piece of land may affect the activity on it.

(9) Interrelations: The activities on land are closely related to other activities, such as employment, income investment etc.

We will soon see that the distinctions specified by Clawson and Steward 40 years ago are still valid today. Burley (1961) pointed out the confusion and clarified the meaning of land use. He traced the original definition of land use back to the definition provide by Sauer[1] as the use to which the entire land

---

[1] Sauer, C.O. Mapping the Utilization of the Land, *Geographical Review*, Vol. 8, 1919, p.48. Cited in (Burley, 1961).

surface is put. According to Burley, land use consists of two interrelated phenomena— land cover and land utilization. Land cover describes the natural and human altered land surface on which activities takes place. Land utilization, on the other hand, describes the action on the land. This clarification is significant since most land use studies consider both. Naturally, a certain type of land use is normally associated with specific types of land cover. On the one hand, human activities are limited by the setting and on the other hand, human activities alter the land cover. This connection is the basis for the designation of land use types from interpretation of land cover characteristics.

Because of the close connection between land and human activities, land use analysis is called upon in an area where a change is expected. If there is no human desire to develop an area, there is no need for land use analysis. The purpose of land use analysis is to help answer questions such as "What should be built?", "Where should it be built?", "When and how should it be built?" and "What impact will it generate?". The reason these are important questions is that the goal of land planning is to produce good communities. Although there is much to be debated about what constitutes a "good" community among the stakeholders, they all need land use analysis to provide a base for their reasoning.

Kaiser et al. (1995) have identified three major types of institutional stakeholders, in addition to planners, who have an interest in land. The market group includes land owners, developers, builders, realtors, and bankers. Their interest in land is to seek profit. They will need land use analysis to help identify the land where land use changes can generate profits. The government group includes elected and appointed government officials who are charged with making land use changes that meet the public's interest. They need land use analysis to produce knowledge about which the types and locations of land use change can lead to a well-built environment. The third group includes stakeholders who have special interests, such as environmental preservation, economic development, or farming. They also need land use analysis to evaluate the potential impact on their interests.

In short, land use analysis is a set of tools that helps to understand: (1) how land is currently used; (2) what land use changes can be made in accordance to a set of rules; and (3) what are the impacts of land use changes. Within this context, we will discuss two types of land use analysis in this chapter. The first type describes land use patterns and distributions within a study area. The second type determines the developability a proposed land use. Both of these analyses are based on the spatial variation of land characteristics. Consequently, people have different preferences when they make decisions about what to do with a piece of land. The difference is reflected in the various land uses. Therefore, the foundation of land use analysis is land classification, which reflects such variation. Only after a study area is divided into smaller land parcels with different uses can we analyze and compare different human activities. In this chapter, we will first explore the relationship between land use and human activities. Then, we will discuss ways of classifying land uses, which is followed by the analysis of land use distribution patterns and land developability.

6.1   Land Use and Human Activities

The prevailing consideration for land management has an anthropocentric basis. Land value is often a reflection of its direct usefulness to humans. In land use analysis, human activities can be divided into three major categories—residential (where people live); employment (where people work); and others (non-residential and non-employment activities). The importance of land to human activities is reflected in the interaction between the two. As shown in Fig. 6.1, on the one hand, land provides resources for meeting human demand, such as space, materials, and energy. For example, a manufacturing plant must have a piece of land large enough for buildings and production lines. A person must intake water regularly. Therefore, a human settlement must be close to surface or underground fresh water resources. The history of human settlements around the world is full of such evidence. This represents the material and energy flow from land to humans. On the other hand, human activities modify the nature of the land. These changes of physical characters and composition of land have the purpose of supporting human activities. For example, people clear natural vegetation to plant crops for food, to build houses for shelter, to level hills or dig tunnels for roads. Also, people add chemicals to farm fields and lawns and, dispose municipal waste in to the ground.

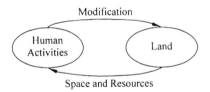

Figure 6.1   Human-land relationship

People can easily see the benefit of withdrawing resources from land and modifying land. After a new road is built people can start to enjoy the improved travel right away. On the other hand, it is less obvious and more difficult for people to realize that the changes on land can actually harm people. For example, the increased area of impervious surface as a result of a new road may contribute to loss of property and human lives in a storm event. Increased water consumption due to growing population and higher consumption rates may lead to the shortage or exhaustion of water resources in a city. However, it is difficult to link such damage to any particular development. It is often the result of an accumulation of many development activities. Even though such linkage can be established in some cases, the problem may occur long after the development is completed. As such, many unpleasant consequences of poor development are readily and frequently observed around the world. To ensure high quality land development that maximizes benefits and minimizes damage to humans, urbanization and its accompanying development require careful planning.

The previous discussion is based on the idea that only people are valuable and non-human species have value only as means to meet human needs. An alternative perspective is the biocentric view, which says that non-human species are valuable in and of themselves, regardless of their use to humans. Meanwhile, humans have moral obligations to recognize and respect their values. These two schools of thought affect how an individual considers the benefit and impact of a particular development. Those who take the biocentric view may differ on which species are worthy of people's consideration (Ortolano, 1997). Discussion of those philosophical differences goes beyond the scope of this book. However, there is no argument that people's activities are different and different land uses exist to support the variety of human activities. The methods of analysis to be presented in this book can be used in any research to advance the knowledge of human-land relationship.

Intensity is a measure of human activities, which is related to the number of people at a place and what they do there. The kind of human activities at a place determines the resource demand and alteration to the land. Some human activities do not need a lot of resources from land and require minimal change to the natural environment. For example, parks are where people go to enjoy nature. The only changes to the land to provide access and vital needs, such as drinking water and sanitation. People walk and play in a park, these activities do not require a great deal of resources and do not generate much waste. If the park land is converted for agricultural activities, the slope may be leveled, drainage ditches may be installed and chemicals, such as fertilizers and pesticides may be applied. If the land is converted to a residential area, houses and roads will be built and utility and power lines will be installed. During the process, the landscape may be altered and part of the land surface will be covered with pavement.

Construction of an office or commercial complex would require the replacement of all natural vegetation with concrete structures below and above ground. While the demand for water, electricity and other resources for a park may be little, a manufactory would requires more resources to support the production activities. People may build a narrow street to provide access to a residence while access to a commercial area requires more and wider streets.

In general, land use changes tend to lead to higher intensity levels. For example, land in its natural condition is less intensive than residential land because the vegetation land cover is converted to buildings and streets. Commercial or industrial land uses are more intensive than residential land use. For example, in its early days, farming was one of Boone County's primary activities along the 70 kilometer portion of the Ohio River. Now, 34% of the

276

County is for agriculture and 31% for various development activities, including residential, industrial, commercial, and institutional uses.

In addition to land use types, the number of people on a given land can affect the intensity level of human activities. Taking Boone County as an example, there were about 1,500 people when the county was officially established in 1799 Two hundred years later, on the same 666 square kilometer land area, the County population has increased to 85,991 (U.S. 2000 Census). This results in higher intensity of human activities.

Urbanization, which is part of the comprehensive phenomenon of societal change, manifests human history (Gilbert and Gugler, 1981). To a large degree, urban functions have determined the physical features of land. Using the United States as an example, we can describe urbanization in four phases that reflect the transition of urban functions. In general, the intensity of human activities has been increasing along with urbanization.

The first phase is the pre-industrial era, dating from the late 17th century to 1820. There were two types of cities formed—political centers where the administrative sovereign lived and commerce and finance centers where agricultural surplus were assembled, traded and redistributed (Melosi, 1980). People gathered in those cities for security, or to exchange goods, services and ideas. Cities became markets for agricultural products and subsequently locations for supplementary industries such as flour milling and ship-building. Those cities became economic, political and cultural centers. The population of cities in the pre-industrial era was relatively small compared to that in the later era. For example, at the beginning of the eighteenth century, 7,000 people lived in Boston, the largest city in the U.S. New York City housed 5,000 people (Nash, 1997). The physical size of the cities was also small. The core of urban areas was normally related to walking distance.

The second phase of urbanization started as early as 1820 when industrial cities emerged as the dominant urban form. During the beginning of the industrial revolution, cities were concentrated with manufactory that helped to significantly increase the nation's prosperity. New cities such as Pittsburgh, Cleveland and Milwaukee began to experience rapid growth and vast economic prosperity. Some old cities, such as Boston and Philadelphia, also attracted major industries. The value added by manufacturing increased ten-fold in the half-century, almost trebling the increased value of farm products (McKelvey, 1963). For the most part, proximity to large cities meant the difference between economic success and failure. The increasing use of machines reduced the need of the farming labor. The excess farm workers had moved to cities for better job prospects and opportunities. In short, the industrial revolution attracted people to cities. Along with the urban population increase, industrial activities took more land, extracted more resources, and discharged more pollutants. Some of the pollutants resided on land. The result was an increase of human activities, which led to more land being built. Due to the nature of the industrial process, industrial cities experienced environmental challenges posed by rapid large-scale industrialization and urbanization that were never experienced before, such as overcrowded tenements, congested traffic, poor health, smoky skies, wastes, polluted waterways, and noise (Melosi, 1980).

The third urbanization phase started about 1920 as a product of accelerating technological revolution, such as electric power, the automobile, and the telephone. In this phase, technological revolution made it possible to diffuse people and industry over a much wider area (Hauser and Schnore, 1965). Manufacturing plants in cities were moved to rural/suburban areas, as well as to cities in less developed regions. The original industrial cities have been transformed from centers of local significance to the core of much larger metropolitan areas functioning as centers of the regional, national, and world economics. In central cities, financial institutions and service sectors, such as retail, office, restaurants, government, education, medical care, etc., gradually replaced manufacturing industries. As the urban areas grew outward, more land was converted to roads and buildings.

The fourth phase started about the third quarter of the 20th century. The unique feature that separates this phase from previous phases is that by now urban population stopped increasing while areas with urban services kept expanding. Many service sectors, such as government offices, business offices, schools, and medical care moved to suburbs. Meanwhile, the need for face-to-face transaction and for centrally located office space had diminished (Lampard, 1983). The difference between urban population and rural population in suburbs became fuzzy. Someone working in an urban center may live 50 kilometers away in a suburb with all the services that used to only available in urban areas— telephone, electricity, tap water, sewerage service, garbage pickup, neighborhood parks and entertainment. While some cities remained service and financial centers, many other cities, especially central cities, were left with hollow areas of abandoned buildings and contaminated land.

The increasing number of towns within or beyond metropolitan boundaries manifests this pattern. What is commonly known as the "Edge City" phenomenon (Garreau, 1988) has given rise to the creation of a new urban landscape characterized by the loss of sense of place and identity, the rise of urban sprawl, and, particularly, office development. According to Garreau (1988 (p.5)), "by the mid-1980s, there was far more office space in Edge Cities around America's largest metropolis, New York, than there was at its heart—midtown Manhattan". The impact on land from this phase was more related to the type of activities than to the population density. Take the American dream—single-family home as an example. We have seen the increase of the size of new houses in the Cincinnati area. Houses built in the early 1900s are about 1,500 square feet. Most recently built houses in the suburbs are larger than 3,000 square feet. This phenomenon is translated to more land needs that support the same number of people. The additional land can only be found by converting more farmland and woodland.

Kelbaugh (2002) asserts that urban sprawl reflects the historical propensity of Americans to depend on expansion, growth, and start-over somewhere else as a way to solve difficult problems. With abundant space and resources, Americans feel no reason to crowd together in small dwellings in tightly packed cities. Automobiles are now deeply rooted in American culture. Together with the extensive publicly funded highway system, people are willing to drive alone much farther to live in large houses.

The American style of urbanization has resulted in many changes to land. Those changes have put more pressure on increasing land use intensity. In order to maintain the desirable life standards, people make more changes to and withdraw more resources from land. Along with the rapid urbanization in the world, resource consumption has been rising faster than population growth. One example is in the United States, the amount of urban land has increased faster than the urban population growth rate as a result of residents and businesses moving to "Green fields" in the suburbs and leaving inner city land behind as "Brownfields" or abandoned land. The pressures for more land are even greater in developing countries where population growth rates are higher. Urban growth has taken prime agricultural and forest land. When less land is available to accommodate the increased demand, development takes more land in less desirable areas, such as steep slopes, floodplains, and wetlands.

A review of the human history reveals the increased intensity of human activities. This leads to the importance of land use planning, which should help guide urban development to be more environmentally friendly while providing adequate land for urban activities. Currently, the demand for resources and land has increased to a point such that humans need to be concerned about resource and land availability. Within this context, land use analysis helps examine land developability based on feasibility and impact of a particular use of land. In short, land developability analysis reviews what requirements a proposed human activity imposes for a site, the capacity of land to support such proposed use, and the impact and compatibility of such use to existing uses on surrounding land. Both feasibility and impact must be determined from physical, economical, and political aspects. In order to conduct such land analysis, the first step is to classify land into categories that are reflective of different land uses for various human activities.

6.2   Land Classification

The principal concept of land classification is to separate human activities of different intensity levels. Normally, land classes are ranked from low to high intensity for human activities. There are several different approaches of land classification. The most common approaches are based on ownership, structure, ground coverage, or use of land. Sometimes a single land classification may use more than one of those features.

Harland Bartholomew (1955) first adopted a land use classification in the early 1950s. Bartholomew applied a two-level land classification system (Table 6.1). At the first level, one category is vacant land and the rest are developed land. Some of the developed land categories are publicly developed and others are privately developed. Some of the categories are further divided at the second level.

Table 6.1   Bartholomew land use classification

Level 1	Level 2
Residential	Single-family homes
	Two-family homes
	Multiple dwellings (apartments)
Commercial	
Industrial	Light industry
	Heavy industry
Public and Semi-public	Schools, churches, hospitals,
	institutions, golf courses, etc.
Public Parks	
Railroads	
Streets	
Vacant Land	Undeveloped or agricultural

Source: Lovelace, 1993

Bartholomew developed his classification system based on a land survey approach using large-scale land plat maps. The rationale for Bartholomew's land classification was to set up a simple system that can be standardized for data collection and comparison. When more detailed data became available, the system was made more complex (Lovelace, 1993), such as using ownership to separate the developed land. Within each ownership category, the system groups land by the use types. We can tell that a piece of land can be classified from a field survey and review of ownership data.

The Standard Land Use Coding Manual (SLUCM) published by the Bureau of Public Roads and the Urban Renewal Administration in 1965 introduced a land-use classification based on the Standard Industrial Classification (SIC) system (Urban Renewal Administration and Bureau of Public Roads, 1965). This coding system uses numeric digits that match the SIC codes to identify land-use activities. Table 6.2 lists some examples of land use classes. There are nine one-digit categories, 67 two-digit categories, 294 three-digit categories and 772 four-digit categories.

Table 6.2   The SLUCM land use activity classification

1	Residential units	
	11	Household
	12	Group quarters
		121 Rooming and boarding houses
		122 Membership lodgings
		123 Residence halls or dormitories
		1231 Nurses homes
		1232 College dormitories
		1239 Other residence halls or dormitories, NEC
		124 Retirement homes and orphanages
		125 Religious quarters
		129 Other group quarters, NEC
	13	Residential hotels
	14	Mobile home parks or courts
	15	Transient lodgings
	19	Other residential, NEC (Not elsewhere coded)
2	Manufacturing	
	21	Food and kindred products—manufacturing
		211 Meat products—manufacturing
		2111 Meat packing—manufacturing
		2112 Sausages and other prepared products—manufacturing
		...
	...	
...		
3	Manufactuing	
	31	Rubber and miscellaneous plastic products—manufacturing
		311 Tires and inner tubes—manufacturing
		312 Rubber footwear—manufacturing
		3120 Rubber footwear—manufacturing
4	Transportation, communication, and utilities	
5	Trade	
6	Services	
7	Cultural, entertainment, and recreational	
8	Resource production and extraction	
9	Undeveloped land and water area	

Source: URA and BPR, 1965

Additional digits are used to represent ownership and structure type. Table 6.3 lists the ownership and structure coding systems. In addition, the system also uses a set of one-digit auxiliary categories to link certain significant auxiliary functions and the parent activities they serve. For example, an automobile parking area for a meat packing plant (2111) would be coded as 2111-5.

Table 6.3   SLUCM ownership and structure coding systems

A. Coding system for identifying ownership	
1	Public
11	Federal
12	State
13	County
14	Township
15	Municipal
16	Special district
19	Other publics, NEC
2	Private
20	Private
B. Coding system for identifying structures containing household units	
1	Single-family structure
11	Single units—detached
12	Single units—semi attached
13	Single units—attached row
2	Two family structure
3	Multifamily structure
4	Converted structures
5	Mobile homes
51	Mobile homes—on permanent foundation
52	Mobile homes—not on permanent foundation
9	Nonresidential structures
90	Nonresidential structures

Source: URA and BPR, 1965

Anderson et al. (1976) developed a four-level hierarchical classification system. The Anderson Classification System is a land-cover-based classification of land uses. The first-level of categories include nine land use types: urban or built-up land; agricultural land; rangeland; forest land; water; wetland; barren land; tundra; and perennial snow or ice. These multiple levels allow a uniform classification in large areas at the first level, such as nationwide, and at the same time, permits flexibility at the third and fourth levels to meet particular needs at a local level. Table 6.4 illustrates the first two levels of classification.

The Anderson Classification System was designed to use with remote sensing images. Different land use/covers reflect light differently, from which one can distinguish one type of land use from another. In the image interpretation process, the correlation of reflections and the land use types are statistically established. The image interpretation is often supported with field survey. The spectrum of the characteristics of a particular land cover is analyzed and categorized. Any other land that shares the same characteristics will be classified in the same group.

Table 6.4   Level II Anderson land use/land cover classification

Level I		Level II
1 Urban or built-up land	11	Residential
	12	Commercial and services
	13	Industrial
	14	Transportation, communications, and utilities
	15	Industrial and commercial complexes
	16	Mixed urban or built-up land
	17	Other urban or built-up land
2 Agricultural land	21	Cropland and pasture
	22	Orchards, groves, vineyards, nurseries, and ornamental horticultural areas
	23	Confined feeding operations
	24	Other agricultural land
3 Rangeland	31	Herbaceous rangeland
	32	Shrub and brush rangeland
	33	Mixed rangeland
4 Forest land	41	Deciduous forest land
	42	Evergreen forest land
	43	Mixed forest land
5 Water	51	Streams and canals
	52	Lakes
	53	Reservoirs
	54	Bays and estuaries
6 Wetland	61	Forested wetland
	62	Non-forested wetland
7 Barren land	71	Dry salt flats.
	72	Beaches
	73	Sandy areas other than beaches
	74	Bare exposed rock
	75	Strip mines quarries, and gravel pits
	76	Transitional areas
	77	Mixed barren land
8 Tundra	81	Shrub and brush tundra
	82	Herbaceous tundra
	83	Bare ground tundra
	84	Wet tundra
	85	Mixed tundra
9 Perennial snow or ice	91	Perennial snowfields
	92	Glaciers

Source: Anderson et al., 1976

Since remote sensing data can cover large areas, land classification based on such data is often prepared for large areas. For example, the National Land Cover Data (NLCD) developed in early 1990s are interpreted from the Landsat Thematic Mapper data, using Level II Anderson classification scheme.

In 1994, the Research Department of the American Planning Association assisted Federal agencies in updating the 1965 Standard Land Use Coding Manual. The outcome of the project was a set of Land-Based Classification Standards (LBCS) that classify land uses. Expanded from the 1965 SLCUM, LBCS is a multi-dimensional and multi-scale hierarchical land use classification model. The five dimensions are activities, functions, building types, site development character, and ownership. The land use classes for each dimension are defined at different levels. These multiple dimensions allow users to have precise control over land-use classifications.

The activity dimension directly describes human use of land. Table 6.5 is the first-level activity-based LBCS land classification. The class name defines the types of human activity that occur on land. People live on land classified as residential activity and shop on land classified as shopping, business, or trade activity. All transportation-related activities are in category 5000, travel or movement. The activity category 6000, mass assembly of people, includes activities associated with mass assembly, such as sports or entertainment. Abandoned buildings and vacant lots are examples included in the activity category 9000, no human activity or unclassifiable activity.

Table 6.5 Land II Based Classification Standards—Activity Dimension

Code	Description
1000	Residential
2000	**Shopping, business, or trade**
	2100 Shopping
	2110 Goods-oriented shopping
	2120 Service-oriented shopping
3000	Industrial, manufacturing, and waste-related
4000	Social, institutional, or infrastructure-related
5000	Travel or movement
6000	Mass assembly of people
7000	Leisure
8000	Natural resources-related
9000	No human activity or unclassifiable activity

Source: http://www.planning.org/lbcs/standards/view.htm

The class can be further divided to reflect the variation of the same activity class. There are three second-level classes under residential activity—1100 for household activities, 1200 for transient living, and 1300 for institutional living. The household activities include those activities associated with single-family, multifamily, or town houses, etc. Activities associated with hotels, motels, tourist homes, bed and breakfast, etc. are part of the transient living class. The institutional living class is for residential living activity associated with dormitories, group homes, barracks, retirement homes, etc. Some classes may expand to the third or fourth level. For example, service-oriented shopping (2120) is part of the shopping class (2100) under shopping, business, or trade activities (2000).

The function dimension reflects the economic function or type of establishment on land, regardless of the activities occurring on the land. One establishment may have multiple activities while serving one economic function. This economic function would then be used to classify land. Table 6.6 lists the first level function used in the LBCS land classification. The 1000 category includes residence or accommodation functions. Homes, apartments, as well as hotels are examples of this category. The 2000 category covers commercial functions, such as sales and services. The manufacturing and wholesale trade category, 3000, represents production functions in plants, factories, or mills. The 4000 category includes the land area where the major function is for transportation, communication, information, and utilities. The establishments with functions related to cultural, entertainment, and recreation are in the 5000 category. Many of the institutional functions, such as education and health care, are included in the 6000 category. The 7000 function category refers to establishments changing land surface, such as construction and demolition services. Establishments that

Table 6.6   Land Based Classification Standards—Function Dimension

1000	Residence or accommodation functions	
2000	General sales or services	
3000	Manufacturing and wholesale trade	
4000	**Transportation, communication, information, and utilities**	
	4100 Transportation services	
	4200 **Communications and information**	
		4210 Publishing
		4220 Motion pictures and sound recording
		4230 Telecommunications and broadcasting
		4240 **Information services and data processing industries**
		4241 Online information services
		4242 **Libraries and archives**
		4243 News syndicate
	4300 Utilities and utility services	
5000	Arts, entertainment, and recreation	
6000	Education, public admin., health care, and other inst	
7000	Construction-related businesses	
8000	Mining and extraction establishments	
9000	Agriculture, forestry, fishing and hunting	

Source: http://www.planning.org/LBCS

extract natural resources (minerals and natural gas) are in the 8000 function category and all establishments related to farming, forestry, fishing and hunting are in the 9000 category.

Similar to the activity dimension, the function dimension classification may have up to four levels. Table 6.6 illustrates how a library is classified in the four-level function classification. The first-level function class is transportation, communication, information, and utilities (4000). The second-level function class, communications and information (4200), contains four third-level function classes. Information services and data processing industries (4240) is the last one. Under the 4240 class, a library belongs to libraries and archives (4242).

The structure dimension reflects structure types on land. Table 6.7 illustrates the first level classification for the structure dimension. All buildings for residential usage are in the Residential buildings category (1000). Buildings for commercial usage are in the 2000 category. The 3000 category includes buildings where people gather such as theaters, sports stadium, airport terminal, churches, or convention centers. Other types of buildings are places where people may congregate, such as schools, hospitals, libraries, or museums, and are included in the 4000, "Institutional or community facilities" category. The 6000 category covers many utility and other non-building structures. A highway interchange,

Table 6.7   Land Based Classification Standards—Structure Dimension

Code	Description
1000	**Residential buildings**
	1100 **Single family building**
	1110 Detached units
	1120 **Attached units**
	1121 **Duplex structures**
	1122 Zero lot line, row houses, etc.
	1130 Accessory units
	1140 Townhouses
	1150 Manufactured housing
	1200 Multifamily structures
	1300 Other specialized residential structures
2000	Commercial buildings and other specialized structures
3000	Public assembly structures
4000	Institutional or community facilities
5000	Transportation-related facilities
6000	Utility and other non-building structures
7000	Specialized military structures
8000	Sheds, farm buildings, or agricultural facilities
9000	No structure

Source: http://www.planning.org/lbcs/standards/view.htm

water-supply pump station, dam, levee, power plants, landfill facility, or communication towers are examples in this category. Military and defense related structures are classified in the 7000 category and agricultural structures are in the 8000 category. A place without structures, however, having specific functions and activities, should be in the 9000 category—"no structure". Golf courses are such an example.

There can be up to four levels of sub-categories for the structure dimension. A single family building (1100) class is one of the three second-level classes under the residential buildings class (1000). This class can be further classified, such as detached units (1110), attached units (1120), or manufactured housing (1150). Duplex structures is one of the fourth level classes under attached units. This dimension is independent to the actual activities on the land. If a neighborhood convenience store is operating in a residential building, the classification of the Structure dimension would still be in the residential building class.

The site development dimension refers to the physical character of the land. Table 6.8 lists the first level site development dimension classification. Category 1000 includes any area that is not yet developed, such as an open space. The 2000 category is for site that is under construction. All developed sites are in categories 3000 through 7000. Farm land is in the 3000 category. Non-farming sites without buildings, such as a landfill site or a parking lot, are examples of the 4000 category. Sites with non-building structures are in the 5000 category. For example, roads are considered to be developed land, although there are no building structures on them. With the site development dimension, roads are classified as the "Developed site with roads, train tracks, and other linear structures" (5300),

Table 6.8   Land Based Classification Standards—Site Development Dimension

Code	Description
1000	Site in natural state
2000	Developing site
3000	Developed site—crops, grazing, forestry, etc.
4000	Developed site—no buildings and no structures
5000	Developed site—non-building structures
	5100 Developed site with landscaped or ornamental features
	5200 Developed site with billboards, signs, etc.
	5300 Developed site with roads, train tracks, and other linear structures
6000	Developed site—with buildings
7000	Developed site—with parks
8000	Not applicable to this dimension
9000	Unclassifiable site development character

Source: http://www.planning.org/lbcs/standards/view.htm

which is a second-level class under the first-level class of Developed site—non-building structures (5000). Sites with building structures are in the 6000 category. Parks have a separate category (7000) regardless if there are buildings or structures, developed or undeveloped. A site that cannot be classified in any of the other categories in this dimension is assigned to the 8000 category, while a site is in the process to be classified is temporarily assigned to the 9000 category.

The ownership dimension reflects the ownership of the land. In general, properties are owned by the private, public, and nonprofit sectors, or may be jointly owned. Table 6.9 contains the first-level class for the ownership dimension. Based on this dimension, privately owned properties are in the 1000 category and publicly owned properties are in the 4000 and 5000 categories. The 5000 category is for special government agencies, such as a port authority or water district. All other properties are in other categories. The 2000 category includes the properties that have easement restraint. An easement refers to a land owner who does not have the sole right of use of the property. For example, a public easement on a private property means that the public can use property that is privately owned. A leased property is under the 3000 category, if the owner and the tenant are in different ownership categories. An example would be a private establishment that leases a publicly owned property. Properties owned by nonprofit organizations are in the 6000 category. The 7000 category includes joint ownership of different public agencies and the 8000 category includes joint ownership of public and private entities. The 9000 category covers all other land where ownership may not be determined. Like other dimensions, the ownership

Table 6.9 Land Based Classification Standards—Ownership Dimension

Code	Description
1000	No constraints—private ownership
2000	Some constraints—easements or other use restrictions
3000	Limited restrictions—leased and other tenancy restrictions
4000	**Public restrictions—local, state, and federal ownership**
	4100 Local government
	4110 City, Village, Township, etc.
	4120 County, Parish, Province, etc.
	4200 State government
	4300 Federal government
5000	Other public use restrictions—regional, special districts, etc.
6000	Nonprofit ownership restrictions
7000	Joint ownership character—public entities
8000	Joint ownership character—public, private, nonprofit, etc.
9000	Not applicable to this dimension

Source: http://www.planning.org/lbcs/standards/view.htm

can be classified at different levels. For example, city owned land categorized as City, Village, Township, etc. (4110) under the Local government, is part of the first-level class, Public restrictions—local, state, and federal ownership (4000).

The multi-dimension classification approach helps to accurately categorize the use of land with any single dimension. For example, a doctor's office in a residential building can be classified as a:

(1) Social, institutional, or infrastructure-related activity (activity dimension 4000);

(2) General sales or services function (function dimension 2000);

(3) Residential buildings structure (structure dimension 1000);

(4) Developed site—with buildings (site development dimension 6000);

(5) No constraints—private ownership (ownership dimension 1000).

The purpose of the LBCS system is to support planning applications at different geographical scales or different emphasis. At the neighborhood scale, the land coding schemes applied are site specific. That is, a local-based classification scheme is adopted to best describe the land use for a given site. Depending on the purpose, the land classification can be related to any of the five dimensions. At the citywide or countywide scale, normally land-uses are classified for each land parcel. This scale level is the closest to the 1965 SLUCM. At the Regional scale, the land classification is to support regional coordination and planning. Currently a uniformly applicable system is not yet available. At the state scale most classification is used for resource management and coordination of regional development.

6.3   Land Database and Land Mapping

Before computers became available, land use data were normally stored as hard copy maps and narrative descriptions. Typically, parcel map books are the basis for land use data. Most local agencies use parcel plat maps to describe the location and dimension. Each parcel is labeled with a unique **property identification number** (PIN). A parcel map book contains PINs, ownerships, structures, land use types, property values, and other data for the listed parcels. To know the features of a parcel, a user first locates the parcel on a map, gets the PIN for the parcel, and looks at the associated data record.

6.3.1   Land Database

The computerized land database follows a similar style as its paper counterpart. The early land database contained graphics of land parcels. Lines were used to portray the property boundaries and each parcel was labeled with its PIN. A separate file contained the descriptive data of the parcels in tabular format. A user followed the same procedure of using paper maps to find parcel data. The difference is that the search can be done with computer files.

Most likely, a land database is a relational database. A relational database consists of multiple tables. In the tables, data records are stored as rows and each column, also called field, of the table represents one variable. As shown in Table 6.10, the first row of a table contains variable names. The table has two columns. The first column, LUCODE, represents the land use code and the second column, DESCRIPTION, contains land use classification names associated with the land use code. Looking at the first record in the table, we can tell that the letter "A" represents Agriculture use.

Table 6.10 Table of land use description

LUCODE	DESCRIPTION
A	Agriculture
SF	Single family residential
C	Commercial
W	Water
MF	Multi-family residential
LI	Light Industrial
HI	Heavy Industrial
VA	Vacant

The power of a relational database is that any two tables can be related to each other with a key field. A key field is a variable in a table which contains values representing special characters of the records in the table. Once the key field value in a table matches the key field value in a different table the relationship of the two tables is established. There are four different relationship types between two tables:

(1) One-to-one,
(2) Many-to-one,
(3) One-to-many,
(4) Many-to-many.

Along with the development of Geographic Information Systems (GIS), the land database has been improved to a more integrated stage. A GIS database internally connects two parts—a graphic component (map data) and an attribute component (tabular data) with a one-to-one relationship. In a one-to-one relationship the key fields in both tables have unique values. Therefore, the one key value (representing one record) in the first table has, at the most, one matching key value (one record) in the second table. You may image that the two components of a GIS land database as two separate tables. Each map feature is stored as one record in the map table, which contains geometric description of the feature. There is a companion data table that contains other descriptions of the map features. This data table is also called an attribute table. The connection between the two tables is established through a key variable in the two tables. This key variable is normally called the feature identifier field. Each map feature is assigned a unique identifier and for each unique identifier in the map data table, there is a record in the attribute table having the same identifier. As shown in Fig. 6.2, the parcel map data contain a key variable, PIN, for each parcel. A separated table stores data describing parcel features, such as land use code. The two tables are linked through a one-to-one relationship using the PIN field. Therefore, we can tell, from the two tables, that the land use code for the parcel with a PIN of 52002920074 is "C".

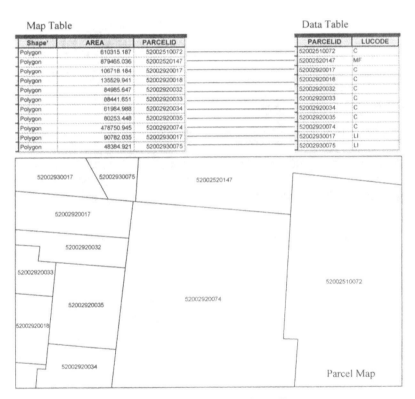

Figure 6.2   Parcel map and its attributes

The many-to-one relationship represents a case that the key field in the first table may have duplicated values while the key field in the second table has unique values. Consequently, the multiple records in the first table that have the same key value can be linked to one unique key record in the second table. Only, based on the one-to-one relationship shown in Fig. 6.2, a user may not know the meaning of the letter "C" in the data attribute table. Therefore, we need to link the data table to the land use description table (Table 6.10).

Figure 6.3 displays a two-step relation of three tables to derive land use description for each parcel. The table on the left represents a map file of parcels. It contains two variables—the identifier, PARCELID, and a variable, AREA, for parcel size data. The table in the middle is stores land use codes for the parcels. It also contains a PARCELID variable and a land use code variable, LUCODE. The table on the right contains descriptions of the land use codes used in the middle table. The key fields connecting the left and middle tables are the PARCELID variables while the key fields connecting the middle and the right tables are the LUCODE variables.

Parcel Map		Land Use Table		Land use description Table	
PARCELID	AREA	PARCELID	LUCODE	LUCODE	DESCRIPTION
52002510072	37404	52002510072	C	A	Agriculture
52002520147	4118	52002520147	MF	SF	Single family
52002920017	7635	52002920017	C	C	Commercial
52002920018	21334	52002920018	C	W	Water
52002920032	50226	52002920032	C	MF	Multi-family residential
52002920033	35491	52002920033	C	LI	Light Industrial
52002920034	37510	52002920034	C	HI	Heavy Industrial
52002920035	62175	52002920035	C	VA	Vacant
52002920074	20767	52002920074	C		
52002930017	69025	52002930017	LI		
52002930075	4638	52002930075	LI		

Figure 6.3 Relational database tables

Once the two key variables that link the three tables are identified, we can navigate the tables to find out the land use for each parcel. Comparing the left and middle tables, we can tell that the land use code for the first parcel (PARCELID = "52002920074") is "C". When we further look for "C" in the LUCODE column in the last table, we can see that "C" represents "Commercial" land use. Therefore, we know that the land use for parcel "52002920074" is commercial. In this example, the connection between the middle and right tables is many-to-one relationship.

Tables in a relational database can be joined to form a single table. After the land use table (the middle table) is joined to the Parcel Map table (the left table) using the PARCELID as the key variables, the land use code (LUCODE) for each parcel is appended to the right of the original parcel map table. Then we can use the LUCODE as the key variable to join the Land Use Description table to the Parcel Map table. The end result is that each record (a parcel) in the Parcel Map table has a land use description (Table 6.11).

Table 6.11   A joint parcel level land use description table

PARCELID	AREA	LUCODE	DESCRIPTION
52002510072	37404	C	Commercial
52002520147	4118	MF	Multi-family residential
52002920017	7635	C	Commercial
52002920018	21334	C	Commercial
52002920032	50226	C	Commercial
52002920033	35491	C	Commercial
52002920034	37510	C	Commercial
52002920035	62175	C	Commercial
52002920074	20767	C	Commercial
52002930017	69025	LI	Light Industrial
52002930075	4638	LI	Light Industrial

The one-to-many relationship is a case that the key field in the first table has unique values and the key field in the second table has duplicated values. One record in the first table can therefore be connected to multiple records in the second table with matching values. Figure 6.4 illustrates a case of on-to-many relationship. From the previous discussion we know that land use classification often has multiple levels. In the left table in Fig. 6.4, the LUCODE values represent the first-level land class. The table on the right includes the second-level land use classes stored in the column labeled as "CLASS". The key field connecting the two tables is LUCODE. The one LUCODE value in the first table may have

Land Use Description Table

LUCODE	DESCRIPTION
A	Agriculture
SF	Single family residential
C	Commercial
MF	Multi-family residential
LI	Light Industrial
HI	Heavy Industrial
VA	Vacant

Land Use Sub-class Table

LUCODE	CLASS
A	100
A	101
A	102
C	410
C	422
C	435
HI	210
HI	220
HI	230
HI	240
HI	250
HI	260
LI	340
MF	530
MF	550
SF	510
VA	500
VA	508

Figure 6.4   One-to-many relationship

multiple matches in the second table. For example, the agriculture category has three secondary classes, labeled 100, 101 and 102.

The last type, many-to-many relationship, is the most complicated case in that both key fields may have duplicated values. As a result, one record in the first table may be linked to multiple records in the second table and one record in the second table also may be linked to multiple records in the first table. In planning studies, we often need to analyze land use distribution with other variables such as population distribution. Population data are normally summarized by census tract. We may expect that one census tract can have more than one land use type and, at the same time, one land use type may appear in multiple census tracts. This represents an example of many-to-many relationship between the census tract table and the land use table. In a relational database, the many-to-many relationship needs special treatment. One approach is to create a connecting table with two key fields. The first key field is used to connect to the first table and the second key field is used to connect to the second table. In this case, census tract name is the first key field and land use type is the second field. Figure 6.5 illustrates this example.

Census Tract Table			Connecting Table			Land Use Description Table	
TRACT	SQKM		TRACT	LUCODE		LUCODE	DESCRIPTION
701	4.6		703.04	A		A	Agriculture
702	4.2		703.04	SF		SF	Single family residential
703.01	11.8		703.04	LI		C	Commercial
703.04	39.8		703.04	SF		MF	Multi-family residential
703.05	5.8		703.04	C		LI	Light Industrial
703.06	11.0		703.04	LI		HI	Heavy Industrial
703.07	19.7		703.04	VA		VA	Vacant
703.08	10.0		703.05	VA			
703.09	7.6		703.05	VA			
704.01	65.1		703.05	A			
704.02	74.8		703.05	A			
705.01	21.5		703.05	LI			
705.02	156.7		703.05	SF			
706.01	95.3		703.05	SF			
706.03	53.8		703.05	C			
706.04	84.0		...	...			

Figure 6.5   Many-to-many relationship

The advantage of a relational database is its flexibility. Tables are added, maintained and edited separately. The change of one table can be reflected in other tables through the connections. This can keep the small database size and substantially reduce the maintenance effort. The three tables in Fig. 6.4 and the one table (Table 6.11) contain the same amount of data. In the three-table option, land use description is stored once in a separate table. If there is any need to change the description, we can simply modify one record. For example, if we detect a spelling error in Commercial we can easily change it to "Commercial". It will require much more effort to make the similar change in the one-table option. This storage efficiency becomes more important if there are multiple parcel files using the same data. Such an example is that several municipalities in a county adopt the same land use classification. In a relational database, while there are individual parcel data tables for the municipalities, only one land use description table is needed, which can be joined to any one of the parcel tables.

6.3.2   Land Data Sources

There are multiple ways of collecting land use data. Field survey is the most direct approach of collecting land use data. In a field survey, land surveyors identify the major landmarks and measure the relative location of lines and areas in reference to the landmarks. The product of a field survey is essentially a map of points and lines representing land features to a scale.

When the object of a survey is a property boundary, the map produced is called a cadastral data file. Cadastral data describe the location and extent of a land parcel, normally expressed as direction and distance from a nearby landmark. In the United States, cadastral data are the legal description of land parcel. In preparing cadastral data, surveyors measure the land and review the history of land use and legal ownership documents. Generally, cadastral data are the basis for taxation.

Remote sensing data have become common as the source of land use data. The data are land surface imageries captured by satellite sensors. Different land surfaces have different reflections of energy, which are shown on the imageries as different spectrums. Remote sensing specialists analyze and identify certain spectrum characteristics for a known land use. Knowledge obtained from such an analysis is then applied to a larger area to classify land surface by interpreting satellite images. Most land uses from remote sensing data follow the Anderson land use classification system.

Building permits are a common data source for land use. Local governments issue building permits for new developments. A building permit specifies the type of intended use for the structure from which the type of land use can be derived.

6.3.3   Land Mapping

Land mapping is used to present the spatial distribution of land classes. Using different colors, a land use map can display the location and size of each land use type and the spatial relationship of different uses. Throughout the years of land use classification, color standards have been adopted in communications and presentations. Although there are variations, the following color scheme is commonly used (Table 6.12).

Table 6.12   Example of a land use mapping color scheme

Color	Land Use
Light green	Agricultural
Yellow	Residential
Red	Retail and commercial
Purple	Industrial
Pink	Institutional and public facilities
Green	Recreational
Gray	Transportation
Dark green	Natural
Blue	Water

The Land-Based Classification Standards System adopts a color coding system for each dimension. Table 6.13 lists the color assignment for the first-level class in the five LBCS dimensions. Land use mapping provides a visual presentation of the spatial distribution of land uses. While making maps we need to be careful of the consistency of color presentation. Same color may appear differently on different presentation media, such as print or computer screen. You should try to use the RGB (Red, Green, Blue) or hexadecimal values for accurate color assignment. Another issue related to the color land use map is color differentiation of a map. There are nine colors only for the first-level class. If we are using the second-level classification there will be many more colors required. The LBCS document suggests the use of color ramp. That is, the color is defined by the first-level category and the secondary categories use different shades for the same color.

Table 6.13   LBCS color assignment

Dimension	Code	Color Name	RGB Value	RGB Code Hex
Activity	1000	Yellow	RGB(255,255,0)	FF00FF
Activity	2000	Red	RGB(255,0,0)	FF0000
Activity	3000	Purple	RGB(160,32,240)	A0F020
Activity	4000	Blue	RGB(0,0,255)	00FF00
Activity	5000	Gray	RGB(190,190,190)	BEBEBE
Activity	6000	Dark slate gray	RGB(47,79,79)	2F4F4F
Activity	7000	Light green	RGB(144,238,144)	9090EE
Activity	8000	Forest green	RGB(34,139,34)	22228B
Activity	9000	White	RGB(255,255,255)	FFFFFF

Continued

Dimension	Code	Color Name	RGB Value	RGB Code Hex
Function	1000	Yellow	RGB(255,255,0)	FF00FF
Function	2000	Red	RGB(255,0,0)	FF0000
Function	3000	Purple	RGB(160,32,240)	A0F020
Function	4000	Gray	RGB(190,190,190)	BEBEBE
Function	5000	Light green	RGB(144,238,144)	9090EE
Function	6000	Blue	RGB(0,0,255)	00FF00
Function	7000	Dark cyan	RGB(0,139,139)	008B8B
Function	8000	Purple4	RGB(85,26,139)	558B00
Function	9000	Forest green	RGB(34,139,34)	22228B
Ownership	1000	Beige	RGB(245,245,220)	F5DCF5
Ownership	2000	Blue	RGB(0,0,255)	00FF00
Ownership	3000	Blue4	RGB(0,0,139)	008B00
Ownership	4000	Light green	RGB(144,238,144)	9090EE
Ownership	5000	Dark green	RGB(0,100,0)	000064
Ownership	6000	Olive drab	RGB(107,142,35)	6B238E
Ownership	7000	Gray	RGB(190,190,190)	BEBEBE
Ownership	8000	Black	RGB(0,0,0)	000000
Ownership	9000	White	RGB(255,255,255)	FFFFFF
Site	1000	Light green	RGB(144,238,144)	9090EE
Site	2000	Beige	RGB(245,245,220)	F5DCF5
Site	3000	Bisque3	RGB(205,183,158)	CD9EB7
Site	4000	Wheat4	RGB(139,126,102)	8B667E
Site	5000	Tan4	RGB(139,90,43)	8B2B00
Site	6000	Brown4	RGB(139,35,35)	8B2323
Site	7000	Forest green	RGB(34,139,34)	22228B
Site	8000	Light gray	RGB(211,211,211)	D3D3D3
Site	9000	White	RGB(255,255,255)	FFFFFF
Structure	1000	Yellow	RGB(255,255,0)	FF00FF
Structure	2000	Red	RGB(255,0,0)	FF0000
Structure	3000	Purple	RGB(160,32,240)	A0F020
Structure	4000	Blue	RGB(0,0,255)	00FF00
Structure	5000	Gray	RGB(190,190,190)	BEBEBE
Structure	6000	Gray52	RGB(133,133,133)	858585
Structure	7000	Pink	RGB(255,192,203)	FFCBC0
Structure	8000	Forest green	RGB(34,139,34)	22228B
Structure	9000	White	RGB(255,255,255)	FFFFFF

Source: http://www.planning.org/lbcs/standards/colorcodes.htm

6.4   Land Suitability Analysis

As we discussed earlier, the intensity levels of different human activities vary. It is important for a sustainable society to be able to retain those human activities for a very long time. Different human activities require different land uses. It is unrealistic to restrict one type of land use in favor of the other everywhere.

Therefore, we need to allocate different land uses in a way that will support one type of land use while respecting other uses. Land suitability is a factor to be considered in land use allocation. The meaning of suitability is that a piece of land has the required feature to support a proposed land use, considering social, physical, spatial, and economic factors.

6.4.1   The Eight-Step Land Suitability Analysis

In general, different factors considered in a land suitability analysis fall into one of three categories: (1) physical constraints, such as slope, soil, groundwater aquifers, and flood plains; (2) access, such as distance to roads, surface waters, sewer lines, or water lines; and (3) costs and benefits of the development. New developments could impact the physical environment or human society, such as an aquifer, a wildlife habitat, or historical sites. Land suitability analysis is a systematic procedure for examining combined effects of a related set of factors that an analyst assumes to be the important determinants of locational suitability (Kaiser et al., 1995). Specifically, a land suitability analysis examines selected land characteristics to determine the level of suitability, and ranks available land accordingly. The most suitable land will be used for development first. The selection of land characteristics is normally a judgment of the person in charge of the study. Those characteristics are represented with a set of factors. In general the process follows the following eight steps:

(1) Select a land use type for analysis;
(2) Select factors to be considered and attribute values of each factor;
(3) Determine a score for each factor attribute;
(4) Weigh the factors;
(5) Calculate a composite score from the attribute values and weight it for each factor;
(6) Rank the combined scores to establish suitability levels;
(7) Identify available land based on existing land uses;
(8) Compare with comprehensive plan, zoning or other land use controls that further remove unavailable land.

A land suitability analysis should be conducted for each land use proposed for the future. As we discussed before, different land uses require different land conditions and pose different impacts to the land and surrounding areas. These differences are reflected in the land suitability analysis. In order to decide land suitability, multiple factors are combined into a composite value. Two aspects are considered during this process. The first is the suitability score for each individual factor. After a score range is decided, a score can be assigned based on the attribute of a factor to reflect the suitability level. The more suitable, the higher the value is. The second is to weigh each factor based on its relative importance level, compared with other factors. The weighed total of scores, which is also called a composite score, is the final suitability score for the site. Everything else equal, the site with a higher composite score should be developed prior to the site with a lower composite score. We will use the Boone County data to work through an example of land suitability analysis.

Step 1   Select a land use type for analysis

A land suitability analysis focuses on one type of land development at a time. Normally, the development can be grouped as commercial, industrial, or residential use. When there is more than one land use type in the analysis, a suitability analysis of each land use type will be conducted. In the end, a preference order needs to be developed for areas suitable for multiple uses. As an example, we will use residential development in the following discussion. The same approach can be applied to any land use types.

Step 2   Select factors to be considered and attribute values of each factor

The purpose of a land suitability analysis is to analyze the physical and locational attributes of land in relation to a particular land use. Based on such analysis, the location for future land use in a study area can be identified so as to increase economic benefits with minimum degradation of environmental quality.

The factors considered here are those that can help us decide on the priorities for land development. Some factors are related to the physical conditions that may determine the impact of the proposed land use to the area or to the development itself. Other factors reflect the demands posed by the proposed development. The factors could also be related to the costs and benefits of the proposed land use. Examples of factors commonly included in land suitability analysis are floodplain, aquifer, soils, slope, wetland, habitat, distance to streams, special landmarks (for instance historical buildings), transportation (e.g., streets and railroads), and utility services (e.g., sewer and water).

Land suitability analysis is a systematic procedure for examining the combined effects of a related set of factors that the analyst assumes are the important determinants of locational suitability (Kaiser et al., 1995). There is no uniformly applicable list of factors. We need to review the local situation and engage in discussions with the stakeholders in order to determine which factors should be included in the land suitability analysis. For illustration purposes, we will use five factors. They are slope, floodplain, soil features related to construction, distance to sewer lines, and distance to highways.

The slope factor is one of the main determinants for future land uses. For instance, flat land is the most desirable land for an industrial land use. It may become unsuitable for industrial uses if the slope is greater than 5%. The slope also affects road construction. The higher the road class, the lower the allowable maximum grades (Marsh, 2005). A slope greater than 25% will be the least desirable place for any kind of construction, based upon three considerations. The first is related to construction cost. The steeper the slope, the higher the construction cost is. When the cost exceeds a certain amount, it makes the development economically unfeasible. The second is related to the safety of land use. A structure built on steep slope may not be stable because of erosion or land sliding, which may cause property damage or become unsafe for humans. The third is related to the impact of surrounding areas. For example, a steep slope may increase runoff and soil loss, which could affect the environmental quality in downstream areas.

Protection of property and people from natural environmental hazards such as flooding is a major consideration in development decisions. A floodplain defines areas that may be affected by a storm statistically reoccurring on at a given frequency. For example, a 100-year flood plain delineates the areas that will be affected by a storm of the possibility of occurring once every 100 years. Any structures built on a floodplain may alter the water flow during a storm event. The structures themselves may also be damaged. Therefore, land development within a floodplain should be avoided. To encourage communities to adopt measures for reducing flood damage, the Federal Emergency Management Agency (FEMA) provides a National Flood Insurance Program (NFIP) to residents and business owners voluntarily adopting and enforcing floodplain management to reduce future flood damage. In general, floodplain management includes zoning or special-purpose floodplain ordinances (http://www.fema.gov/fima/floodplain.shtm).

To further encourage communities to go beyond the NFIP minimum requirements, FEMA has created a Community Rating System (CRS, http://www.fema.gov/nfip/crs.shtm), a voluntary incentive program. The goals of CRS are to reduce flood loss, to facilitate accurate insurance ratings and to promote awareness of flood insurance. FEMA offers discounted NFIP premium rates 5%~45% to local communities participating in one or more of 18 creditable activities, organized under four categories: (1) Public Information, (2) Mapping and Regulations, (3) Flood Damage Reduction, and (4) Flood Preparedness.

Soil is a factor that has multiple effects on the suitability of a proposed land use. In less populated areas, septic systems are often used for individual homes to dispose of human waste. If soil does not drain well, it is not suitable for septic systems. In a septic system, the septic tank collects the solid portion of the waste and the liquid flows to a drainage field where water seeps through the soil. During the process, the soil absorbs and filters wastewater. Therefore, the water will be purified before it eventually reaches the groundwater aquifer. If the soil does not have good permeability, such as clay soils, the wastewater will not be able to drain through the soil easily. Consequently, the septic system will not be able to handle the human waste without an outflow. Soil with good drainage is preferred for development. Another aspect of the soil features related to development is the suitability for construction. Certain types of soil restrict building construction because of their slope or wetness.

Accessibility refers to considering whether the proposed land use is compatible with adjacent land uses and whether it has adequate access to services, such as transportation (streets, railroads and ferries), utilities (water or sewer lines), recreation (parks and recreational facilities), and education (schools). In populated areas, most municipalities have installed sewerage systems to collect wastewater and transport it to centralized treatment plants. The treatment plants are connected to individual houses through a network system that consists of different sized pipes. Normally, a sewerage system follows the gravity force. The cost of accessing the sewerage system is directly related to the distance of the sewerage network. Consequently, the area within the service area will have higher preference. Quality residential land developments must have access to the network of supporting infrastructure and community facilities (Kaiser et al., 1995). Areas closer to the facilities are more likely to be developed before the more remote areas. The last two factors we will consider in the Boone County example are sewer and water service areas and distance to major roads.

Step 3   Determine the score for each attribute of each factor

Once the factors are determined, their attributes need to be determined. Attributes of a factor reflect its variation, which may be measured at any of the four levels of measurement—nominal, ordinal, interval, or ratio. For example, the floodplain data are at the nominal level, with two values—inside or outside the 100-year floodplain. The soil data regarding construction suitability has three values at ordinal level—severe, moderate, and slight, referring to the level of limitations a type of soil posted on construction. The slope measured in degrees is an example of ratio level of measurement. The slope can be any numerical value between 0 and 90 degrees. The sewer service factor is measured as inside or outside a sewer service district. The distance to major roads is measured as kilometers.

The idea of a suitability analysis is to review relevant factors together, which requires a unified measurement of different factors. In order to link suitability to a factor, the relationship between the suitability measurement and the original factor attributes must be established. Scores, which are the suitability measurement, should always be at the interval level using a few manageable values. A higher score corresponds to a higher level of suitability and a lower score represents a lower level of suitability. The first step of measuring individual suitability is to decide the lowest and highest possible scores. For example, the scores can be any values between 1 and 5. A score of 0 reflects the least suitable use and a score of 5 indicates the most preferable use. A land with a score of 4 can be interpreted as twice as suitable as the land with a score of 2. Table 6.14 is an example of the land suitability scores for the factors used in the Boone County case study.

Assigning scores is one of the most challenging tasks in land suitability analysis due to the subjective nature of the process. First, the original attributes need to be reclassified or ordered. As shown in Table 6.14, the slopes are measured as continuous values, which need to be reclassified into four categories.

Table 6.14 Land suitability scores for a residential development

Factor	Attribute	Score
Slope	≤ 5%	5
	5% ~ ≤ 15%	4
	15% ~ ≤ 25%	2
	> 25%	1
Floodplain	Inside 100-year floodplain	1
	Outside 100-year floodplain	5
Soil classified based on restrictions to construction	Slight	5
	Moderate	3
	Severe	1
Sewer service district	Inside the district	5
	Outside the district	2
Distance to major roads	≤ 1 kilometers	5
	1 ~ ≤ 2 kilometers	4
	2 ~ ≤ 5 kilometers	3
	> 5 kilometers	2

The two values of the floodplain factor must be arranged in an order to reflect the level of suitability. Second, scores are assigned to the reclassified factor values. Although the process is subjective, some approaches may be more reliable than others. A simple way is for the analysts, who conduct the study, to and assign scores based on the best knowledge available about the factors. This approach is subject to the challenge of validity.

Another approach is to involve professionals, citizens, decision makers and other stakeholders in the score assignment process. One method often recommended to implement this approach is the Delphi method. The Delphi method recognizes human judgment as a legitimate and useful input. The literature has shown that the method can help to translate scientific knowledge into an informed judgment on evaluating and analyzing decision options (Linstone and Turoff, 1975). Experts (or stakeholders) work corroboratively towards a common problem. During the process, participants can clarify the issue and the reasoning process, as well as increase the understanding of other participants' positions (Buckley, 1995). To avoid an individual dominating a group meeting, the Delphi method keeps all the responses anonymous (Scheele, 1975). A facilitator collects input from the participants and presents results statistically. From the summary, participants can review information and judgment from other participants. After that, the participants are asked to offer their input again, during which an individual may alter or revise his/her views. The facilitator then summarizes the results again for review. Although the Delphi method does not require participants reach a consensus on the issue, this process may be repeated until the participants feel they have obtained a useful result for their objective (Linstone and Turoff, 1975). The Delphi method addresses the following concerns in decision-making:

(1) Representative: Individual bias is a fact. Nobody can be completely objective in reaching a decision due to human nature and the knowledge of individual processes. The Delphi method collects input from a wide range of participants representing different groups, each having different priorities, concerns, and values.

(2) Dominating personality: It is a common concern in group discussions and the decision making process that one or a few participants dominate the outcome. By preserving the anonymity of participants, individuals only expresses their opinions through questionnaire responses.

(3) Consensus building: As diverse as participants may be, they share a common goal—to identify land development that maximizes benefits and minimizes costs. They are willing to have an open mind, listen to each other, and adjust their opinions during the process. The facilitator collects and statistically summarizes the responses. The participants then build on the similarities and resolve the differences in another round of responses.

Step 4   Weigh the factors

In this step, the relative importance of each factor is reflected in the weights assigned to each factor. The simplest weighing system assumes all factors are equally important; therefore, an equal weight will be assigned to each factor. When some factors are more important than others, those factors will be assigned a higher weight. Consequently, other factors will have a lower weight. When weights are expressed as percentages, the total of all weights must be 100%. This requirement ensures that the final composite score derived from the factors will have the same data range as each factor.

Using Table 6.15 as an example, the most important factor in determining residential land suitability is slope and the least important factor is distance to roads. The weight for slope is 30% and the weight for soil is 15%. Therefore, the slope factor is treated twice as important as the soil factor.

Table 6.15   Weights of land suitability factors

Factor	Weight
Slope	30%
Floodplain	20%
Soil classified based on restrictions to on-site septic systems	15%
Sewer district	25%
Distance to major roads	10%

Different individuals or groups are very likely to rank the importance of factors differently. One group may think that the slope factor is most important while another group may think that distance to utility service is even more important. The process of assigning weights is similar to the process of assigning scores. The Delphi method can be used to allow participants to go through several iterations until they reach an agreement of weights.

Step 5 Calculate a composite score from attribute value and weight for each factor

After assigning factor scores and weights, we can calculate the composite suitability score using the following formula.

$$S = \sum s_i \cdot w_i \tag{6.1}$$

where, the composite score, S, is the sum of the product of the individual weight, w_i, and the score, s_i for each factor, i. For example, consider a piece of land with a slope of 20% $(s_1 = 2, w_1 = 0.3)$ outside the 100-year floodplain $(s_2 = 5, w_2 = 0.2)$ and within the sewer service district $(s_3 = 5, w_3 = 0.25)$. The soil has moderate restrictions $(s_4 = 3, w_4 = 0.15)$ to building site development and the major roads are two kilometers away $(s_5 = 4, w_5 = 0.1)$. The composite suitability score for this land would be calculated as:

(slope score × slope weight) + (floodplain score × floodplain weight) + (sewer score × sewer weight) + (soil score × soil weight) + (highway score × highway weight), that is,

$$S = (2 \times 0.3) + (5 \times 0.2) + (5 \times 0.25) + (3 \times 0.15) + (4 \times 0.1)$$

$$= 0.6 + 1 + 1.25 + 0.45 + 0.4 = 3.7$$

Step 6 Rank the combined scores to establish suitability levels

Once composite scores are calculated for each piece of land, the land can be compared and ranked based on scores. The highest scores will be the most suitable land for the proposed use and the lowest scores will be the least suitable land. The suitability scores can be used as a guide for land use decision-making. A possible classification is shown in Table 6.16. The most suitable land has a value above 4 and the least suitable land has a value of 0.

Table 6.16 Land suitability classification

Composite score	Land suitability class
0~1	Least suitable
1.1~2	Less suitable
2.1~3	Moderate suitable
3.1~4	More suitable
4.1~5	Most suitable

With the scores and values we used in the example, the lowest possible scores for the five factors are: 1 for slope, 1 for floodplain, 1 for soil, 2 for sewer service district and 2 for distance to major roads. Therefore, the minimum possible composite score is:

$$S = 1 \times 0.3 \text{ (slope)} + 1 \times 0.2 \text{ (floodplain)} + 1 \times 0.25 \text{ (soil)} + 2$$

$$\times 0.15(\text{sewer}) + 2 \times 0.1(\text{roads}) = 0.3 + 0.2 + 0.25 + 0.3 + 0.2$$

$$= 1.25$$

This means that no land in this study will be classified as least suitable. The worst possible case will be in the less suitable category, a composite score between 1.1 and 2. This result is because none of the factors has a minimum score of 0. The minimum score for "the distance to major roads" is 2 and other minimum scores are 1.

Step 7   Identify the available land based on existing land use

Unless development occurs in an area never touched by humans, it will require a conversion from an existing use, which has to meet certain people's needs, to the proposed use. As discussed before, land uses vary in intensity. It is rare that a land use with higher intensity is changed to another use with less intensity. In general, different land uses can be ranked based on human impact. Undeveloped land, such as forest area or barren land, is the area where human impact is the least. Consequently, the new development would most likely occur on undeveloped land. Within the intensity scale, farming is less intense than residential use; therefore, farmland can be treated as available land for residential development. We would normally not convert a higher intensive land use to a lower intensive land use. From the existing land use data, we can identify those land parcels where the proposed land use is not appropriate or not desirable. For example, in Boone County, only open space, agricultural, and woodland areas can potentially be changed to residential use. After the land suitability is compared with the available land, we can quickly focus attention on areas that are suitable and available for future residential land development.

Step 8   Constraints with comprehensive plans, zonings or other land use controls to further remove unavailable land

Comprehensive plans, zonings, and/or other regulations specify the permitted uses in an area. Unless there is a zoning change of zoning, future residential development can only be considered in permitted areas. Additional constraints may exist based on existing land uses or other physical conditions. For example, if certain areas are designated for conservation purposes, no residential development will be allowed there. In the Boone County example, let's assume that no residential development should be placed within 400 meters of major highways. Excluding the areas not residentially permitted from the suitable and available land, we will derive the final areas that can be considered for future residential development. The next section discusses the implementation of land suitability analysis with Geographic Information System (GIS) tools.

The land suitability analysis is a process of comprehensively considering multiple factors used to eliminate areas where future development should not be considered. In addition, for areas where future development is permissible, land suitability analysis helps rank them in terms of future development preference. The benefit of land suitability analysis in planning is built upon these two outcomes. The unsuitable land will be excluded from consideration of future development. For areas that are suitable for new development, the more suitable land will be considered prior to the less suitable land.

6.5   GIS-Based Land Suitability Analysis

The legendary landscape architect and city planner Ian McHarg (1920 – 2001) recognized interaction between humans and the environment and advocated for the consideration of the environment in land use decisions. In his landmark book, *Design with Nature* (McHarg, 1969), McHarg illustrated a new method to support such consideration—overlay analysis. In the example of a road construction project in Staten Island, New York, McHarg considered social benefits and cost factors such as historic, water, forest, wildlife, scenic, recreation, residential, institutional, and land values. A series of maps were prepared, one for each factor, with transparencies and magic markers. The colors and gray tones reflected an ordinal scale. The darkest areas were the areas of greatest social benefits and the lightest areas were the areas of greatest social costs. These maps were drawn on transparencies as individual layers. The layers were put on top of other layers on a light projector. The final product is a composite layer of different tones reflecting different social benefits and costs at different locations. This composite layer provides the basis for identifying areas where a future road can provide the most social benefits. McHarg emphasized that the product must be a comprehensible and complete representation of the study area. McHarg's method has become the foundation of GIS overlay analysis.

Two types of GIS analysis, raster based and vector based, can be used to implement this overlay process. In raster-based analysis, the overlay is accomplished through a cell-based calculation. With vector based overlay analysis, all factors are saved as polygon layers. Those polygons are then intersected together, two at a time, until all the factors are included in the final layer. The vector based overlay procedure will create many intermediate layers. As the number of factors increase, the intersected data layers will have many small polygons, which may take a long time to process. Therefore, a raster-based analysis is generally preferred. One important consideration in a raster analysis is cell size. The larger the cell size, the faster the process, however, the resolution is lower. If we reduce the cell size, the process is significantly slower. The choice of cell size is based on the resolution requirement and the size of the study area. You must select the cell size that provides enough resolution and that also allows you to complete the analysis for the study area within a reasonable time frame.

After the factors to be considered in land suitability analysis for a particular land use type are determined, we can use GIS to prepare a data layer for each factor. We used ArcGIS, a product of ESRI, Inc. (Redlands, CA), to illustrate the process with the raster GIS overlay functions. Many other commercial and non-commercial GIS software packages can be used in land suitability analysis, based on the raster or vector data model. In a GIS based land suitability analysis, the factors are treated as individual layers. The scores for the classes of each layer are the layer values. The land suitability at a location is determined by accumulating the scores from all of the layers, and then multiplying the weight for each layer.

6.5.1 Data Preparation

In order to perform the overlay analysis, the layers must be developed. Conversion and other management functions are necessary to make the layers in raster format. A raster format data layer represents a study area with uniformly distributed grids. The grids, also called cells, have a fixed size. The cells are arranged in rows and columns. The location of a cell is defined by a row number and column number, which represents the row and column intersecting at the cell. The cell size determines the resolution of the data layers. To be comparable among the layers, different layers should have the same cell size. In addition, the data layers should be in the same projected coordinate system.

6.5.1.1 Slope Layer

A slope is defined as the difference in land surface elevation divided by the horizontal distance between two points on the land. In a raster based data file, the slope of a cell is the steepest downhill slope of a cell. It is calculated by determining the largest elevation difference between a cell and an adjacent cell of lower elevation and dividing it by the distance between the centers of the two cells. The result is expressed as a percentage. A slope can also be expressed as an angle. Any cell can have up to eight adjacent cells. Four of them share the borders and four meet at diagonal corners. Figure 6.6 illustrates the spatial arrangement of cells. The number in each cell represents the elevation of the cell in meters. In this illustration, only the three cells in the bottom row have elevations lower than the center cell, therefore, the steepest slope is from the center cell to one of the three cells. If the cell size in this illustration is 30 m, the distance between the center cell and cell below it would be 30 m, and the distance between the center cell and the two cells at the corner of the bottom row would be $30 \times \sqrt{2} = 42.4$.

Therefore the slope from the center cell to the lower left cells would be:

Left cell	$1/42.4 = 0.024$ or 2.4%
Middle cell	$2/30 = 0.067$ or 6.7%
Right cell	$5/42.4 = 0.118$ or 11.8%

Therefore, the steepest slope is facing the southeast corner, from the center cell to the lower right cell.

350	360	355
345	345	350
344	343	340

Figure 6.6   Illustration of adjacent cells

Elevation data represent the height of land surface. Land surface is a continuous field, which can only be approximated. There are many different types of elevation data. Among them, two major types are commonly used.

The vector format elevation data include elevation contour lines or elevation points. An elevation point is a location defined by x and y coordinates and a z value for elevation. The contour lines connect points of the same z values so the elevation along a line is always the same. In an area with significant elevation change, the contour lines are placed close to each other. In an area where land surface is flat or with little variation, the contour lines are far apart. The vector based elevation data can also take the form of a Triangulated Irregular Network (TIN). TINs represent a surface as a set of irregular triangles. Elevation values are associated with each node of triangles. The lines connecting those nodes are called edges.

The second type is raster format elevation data which contain elevations as cell attributes. A variation of the raster elevation data is the Digital Elevation Model (DEM), which contains evenly distributed sampling points. There is an elevation value at each sample point.

An elevation grid is needed to create the slope grid. If the input elevation data are not in the raster grid format, a conversion is required. Several ArcGIS functions are available for converting other formats to the raster data format. For example, the DEM to Grid function can convert DEM format to raster format. Launch ArcToolBox, go to the Conversion Tools, click Import to Raster, then double click the DEM to Grid function. Select the DEM file as input file and give a name to the output raster file.

If the original data are in the vector format, the 3D Analyst extension is required to create a Triangular Irregular Network (TIN) from the vector lines or points. You will first launch ArcMap and add the 3D Analyst extension. Add the contours and elevation point files as layers to ArcMap. From the 3D Analyst toolbar, select the **Create/Modify TIN** option, then select the **Create TIN From Features** option. In the dialog box, select the input vector files and specify the height source field for each file. Make sure to give the output TIN name and click **OK** to proceed. After the process is completed and the TIN file is added to ArcMap automatically, select the **Convert/TIN to Raster** option from the 3D Analyst toolbar. In the dialog box, specify the input TIN and the output raster grid name. Click **OK** to proceed. The elevation grid from the process will be added to ArcMap automatically. To create a slope grid from an elevation grid, select the **Surface Analysis** option from the Spatial Analyst toolbar and select **Slope** from the pull-down list. Specify the input elevation grid, give a name to the output slope grid, and select the slope unit as percent. Click **OK** to proceed. After the process is completed, a slope grid is created and added to ArcMap (Fig. 6.7).

The final step of preparing the slope factor layer is to convert the slope grid to a slope score grid. From the Spatial Analyst toolbar, select **Reclassify**. Select

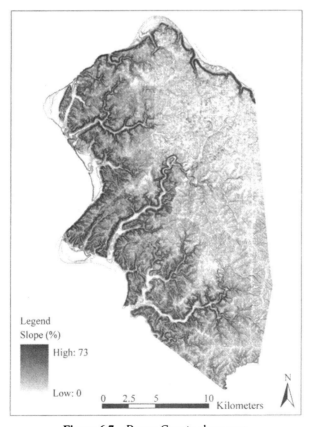

Figure 6.7   Boone County slope map

the slope grid as the input file, and specify four categories for the reclassification. Using Table 6.14 as the guide, enter the category range for the classification and give the corresponding score. Enter the output grid name and click **OK** to proceed. The result is a grid whose values are the slope scores (Fig. 6.8).

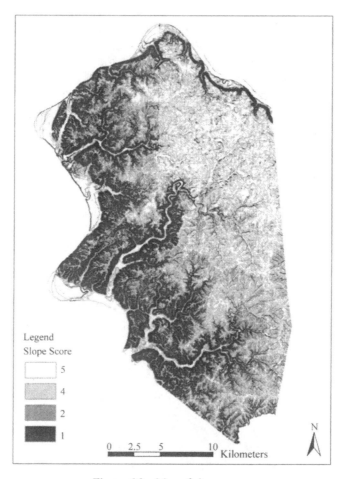

Legend
Slope Score

	5
	4
	2
	1

0   2.5   5   10
▬▬▬▬▬▬▬▬▬▬▬▬▬ Kilometers

N

Figure 6.8   Map of slope scores

6.5.1.2   Soil Layer

The second layer, soil data are normally in vector format using polygons to represent different soil types. In the United States, the U.S. Department of Agriculture Natural Resource Conservation Service (NRCS)[1] continuously conducts field soil surveys and publishes them to the Soil Survey Geographic

---

[1] U.S. Department of Agriculture Natural Resources Conservation Service (NRCS), http://www.nrcs.usda.gov.

(SSURGO) Database. The SSURGO database contains the most detailed soil data normally found in county soil survey books. The soil data are available in several formats that can be used directly in ArcMap. Each soil type is labeled with a soil symbol.

In addition to the map data, NRCS has prepared county level tables of soil features. Two tables that are especially relevant to a land suitability analysis are the tables for on-site septic systems and building construction. Those tables can be linked to the soil map by matching the soil symbol. Figure 6.9 is a soil type map with the associated table regarding soil restrictions to construction. The soil graphic data contain soil symbol and shape for each soil polygon, which are shown on the map. The first column of the soil table contains one record for each soil symbol. The second column is the soil characteristics for the soil type.

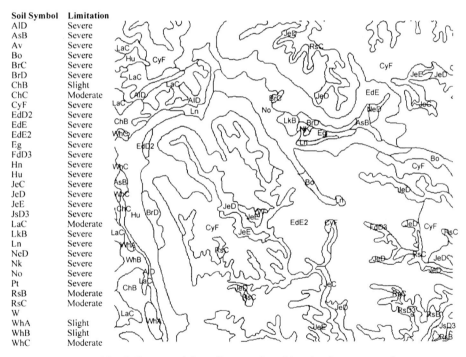

Soil Symbol	Limitation
AlD	Severe
AsB	Severe
Av	Severe
Bo	Severe
BrC	Severe
BrD	Severe
ChB	Slight
ChC	Moderate
CyF	Severe
EdD2	Severe
EdE	Severe
EdE2	Severe
Eg	Severe
FdD3	Severe
Hn	Severe
Hu	Severe
JeC	Severe
JeD	Severe
JeE	Severe
JsD3	Severe
LaC	Moderate
LkB	Severe
Ln	Severe
NcD	Severe
Nk	Severe
No	Severe
Pt	Severe
RsB	Moderate
RsC	Moderate
W	
WhA	Slight
WhB	Slight
WhC	Moderate

Figure 6.9   Soil map and the soil constraint table related to construction

Once the tables and the soil map file are ready we can use ArcMap to create the soil layer. The procedure has three steps. In the first step, the soil characteristics table is joined to the attribute table of soil map data with the join by attributes function. From the Join Window, select the soil characteristics table and soil symbol as the join field. Click **OK** to join the two tables. Then the soil score lookup table is joined to the map attribute table with the same procedure, using soil characteristics as the join field. Finally, the vector soil layer is converted to a soil score grid. From the Spatial Analyst Tool Bar, select **Convert** then **Feature to**

Raster using the score field as the raster grid values. Click **OK** to start the conversion. After the process is completed the soil score grid will be added to ArcMap. Figure 6.10 is an example of the map of soil suitability scores.

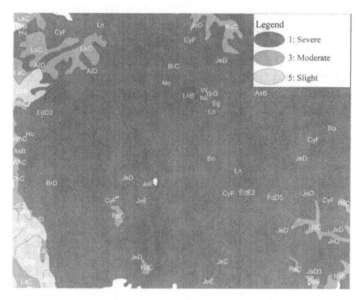

Figure 6.10   Map of construction related soil suitability scores

6.5.1.3   Floodplain and Sewer Service District Layers

The Federal Emergency Management Agency produces a series of maps showing areas subject to flooding, such as Flood Hazard Boundary Maps (FHBMs), Flood Insurance Rate Maps (FIRMs). Many communities also have maps showing the floodplains. Sometimes the maps are in hardcopy, though digital maps have recently become more common. Once vector polygon floodplain data are obtained or digitized, a new field can be added to store the suitability scores for the floodplain layer. From the Spatial Analyst Toolbar, select Convert then Feature to Raster using the score field as the raster grid values. Click **OK** to start the conversion. After the process is complete, the floodplain score grid is added to ArcMap. Figure 6.11 is the map of floodplain scores in Boone County.

Similarly, scores for sewer and water service can be assigned to the polygons, representing service districts. Raster data layer of service scores can then be created as shown in Fig. 6.12.

6.5.1.4   Distance to Roads Layer

To create the distance to roads suitability score, a data layer of major roads is required. Most communities have developed roads as part of the baseline database. With such a file, we can use the GIS Buffering function to create

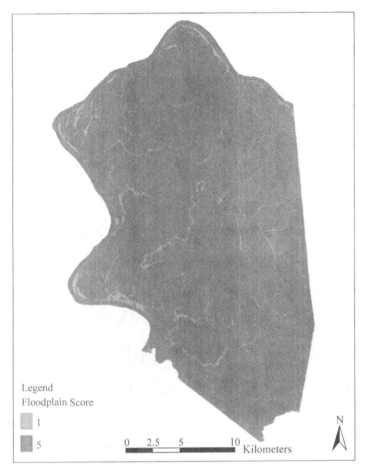

Legend
Floodplain Score

1

5

0   2.5   5   10
                              Kilometers

N

Figure 6.11   Map of floodplain scores in Boone County

distance buffers to roads and reclassify the buffers to reflect the distance classes for different suitability scores. To create the buffer, click the distance option from the Spatial Analyst Tool Bars, select the **Straight Line** option. Select the street layer as the **Distance to** layer, the cell size and the output raster layer name, and then click **OK** to proceed. A new layer showing the continuous distance to streets is created and added to ArcMap. Following the distance classification in Table 6.14, we can reclassify the distance into 4 groups by executing the **Reclassify** option from the Spatial Analyst Toolbar. From the Reclassify window, click the **Classify...** button to specify the number of classes for the output layer. Then the appropriate break values are entered for the classification. After clicking the **OK** button, you will see that the new classes are assigned accordingly in the Reclassify window. Corresponding scores for individual distance classes are then entered to proceed with the process. Figure 6.13 displays the map of distance to roads scores.

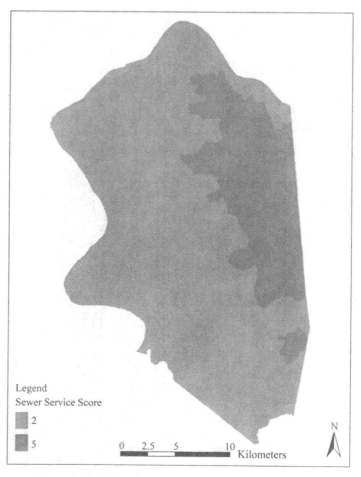

Figure 6.12   Map of sewer service scores in Boone County

6.5.2   Calculate Composite Scores

By now we have prepared all five suitability factor layers. In the next step, those layers are used to create a composite suitability layer. This process is implemented with raster map algebra calculation. Map algebra calculates a cell value based on the values of other layers for the cells representing the same location. Such an overlay analysis can easily derive the cumulative effects of multiple layers. Weights for the factor layers can be simply incorporated into the formula. As shown in Fig. 6.14, the center cells have values representing the scores for the individual factors at the location. The weights for individual layers are shown in parentheses. The value for the center cell in the composite layer is calculated from the individual cell values and weights for the layers.

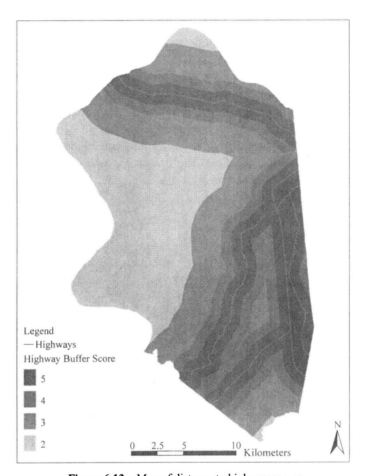

Figure 6.13   Map of distance to highway scores

Factor	Score	×	Weight	
Slope	5		0.3	1.5
				+
Floodplain	1		0.2	0.2
				+
Sewer	5		0.25	1.25
				+
Soil	1		0.15	0.15
				+
Roads	3		0.1	0.3
Composite	3.4			3.4

Figure 6.14   Illustration of map algebra

To implement this calculation with ArcMap, select the **Raster Calculator** from the Spatial Analyst Toolbar, and enter the following formula:

$$[\text{slope}] \times 0.3 + [\text{floodplain}] \times 0.2 + [\text{sewer}] \times 0.25 + [\text{soil}] \times 0.15 + [\text{roads}] \times 0.1$$

Click the **Evaluate** button, a composite suitability layer is created and added to ArcMap. The composite score for the cell in the above formula is 3.4. The final task is to reclassify the composite scores into groups, as shown in Table 6.16. Figure 6.15 displays a suitability analysis result for Boone County data. This map clearly shows where land is suitable for residential development and where land is not suitable based on the scores and weights assigned in this chapter.

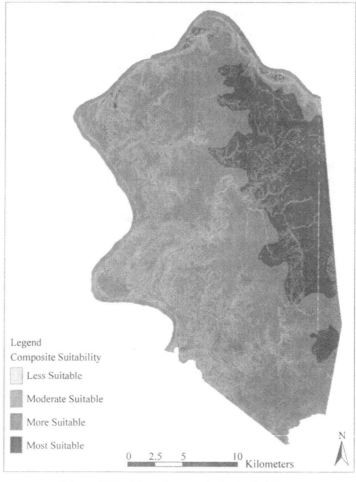

Figure 6.15   Map of composite land suitability

6.5.3   Delineation of Developable Land

However, not all of the land is available for residential development. Some of the land has already been developed which should not be converted to future residential land. Some of the areas are not permitted for residential land development. Figure 6.16 displays areas where land is available for residential development. The constraints for land availability are derived from existing land uses to indicate currently undeveloped (open space or woodland) land or farmland. Other constraints may be imposed by government rules or regulations as a way to guide where development may go. Figure 6.16 also displays a map of the land that is permitted for residential development in accordance to the zoning regulations. We can clearly see that the zoning requirement further limits where the future residential development may take place.

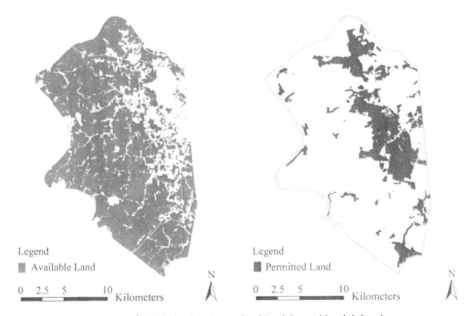

Figure 6.16   Available land and permitted land for residential development

Combining the three layers—land suitability, land availability and permitted land, we can derive the land that may be considered for future residential development. Those areas which are shown in Fig. 6.17 and represent the developable land that is suitable for residential development, currently is not developed, and is permitted by the zoning regulations. The map can be derived from three layers with GIS overlay functions. For example, in ArcMap, one may select **GeoProcessing Wizard** from the Tool menu bar, choose the "Intersect two layers" and click **Next**. In the next window, specify the two layers and the

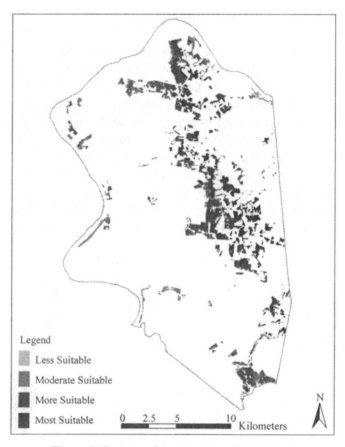

Legend

Less Suitable

Moderate Suitable

More Suitable

Most Suitable

0   2.5   5   10
Kilometers

N

Figure 6.17   Map of developable residential land

output layer name. Click **OK** to execute the process. A new layer is added to ArcMap, which only has the areas available and permitted for future residential land development. The final product is produced after this new layer is overlaid with the land suitability layer. Since the land suitability layer is in raster format, the overlay process is different. Select **Option** from the Spatial Analyst Toolbar. For the mask option, select the intersected available-permitted layer from the pull-down list. Click **OK** to finish. A mask functions is like a cookie cutter. Any areas outside of this mask will not be included in output file. Use the **Raster calculator** to calculate a new layer from the suitability layer. Because we have set up the intersected layer as the mask, the new land suitability layer is limited to the available and permitted land only. When a residential development decision needs to be made, only those areas suitable, available, and permitted should be considered. Among those areas, the most suitable area should have priority over the less suitable land.

6.6   Impact Analysis

We will conclude this chapter with a brief discussion of impact analysis of land development. The impacts of land development should be analyzed with a systems approach. A human settlement is a dynamic system that demands additional resources than the natural condition. The process of creating and maintaining the settlement leads to various types of impacts.

When we examine what is affected, the impacts could be on humans or on the environment. There are various social, economic, or cultural impacts of human development. People's needs are the driving force for most land development. Land development modifies the existing land use, which normally increases the intensity of human activities and land value. This happens often as we see that farm land is converted to residential, industrial or commercial uses. The human impact may be that land owners and developers get profit from the land development and the buyers get to the use the land as they want. Along with the development, the characteristics of the area may be changing as well. The fast expansion of urban areas around the world is such an example. The land development often results in the change of social dynamics and life style. It is not uncommon to read in the newspaper that in fast growing areas, residents complain about the smell from nearby farms and that the tractors move too slowly. Farmers who want to stay in farming complain about the difficulty of maintaining a business; some may be under extreme pressure to sell their land.

Environmental impacts refer to the degradation of quality in water, air, and land as a result of land development. Many of the by-products of human activities are the sources of environmental pollution. For example, water quality reflects the physical, biological and chemical status of a water body. Surface water such as streams, lakes, and estuaries are typically diverse and biologically productive environments in their natural form. It has been recognized that the quality of receiving waters is affected by human activities in a watershed via point sources, such as wastewater treatment facilities, and non-point sources, such as runoff from urban area and farm land. Industrial waste water may contain chemicals that do not exist in natural water. The application of fertilizers, pesticides and herbicides to lawns and farm fields may increase the concentration of nutrient or chemical concentrations in the water after a storm event. Physical and chemical factors, such as temperature, suspended solids, PH, nutrients, and chemicals determine the presence, abundance, diversity, and distribution of aquatic species in surface waters. The concept of biological integrity refers to the condition with little or no human impacts (Angermeier and Karr, 1994). Therefore, those water bodies that have been impacted by human activities to various degrees would demonstrate changes in biological integrity. Countries like the United States have set up policies to restore and maintain the integrity of the Nation's waters. To achieve this goal, we must limit the land use impacts on waters to maintain water integrity, that is, the capability of supporting and maintaining a community of

319

organisms comparable to that of a natural habitat (Karr and Dudley, 1981).

The impacts of land development are also reflected in the change in demand for resources, such as water, minerals, and energy; or for services such as schools, fire protection, sewage treatment, or garbage removal. For example, a change from farm land to residential use will significantly increase the number of people on the land; therefore, the demand for resources and services will increase as well.

The human and environmental impacts can vary in terms of spatial extent. Some impacts are limited to the development site. For example the land value may increase substantially after development. An urban heat island is another example, which refers to the high temperature in urban area, as a result of a high proportion of paved land and the extensive use of air conditioners. The development impacts also can go beyond the site boundary. One such example is the induced traffic from development. After a site is developed, for example, as residential or commercial use, there will be traffic coming and leaving the site. The roads connecting to the site will experience an increase in traffic volume. If the increased volume exceeds the design volume of the roads, we will expect traffic congestion to occur on those roads. People living in other areas and using the same roads will experience increasing difficulties when traveling.

It has been well documented that increased imperious surface in urbanized areas can significantly increase the risk of flooding because of the reduced infiltration and increased amount and flow rate of runoff. Communities downstream from a development site may be at higher risk of flooding damage.

Land development impacts may also vary along the temporal dimension. Some of the development impacts may be seen immediately and some other impacts will only appear in the future. For example, residents may experience the convenience of shopping as well as the traffic congestion after a retail development is completed in nearby area. Land and groundwater contamination from a gas station may become evident many years after the gas station is closed. The effect of such contamination may last much longer than the period of time the gas station was in operation.

The land development impacts can easily have a chain effect. The addition of nutrients into lakes may cause excess algae growth. Fertilizers applied on land, such as residential lawn, golf course, or agricultural fields can reach surface water body. The dissolved mineral nutrients, such as phosphorus and nitrogen, stimulate the growth of aquatic species and increase the organic mass in the water body. The consequence is the depletion of dissolved oxygen and the mortality and replacement of aquatic species.

Environmental impacts may lead to social and economic impacts. The urban sprawl phenomenon in the United States clearly demonstrates such effect. Once a real property is developed, used, and abandoned, the expansion, redevelopment, or reuse of the property may be complicated by the presence or potential presence of pollutants. Most such properties are in the urbanized areas. Two consequences

320

are common as developers and investors stay away from those properties: The urban areas lose taxes, population, jobs, and prosperity. At the same time, much of the undeveloped land is developed. Land use efficiency is low at the edge of urban areas because of the waste of land and infrastructure (Bertaud, 1994). As people move out the center cities much land is converted to highways, people spend longer times commuting to work. Such development patterns are called urban sprawl. A critical consequence of reliance on highways as a principal means, of transportation is pollution from motor vehicles. The increasing air pollution elevates health problems, such as asthma, lung cancer, and premature death. A recent study sponsored by the U.S. Federal Transit Administration shows that "[urban sprawl] has thwarted mass transit development, separated rich and poor, caused unnecessary travel, consumed fragile land, and generated excessive public expenditures" (Burchell et al., 2002).

There are many different approaches to quantify various impacts. Environmental impact analysis focuses on locally significant environmental quality, such as the alteration of wildlife habitat, the increase of soil erosion, the type and amount of pollutants discharged to local surface or ground water and emissions to air, or the increase of storm water runoff. [①] Traffic impact analysis calculates the traffic volume associated with a proposed development, which in turn to assess the carrying capacity of the existing roads. If the existing roads cannot support the proposed development, additional roads will be required in order to avoid traffic congestion. The impact to traffic will be the subject of the next chapter.

Detailed discussion of land use impact analytical methods goes beyond the scope of this book. Kaiser et al. (1995) propose two land use analytical approaches that serve a good example of the foundation for impact analysis. A "carrying capacity analysis" method is used to identify the maximum amount development without causing a breakdown of a natural or artificial system. A "committed lands analysis" is a method used to identify areas where the benefits of a proposed development exceed costs of the development. These two methods analyze the impact of a proposed development. The carrying capacity refers to the extent to which the land can support the proposed use. The rationale behind the carrying capacity is that the actual intensity level of a suitable land use development may vary. For example, a land suitable for residential development may be developed as low density or high density, consequently the impact of the land development would be different. Since there are more people on a high density residential land than a low density residential land, the former will have greater impact on the land. Examples of the impact may be the demand for water, if there is enough water resource to support the development, or the demand for roads, if the road network can support the added traffic from the residential

---

① Community Guide to Development Impact Analysis by Mary Edwards (http://www.lic.wisc.edu/ shapingdane/facilitation/all_resources/impacts/analysis_intro.htm). Accessed May 2005.

development. Other examples of impact may be the amount of runoff from the new development can be safely drained or the pollution generated from the development does not degrade the receiving water.

The committed land analysis reviews the benefit and cost related to a proposed development. Land development requires services such as water, sewer, school, and transportation. Although the development pays for the service sometimes the cost to provide the service may be higher than the revenue generated from the development. Let's compare two similar developments one in an area supported by an existing sewer line and the second requires building a new line. The cost for the second development will certainly be higher than the first. If both developments can provide enough revenue for the sewer service, economically it makes sense to commit to any of the developments, although the first development will be more efficient than the second development. If the cost to provide the sewer service is higher than the revenue from the second development, we should not commit to the second development. The purpose of committed land analysis is to identify the suitable land development that the benefit of development exceeds the cost. Kaiser et al. (1995) gave an example of the cost and revenue comparison. If the new development requires water service for 150 families and the charge for using the service is $50 per year per family, the total annual revenue from the 150 families will be $7,500. If the costs for expanding the water service lines are $30,000 per kilometer, the revenue associated with the development in the first year can support the expansion of service of 250 meters.

Another factor in land use development is the consideration of the compatibility of a proposed land development with existing land uses in the surrounding area. For example, industrial use in the middle of a residential area is not considered as compatible use. The compatibility consideration recognizes that the affect of human activities on a piece of land may cross the parcel boundary. Such impacts may be reflected in many aspects, such as environmental, economic, traffic, services, or aesthetics.

The impact analysis aims to assess and compare impacts of various development alternatives to the community by comparing the asset addition and the accompanied cost. A desirable development should minimize the fiscal, environmental, social, and traffic impacts; help to maintain or create the community characters desired by the residents: and efficiently use the available capacity of existing infrastructure, or be able to bring benefits to justify the expansion of existing infrastructure.

This chapter introduces two major types of land analysis: land classification and land suitability analysis. Land classification is the base of describing human activities on land, which makes it possible to analyze the spatial distribution and relationship of land uses. Built upon the knowledge gained from land classification, we can assess the compatibility and impacts of different land uses. Like any other classifications, the purpose of classification is to use a discrete number of classes to describe a real world phenomenon. This is necessary to be manageable, and at the same time, introduces errors. The classification is a process that requires individual judgment. Different operators may derive different classes, especially in the case of mixed uses. Also, there is sometimes no clear boundary between adjacent and different land uses. However, the nature of land classification requires artificial separation of uses.

The land suitability analysis as presented in this chapter is primarily based on the impacts of a proposed land use. From the land suitability analysis we can identify the use that is most suitable for the land. Sometimes, a site that is suitable for development if reviewed in isolation may become unsuitable if reviewed in conjunction with the surrounding land uses. For example, a new commercial development on a piece of suitable land may introduce too much automobile traffic. For the site to be properly functional, it may be necessary to widen the existing roads or to build new roads. There may not be suitable land to accommodate road expansion. However, this problem is not considered in the original land suitability analysis.

Review Questions

1. Why is land used differently by humans?
2. What are the characters that separate one type of land use from the other?
3. What is the purpose of land classification?
4. The two land classification systems that are used widely are the Anderson land classification system and the Land-Based Classification Standard (LBCS) system?
5. Why do we say that a GIS land use database is a relational database?
6. Why do we need to assign scores to different factor attributes in a land suitability analysis?
7. What does the factor weighting do in land suitability analysis?
8. Make a list of five different factors you may use in a land suitability analysis. Justify your choice by explaining the importance of each factor.
9. Describe the function of constraints in identifying available land for future development.
10. What is the next step after land suitability analysis?

Exercises

1. Conduct a literature review on an issue that is related to land development, such as urban sprawl, brownfield development, traffic congestion, farm land

protection. Use the issue to illustrate the human-environment relationship. Why is it important to consider resource consumption and land developability?

2. Look for land use maps or documents describing land uses of your city or town at different times in history. Prepare a series of hard copy land use maps, using the Anderson classification. If the land use classes in the data differ from the Anderson classification system, use your judgment to convert the classes. Prepare a detailed description of the final land use map, including the class description, classification approach, and data sources. If time permits, create a land use database using any GIS software. The description will be part of the data dictionary.

3. Compare the historical land use maps and describe the chronological land use change. What are the connections between the spatial distribution of land uses and the development of the place?

4. Zoom in to a few blocks in your city or town and follow the Land Based Classification Standards to prepare a set of first level land use classifications for activities, functions, building types, site development character, and ownership.

5. The most challenging and controversial tasks in land suitability analysis is to identify factors to be included in analysis, assign scores and weights to the factors. Assume there is a development proposal in your community (It can be residential, commercial, or industrial development; which ever you think would help the community). Organize a group of students to complete the tasks using the Delphi method. Each will represent a different stakeholder group in the community (i.e., developers, investors, residences, special interest groups, government officials). Make sure you think and act as the group you represent. One person acts as the facilitator. Your goal is to reach a consensus on the factors, scores and weights, taking as many rounds as needed. Make notes along the process. After the exercise, the get together as a group and compare notes. Summarize your experience of the exercise.

References

Anderson, James R. et al. 1976. *A Land Use and Land Cover Classification System with Remote Sensor Data.* Washington, D.C.: U.S. Government Printing Office.

Angermeir, P.L. and J.R. Karr. 1994. Biological integrity versus biological diversity as policy directives. *Bioscience*, 44 (10): 690 – 697.

Bartholomew, Harland. 1955. *Land Uses in American Cities.* Cambridge, MA: Harvard University Press.

Bertaud, Alain. 1994. Overview. In: Ismail Serageldin, Michael A. Cohen, and K.C. Siva-ramakrishnan (eds). *The Human Face of the Urban Environment, Proceedings of the Second Annual World Bank Conference on Environmentally Sustainable Development.* Washington, DC: The World Bank.

Burchell, Robert W., Lowenstein, George, Dolphin, William, Galley, Catherine C., Downs, Anthony, Seskin, Samuel, Still, Katherine g., and Moore, Terry. 2002. *Costs of Sprawl 2000*. Washington, DC: National Academy Press, Transit Cooperative Research Program. Report 74.

Buckley, Chris. 1995. Delphi: a methodology for preferences more than predictions. *Library Management*, 16 (7): 16 – 19.

Burley, Terence M. 1961. Land use or land utilization? *Professional Geographer*, 13: 18 – 20.

Clawson, Marion and Charls L. Stewart. 1966. *Land use Information; a Critical Survey of U. S. Statistics, Including Possibilities for Greater Uniformity*. Baltimore, MD: Johns Hopkins Press.

Fraser, Derek and Anthony Sutcliffe (eds.) *The Pursuit of Urban History*. London: Edward Arnold.

Garreau, Joel. 1988. *Edge City: Life on the New Frontier*. New York, NY: Doubleday.

Gilbert, Alan and Josef Gugler. 1981. *Cities, Poverty, and Development: Urbanization in the Third World*. London: Oxford University Press.

Hauser, P.M. and L.F. Schone. 1965. *The Study of Urbanization*. New York, NY: John Wiley & Sons, Inc.

Jeer, Sanjay. 2001. *Land-Based Classification Standards*. Chicago, IL: American Planning Association. Available online at http://www.planning.org/LBCS.

Kaiser, Edward J., David R. Godschalk and F. Stuart Chapin, Jr. 1995. *Urban Land Use Planning*. Urbana, IL: University of Illinois Press.

Karr, J.R. and D.R. Dudley. 1981. Ecological perspective on water quality goals. *Environmental Management*, 5: 55 – 68.

Kelbaugh, D.S. 2002. *Repairing the American Metropolis*. Seattle, WA: University of Washington Press.

Lampard, Eric E. 1983. The nature of urbanization. In: Derek Fraser and Anthony Sutcliffe (eds.). *The Pursuit of Urban History*. London: Edward Arnold.

Linstone, Harold A. and Murray Turoff (eds.) 1975. *The Delphi Method: Techniques and Applications*. Reading, MA: Addison-Wesley Publishing Company.

Lovelace, E. 1993. *Harland Bartholomew: His contributions to American Urban Planning*. Urbana, IL: University of Illinois Office of Printing Services.

Marsh, William M. 2005. *Landscape Planning: Environmental Applications*, 4th ed. New York, NY: John Wiley & Sons, Inc.

McHarg, Ian L. 1969. *Design with Nature*. Garden City, NY: Natural History Press.

McKelvey, Blake. 1963. *The Urbanization of America, 1800 – 1915*. New Brunswick, NJ: Rutgers University Press.

Melosi, Martin V. 1980. *Pollution and Reform in American Cities, 1870 – 1930*. Austin, TX: University of Texas Press.

Mohl, Raymond A. (ed.) 1997. *The Making of Urban America,* 2nd ed. Wilmington, DL: Scholarly Resources Inc.

Nash, Gary B. 1997. The social evolution of pre-industrial American cities. In: Raymond A. Mohl (ed.). *The Making of Urban America*, 2nd ed. Wilmington, DL: Scholarly Resources Inc.

Ortolano, Leonard. 1997. *Environmental Regulation and Impact Assessment.* New York, NY: John Wiley & Sons, Inc.

Scheele, D. Sam. 1975. Reality construction as a product of Delphi interaction. In: Harold A. Linstone and Murray Turoff (eds.). *The Delphi Method: Techniques and Applications.* Reading, MA: Addison-Wesley Publishing Company.

Urban Renewal Administration, Housing and Home Finance Agency, and Bureau of Public Roads, Department of Commerce (URA and BPR). 1965. *Standard Land Use Coding Manual: A Standard System for Identifying and Coding Land Use Activities.* Washington, DC: Government Printing Office.

Chapter 7 Transportation Analysis

Transportation analysis is the last part of the four planning analytical methods covered in this book. Various economic activities for a given population in an area occur at different locations, which are associated with different land uses. The interaction of those activities requires a network to connect places for moving people and goods. The function for such a system is the focus of transportation analysis. Transportation analysis provides the basis for transportation planning. Transportation planning is a process of finding feasible alternatives and components of a transportation system to support human activities in a community. A transportation system consists of many different subsystems to accommodate different modes of transportation. Transportation is a broad category which includes air, water, and land transportation systems. The land-based system includes motor vehicles, pedestrians, bicycles, and rail and public transits. In addition to the modes of transportation, a transportation system consists of networks such as roads, and supporting facilities, such as traffic lights.

A comprehensive plan can give indication of the future land uses in a community. Transportation planners estimate the amount of traffic associated with the planned land use allocation, the options of travel modes, the alternative routes, and the required roadway features to support the estimated traffic volume. During the process of evaluating the various transportation alternatives required to meet the future demand, planners must consider community characteristics, available funds, environmental impacts, and other factors. Transportation engineers design appropriate transportation systems to support a community's desired mobility. For example, after traffic volume increases and congestion occurs in a community, a transportation engineer can design additional roadway lanes needed to accommodate the additional traffic volume while maintaining the original travel speed.

The most critical challenge for transportation engineers and planners is the dynamic feature of a transportation system, both spatially and over time. Transportation facility and traffic volume are constantly affecting each other. Unlike housing development, where a house or an apartment is built for one family and the demand for housing can be met by building more houses, roads are built and shared among travelers. On any particular road, bad traffic indicates that more people are traveling on the road than has capacity to handle. One common practice to improve traffic conditions is to increase the road capacity, such as adding a new lane to an existing road. However, this increased capacity can effectively relieve the traffic congestion only for a short period. More people start to enjoy the easy travel from the road expansion and soon the traffic congestion occurs again. The theory of induced traffic explains this phenomenon as the increases in the carrying capacity of a road attracts more vehicle traffic to the road (Norland, 2001).

People's travel choices can be summarized as the time of departure, travel mode, and route. Many people travel to work within a short time period, called morning rush hours. Because many work places are close to each other in areas such as Central Business Districts (CBD), traffic volume tends to increase on roads that lead to the work places. People may choose to drive private cars or take public transit to work. People's decisions regarding the three choices are often based on the comfort level, convenience, flexibility, privacy, and travel time. In the United States, the majority of the travelers drive private vehicles for those reasons. The trend in China shows similar pattern as automobiles become affordable to more and more people. Although effort has been made to have different work hours, the nature of business determines the vast majority of businesses will have similar working hours. Once on the road, travelers normally want to reach their destination quickly. This leads to the route choice as the only major factor affecting the traffic volume. Travelers can easily switch routes on the way. Radio stations in many metropolitan areas report road traffic conditions and suggest alternative routes.

Assume a CBD is connected by a highway and a local street, more people would choose the highway in order to avoid traffic lights and to able to travel at higher speeds. As more people get on the highway, the vehicle moving speed will decrease. Eventually, there will be no difference in travel time between traveling on a highway and the local streets, which indicates that traffic has reached equilibrium.

Now assume a new lane is added to the highway to solve the highway congestion problem, the immediate outcome is that travelers on the highway will be able to move faster. However, people who travel on the local streets realize that they may travel faster on highway and, consequently, switch their route to the highway. As a result of this switch, the travel speed on the highway will decrease. If this is the only consequence we may still expect that the new lane has relieved the traffic congestion to some degree. In reality, those who use public transit may realize the highway improvement switch to driving private vehicles. And those who leave to work earlier or later than their preferred time to avoid congestion may switch back to their normal time. This switch of routes, modes, and time is called "triple convergence" (Downs, 2004). According to the triple convergence principle, increasing the roadway capacity does not alleviate traffic congestion during the rush hours unless the roadway capacity is increased to the level that can accommodate all the traffic, which is spatially and financially impossible for many metropolitan areas. In short, the net affect of roadway improvement is that the improved travel condition induces more trips during the rush hours. This dynamic phenomenon presents a big challenge to transportation planners.

Detailed discussion of transportation engineering and transportation planning goes beyond the scope of this book. Students who are interested in further study should look into transportation courses offered in planning and transportation engineering programs. The goal of this chapter is to introduce the fundamental concepts and calculations in transportation analysis. You will be able to understand the travel demand modeling and its applications in planning.

7.1   Basic Concepts in Transportation Analysis

Let us begin by reviewing some terms commonly used in transportation analyses, using Fig. 7.1 as an example. A transportation study analyzes the traffic conditions on road networks. A road network is a special application of the "network flow problems", which is part of linear programming theory. The mathematical base of network analysis is to determine a static maximal flow from one point to another in a network, subject to capacity limitations of the network (Ford and Fulkerson, 1962). A road consists of multiple segments and one road connects to other roads at intersections. The collective features of each road segment represent the overall traffic conditions in a region.

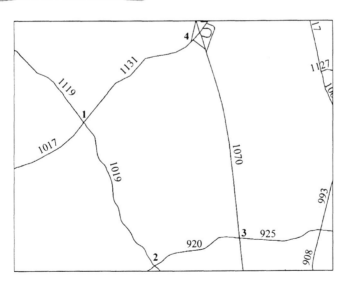

Figure 7.1   Illustration of a street network

A **street network** refers to all the surface roads that are connected to each other and to different places of human activities. A street network consists of segments and nodes. A network may be a real geometric representation of roadways or straight lines connecting the nodes.

A **node** is an intersection where two or more streets are connected or the end of a street. For example, in Fig. 7.1, four street intersections are labeled as nodes 1 through 4.

A **segment** is a line connecting two nodes. The traffic on a segment remains same and may only change from one segment to another. Figure 7.1 shows four complete segments (labeled as 920,1070,1019, and 1131).

A **link** is a segment associated with direction. If we use letter L to represent a link, the link from node i to nod j is often represented as L_{ij}. A one-way street is represented as a link with only one direction. A link representing a two-way street will have traffic data for two opposite directions. Therefore, a street network segment may be represented as L_{ij} and L_{ji}. A link is the smallest unit of analysis in transportation studies. Many of the basic features of a street network are associated to links. Variables normally describe link-based traffic include design capacity, design speed, number of lanes, traffic volume, and actual travel speed.

A **chain** is a series of connected links directed the same way. The travel from a node i to a node j may go through a link or a chain of links.

A study area is divided into areas, instead of points. Those areas are called **Traffic Analysis Zones (TAZs)**. A traffic analysis zone is delineated as the smallest area of the study region. Although there may be numerous residential locations in a TAZ, to include each location in the model would be rather cumbersome in practice. Therefore, travelers within a TAZ are treated in the same way as an aggregated group (Oppenheim, 1995). Although people living in the same TAZ may access to the street network at many different nodes, transportation studies treat all traffic from a **centroid** of the zone. Traffic generated from a TAZ or end at a TAZ is connected to street networks through one or more **connectors**. One end of a connector is a node on the street network. The other end is the centroid of a TAZ. Connectors may not be real roads. Figure 7.2 illustrates TAZs and their connectors to the street network.

A **trip** is normally the focus of a transportation analysis. It represents the path people make from one place to another, for instance, from home to office. One type of trip is a **vehicle trip**—the number of automobile trips traveling in a transportation system. Another type of trips is a **person trip**—the number of people traveling through the transportation system. When there is more than one passenger in a vehicle it becomes necessary to distinguish the two. In this case, an estimation of number of people per vehicle is required to convert person trips to vehicle trips.

The two places connecting a trip are called **trip ends**. Trip ends can be further divided into two categories when trip direction is considered. The trip end at the beginning of a trip is called **origin** and the trip end at the end of a trip is called **destination**.

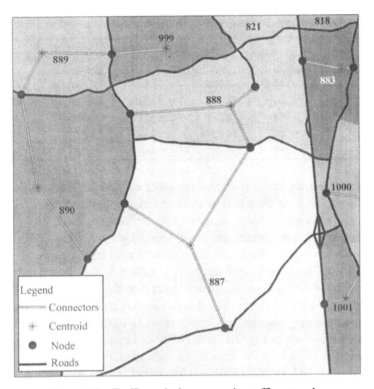

Figure 7.2   Traffic analysis zones and a traffic network

Travel Time Index measures the additional time for a peak hour trip when it is compared with the same trip during non-peak hours. It is expressed as the ratio of the peak hour trip time and the non-peak hour trip time. For example, the trip from my house to office takes 40 minutes during the peak hours and 25 minutes during non-peak hours. The travel time index is $40/25 = 1.6$.

Traffic flows between TAZs are normally expressed in an **origin-destination (O-D) matrix.** Table 7.1 illustrates an O-D matrix for a study area of four TAZs. Reading horizontally, the matrix shows that the traffic volume generated from Zone 1 is 11,774, among which 4,340 trips go to other parts of the same zone. Three other numbers represent the trips from Zone 1 to Zones 2, 3 and 4. For example, 3,180 trips go from Zone 1 to Zone 2. Reading vertically, the matrix shows the number of trips ending in each zone. For instance, 8,220 trips originate in Zone 2 and end in Zone 1. Numbers in the last column are trips that start from each origin zone. Numbers in the last row represent trips ending in each destination zone. The matrix shows that Zone 1 generates fewer trips than the other three zones. Zone 2 receives more trips than other zones. This could be an indication that Zone 2 may be dominated by industries or shopping centers that make Zone 2 the major employment center.

Table 7.1   An O-D matrix for a hypothetical study area of four TAZs

From \ To	1	2	3	4	Total Trip Origins
1	4,340	3,180	1,769	2,485	11,774
2	8,220	16,493	5,804	10,525	41,042
3	4,954	6,287	6,828	5,179	23,247
4	8,989	14,727	6,691	20,347	50,754
Total Trips	26,502	40,687	21,092	38,536	126,817

Design capacity is the maximum number of vehicles that can pass the end of a link within a given time period without causing traffic delay. It is measured as number of vehicles per hour, such as 1,000 vehicles per hour.

Design speed is the maximum travel speed for a given link when there is no delay[1]. A design speed reflects the function of a road and is normally limited by physical, social, economic, and aesthetic conditions. For example, the design speed of a link on steep slope is usually lower than the design speed of a road on flat land due to safety concerns. The design speed is also related to road functions. A local road passing through residential areas is likely to have a lower design speed than a highway. In Fig. 7.1, link 1070 has larger design capacity and faster design speed than link 1019. This is an indication that link 1070 represents a major road while link 1019 represents a local road.

Number of lanes represents the lanes available for travel. The number of lanes can be the total lanes for both direction or be counted by the travel direction.

Volume is the actual number of vehicles going through the link within a given time period. The volume can be measured as daily volume (24-hours) or one-hour volume. The one-hour volume is usually used to represent the traffic during peak hours.

Average Daily Traffic (ADT) represents the typical daily traffic volume for a link. In transportation planning analysis, traffic volume data are normally collected during a long period in order to calculate ADT. The daily traffic can further be divided into weekday and weekend volume.

Average Peak Hour Traffic (PHV) can be calculated when traffic data are collected only during peak hours on multiple days and the average is calculated from the data.

Vehicle occupancy is the number of people traveling together in one mobile vehicle. It is normally calculated as the number of travelers divided by the number of traveling vehicles in a geographic area such as a traffic analysis zone, or a region.

---

[1] A Policy on Geometric Design of Highways and Streets, American Association of State Highway and Transportation Officials, Washington, DC 1994.

In transportation analysis trips are normally classified by **trip purpose** based on the location of the origin and destination.

(1) If one of the trip ends is home and the other trip end is a workplace, the trip purpose is defined as **home based work** (HBW). A typical HBW trip is the trip from home to work in the morning or going home from work in the evening.

(2) If one of the trip ends is home and the other trip end is not a workplace, the trip purpose is **home-based-non-work** (HBNW). Sometimes this trip purpose is called **home based other** (HBO). When a family goes to a restaurant for dinner, the trip purpose is qualified as HBO.

(3) If neither of the two trip ends is home, the trip is defined as **Non-home based** (NHB) purpose. A good example of a NHB trip is for a person to go shopping at lunch break. One trip end is the office and the other trip end is the store.

(4) Two trips between two trip ends (back and forth) are called a **round trip**. For example, a person goes to work from home in the morning and returns home in the evening will count as one round trip, consisting of two trips.

(5) The above discussed trips can be called simple trips. As the trip making behavior becomes more complex, people may make intermittent stops on a trip. **Trip chaining** is the succession of trip segments (Hensher and Reyes, 2000).

Figure 7.3 illustrates the different trip terms. It shows three round trips. The round trip on the left consists of two HBN trips. The round trip in the middle has two HBW trips. The trip from WORK to BANK then HOME is an example of trip chain. The round trip on the right is made up of two NHB trips.

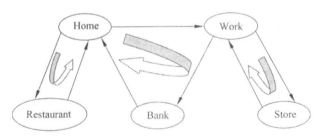

Figure 7.3   Illustration of trips

7.2   Overview of Transportation Analysis

In general, transportation planning consists of two tasks. The first task is to estimate the traffic flow based on population and economic activities. Human activities are normally reflected in land use composition. The second task is to evaluate the social, economic, and environmental impacts of transportation projects.

Traffic demand analysis (freight and passenger) aims to derive the traffic volumes of a traffic network. The volumes are calculated from a set of origin-destination matrices related to a proper traffic analysis zone subdivision. Computer models are often developed to simulate traffic demands. Most of these types of models work best on a corridor or regional scale for planning purposes. They are not designed for estimating traffic volume on a particular street.

The purpose of a traffic impact analysis is to identify the traffic-related consequences of a proposed development, such as a new commercial center. Normally, the outcome of the analysis is recommendation for minimizing undesirable impacts. In order to do so, the analysis will determine specific traffic volumes associated with a proposed development, the capacity of existing transportation systems to absorb additional traffic volumes, the significant traffic impacts, and possible mitigation measures for those impacts. The traffic impact study results are used to identify and assist in the design of specific transportation improvements required for a project. These improvement requirements are normally incorporated into the conditions of the project approval.

While transportation project is intended to improve mobility, it also incurs implementation costs. The comparison of costs and benefits of different alternatives is often used as the basis for selecting a desirable course of action. A commonly used measure is the **ratio of benefits to costs** (B/C ratio). If the ratio of a project is greater than one, the project is expected to have greater benefits than costs. Everything else being equal, the project with the higher ratio would most likely be the preferable choice.

The challenge of a cost-benefit analysis is the measurement of cost and benefit. Costs may be monetary or non-monetary. The costs to build or maintain a street are an example of monetary costs. The costs incurred from automobile accidents and congestion are examples of non-monetary costs. In addition, a transportation project may affect the land use pattern, air quality, and quality of life in the surrounding areas, which may also be non-monetary costs and/or benefits. Examples of benefits include increased efficiency of the transportation system, positive economic development impacts, and increased real estate values. In general, a Benefit-Cost Analysis (BCA) identifies alternative projects that have positive net social benefits and then selects one from the list as the preferable choice. The final selection could be solely based upon the net benefit or other additional considerations. What can complicate the Benefit-Cost Analysis is that the costs and benefits may be short-term or occur over time.

7.3   Street Classification

Streets have two functions—providing access and facilitating movement. Both functions are critical for an effective transportation system. **Access** refers to connecting the points of interest to the street network. **Movement** means that one can travel fast along a street. Streets with good access are easy to get on and off. Such a street does not allow high-speed travel. Streets with good movement have limited number of access points; so, traffic can move uninterrupted. Most of the time, a street is normally designed to have one primary function. Some streets are designed to move vehicles quickly and efficiently from one point to another; others are connecting to as many places as possible. At one extreme, a street used for fast moving vehicles has limited access, such as express highways. Local streets are at the other extreme, which connect to individual buildings and have low travel speed limits. This allows the transportation system to provide connections to places of human activities with a safe and smooth traffic flow.

Street classification is a method that reflects the various street functions. A local municipality may use a variation of this general street classification system to accommodate the specific local circumstance. In general, a street classification consists of the following categories:

Expressways or freeways (movement $\gg$ access): The most important function of expressways or freeways is to provide rapid vehicular mobility between cities and major attractions. The access of these roads is limited to major regional destinations, such as airports, large shopping malls, or hospitals. The limited number of access points allows automobile travel at high speeds without much interruption between origin and designation. An expressway traveling through a city only has a few exits for connecting the city and the transportation system and with minimal delay for the through traffic.

Arterials (movement > access): The primary function of arterial streets is still to provide a high degree of vehicular mobility. However, this class of roads can connect more areas to a transportation system within an area, such as a city or a town. Once a vehicle gets on an arterial, the purpose is to enter to an express highway within a short distance or travel to a place that is not too far away. Because of its emphasis on mobility, these streets should be designed to maintain high traffic capacity.

Collectors (movement = access): Access and mobility are equally important for collector streets. The access refers to linking the interior of an area to the transportation system by providing a short travel to the nearest arterial streets. One example of the consideration of movement is the left turn lane and restricted turning movements.

Local streets (movement < access): Local streets primarily provide a high degree of access. Vehicles are constantly merging or leaving traffic along streets, as well as containing pedestrian crossings. Another feature of local streets is on-street parking. Easy access to local streets is much more important than fast vehicle movement. In fact, most local streets impose low travel speed limits.

The U.S. Census Bureau developed a street classification system as part of its Census Feature Class Code (CFCC), based on the U.S. Geological Survey (USGS) classification code in the DLG-3 file. The CFCC is a hierarchical three-character system for linear features. The first character, A, is used for roads.

335

The second character is a number representing the major street category. The third character, also a number, describes sub-categories for each major category.

Table 7.2 displays the major CFCC Road categories. For example, A1 represents a "Primary highway with limited access". In this category, A11 is a "Primary road with limited access or interstate highway, unseparated"; and A12 is the "Primary road with limited access or interstate highway, unseparated, in tunnel." Most of the street classifications were field verified by census staff during field operations or through the use of aerial photography or imagery.

Table 7.2   Major Census Feature Class Code road categories

CFCC Category	Description
A0—Road With Category Unknown	Source materials do not allow determination of the road category
A1—Primary Highway With Limited Access	Interstate highways and some toll highways, which are accessed by way of ramps and have multiple lanes of traffic. The opposing traffic lanes are divided by a median strip
A11	Primary road with limited access or interstate highway, unseparated
A12	Primary road with limited access or interstate highway, unseparated, in tunnel
A13	Primary road with limited access or interstate highway, unseparated, underpassing
A14	Primary road with limited access or interstate highway, unseparated, with rail line in center
A15	Primary road with limited access or interstate highway, separated
A16	Primary road with limited access or interstate highway, separated, in tunnel
A17	Primary road with limited access or interstate highway, separated, underpassing
A18	Primary road with limited access or interstate highway, separated, with rail line in center
A2—Primary Road Without Limited Access	Nationally and regionally important highways that do not have limited access as required by category A1. It consists of highways that connect cities and larger towns. A road in this category must be hard-surface (concrete or asphalt). It has intersections with other roads, may be divided or undivided, and have multi-lane or single-lane characteristics
A3—Secondary and Connecting Road	Highways that connect smaller towns, subdivisions, and neighborhoods. The roads in this category are generally smaller than roads in Category A2, must be hard surface (concrete or asphalt), and are usually undivided with single-lane characteristics. These roads usually have a local name along with a route number and intersect with many other roads and driveways

Continued

CFCC Category	Description
A4—Local, Neighborhood, and Rural Road	Roads for local traffic with a single lane of traffic in each direction. In an urban area, this feature is a neighborhood road and street that is not a thorough-fare belonging in categories A2 or A3. In a rural area, this is a short-distance road connecting the smallest towns
A5—Vehicular Trail	Usually a one-lane dirt trail, and is found almost exclusively in very rural areas
A6—Road with Special Characteristics	Roads, portions of a road, intersections of a road, or the ends of a road that are parts of the vehicular highway system and have separately identifiable characteristics
A7—Road as Other Thoroughfare	Roads used by bicyclists or pedestrians, and is typically inaccessible to mainstream motor traffic except for private-owner and service vehicles

Source: U.S. Census Bureau. 2004.

The street classification reflects the variations of road functions. The physical characteristics of streets in different categories vary significantly. The major function of roads in the A1 class is movement. Therefore the roads are wide and have limited access, such as the expressways. The length of streets between exits is long. This is consistent with people that use the A1 class streets for long distance travel, such as between cities. Travelers do not need to make frequent stops and speed is the major concern. Compared to the A1 class, roads in the A4 category are used more provide access than movement. Travel speed is less of a concern for people traveling on roads in the A4 category. The primary purpose of using these roads is to get to the point of interest. The connection to residential, commercial and work places is provided through local streets. Those streets are the most widely dispersed and span to every place of human activities. Each lower category street feeds traffic to the higher category streets. The need for higher category streets is less since there are fewer areas to be connected.

7.3.1   Level of Service

The travel quality of a road is normally expressed with the measurement of level of service (LOS). In the United States there are six LOS categories represented by the letters "A" to "F", where A is for the best traffic condition and F, the worst. In general, the LOS system reflects a user's actual travel experience in relation to desired travel condition. It can be used to measure different modes of transportation, such as automobiles, bicycles, pedestrians, and public transit. Although the scale system may be similar for all transportation modes, the measurement varies. Even for the automobile traffic alone, different measurements are normally adopted for highways and urban streets.

It should be noticed that LOS measures the quality of traffic flow, or the levels of congestion. Although traffic can be by automobile, bicycle, or public transit, the discussion below is specific to automobile traffic. In designing a street, traffic engineers use LOS as the base for selecting design parameters.

7.3.1.1 Highway Level of Service

Highway LOS is calculated according to the volume/capacity ratio as shown in Table 7.3.

Table 7.3 Highway level of service classification

LOS	Volume/Capacity Ratio	Description (TRB, 2000)
A	Less Than 60%	Free-flow operation
B	60% to Less Than 70%	Reasonably free-flow
C	70% to Less Than 80%	Flow at or near free-flow speed
D	80% to Less Than 90%	Borderline unstable
E	90% to Less Than 100%	Operation at capacity
F	100% or Greater	Breakdown

Level-of-service A represents free-flow operations. A traveler can travel at the designed speed almost completely unimpeded. The distance between vehicles is large enough for the motorist to feel comfortable. The effect of minor incidents can be easily absorbed.

Level-of-service B describes a condition in which a motorist still can experience reasonably free flow at free-flow speeds. Although slightly restricted, the ability to maneuver and level of comfort are still high and minor incidents do not cause much delay.

Level-of-service C is the lowest level in which a motorist can move at, or close to, the free-flow speed. The ability to maneuver is noticeably restricted. Drivers may feel tense while driving due to the additional vigilance required for safe operation. Although minor incidents can still be absorbed, local deterioration in service will be substantial.

Level-of-service D depicts a condition in which motorists can experience reduced travel speeds. The ability to maneuver is severely limited. Drivers may start feeling uncomfortable physically or psychologically. The network has little capacity to absorb minor incidents.

Level-of-service E is a condition in which traffic is at its design capacity. There is no room for any disruption of traffic flow. A simple lane change may significantly affect the traffic. The level of maneuverability is extremely limited and driving is no longer a comfortable experience. Serious breakdown with extensive queuing can result from minor incidents.

Level-of-service F describes a condition of breakdowns in the traffic flow. Queuing and congestion are the norm for LOS F. The traffic flow exceeds the design capacity. There is almost no ability to maneuver and no one will feel comfortable driving.

In planning and designing a transportation network, transportation authorities set up LOS standards for each roadway segment, which specify acceptable LOS. It is critical to set up adequate LOS standards. Achieving a better level of service normally costs more for construction and maintenance. It may also require more land to be committed to transportation. In order to maintain the level of movement that matches the development level of a community within the affordable budget, planners and decision makers must carefully select a proper LOS for new transportation, as well as improvement of the existing transportation system. For example, the designation of LOS can be the basis for establishing a traffic impact mitigation fee system to provide "fair share" funding for transportation improvements. The level of service can also be used as environmental impact review criteria that provide a basis for accepting, modifying, or denying a proposed development.

7.4 Travel Demand Modeling

A travel demand model is used to forecast the transportation arrangement. Because of the difference of various conditions, such as those discussed in the land suitability analysis, human activities in an area are not evenly distributed. Certain areas may not be suitable for all types of development. For those areas that can support development, some may be more suitable for industrial development, while other areas are more suitable for residential development. In addition to the natural condition, the layout of existing land uses also determines the potential for future development. For example, it would normally be considered inappropriate to build a factory in a residential area. The outcome of the suitability and compatibility considerations is the uneven distribution of human activities. Certain areas are predominately for residential uses, some for commercial uses, and some for industrial uses. Such distribution makes it necessary for people to travel among different areas using the transportation system. In addition to the connections, the demands for carrying capacity and other facilities, such as parking, vary spatially and temporarily. The trips to and from a factory may have morning and afternoon peaks while such patterns may not exist for trips to a shopping mall.

In order to estimate the traffic associated with different human activities, a region is divided into TAZs and the TAZs are connected to the transportation network. TAZs are the smallest unit of analysis in travel demand modeling. Two general rules are normally used in delineating TAZs:

(1) A zone should be bounded by the transportation network or natural boundaries, such as rivers.

(2) The zone boundaries enclose a relatively homogeneous area in terms of land use characteristics and traffic conditions and separate the areas that are different. TAZ boundaries may follow community or neighborhood boundaries.

The study area where a travel demand model can be developed must be small enough so that people are likely to travel between all zones within the area. At the same time, the study area must be large enough so that the trips crossing the study area boundary can be ignored. A metropolitan region is normally used as a study area.

Although there are different travel demand models using different variables, the application of travel demand modeling in general contains the following six components, normally arranged in a sequential order:

(1) Specify the regional population and economic activities for the study area. This component focuses on what is expected to occur in the study area. The population and economic analysis methods discussed in Chapters 3 – 5 are used to determine the characteristics of human activities.

(2) Allocate these population and economic activities to each TAZ based on land uses. All human activities concerned in this context require the use of land. The methods discussed in Chapter 6 are used to identify and allocate land for human activities specified in the first component. Traffic Analysis Zones are the smallest areas used to summarize human activities.

(3) Choose a proper model structure and relevant variables to be included in the travel demand model. This process is called **model specification**. Modelers analyze the trend and special features of the study area and construct a model that describes the connection between human activities and the traffic demand. Such a model incorporates the most important variables in establishing the connection. In addition, model specification also determines how those variables are used to quantify the connection.

(4) Use the travel demand model to calculate traffic flows between TAZs. In this component, the travel demand model is used to calculate the traffic from one TAZ to another. The total traffic can be summarized by the modes of transportation and different routes that connect the TAZs.

(5) Collect actual traffic flow data and calibrate the travel demand model for the study area. The purpose of calibration is to adjust model structure and/or parameters in order to match model outputs with observed data. A model is only useful if its prediction matches the observed data. In this component, the travel demand model is fine tuned with real world data.

(6) Use the calibrated travel demand model to predict traffic flows for different growth scenarios. After the model calibration, the travel demand model is believed to be capable of predicting traffic for a given human activity scenario. Additional predictions may be derived from the traffic forecast, such as travel time and travel costs, street alignment and construction costs, and other social,

economic, and environmental impacts. The modeling results are used to support decisions about different alternatives.

Traffic planners and engineers spend a considerable time and resources to design a model and to analyze issues related to the structure, parameter and application of travel demand models. The rest of the Chapter introduces the general components of travel demand models. Although not all planners need to develop or operate a travel demand model, it is important for planners to understand how a travel demand model establishes the connection between human activities and traffic.

This travel demand modeling covers major travel behaviors that affect travelers' decisions on choice of traveling, destinations, transportation modes, and travel paths. The modeling process consists of four individual parts, commonly referred to as the four-step travel demand forecast modeling process.

(1) Trip Generation: Forecast the number of trips originated from and attracted to each TAZ.

(2) Trip Distribution: Allocate the trips within and between the TAZs.

(3) Mode Choice: Divide trips among different modes of travel.

(4) Trip Assignment: Assign the trips to different routes connecting the TAZs.

These four steps were developed in the 1950s and 1960s. Since then, although the four components are kept intact, many significant modifications have been made to the models in response to the advancement of understanding travel behavior by modelers (Chang and Meyers, 1999).

7.4.1   Trip Generation

As we discussed earlier, a trip is defined as a connection between an origin (O) and a destination (D). Consequently, trip generation is a process to determine the number of trips from and to a particular site or area.

Trip generation establishes the connection of transportation analysis to demographic analysis and economic analysis (Gazis, 2002). The subject of transportation analysis is how people travel. The number of trips generated in a zone depends on the zone's population. In general, the more people, the more trips expected. In addition, people with different characteristics travel differently. One observation from various studies shows that people with higher income levels tend to travel more than those with lower income. A young aged person who is not permitted to drive will have to ride with someone else in a private vehicle or use transportation modes other than the private vehicle. The demographic analysis discussed in Chapter 3 gives the base for estimating trip generation.

Some people may travel for the purposes other than to reach a destination.

For example, one may want to get in his/her car to be alone for awhile. However, the majority of trips have an origin and a destination. The destination is closely related to the trip purposes, such as to go to work, to shop, to dine, or to entertain. All those human activities are closely related to the economics of a region. The availability of employment opportunities can determine the number of people who travel to work. The type and size of retail stores can affect the number of people who travel to shop. Understanding the economic activities in a TAZ can help estimate the number of trips that may end in the zone.

As we discussed in Chapter 6, most human activities require the use of land. A region is divided into different pieces of land that are associated with different human activities. Majority people do not live and work in the same place, although the number of people who do so may increase. With advances in technology, such as high speed internet connection, people may work at home. However, majority of the jobs will still require face-to-face interaction in a traditional work-place. The inventory of land uses, therefore, provides the base for estimating trip generation. For example, the Institute of Transportation Engineers publishes trip generation rates for different land use types. The trip generation rate can be calculated as daily trips or peak hour trips. Trip generation rate are presented as vehicle trips or person trips. A vehicle occupancy variable can be used to convert the two rates:

$$TG_v = TG_p \ / \ VO \qquad (7.1)$$

where,

    TG_v — vehicle trip generation rate;

    TG_p — person trip generation rate;

    VO — vehicle occupancy rate.

As shown in Table 7.4, trip generation rate can be calculated for a particular site. Depending on the type of land use, trip generation rates may be expressed as number of trips per employee, number of trips per unit land area (i.e., trips per acre), or number of trips per occupied dwelling unit. The ITR report also separates the trips by direction—entering or exiting the site. These trip generation rates are normally derived from observed data, using regression analysis.

The origin and destination are normally represented as Traffic Analysis Zones. After a study area is divided into TAZs, the amounts of different land use types in each zone can be determined. There are two components of estimating trip generation and both are closely related to TAZ-level land uses. Trip production refers to the number of trips that originate from a TAZ. Trip attraction reflects the number of trips that end in a TAZ. The combination of trip production and trip attraction is the outcome of trip generation analysis. People's travel behaviors vary for different trip purposes. To improve the accuracy of trip estimation, the trip generation analysis is usually done separately for different trip purposes.

Table 7.4 Selected trip generation rates

Code	Land Use	Vehicle Occupancy	Vehicle Trip Generation (Weekday)						Unit
			Am			Pm			
			Rate	Enter	Exit	Rate	Enter	Exit	
21	Airport	1.79 2.42	1.21	45%	55%	1	47%	53%	Trip/Employee
110	General Light Industrial	1.3	0.48	87%	13%	0.42	21%	79%	Trip/Employee
110	General Light Industrial	1.3	7.96	85%	15%	7.26	22%	78%	Trip/Acre
120	General Heavy Industry	1.3	0.4			0.4			Trip/Employee
120	General Heavy Industry	1.3	6.41			4.22			Trip/Acre
130	Industrial Park	1.8	0.43	87%	13%	0.45	21%	79%	Trip/Employee
130	Industrial Park	1.8	8.29	87%	13%	8.67	21%	79%	Trip/Acre
140	Manufacturing	1.3	0.39	80%	20%	0.4	48%	52%	Trip/Employee
140	Manufacturing	1.3	9.3	72%	28%	9.21	48%	52%	Trip/Acre
150	Warehousing	1.3	0.55	50%	50%	0.58	22%	78%	Trip/Employee
150	Warehousing	1.3	8.34	50%	50%	8.77	22%	78%	Trip/Acre
210	Single-Family Detached Housing		0.77	25%	75%	1.02	64%	36%	Trip/Occupied Dwelling Units
210	Single-Family Detached Housing					2.73	66%	34%	Trip/Acre
220	Apartment		0.56	28%	72%	0.62	67%	33%	Trip/Occupied Dwelling Units
221	Low-Rise Apartment		0.51	20%	80%	0.62	65%	35%	Trip/Occupied Dwelling Units

Continued

Code	Land Use	Vehicle Occupancy	Vehicle Trip Generation (Weekday)						Unit
			Am			Pm			
			Rate	Enter	Exit	Rate	Enter	Exit	
222	High-Rise Apartment		0.34	22%	78%	0.35	61%	39%	Dwelling Units Trip/Occupied
223	Mid-Rise Apartment		0.35	29%	71%	0.44	59%	41%	Dwelling Units Trip/Occupied
230	Residential Condominium Low-Rise Residential		0.44	18%	82%	0.54	65%	35%	Dwelling Units Trip/Occupied
231	Condominium/Townhouse Luxury		0.51	17%	83%	0.83	57%	43%	Dwelling Units Trip/Occupied
233	Condominium/Townhouse		0.65	32%	68%	0.65	60%	40%	Dwelling Units
240	Mobile Home Park		0.43	26%	74%	0.58	62%	38%	Dwelling Units
250	Retirement Community		0.29	51%	49%	0.27	56%	44%	Trip/Occupied Dwelling Units
253	Elderly Housing-Attached Residential Planned Unit		0.06	50%	50%	0.11	53%	47%	Trip/Occupied Dwelling Units
270	Development Residential Planned Unit		0.58	23%	77%	0.62	65%	35%	Dwelling Units
270	Development		3.27			4.13			Trip/Acre
310	Hotel		0.52	55%	45%	0.61	53%	47%	Trip/Room
412	County Park		0.52	71%	29%	0.59	35%	65%	Trip/Acre
430	Golf Course		0.33	47%	53%	0.39	43%	57%	Trip/Acre

Source: Institute of Transportation Engineers 1997

The TAZ-based trip generation is calculated in two steps. In the first step, TAZ-based trip productions are calculated. Then TAZ-based trip attraction rates are estimated. The attraction rates reflect the relative attractiveness of a TAZ in relation to other TAZs in the study area.

The difference between trip production/trip attraction and trip origin/trip destination is worth noticing. An individual trip has two ends, one end is the trip origin and the other end is the trip destination. Trip production and trip attraction refer to aggregated trips associated with traffic analysis zones, rather than individual trips. This distinction is important and becomes the basis of trip generation studies. Furthermore, trip production is only related to residential land in a zone. That means, only the TAZs having residential land can produce trips. Trips can be attracted by both residential and non-residential land uses.

Figure 7.4 illustrates the difference of trip origin-destination and trip production-attraction. The graphic represents a three-zone area. Zone A is residential only and Zones B and C only have non-residential land uses. Assume a person who lives in Zone A goes to Zone B to work. After work the person goes shopping in the same zone (Zone B) and then to a take-out restaurant in Zone C before going back home in Zone A. There are total of four trips. Zone A and Zone C each has one trip origin and one trip destination and Zone B has two trip origins and two trip destinations. For Trip 1, which starts from Zone A and ends at Zone B, Zone A is the origin and Zone B is the destination. For Trip 2, which starts from Zone B and ends in Zone B, Zone B is both the origin and the destination. The origin for Trip 3 is Zone B and destination is Zone C. For Trip 4, Zone C is the origin and Zone A is the destination.

In a trip generation study, trip direction is ignored and all trip productions are only associated with residential land use. Therefore, in the three-zone example in Fig. 7.4, only Zone A, the zone with residential land use, can be associated with trip production. Zone A can also attract trips. The other two zones are only associated with trip attraction, not trip production. In the simplified example of four trips shown in Fig. 7.4, all four trips are treated as being produced in Zone A. Zone B and Zone C attract two trips, respectively. No trips are generated in either Zone B or Zone C.

This certainly introduces errors. For example, Trip 2 does not start from Zone A, nor does it end in Zone A. However, there is no residential land use in Zone B, Trip 2 is still treated as if it is produced in Zone A. In addition, the model assumes that there are no trips being generated in Zone B and attracted to Zone C. This limitation is attributed to the practical operation of a travel demand model. Only with such assumption is it feasible to simulate the traffic. Another reason for such model design is that trips generated from workplaces are much smaller than the trip production from residential land. In addition, most TAZs contain residential and non-residential land, which helps to hide the problem.

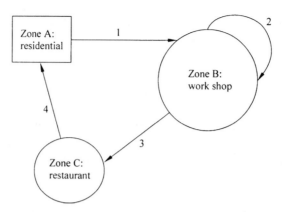

Figure 7.4 Difference of trip origin-destination and trip production-attraction

7.4.1.1 Trip Production

A common practice of estimating trip production from a TAZ is based on variables related to population in the zone. The most commonly used variable is number of households. It should be emphasized that the trip production is more complicated than simply house counting. For example, households with automobiles are more likely generating more vehicle trips than households without an automobile. Households of higher incomes generally make more non-work related trips (for example, shopping) than lower income households. The following list contains some of the variables commonly used in calculating trip production. Not all of them need to be considered in a single model. In fact, many of these variables are correlated and should not be included in the same model.

Workers per household. Workers are the most likely people who travel. The more workers in a household the more trips will be made.

Number of households. Trips are generated by residents. The more households in a zone the more trips will be made.

Family income. Costs are associated with travels. The higher the family. income, the more trips will be made.

Number of automobiles available. People with a car likely travel more than those without a car.

Education level. People's travel behaviors may vary depending on the level of education.

Family size. It is likely that large families travel more than smaller sized families.

Family's age distribution. People at different ages levels travel differently. For example, school aged children and retirees are not likely to travel to work.

Number of occupied dwelling units. The dwelling unit occupancy rate is an indicator of the number of residences. With the same dwelling units in a zone, the more occupied dwelling units, the more trips that can be expected from the zone.

Dwelling unit type. Home ownership is normally an indicator of family income.

Residential density. The residential density on one hand reflects the number of residents in a zone. The more people living in a zone the more trips are expected to be generated in the zone. On the other hand, residential density may reflect people's living style and travel pattern. For example, a high density area has more public transit services than a low density area.

Two methods are used most often in estimating trip production from traffic analysis zones.

The first method uses **aggregated zonal characteristics**. The trip production of a zone is the dependent variable and independent variables are those in the list above or zonal summary statistics derived from them. The following formula illustrates an example of the functional relationship between the number of trips produced by zone and three zonal independent variables.

$$\text{Trip Production} = f(\text{median family income, residential density,}$$
$$\text{mean number of automobile per household}) \qquad (7.2)$$

Regression analysis is a common approach to specifying the formula. After zonal variable data for the entire study area are collected, linear regression analysis is applied to derive the coefficients for the prediction model. A major concern of this type of trip production model is that the overall zonal characteristics may not accurately reflect the driving forces of trip production. In other words, the number of trips generated from a zone is not necessarily related to the aggregated zonal variable values. For example, Fig. 7.5 shows the family income distribution for two hypothetical zones.

There are 387 and 349 families in each zone, respectively. The median family income values for the two zones are quite close. If all other independent variables also are similar, an aggregated model using median family income as an independent variable would predict that the two zones produce similar number of trips. However, the family income distribution as shown in Fig. 7.5 reveals the difference between the two zones. Family income in Zone 1 spreads a much wider range than that in Zone 2. If the rationale behind the model is that family income affects people's travel behavior, the trips produced in the two zones are very likely different. However, the aggregated model is unable to reflect the difference.

The second method, **cross-classification method**, addresses this deficiency by classifying zonal households into categories based upon socio-economic characteristics. Trip generation rates are then developed for each individual category. The rationale of this method is that households with similar characteristics are likely to have similar travel patterns. Therefore the trips generated for each individual household category should be calculated separately. The trips from different household categories are added together to provide a more accurate estimate of zonal trip generation.

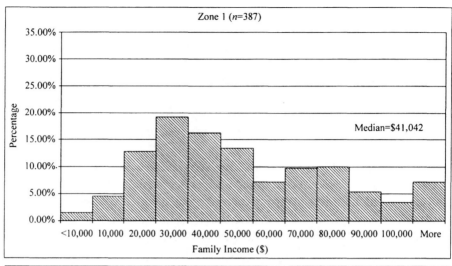

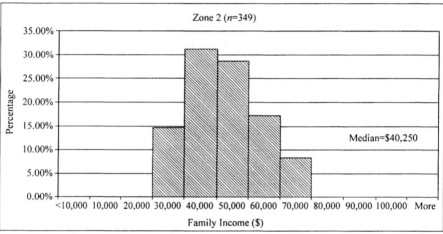

Figure 7.5 Family income distribution in two hypothetical traffic analysis zones

Normally, no more than three to four variables such as family size, automobile ownership, or household income, are used in household classification. Each variable has a few discrete categories. The cross-classification method requires much more data than the zonal method. For example, if four variables are used in household classification and each has three categories, there would be $3^4 = 81$ household categories in a zone.

The following formula is an example for calculating trip generation for families of different household income categories:

$$T_p = \sum_{i=1,n} (r_i \cdot H_i) \tag{7.3}$$

where,

T_p — trips generated;

i — household category;

n — number of household categories;

r_i — trip production rate for household category i;

H_i — number of households in category i.

Data used in trip generation can be obtained from government agencies or field surveys. In the previous chapters, we have discussed land use data and census data. Those data are often used for estimating trip generation. It may take considerable effort to collect data for the study area. Once relevant data are collected, regression analysis is a common tool used to derive the trip production rate for each category. Trip production rates from similar cities or regions can be used if no local data are available.

The following example illustrates that the amount of person trips per household is based on the number of households classified by household income. In addition, the distribution of trip purpose varies by household income level. As shown in Table 7.5 households in the lowest income groups make fewer trips than the higher income group.

Table 7.5　Number of person trips per day by trip purpose and by household income

Income Level: $1,000 Personal Trips Per Day Per Household by Trip Purpose	$\leqslant 15$	$15-25$	$25-35$	$35-45$	> 45
Home based work (HBW)	0.443	0.873	1.260	1.867	2.766
Home based non-work (HBNW)	2.283	2.593	2.643	2.826	3.022
Non-home based (NHB)	1.423	1.567	2.092	2.604	3.241

The person trips by household income category are calculated as:

$$PT = N_{hh} \cdot PTPH \qquad (7.4)$$

where,

PT — person trips;

N_{hh} — number of households;

PTPH — person trips per household.

For example, Table 7.6 shows that there are 352 households in the first household income category ($\leqslant \$15,000$), the daily HBW person trips produced by those households are estimated as:

$$352 \times 0.443 = 156$$

Table 7.6 Trip production by household income and trip purpose

	< 15	15 – 25	25 – 35	35 – 45	> 45	Total	Automobile Occupancy	Vehicle Trips
Number of Households	352	478	491	892	543	2,756		
	Person Trips						Automobile Occupancy	Vehicle Trips
HBW Person Trips	156	417	619	1,665	1,502	4,359	1.37	3,182
HBNW Person Trips	804	1,239	1,298	2,521	1,641	7,502	1.81	4,145
NHB Person Trips	501	749	1,027	2,323	1,760	6,360	1.43	4,447
All Purposes						18,222		11,774

The number of daily HBW person trips produced by the 543 households in the last household income category (> $45,000) is calculated as:

$$543 \times 2.766 = 1,502$$

Similar calculations can be made to the other household categories. Using the number of households by category in Table 7.5, the total HBW person trips is calculated as the sum of trips in all household categories:

$$T_p = \sum_{i=1,n} (r_i \cdot H_i)$$

$$= 352 \times 0.443 + 478 \times 0.873 + 491 \times 1.260 + 892 \times 1.867 + 543 \times 2.766$$

$$= 156 + 417 + 619 + 1,665 + 1,502$$

$$= 4,359$$

The result shows that 4,359 daily home-based-work person trips are expected from this zone. The same calculation can be made for other two trip purposes. The results shown in Table 7.6 are a total of 7,502 person trips for the home-based-non-work purpose and the trips that belong to the non-home-based trip purpose are 6,360.

Another variable—vehicle occupancy—is needed to convert person trips into vehicle trips. This information is normally collected at the local level. In general, the vehicle occupancy for work-related trips is lower than other trips because it is more likely for people to travel alone to work. Table 7.6 includes illustrative vehicle occupancy values for different trip purposes. Using the vehicle occupancy, we can then calculate the vehicle trip production for the zone as follows:

HBW vehicle trips = 4,359 / 1.37 = 3,182

HBNW vehicle trips = 7,502 / 1.81 = 4,145

NHB vehicle trips = 6,360 / 1.43 = 4,447

From the result, we can see the impact of vehicle occupancy on the vehicles on the road. Because people are more likely to travel together for trips from home to non-work places than the trips not starting from homes, the HBNW vehicle occupancy is greater than that of NHB. Although more people travel for the HBNW purpose (7,502) than the NHB purpose (6,360), there are fewer HBNW vehicle trips (4,145) than the NHB vehicle trips (4,447).

7.4.1.2   Trip Attraction

Trip attraction predicts the number of trips to be attracted to (end in) each zone. The attractiveness of a zone is related to the size and type of land uses that are the destination of trips. The majority of such land uses are non-residential land, such as stores, offices, libraries, etc. The trip attraction is normally expressed as the number of vehicle trips per household or per unit area of non-residential land use. In addition to the zonal characteristics, the number of trips attracted to a zone is related to the attractiveness of other zones in the region. All trip attracting zones in a region compete for the number of trips produced in the region. Zones that are more attractive will attract more trips than the zones that are less attractive.

For example, Table 7.7 lists trip attraction rates for residential and some non-residential land uses. For the residential land use, the trip attraction rate is expressed as number of trips per household. The value of "0.079" in Table 7.7 means that each household can attract 0.079 HBW vehicle trips per day. This can be explained as on average, each 1,000 households can attract 79 trips from home to work. An example of HBW trip to a residence is a nurse who leaves home to take care of a patient at the patient's home.

Table 7.7   Daily vehicle trip attraction rates

Type of Activity	Trip Purpose		
	HBW	HBNW	NHB
Households (unit)	0.079	0.518	0.302
Retail (sq · km)	155.7	560.0	467.6
Basic (sq · km)	131.9	84.3	93.8
Service (sq · km)	112.3	64.3	126.6

The vehicle trip attraction rates associated with non-residential land uses are functions of the land use type and the size of land uses. The values in Table 7.7 are the per unit area trip attractions by different land use types. The table shows that retail trade sector is more attractive than basic or service sectors. Similar to the residential land, the trips attracted by different nonresidential land can be divided into different trip purposes. For the retail land use, the rate of home-based work trips (155.7, those who work in retail stores) is lower than that of home based non-work trips (560.0, those who come to stores from home to shop).

Similar to trip generation, data required for calculating the trip attraction rates can be obtained from government agencies or field survey. The types and amount of different land uses by traffic analysis zone can be derived by overlaying the TAZ and land use data (as discussed in Chapter 6). The number of households is usually part of the census data regularly collected. Once the data are collected, regression analysis is a common tool used derive the trip attraction rate for each land use category. When local data are not available, trip attraction rates from similar cities or regions can be used.

The HBW vehicle trips attracted to a zone is then calculated as:

$$TA_{HBW\_H} = N_{hh} \cdot TAR_{\_R} \quad (7.5)$$

where,

TA_{HBW_R}— home-based work vehicle trip attractiveness of the zone by households;

N_{hh}— number of household in the zone;

$TAR_{\_R}$— trip attraction rate by households.

The HBW trips attracted by retail are calculated from the size of retail land use and the retail trip attraction rates.

$$TA_{HBW\_NR} = A_{\_NR} \cdot TAR_{\_NR} \quad (7.6)$$

where,

TA_{HBW_NR}— home-based work vehicle trip attractiveness of the zone;

$A_{\_NR}$— non-residential land use size in the zone;

$TAR_{\_NR}$— trip attraction rate of the non-residential land use.

Table 7.8 lists an example of the types of land use that attract trips for a zone. The unit for the residential land is the number of households and the units for other land uses are square kilometers. The HBW vehicle trips attracted to the zone by the 2,756 households in the zone are calculated as:

HBW trip attractiveness = number of households × residential trip attraction rate
$$= 2,756 \times 0.079$$
$$= 218$$

For example, the HBW trip attractiveness of the zone is:

HBW trip attractiveness = size of retail land use × retail trip attraction rate
$$= 14.53 \times 155.7$$
$$= 2,263$$

The trips attracted by different land uses can be calculated in the same fashion. The results are included in Table 7.8. The last row shows the total vehicle trip attractiveness of the zone.

Table 7.8 Trip attractiveness by trip purpose

Land Use	Size	Trip Attractiveness			
		HBW	HBNW	NHB	Total
Households (unit)	2,756	218	1,428	832	2,478
Retail (sq · km)	14.53	2,263	8,138	6,796	17,197
Basic (sq · km)	5.51	727	464	517	1,708
Service (sq · km)	1.92	216	123	243	582
Total		3,424	10,153	8,388	21,965

After the same procedure is applied to all the zones in the study area, a trip production and attraction table is constructed. The following tables are the results for a hypothetical study area of four TAZs. From the number of households by income level in Table 7.9 and trip production rates in Table 7.5, we can calculate the trip productions by income level, as shown in Table 7.10.

Summarizing the trip generations by income level in Table 7.10 we can derive the person-trips by purpose, which is displayed in the left portion of Table 7.11. The vehicle occupancy ratios are then used to convert the person-trips to vehicle-trips. The bottom row of Table 7.11 shows the total trips produced in each zone. From the result, we can see that Zone 4 produces many more trips (50,754) than other zones.

The trip attraction by zone is calculated using the trip attraction rates in Table 7.7 and the land use by zone for the study area, in Table 7.9. The results are displayed in Table 7.12. Table 7.12 is an expansion of Table 7.8. The total trip attraction summarized by trip purpose and zone is included in Table 7.13.

Table 7.9 Trip production data by traffic analysis zone

Number of Households by Zone and Income Level				
Income Level (1,000 dollars) \ Zones	1	2	3	4
< 15	352	141	70	70
15 – 30	478	239	598	956
30 – 45	491	4,419	2,946	7,365
45 – 60	892	1,427	714	1,784
> 60	543	2,715	1,086	1,810
Total	2,756	8,941	5,414	11,985
Land Use by Zone				
Land Use \ Zones	1	2	3	4
Households (unit)	2,756	8,941	5,414	11,985
Retail (sq · km)	14.53	12.10	8.62	10.19
Basic (sq · km)	5.51	14.20	7.38	14.19
Service (sq · km)	1.92	2.73	1.63	2.57

Table 7.10 Number of person-trips by income level and trip purpose

Income Level (1,000 dollars) \ Zones Trip Purpose	1 HBW	HBNW	NHB	2 HBW	HBNW	NHB	3 HBW	HBNW	NHB	4 HBW	HBNW	NHB
<15	156	804	501	62	321	200	31	161	100	31	161	100
15 – 30	417	1,239	749	209	620	375	522	1,549	936	835	2,479	1,498
30 – 45	619	1,298	1,027	5,568	11,679	9,245	3,712	7,786	6,163	9,280	19,466	15,408
45 – 60	1,665	2,521	2,323	2,665	4,033	3,716	1,332	2,017	1,858	3,331	5,042	4,646
>60	1,502	1,641	1,760	7,510	8,205	8,799	3,004	3,282	3,520	5,006	5,470	5,866
Total	4,359	7,503	6,360	16,013	24,859	22,335	8,601	14,795	12,577	18,483	32,617	27,518

Table 7.11 Trip production by trip purpose and zone

Purpose \ Zones	Person-Trips by Trip Purpose 1	2	3	4	Vehicle Occupancy	Vehicle-Trips by Trip Purpose 1	2	3	4	Total
HBW	4,359	16,013	8,601	18,483	1.37	3,182	11,688	6,278	13,491	34,640
HBNW	7,503	24,859	14,795	32,617	1.81	4,145	13,734	8,174	18,020	44,073
NHB	6,360	22,335	12,577	27,518	1.43	4,447	15,619	8,795	19,243	48,105
Total	18,221	63,207	35,973	78,617		11,774	41,042	23,247	50,754	126,818

Table 7.12 Trip attractiveness by land use and trip purpose

Land Use \ Zones Trip Purpose	1 HBW	HBNW	NHB	2 HBW	HBNW	NHB	3 HBW	HBNW	NHB	4 HBW	HBNW	NHB
Households	218	1,428	832	706	4,631	2,700	428	2,804	1,635	947	6,208	3,620
Retail	2,263	8,138	6,796	1,885	6,778	5,660	1,343	4,829	4,032	1,587	5,708	4,766
Basic	727	464	517	1,874	1,197	1,332	974	622	692	1,872	1,196	1,331
Service	216	123	243	306	175	345	183	105	206	289	165	326
Total	3,423	10,154	8,388	4,771	12,783	10,038	2,927	8,360	6,565	4,695	13,278	10,043

Table 7.13   Trip attraction by trip purpose

Zones Trip Purpose	1	2	3	4	Total
HBW	3,423	4,771	5,853	4,695	18,741
HBNW	10,154	12,783	16,719	13,278	52,934
NHB	8,388	10,038	13,130	10,043	41,599
Total	21,964	27,591	35,703	28,016	113,274

Number of Vehicle-Trips Produced by Trip Purpose and Zone

For trip generation modeling, the number of trips produced must be compared with the observed trips to select independent variables (predictor variables) and the parameters that connect them to the trip generation.

7.4.2   Trip Distribution

The purpose of the trip distribution process is to allocate the trip productions and trip attractions. "To allocate" means to specify where the trips generated from a particular TAZ will go. From Tables 7.11 and 7.13, we can see that Zone 1 produces 11,774 trips and attracts 21,964 trips. However, we don't know where the 11,774 trips produced at zone 1 end and where the 21,964 trips attracted by zone 1 originate. Trip distribution analysis addresses this question. The rationale behind the trip distribution is quite simple. The trips between any trip production zone, i, and trip attraction zone, j, are a function of the number of trip production, P_i, the trip attraction, A_j, and the effort associated with the travel between the two zones, W_{ij}. W_{ij} is normally expressed as the costs or time taken to travel from the production zone to the attraction zone. The equation below is a formula for calculating the trip distribution between the two zones, T_{ij}. Such an equation is called gravity model.

$$T_{ij} = C \frac{P_i \cdot A_j}{W_{ij}} \tag{7.7}$$

where,

i — the zone of trip production;

j — the zone of trip attraction;

T_{ij} — number of trips produced in Zone i and attracted to Zone j;

P_i — number of trips produced in Zone i;

A_j — number of trips attracted to Zone j;

W_{ij} — the impedance between Zones i and j;

C — constant.

The formula is named after Newton's law of gravity, which states that the attractive force between any two bodies is directly related to the masses of the bodies and inversely related to the distance between them. In the case of a trip distribution, the attractive force is the number of trips between two zones, the masses are the trip production and attraction, and the distance is the impedance factor between the two zones. Accordingly, large numbers of trip productions or trip attractions increase the number of trips any two zones, while higher impedance factors reduce the trip volume. Conceptually, the gravity model is straightforward. The challenge in applying the model is to assign proper values to the impedance, W, and the constant, C.

As we discussed before, the travel demand model assumes there is a balance between the total trip production and attraction. This means that trips produced in Zone i must equal to the total of all the zones that receive trips that originated in Zone i. That is,

$$P_i = \sum_j T_{ij} \tag{7.8}$$

The implication is that all zones compete for the trip production, P_i, based on the zonal attractiveness and impedance. For a study area of n zones, the balance can be expressed as:

$$P_i = \sum_{j=1,n} T_{ij} = \sum_{j=1,n} C \frac{P_i \cdot A_j}{W_{ij}} \tag{7.9}$$

Therefore, the constant C can be derived as:

$$C = 1 \bigg/ \sum_{j=1,n} \frac{A_j}{W_{ij}} \tag{7.10}$$

Replacing the constant C, in the trip distribution formula Eq. (7.6), we get:

$$T_{ij} = P_i \left[\frac{A_j / W_{ij}}{\sum_{j=1,n} \left(A_j / W_{ij} \right)} \right] \tag{7.11}$$

The relative attractiveness of Zone j regarding the trips produced in Zone i is expressed in the bracketed term, which is related to the attractiveness and impedance from all other zones.

The impedance, W_{ij}, reflects the level of difficulty when traveling between the two zones. Normally, it is related to the physical condition of roadway network, distance, cost of travel, or time of travel. The model developer must make a decision as to what factors to use for deriving the impedance. As an example, W_{ij} can be a function of travel time between Zone i and Zone j. The impedance increases as the travel time increases:

$$W_{ij} = t_{ij}^a \tag{7.12}$$

where,
  t — travel time;
  W — impedance;
  a — a constant.

Assume the constant, a, for the four-zone study area is 0.5. If we know the travel time as shown in Table 7.14, we can calculate the impedance, W_{ij}. For example, the travel time within Zone 1 is 5 minutes, the impedance for trips inside Zone 1 is:

$$W_{11} = t_{11}^a = 5^{0.5} = 2.24$$

The travel time from Zone 1 to Zone 4 is 25 minutes, the impedance from Zone 1 to Zone 4 is calculated as:

$$W_{14} = t_{14}^a = 25^{0.5} = 5$$

Table 7.14 lists the complete calculation of impedance for all possible travel options. From the table we can see that the travel time between Zones 3 and 4 is the longest of all ($t_{34} = 30$ minutes). Therefore, the impedance between the two zones has the highest value ($W_{34} = 5.48$).

Table 7.14   Travel time and impedance matrix

Travel Time, t_{ij}

From \ To	1	2	3	4
1	5	15	20	25
2	15	6	20	15
3	20	20	7	30
4	25	15	30	8

Impedance, $W_{ij} = t_{ij}^a (a = 0.5)$

From \ To	1	2	3	4
1	2.24	3.87	4.47	5.00
2	3.87	2.45	4.47	3.87
3	4.47	4.47	2.65	5.48
4	5.00	3.87	5.48	2.83

Continued

Friction Factor, $F_{ij} = 1/W_{ij}$				
From \ To	1	2	3	4
1	0.45	0.26	0.22	0.20
2	0.26	0.41	0.22	0.26
3	0.22	0.22	0.38	0.18
4	0.20	0.26	0.18	0.35

You probably have noticed that we have changed the question from finding W_{ij} to finding t_{ij} and a. The travel time, t_{ij}, can be obtained from historical record. The constant, a, is an empirical parameter and its value needs to be estimated and adjusted against observed trip data.

Normally, a friction factor, F_{ij}, which is the inverse of the impedance, W_{ij}, is used in the trip distribution formula to reflect people's wiliness to travel between zones

$$F_{ij} = 1/W_{ij} \qquad (7.13)$$

Considerable effort is spent in transportation modeling finding an appropriate function for friction factor. Equations (7.12) and (7.13) are included only as an example. The friction factor values may be specifically chosen to take into consideration such things as a major barrier between zones or, a toll to cross a bridge. Regardless the form of equations, a friction factor represents the likelihood of trips between any two zones. For example, two zones that are close to each other and connected by an express-way will have higher friction factor value than another pair of zones that are far apart. If two zones are so far apart that no one is willing to travel between the two, the friction factor value will be zero. Placing F_{ij} in Eq. (7.13) into Eq. (7.12) we can derive the gravity model for zonal traffic:

$$T_{ij} = \frac{P_i \cdot A_j \cdot F_{ij}}{\sum_{i=1,n}(A_j \cdot F_{ij})} \qquad (7.14)$$

This model shows that the amount of traffic between two zones is proportion to the number of trip produce in Zone i, the trip attraction of Zone j and all other zones, and the friction factor between all possible pair of zones.

In reality, travel decisions more complete than the trip production, trip attraction, and impedances. Studies have shown that many other factors affect people's travel behavior, such as age, income, gender, vehicle ownership, or availability and quality of public transit services (Hensher and Reyes, 2000;

Taplin and Min, 1997; Turner and Grieco, 2000). As a common practice, trip forecast model developers use a set of inter-zonal socioeconomic adjustment factors, K_{ij}, and include them in the gravity model. The U.S. Department of Transportation has summarized the following rationales for the necessity of including K_{ij} in the gravity model (USDOT, 1985).

First, the gravity model assumes that the trip purpose determines travel pattern. Consequently, the largest proportion of HBW tips will be allocated to the closest zones (small friction) with largest employment establishments (large trip attraction). However, different jobs require different skills and employ certain members of work force.

In a similar manner, some zones are more likely to have jobs and housing for certain income levels. For example, people who work at grocery stores may have quite different incomes than those who work in corporation headquarters in central business districts. In the United States, they are not likely to live in the same neighborhoods.

Last, the friction factor in the gravity model is developed for the entire study area. For example, it implies that travel time and the cost of travel have the same affect to people's travel behavior. This assumption does not consider the different responses to the impedances. For example, the travel cost may affect people differently, depending on their income level. Assume a city is implementing a congestion fee on rush hour highway travels. Low income people may be unable to allocate their limited resources to pay for the congestion fee, and consequently, unable to use the highway. Those who can, and are willing to pay for the fee, will be able to travel on less a congested highway.

In practice, it is too difficult to collect accurate data to allow further stratification of employment opportunities and residents. However, the model may not be valid without considering these factors. With the limited knowledge of these factors, they are included in one adjustment factor— K_{ij}. The gravity model Eq. (7.14) is then revised as:

$$T_{ij} = K_{ij} \frac{P_i \cdot A_j \cdot F_{ij}}{\sum_{i=1,n}(A_j \cdot F_{ij})} \qquad (7.15)$$

The K factors can be added during model calibration to incorporate effects that are not previously captured. Those effects can be interpreted as the extent to which the trips can be increased or decreased because of these unaccounted factors. Because of the complexity of those factors, it is difficult to estimate their values. A common practice is to derive K factors in the model development process. The process of developing travel models is also called **calibration**, during which the model estimations is compared with observed data. Various parameter values are adjusted until the model output satisfactorily matches the observation data.

This Eq. (7.11) shows that the trips between a production Zone, i, and an attraction Zone, j, increase as the trip production or trip attraction increases. When the friction factor increases (for example, as a result of an improved road condition the travel time is shortened), the trips are expected to increase between the two zones. If the friction factor decreases as a result of congestion that leads to longer travel time, the trips between the two zones will decrease. If the socioeconomic factors can lead to more trips between two zones, the K_{ij} value will be greater than 1; otherwise, the K_{ij} value will be less than 1.

To illustrate the use of the trip distribution model, let us ignore the effect of all other socioeconomic factors. That is, $K_{ij} = 1$. The equation becomes the formula:

$$T_{ij} = \frac{P_i \cdot A_j \cdot F_{ij}}{\sum_{i=1,n} (A_j \cdot F_{ij})}$$

The computation of trip distribution can be completed in three steps as shown in the following tables. From the zonal attractiveness A_j of Zone j and friction factor between the Zone i and Zone j, F_{ij}, we can calculate the adjusted attractiveness of Zone i to Zone j, $A_j \cdot F_{ij}$. As shown in Table 7.15, the attractiveness of Zone 1 to Zone 1 is calculated as:

$$21,946 \times 0.45 = 9,823$$

The attractiveness of Zone 1 to Zone 2 is:

$$27,591 \times 0.26 = 7,124$$

Similarly, we can calculate the attractiveness of Zone 1 to Zone 3 and Zone 4:

Zone 1 to Zone 3: $17,851 \times 0.22 = 3,992$

Zone 1 to Zone 4: $28,016 \times 0.2 = 5,603$

The last column in Table 7.15 represents the total of attractiveness of a Zone i to all zones in the region. For Zone 1, the value is calculated as:

$$\sum_j (A_j \cdot F_{1j}) = 9,823 + 7,124 + 3,992 + 5,603 = 26,542$$

Similarly, the trip attractiveness of all zones regarding Zone 2 is calculated as:

$$\sum_j (A_j \cdot F_{2j}) = 5,671 + 11,264 + 3,992 + 7,234 = 28,160$$

Table 7.15   Product of trip attraction and friction factor, $A_j \cdot F_{ij}$

From\To	1	2	3	4	$\sum_j (A_j \cdot F_{ij})$
A_j	21,964	27,591	17,851	28,016	
1	9,823	7,124	3,992	5,603	26,542
2	5,671	11,264	**3,992**	7,234	28,160
3	4,911	6,170	6,747	5,115	22,943
4	4,393	7,124	3,259	9,905	24,681

The values in Table 7.15 reflect the impact of the two factors on the zonal attraction. The product $A_j \cdot F_{ij}$ means that more attractive zones (with higher A_j's) are likely to attract more trips. Meanwhile, as travel from the zone of production to the zone of attraction becames easier (or more convenient), (higher F_{ij}), more trips will be attracted to the zone of destination.

Two more steps are required to calculate the actual number of zonal trips. In the first step, the values in Table 7.15, $A_j \cdot F_{ij}$, were multiplied by the vehicle trip production from the production zone P_i (the last row in Table 7.11 and included as a column in Table 7.16). The result is saved in Table 7.16. For example, the value for Zone 2 to Zone 3 ($i = 2$ and $j = 3$) is calculated as:

$$P_2 \cdot A_3 \cdot F_{23} = 41,042 \times 3,992 = 163,825,554$$

Table 7.16   Individual trip production distribution, $P_i \cdot A_j \cdot F_{ij}$

From\To	1	2	3	4	P_i
1	115,656,054	83,879,411	46,999,480	65,973,213	11,774
2	232,753,561	462,289,433	**163,825,554**	296,879,765	**41,042**
3	114,176,871	143,425,300	156,855,154	118,909,560	23,247
4	222,957,961	361,572,162	165,419,628	502,727,054	50,754

When the value for a trip destination Zone j is divided by the total attractiveness from this zone and all other zones in terms of a trip production Zone i, $\sum (A_j \cdot F_{ij})$, the result is the actual trip distribution from Zone i to Zone j. Table 7.17 displays the trip distribution results for the four-zone illustration.

Comparing the sums of trips ending in Zone j — $\sum_i T_{ij}$ Table 7.17 — with the original trip constant productions — P_i, Table 7.16 — we can see that the row totals, i.e., the trip end productions, remain constant. This shows that the number of trips produced is not related to the travel condition.

Table 7.17 Trip distribution

To\From	1	2	3	4	$\sum_i T_{ij}$
1	4,358	3,160	1,771	2,486	11,774
2	8,265	16,416	5,818	10,542	41,042
3	4,977	6,251	6,837	5,183	23,247
4	9,034	14,650	6,702	20,369	50,754
$\sum_j T_{ij}$	26,634	40,477	21,128	38,580	126,817

$$T_{ij} = P_i \cdot A_j \cdot F_{ij} / \sum (A_j \cdot F_{ij})$$

The advantage of the gravity model is its simplistic form. The calculation is straightforward. For a trip generation zone, the higher the trip production, the more trips will originate from the zone. A zone that produces more trips is expected to have more trips to other zones than another zone that produces fewer trips. Similarly, a zone that has higher trip attractiveness will accept more trips than another zone that attracts fewer trips. The larger the friction factor between any two zones will lead to more trips traveling between the two zones. The challenge of the model in practice is that it only uses two parameters, F_{ij} and K_{ij} to represent travel choices. The lack of behavioral basis to explain how individuals or households decide their travel destinations is the drawback of the method.

7.4.3 Mode Choice

The third step of the travel demand model is to estimate the proportion of travelers using different modes of transportation. There are many alternative modes available for an individual to travel from one place to another, such as driving alone or with someone else, walking, taking the train, bus, taxi, riding a bicycle, etc. Many variables may affect an individual's mode choice. If you take a few minutes to list the reasons you used for choosing particular travel modes for different activities last month, you may have a long list. Of course, you may also find your choices were quite limited. There are so many places in the United States, especially in suburban areas, where there is no public transit. It is quite common to see many streets without sidewalks. People in those areas are forced to drive to travel, even to get the Sunday morning paper. Do you remember how desperate you were last time your car broke down?

The variables affecting mode choice can be organized into three categories — traveler, trip, and transportation system. Traveler characteristics include variables such as automobile ownership, income, number of workers per household, and the place of living and place of work. The University of Cincinnati is in uptown Cincinnati. Many students who live on or near campus simply walk to school. As a commuter campus, there are also many students who commute everyday. They take buses, drive private vehicles, or ride bicycles to school.

The second category of factors affecting mode choice refers to the journey characteristics, such as the trip purpose, length of trip, place of origin and destination, or time of day the trip is taken. If we do not count those who just want to take a ride for the fun of travel, people travel with a purpose. Different trip purposes may determine how to travel. For example, although I can ride my bicycle to work, I would not be able to do so to take two small children to the zoo.

The third category of variables affecting mode choice is related to the characteristics of the transportation system. Those variables may include travel costs, time taken for the travel, comfort level of travel, convenience, reliability, and security of different modes. An individual makes his/her decision on travel mode after comparing the characteristics of different travel modes. For example, a raise in the bus fare may induce people who ride buses to switch to driving private vehicles. After an increase in the parking fee, some people who currently drive to work may switch to other modes.

Even though mode choice is individually based, the mode choice model estimates the aggregated number of trips associated with each of the possible transportation modes. The outcome of mode choice model is the percentage of travelers using each available travel modes. There are many different ways of calculating the mode choice. One approach is to use a diversion curve, which illustrates the split of two modes. Figure 7.6 illustrates a hypothetical mode choice diversion curve. It compares public transit with private automobiles using travel time as the variable. The horizon axis is the ratio of transit-to-auto travel time ratio. A value of 1 represents that there is no difference of travel time for transit or auto travel. When the transit is faster than driving, the ratio would be less than 1. The ratio would be greater than 1 if it is faster to drive than using the transit. The vertical axis represents the proportion of transit trips. According to the diversion curve in Fig. 7.6, about 47% of travelers would use transit if the travel time is the same for transit and driving private vehicles (the solid line). If the transit travel time is 3/4 of the automobile travel time, the number of travelers who use transit equals to those driving private vehicles.

The diversion curve approach is simple to use. However, one curve is unable to reflect the vast number of variables that may affect travelers' mode choices. One approach to improve the method is to stratify trips using some of the important variables, such as trip purpose, income level, or cost of travel. One diversion curve is developed for each stratified group. For example, 160 diversion curves were used in Washington, D.C., USA (Wright, et al., 1997).

Another option is to apply a utility function for each possible mode of transportation. A utility function measures the degree of satisfaction (or cost if

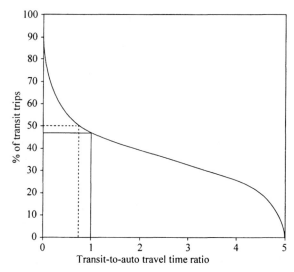

Figure 7.6   An illustrative mode choice diversion curve

negative) that is associated with each mode choice. The market share of all mode choices is then calculated based on the utilities. This approach is based on the assumption that travelers make rational choices between available modes. That is, a traveler selects the mode with highest utility value if he/she has access to perfect information about each travel mode.

   To develop a utility function, we must first decide the relevant independent variables to include in the model. Those variables should reflect the three categories previously discussed: characteristics of travelers, journeys, and transportation system. One example of the traveler characteristics is age. The utility of private vehicles by elderly or underage travelers is limited since they will have to use public transit or travel with others who can drive. Trip purpose and trip destination are examples of the journey characteristics. Easy and mostly free parking of large shopping malls in the outskirts of American cities attract many customers away from downtown areas. The transportation system characteristics are the most common variables to be included in the utility functions. The modes associated with shorter travel times, lower costs, or more convenience are likely have high utility. Sometimes an independent variable may be derived from other variables. As we discussed before, travel costs may have different effects depending on a traveler's income level. A ratio of travel cost to the traveler's income level may be the variable included in the utility function (Papacostas and Prevedouros, 2001). In this example, travel cost is a transportation system variable and income level is a traveler variable.

   The utility function is typically expressed as a linear weighted sum of the independent variables ($X_1, \cdots, X_n$). The effect of variables not specified in the model is included in the constant item, a_0. The general form of the utility function with n variables is:

$$U = a_0 + a_1 X_1 + a_2 X_2 + \cdots + a_n X_n \tag{7.16}$$

where,

U — the utility of the transportation mode;

a_0 — constant;

a_1 — weight for the first variable;

a_2 — weight for the second variable;

a_n — weight for the nth variable;

X_1 — the first independent variable;

X_2 — the second independent variable;

X_n — the nth independent variable.

For a study area with k types of transportation modes, one utility function is established for each mode:

$$\begin{cases} U_1 = a_{01} + a_{11} X_{11} + a_{21} X_{21} + \cdots + a_{n1} X_{n1} \\ U_2 = a_{02} + a_{12} X_{12} + a_{22} X_{22} + \cdots + a_{n2} X_{n2} \\ \vdots \\ U_k = a_{0k} + a_{1k} X_{1k} + a_{2k} X_{2k} + \cdots + a_{nk} X_{nk} \end{cases} \tag{7.17}$$

Any of the factors mentioned before (traveler, trip, and transportation system variables) may be independent variables. A major task in developing the utility functions is the selection of independent variables, which goes beyond this book. Let's assume a set of mode choice utility functions for two modes of three independent variables are developed. The two mode choices are private vehicle and public transit. The three independent variables are cost of travel, travel time, and comfort level.

$$\begin{cases} U_1 = -0.03 - 0.02 X_{11} - 0.015 X_{21} + 0.04 X_{31} \\ U_2 = -0.035 - 0.025 X_{12} - 0.02 X_{22} + 0.05 X_{32} \end{cases} \tag{7.18}$$

where,

U_k — the utility, $k = 1$ for private vehicle travel and $k = 2$ for public transit travel;

X_{1k} — the cost of travel in cents per kilometer, $k = 1$ for private vehicle travel and $k = 2$ for public transit travel;

X_{2k} — the travel time in minutes, $k = 1$ for private vehicle travel and $k = 2$ for public transit travel;

X_{3k} — the comfort level, $k = 1$ for private vehicle travel and $k = 2$ for public transit travel.

You may notice that the coefficients for travel cost and travel time are negative and for comfortable level is positive. The sign of the coefficients reflect the change direction of the independent variables. The negative value implies that as the value of the independent variable increases, the utility will decrease. In the case of travel cost and travel time, people will tend to use the travel mode that costs less and uses less travel time. For the third variable, people will give the travel preference to the mode that is more flexible.

Values for three independent variables are given in Table 7.18. The travel cost is measured as cents and the travel time is measured in minutes. Both variable values may be collected from actual data. The comfort level reflects the travelers' opinion and may be derived from a survey. In this example, the comfort level for automobile travel is twice as much as the transit travel.

Table 7.18 Hypothetical variable values for a utility function

Travel Mode	Travel Cost (X_1) (cent)	Travel Time (X_2) (min)	Comfort Level (X_3)
Private Vehicle (1)	100	20	10
Public Transit (2)	60	40	5

Inserting the variable values into Eq. (7.16), we can calculate the utility for private vehicle and public transit:

$$U_1 = -0.03 - 0.02X_{11} - 0.015X_{21} + 0.04X_{31}$$
$$= -0.03 - 0.02 \times 100 - 0.015 \times 20 + 0.04 \times 10$$
$$= -0.03 - 2 - 0.3 + 0.4$$
$$= -1.9$$
$$U_2 = -0.035 - 0.025X_{12} - 0.02X_{22} + 0.05X_{32}$$
$$= -0.035 - 0.025 \times 60 - 0.02 \times 40 + 0.25 \times 5$$
$$= -0.035 - 1.5 - 0.8 + 0.25$$
$$= -2.05$$

It is worthwhile to point out that the utility-based mode choice model calculates the probability of travelers selecting each travel mode. This is due to the fact that travelers cannot be informed perfectly about the travel modes and the decision making process for a traveler to select a travel mode cannot be perfectly modeled. In the mode choice model, there are many ways to establish the relationship between proportion of travelers using each travel mode and its utility. One such model is the Multinomial Logit (MNL) model.

According to the MNL model, the probability that mode choice k is made under the assumption of utility maximization is the fraction of the total utility. This probability is expressed as:

$$\text{Prob}(k) = \frac{\exp(U_k)}{\sum_{k=1}^{n} \exp(U_k)} \qquad (7.19)$$

where,

Prob(k) — the probability of mode k being selected;

U_k — the utility value for mode k;

n — total number of mode choices.

Using this model, we can calculate the probabilities associated with the two traffic modes in the previous example. We first need to calculate $\exp(U_k)$. For the private vehicle travel, $k = 1$,

$$\exp(U_1) = \exp(-1.9) = 0.150$$

for public transit, $k = 2$,

$$\exp(U_2) = \exp(-2.05) = 0.129$$

then,

$$\exp(U_1) + \exp(U_2) = 0.150 + 0.129 = 0.279$$

From Eq. (7.19) we can calculate the probabilities for the two modes as:

For the private vehicle, Prob(1) = 0.150 / 0.279 = 0.537 = 53.7%
For the public transit, Prob(2) = 0.129 / 0.279 = 0.463 = 46.3%

The model result shows that the market share for private vehicle in this case is 53.7% and the pubic transit share is 46.3%. Use of the multinomial logit model ensures that the sum of trips allocated to all modes of transportation always equal to the total trips.

The multinomial logit model demonstrates that the probability of choosing one transportation mode depends on the utility of the mode and other available modes. The effects of a mode on all other modes are equally distributed, which is far from reality. For example, a trip maker is more easily to switch between a bus and an express bus than from riding a bus to driving a vehicle. To address this uneven effect, researchers have developed nested logit models to expand the MNL model (Koppelman and Wen, 1998; Hensher and Greene, 2002). In a nested logit model, travel modes that are similar are grouped together to form a composite mode choice, which is compared with other mode choices. Figure 7.7 gives an example of a three level nested logit structure.

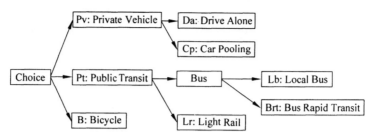

Figure 7.7   A three-level nested logit structure

The probabilities are calculated from the top level then down to the lower level. At each level, the MNL model solution method is used. For the nested logit structure in Fig. 7.7, the MNL model at first level has three choices. The probability for private vehicle is:

$$\text{Prob(Pv)} = \frac{\exp(U_{Pv})}{\exp(U_{Pv}) + \exp(U_{Pt}) + \exp(U_{B})} \tag{7.20}$$

For public transit,

$$\text{Prob(Pt)} = \frac{\exp(U_{Pt})}{\exp(U_{Pv}) + \exp(U_{Pt}) + \exp(U_{B})} \tag{7.21}$$

For bicycle,

$$\text{Prob(B)} = \frac{\exp(U_{B})}{\exp(U_{Pv}) + \exp(U_{Pt}) + \exp(U_{B})} \tag{7.22}$$

At the second level there are two sets of MNL models. For the private vehicle model the probability of driving alone is:

$$\text{Prob(Da|Pv)} = \frac{\exp(U_{Da})}{\exp(U_{Da}) + \exp(U_{Cp})} \tag{7.23}$$

$$\text{Prob(Cp|Pv)} = \frac{\exp(U_{Cp})}{\exp(UD_{Da}) + \exp(U_{Cp})} \tag{7.24}$$

The probabilities in Eqs. (7.23) and (7.24) are called conditional probabilities. That is, the probability of driving alone among those trip makers who use private vehicles. To calculate the unconditional probability of driving alone, we need to use the following formula:

$$\text{Prob(Da)} = \text{Prob(Da|Pv)} \cdot \text{Prob(Pv)} \tag{7.25}$$

The unconditional probability of car pooling is calculated with the following formula:

$$\text{Prob(Cp)} = \text{Prob(Cp|Pv)} \cdot \text{Prob(Pv)} \qquad (7.26)$$

Similarly, the probabilities for bus and light rail modes are calculated with the following formulas.

Bus:

$$\text{Prob(Bus|Pt)} = \frac{\exp(U_{\text{Bus}})}{\exp(U_{\text{Bus}}) + \exp(U_{\text{Lr}})} \qquad (7.27)$$

Light rail:

$$\text{Prob(Lr|Pt)} = \frac{\exp(U_{\text{Lr}})}{\exp(U_{\text{Bus}}) + \exp(U_{\text{Lr}})} \qquad (7.28)$$

The unconditional probability of bus mode can be derived from the probability for public transit and the conditional probability for bus:

$$\text{Prob(Bus)} = \text{Prob(Bus|Pt)} \cdot \text{Prob(Pt)} \qquad (7.29)$$

and the unconditional probability of light rail mode is calculated from the formula below:

$$\text{Prob(Lr)} = \text{Prob(Lr|Pt)} \cdot \text{Prob(Pt)} \qquad (7.30)$$

At the third level, probabilities for local bus and bus rapid transit can be calculated in the same fashion. The following formulas show the conditional and unconditional probabilities for the two travel modes:

Local bus—conditional probability:

$$\text{Prob(Lb|Bus)} = \frac{\exp(U_{\text{Lb}})}{\exp(U_{\text{Lb}}) + \exp(U_{\text{Brt}})} \qquad (7.31)$$

Bus rapid transit—conditional probability:

$$\text{Prob(Brt|Bus)} = \frac{\exp(U_{\text{Brt}})}{\exp(U_{\text{Lb}}) + \exp(U_{\text{Brt}})} \qquad (7.32)$$

Local bus—unconditional probability:

$$\text{Prob(Lb)} = \text{Prob(Lb|Bus)} \cdot \text{Prob(Bus)}$$

$$= \text{Prob(Lb|Bus)} \cdot \text{Prob(Bus|Pt)} \cdot \text{Prob(Pt)} \qquad (7.33)$$

Bus rapid transit—unconditional probability:

$$\text{Prob(Brt)} = \text{Prob(Brt|Bus)} \cdot \text{Prob(Bus)}$$

$$= \text{Prob(Brt|Bus)} \cdot \text{Prob(Bus|Pt)} \cdot \text{Prob(Pt)} \qquad (7.34)$$

7.4.4   Trip Assignment

The trip assignment model is concerned with trip-makers' choice of route between all zones, after the origin-destination matrix for a network has been constructed. The result is the traffic volume on specific road links that make up the network. There are many possible route choices to travel from one zone to another. The concept of "Impedance" plays an important role in estimating vehicular traffic assignments on a roadway network. Impedance, similar to that discussed in trip distribution, is normally related to travel time and travel cost: the longer the trip or the higher the cost, the larger the impedance for the trip along that path. One criterion for trip assignment is to minimize the impedance by assigning trips to different routes. Most trip assignment models are based on one of two theories of minimizing the impedance (Gazis, 2002).

(1) An individual trip maker chooses the route that has the minimum impedance.

(2) The average journey impedance for all users is minimized.

The first theory indicates that the route choice is to minimize the individual traveler's impedance (user optimal) while the second theory is to minimize the collective impedance for all travelers (system-optimal). Using travel time as an example, a model may assign travelers to different paths in a way that each traveler takes the shortest time to travel from the trip generation zone to the trip attraction zone. Alternatively, a model may assign travelers to different routes in a way that the summation of travel time of all travelers is minimized. Studies have shown that the two optimizations are not satisfied at the same time. That is, a user-optimal solution will not lead to a system-optimal solution (Gazis, 2002).

In reality, the decision of travel route is much more complicated than simple optimization. The travel conditions on the routes are likely different. For example, the distance when traveling on local roads may be shorter than on a highway; however, one may travel faster on the highway. Someone may still be willing to travel on the highway even if it will take a little longer time and distance. On the other hand, someone may try as much as possible to avoid traveling on the highway. The trip assignment procedure identifies relevant variables that affect travelers' path choices and predicts how route decisions are made based on certain assumptions, e.g., shortest path.

We should be able to realize, from our own experience that, it is very hard to predict which route people may choose to travel from one place to another. Many factors may affect choice on any given day. Nevertheless, there are some variables that are most relevant to people's choice. The trip assignment procedure of a travel demand model uses those variables to predict the possibilities of people choosing a particular path. Examples of such variables are travel time, travel distance, traffic lights, the width or number of lanes, travel volume, etc.

The level of service is normally used to estimate the impedance for private automobile travel. To estimate the impedance for transit travel, the travel time is normally estimated for different segments, such as time spent in-vehicle, waiting for a vehicle, walking to the transit stop, or transferring to another vehicle. Different weights may be applied to the time segments to reflect people's tolerance level of the time spent. For example, spending 10 minutes on a bus will have a different affect than walking 10 minutes to a bus stop on a person's choice of which way to travel.

The simplest trip assignment model is the "all-or-nothing" method (Wright, et al., 1997). According to this method, all trips between any two zones are assigned to the route with minimum travel time or minimum cost. If two routes have same travel time, the trips are equally split between the two routes. No matter how many other paths are available, no traffic is assigned to them. The traffic volume on any path is the total of the zonal traffics going through the route. If the objective is to minimize the cost of travel, the solution is called **minimum cost route (MCR) algorithm** (Oppenheim, 1995).

Figure 7.8 uses the four-zone example to illustrate the trip assignment using the "all-or-nothing" method. There are eight links connecting the four zones. One intersection, A, connects all four zones. The numbers in the oval box indicates the link number and travel time. Let's use the trip distribution result shown in Table 7.17. Among different ways of traveling between Zone 1 and Zone 2, the

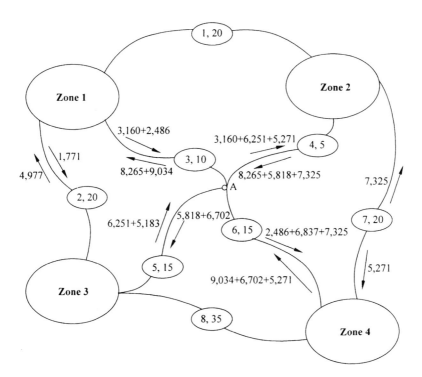

Figure 7.8   "All-or-Nothing" trip assignment

path of the shortest time connects the two zones through Intersection A. Therefore, all 3,160 trips from Zone 1 to Zone 2 are assigned to the two links (3 and 4) from Zone 1 to Intersection A then to Zone 2. Similarly, the 8,265 trips from Zone 2 to Zone 1 are assigned to the two links (4 and 3) from Zone 2 to Intersection A then to Zone 1. The shortest path between Zone 2 and Zone 3 also goes through Intersection A. This path then carries the 5,818 trips from Zone 2 to Zone 3 (Links 4 and 5) and 6,251 trips from Zone 3 to Zone 2 (Links 5 and 4). The total trips along Link 4, from intersection A to Zone 2 are then calculated as summation of the trips from Zone 1 and trips from Zone 3:

Total trips on Link 4 from Intersection A to Zone 2 = 3,160 + 6,251 + 5,271 = 14,682

Similarly, the trips on Link #6 are a combination of trips from Zone 1, Zone 2 and Zone 3 to Zone 4. Other links that are not on the quickest path, such as Link #1 and Link #8 on the other hand, are not assigned any trips.

Apparently, this method does not consider many other variables affecting traffic, nor does it even consider the capacity of any single road. To address these problems capacity restraint methods have been developed. According to capacity restraint methods, the travel time is a function of the volume and capacity of roadways:

$$t = f(V, C) \qquad (7.35)$$

where,

t — travel time on a link;

V — trip volume;

C — roadway capacity.

The initial impedance such as travel time is estimated at the free flow condition. As trips are assigned to road links, the travel time on some links, where the volume exceeds the design capacity, will increase. During the trip assignment process, the initial travel time on all links is calculated and an arbitrary portion of the trip volume (such as 20%) is assigned to the links with the minimum travel time. Then, the travel time on those links are updated to reflect the impact of the assigned travel volume. Based on the updated travel time, new minimum-travel-time links are identified. Another arbitrary portion of trip volume is assigned to the links with the new minimum travel time. This process is repeated until all traffic volumes are assigned.

Equilibrium assignment is another type of traffic assignment method. This method can simulate the fact that people may choose a different route to avoid traffic congestion. When trips are assigned to a roadway link, the volume associated with the link is therefore increased. As a result, the volume/capacity ratio for the link will increase. Because the trip assignment is based on the ratio, the likelihood of assigning additional trips to this link is reduced. The method seeks the trip assignment that every traveler uses paths that minimize the objective function, such as travel time.

Diversion methods also can be used in trip assignment. Similar to its use in mode choice, a diversion method allocates trips between two possible paths. The proportion of trips assigned to a path is a function of the ratio of the impedance of the alternative path over its impedance:

$$P_i = f(1/(W_i/W_a)) \qquad (7.36)$$

where,

P_i— proportion of trips assigned to path i;

W_a— impedance of the alternative path;

W_i— impedance of path i.

Figure 7.9 illustrates a diversion curve for two alternative paths, using travel time as the impedance. The x-axis represents the ratio of the travel time, R:

$$R = T_1/T_2 \qquad (7.37)$$

where,

R — the travel time ratio;

T_1 — travel time for path 1;

T_2 — travel time for path 2.

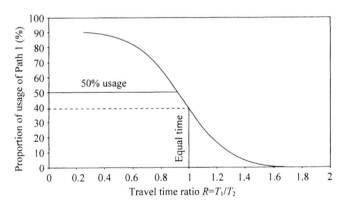

Figure 7.9   Diversion curves for trip assignment

The y-axis is the proportion of the trip volume on path 1. The curve shows that when the travel time on the two paths is the same, $R = 1$, about forty percent of trips are assigned to path 1. As R increases from the equal time point, the travel time on path 1 is greater than that on path 2, the proportion of trips on path 1 decreases. As R decreases from the equal time point, the travel time on path 1 is less than that on path 2, the proportion of trips on path 1 therefore increases. The model shows that the more savings of travel time on a particular path, the higher proportion of trips is expected.

The last words about the travel demand modeling are that once the structure of a model is developed, it must be **calibrated**. The calibration process is to compare the output of the travel demand model with surveyed traffic data, using different parameter values (coefficients). Statistical tests are used to find the set of parameters that can best match the model output with empirical data. Before a calibrated model can be used, it must be **validated**. Model validation is a process of comparing the modeling out with a dataset that is independent from the data used for model calibration. The model validation process tests the model structure and the theories behind it by demonstrating its ability to replicate actual traffic patterns (Edwards, 1999). In order to provide meaningful prediction, a model should only be used after it is validated.

7.5 Critique and Limitations

This chapter introduces the basis of transportation analysis. In particular, the four-step travel demand model describes the traffic features of a transportation system. The trip generation step produces zonal trip production and attraction, which determines the amount of traffic expected to occur in the study region. The challenge in this step is that the estimation of trip production and attraction is based on population characteristics and the types of land use. This calculation may introduce errors because it may not represent other important factors affecting people's travel behavior. Two shopping centers of the same size, however, with different stores which carry different merchants and different brands, may attract people with different travel behaviors. In addition, data used in the model may not accurately reflect reality. For example, in the United States, the Bureau of Census is the main source for population data. Census data are summarized at a given area, such as census tract. It becomes a difficult task to know where people live in a census tract. A common practice is to assume people are evenly dispersed within a census tract. We know this is not correct. One improvement is to limit people to residential land. This can be done once the land use data are available. However, it can be complicated if there is residential land with different densities. There is no single standard procedure to allocate a total population to different residential land densities.

Another limitation of the trip generation is the assumption that all trips originate from the place of residence. We already know that there are non-home-based trips. The traffic demand model cannot assign trip generation to a non-residential zone. For example, it is common to observe heavy traffic during lunch time in a commercial district. These trips will either be ignored or be assigned to one or more residential zones.

The trip distribution model allocates trip production and trip attraction among zones in the study area. One problem, which could be potentially serious, is the assumption that no traffic will go across the study boundary. With the increased travel distance by automobiles it is not uncommon for people to travel long distance, either to go outside the study area or to enter from outside. The model will not be able to catch this portion of traffic.

The third piece of travel demand model is the mode choice or modal split model. It divides trips into different modes of transportation. The current models simulate the choices based on the characteristics of travelers, the trip types, and the service quality of different modes. It could be difficult to assess the performance of a transportation system after introducing a new travel mode since the factors affecting travelers' mode choices are quite localized, which makes it difficult to use study results from other places.

Trip assignment is the last step in the travel demand model. The procedure allocates the trips of different modes to all available roads. The challenge here is that the model must be sensitive to the dynamic changes of the roads. Travelers normally choose the paths based on the level of service of the roads. Their choices will affect the traffic volume on the roads, which in turn affects the level of service. This looping nature often requires that the trip assignment modeling has to be completed in multiple iterations.

The travel demand model applies a linear sequence of the four steps. The trip generation model produces the number of trips from each traffic analysis zone (TAZ). The trip distribution model allocates the trips to all the zones. The mode choice model divides the trips among available travel modes. For each mode, there are normally multiple routes connecting two zones. Therefore, the trip assignment model further allocates the trips between the origin and destination zones in each travel mode to available routes. Hereby, the model assumes that travelers make rational decisions based on the perfect knowledge of traffic analysis zone characteristics, available travel modes, and possible routes. However, this may not reflect reality. For example, travel time is dependent on the travel volumes and traffic congestion can change the friction factors used in the travel demand model. To accommodate the change, a travel demand model has to run under the revised parameter values. However, the impact of congestion on the parameters may not be clear.

A travel demand modeling process does not have to go through these four phases linearly. For example, trip distribution is about where people go, which could very well be affected by the available modes of transportation or the paths connecting the zones. Rosenbloom (1988) summarized the four most common combinations of the four steps. The sequence of trip generation, trip distribution and trip assignment is the same for all four types of combination. The difference is where in the decision process the mode choice is made.

The Type I combination represents a circumstance where a trip maker's decision of making a trip is directly related to the availability of different travel modes. For example, there has been increased traffic in Chinese cities with the increase of automobiles. Assume that an individual who normally takes the bus to work now drives a car. This individual may decide, on the way home, to drive to a place where she has never been because it is not easily accessible by bus. This represents an additional trip that is a result of the availability of the automobile as a mode of transportation. In a different example, in an American city where public transportation has been significantly improved, residents, especially those who do not drive, may make more trips. Similarly, the decision to make those trips is related to the availability of transit service.

The Type II combination reflects a situation that once an individual decides to make a trip, the choice of trip destination is affected by the availability of transportation modes. For example, trips generated can be split into automobile and transit modes before trip distribution. Assume there are two shopping centers with similar merchants. One is easily accessible by bus with no parking space and the other has numerous parking spaces, however it is not close to any bus stops. Where an individual goes shopping is pretty much determined by his/her access to a car or bus. This type is only applicable in an area where transit takes a substantial portion of traffic.

The Type III combination differs from the first two types in which a trip maker decides where to go in conjunction with considering the available mode choices. The available modes may affect trip distribution. For example, whether or not individuals own a car may influence their decision on where to buy groceries.

According to the Type IV combination, the modes of transportation do not affect trip distribution. It represents a situation in which a traveler decides on the transportation mode to use after deciding where to go.

With the travel demand model, a planner can assess the effect of policies and programs on travel demand, the performance of a new or proposed transportation facility, and impacts of a proposed development on traffic. Two primary applications of the traffic demand modeling is Transportation Control Measures (TCM), which is designed to reduce vehicular travel, and Congestion Management Program (CMP), which intends to reduce congestion on the highway network by coordinating land use, air quality, and transportation planning. CMP may provide incentives or implement strategies to affect people's behavior and transportation choices. For example, highway congestion can be alleviated by minimizing single occupancy drivers. Incentives could be provided for people to take the bus or carpool. Although the highway capacity is not increased, the existing capacity is better utilized through a planned process of moving more people.

Researchers have significantly improved the travel demand model since its inception. The behavioral potential has been formalized and their operations are supported by powerful techniques of mathematical programming (Oppenheim, 1995). There are many computer software packages performing the four-step process of traffic demand modeling. Although these models require a large amount of data, including the roadway links, traffic volume, road capacity, and origin-destination tables, the simulation of different scenarios and planning alternatives can be completed quickly.

One caution of using travel demand modeling results is that the model is designed for transportation planning purposes. Therefore it is most suitable for analyzing general traffic patterns in a large area, such as a metropolitan area. The traffic volume on a particular road normally does not reflect the real traffic volume. At least two reasons for the discrepancy can be attributed to the model structure. First, the model simulates an average condition, typically, morning or afternoon peak hours or daily average. The second cause is related to the trip distribution. The model requires that the zonal trip productions and attractions be linked to road network through a limited number of nodes. Therefore, all trips from one traffic analysis zone (TAZ) may be directed to one or two nodes. In reality, people in the same zone may take different roads for travel. If the needs arrive for a more detailed and realistic understanding of traffic on a particular road, readers may refer to other transportation books about the micro level traffic models.

Review Questions

1. Assign trip purpose to each of the trips shown as lines in the diagram. How many trips and how many trip ends have you identified?

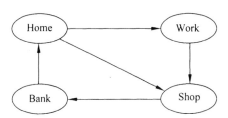

2. Describe the purpose of street classification.
3. Describe the concept of level of service. What are the six level of service classes?
4. What is a travel analysis zone (TAZ)? What are the two general rules in delineating TAZs?
5. What are the four steps in the travel demand modeling process? What is the purpose of each step? What is the outcome from each step?
6. What is the fundamental of the Gravity model?
7. What is a friction factor F_{ij}? How does it affect the trips between Zone i and Zone j?

8. Describe the assumption in the trip distribution model that the total amount of trip generation must equal to the amount of trip attraction.

9. What is a Diversion Method? How is it used in mode choice model?

10. What is the "All-or-Nothing" trip assignment?

Exercises

1. Your instructor will give you a map showing the streets in a portion of the place you live. You will follow the Census Feature Class Code (CFCC) road category scheme shown in Table 7.2 to classify the streets. Allow yourself some time to visit the roads. Prepare a map of the street classification.

2. Download the household income data by census tract for a U.S. County of your choice from the U.S. Census Bureau web site (http://www.census.gov/). Then you will download the census tract map files (i.e., in ArcGIS shapefile format) from the same website. You look for the link to TIGER files. TIGER, which stands for Topologically Integrated Geographic Encoding and Referencing system, is a file format the U.S. Census Bureau used for geographic data. Use the data and the trip generation rates in Table 7.5 to calculate the home-based-work person trips. Then you will make a map showing the spatial distribution of the Home-Based Work (HBW) trips. Describe the spatial distribution of the HBW trips.

3. Use the same data in exercise 2 to complete the calculation for Home-Based-Non-Work (HBNW) and Non-Home-Based (NHB) trips for the county. Use the automobile occupancy data in Table 7.6 to calculate the vehicle trips for each trip purpose.

4. The attached spreadsheet file, ex7_4_trip_distribution.xls (Fig. 7.10) contains a simplified gravity model for trip distribution of a 3-zone area:

$$T_{ij} = \frac{P_i \cdot A_j \cdot F_{ij}}{\sum_{i=1,n}(A_j \cdot F_{ij})} \qquad (7.14)$$

where, F_{ij} is friction factor and is calculated by combing formulas 7.12 and 7.13:

$$F_{ij} = t_{ij}^{-a} \qquad (7.38)$$

The shaded cells in the spreadsheet represent the data or parameters you may change. They are travel time between a pair of zones, t_{ij}, trip production for each zone, P_i, trip attraction for each zone, A_j, and the constant for calculating friction factor, a.

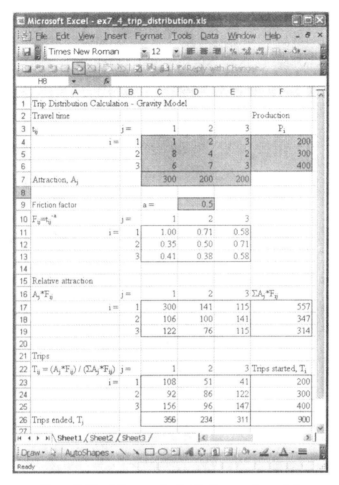

Figure 7.10 A 3-zone trip distribution gravity model

Perform the following tasks:

(1) Open the spreadsheet file and make sure to understand the calculations.

(2) Copy and paste the entire model, Cells A1:F26 to Cell H1. Now you have two identical models side by side. Change any one or several of the trip production values in Cells F4:F6 and compare the new trip distribution in Cells C23:F26 with the original trip distribution in Cells J23:M26. Describe the difference.

(3) Change any one or several of the trip attraction values in Cells C7:E7 and compare the new trip distribution with the original trip distribution. Describe the difference.

(4) Change the constant, a (Cell F9), for instance, let $a = 2$, and compare the new trip distribution with the original trip distribution. Describe the difference.

(5) Summarize your understanding of the gravity model.

5. Figure 7.11 illustrates a hypothetical street network. The network has 8 nodes (101 to 108) and 9 links (1 to 9). The travel time on each link are listed in Table 7.19. Identify the shortest trip from node 101 to node 107. Assume the trip distribution from node 101 to 107 is 1,000, assign trip volume to each link sing the All-Or-Nothing assignment approach.

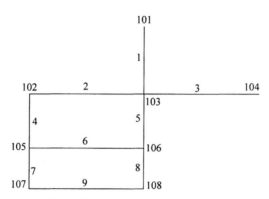

Figure 7.11   Example street network

Table 7.19   Travel time and volume

Link No.	Travel time (min)	Link No.	Travel time (min)
1	5	6	13
2	12	7	4
3	4	8	10
4	6	9	10
5	5		

References

Chang, Cathy L. and Daniel T. Meyers. 1999. Transportation models. In: Edwards, John D. (ed.) *Transportation Planning Handbook*. 2nd ed. Washington, DC: Institute of Transportation Engineers.

Downs, Anthony. 2004. *Still Stuck in Traffic: Coping with Peak-Hour Traffic Congestion*. Washington, DC: The Brookings Institute.

Edwards, John D. (ed.) 1999. *Transportation planning handbook,* 2nd ed. Washington, DC: Institute of Transportation Engineers.

Ford, L.R. and D.R. Fulkerson. 1962. *Flows in Networks*. Princeton, NJ: Princeton University Press.

Gazis, Denos C. 2002. *Traffic Theory*. Boston, MA: Kluwer Academic Publishers.

Hensher, David A. and April J. Reyes. 2000. Trip chaining as a barrier to the propensity to use public transport. *Transportation* 27: 341 – 361.

Hensher, David A. and Greene, William H. 2002. Specification and estimation of the nested logit model: alternative normalizations. *Transportation Research Part B: Me thodological*, 36 (1): 1 – 17.

Institute of Transportation Engineers. 1997. *Trip Generation: Trip Generation Rates, Plots, and Equations*. Washington DC: Institute of Transportation Engineers.

Koppelman, F.S. and C.H. Wen. 1998. Alternative nested logit models: structure, properties and estimation. *Transportation Research* 32B(5): 289 – 298.

Norland, Robert B. 2001. Relationships between highway capacity and induced vehicle travel. *Transportation Research*, Part A 35: 47 – 72.

Oppenheim Norbert, 1995. *Urban Travel Demand Modeling*. New York, NY: John Wiley & Sons, Inc.

Papacostas, C. S and P.D. Prevedouros. 2001. *Transportation Engineering and Planning*, 3rd ed. Upper Saddle River, NJ: Prentice Hall.

Rodwin, Lloyd and Bishwapriya Sanyal (eds.) 2000. *The Profession of City Planning: Changes, Images, and Challenges*. New Brunswick: Center for Urban Policy Research, Rutgers, The State University of New Jersey.

Rosenbloom, Sandra. 1988. Transportation Planning. In: So, Frank S. and Judith Getzels. (eds.) *The Practice of Local Government Planning*, 2nd ed. Washington DC: The International City Management Association.

Taplin, John H. E. and Min, Qiua. 1997. Car Trip Attraction and Route Choice in Australia. *Annals of Tourism Research*, 24(3): 624 – 637.

Turner, Jeff and Grieco, Margaret. 2000. Gender and time poverty: the neglected social policy implications of gendered time. *Transport and Travel, Time & Society*, 9(1): 129 – 136.

U.S. Census Bureau. 2004. Census 2003 TIGER/Line®. Files Technical Documentation. Washington, DC: U.S. Census Bureau. Available online at: http://www2.census.gov/ pub/outgoing/geo/marshall/tgr1990/DOCUMENT/. Accessed March 2005

U.S. Department of Transportation, Federal Highway Administration. 1985. *Development and Application of Trip Generation Rates*. Washington, DC: U.S. Dept. of Transportation, Federal Highway Administration.

Wright, Paul H., Ashford, Norman J. and Stammer, Jr. Robert J. 1997. *Transportation Engineering: Planning and Design*. 4th ed. New York, NY: John Wiley & Sons. Inc.

Chapter 8   Synopsis—An Integrated Analysis

The previous chapters dealt with the four areas of planning analysis separately while repeatedly emphasizing the connections between them. This chapter will further illustrate these connections through a hands-on exercise.

Planners have long realized the close relationship between these different planning areas—the Lowry model, for example, was developed in the 1960s to allocate population and economic activities to different land uses. The fundamental feature of the Lowry model is that human activities in a region are the result of basic sector economic activities. Figure 8.1 is a graphic illustration of such a process. Once an existing basic sector establishment is expanded or introduced to a region, the increased employment can be calculated. The increased population, as well as the additional services needed for the increased population (e.g. retail), can also be calculated. The service sector employment will then lead to a further

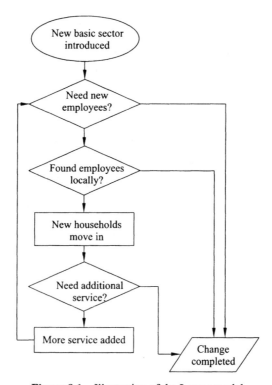

Figure 8.1   Illustration of the Lowry model

increase in population, which in turn, leads to more demand for services. Therefore, the process is repeated until there is no significant increase in population. At that point, a new equilibrium has been reached.

The Lowry model includes three economic sectors—basic, household and retail (Krueckeberg and Silvers, 1974). The land use categories are established accordingly. Although not explicatively shown in the diagram, new economic activities and new households are allocated to one of the three types of land uses in various zones in the region. Depending on the location of activities, the requirement for transportation network will also be determined. For example, in the Lowry model, the service sector is further divided into neighborhood, local, and metropolitan facilities. People's willingness to travel varies, depending on the service categories. A large department store may attract people from long distances while an elementary school normally only serves people living in the immediate neighborhood.

Several planning text books have emphasized on various computer applications in planning. Examples are earlier work by Brail (1987), Klosterman (1990) and Cartwright (1993), as well as the more recent work by Huxhold et al. (1997) and Kaiser et al. (1998) on GIS applications. We agree with Cartwright's (1993) summary that the advantages of spreadsheets are that they are easy to program and easy to modify and therefore, a user may can be more likely to understand how a model works. The rest of the chapter continues to use Boone County as a study area. Since the purpose of this exercise is to illustrate various analytical procedures, several assumptions are made to simplify the calculations. We will use spreadsheet and ArcGIS for most of the calculations. Once you understand the modeling process, you will be able to operate commercial software for a large area with greater amount of data.

8.1   Case Study One: 20-Year Population Projection

Chapter 3 introduced several different methods of projecting population, such as trend extrapolation methods, which simply extend observed historical trends into the future by using regression techniques. Additionally, the more complex cohort-component method was discussed, which divides total population into age cohorts and then projects these cohorts into the near future by using mortality, fertility, and migration rates. In the following exercise, we will project the population in Boone County into the year 2020 using the cohort-component method. All calculations have been done using spreadsheet software (Microsoft Excel) and all individual steps will be described in detail.

Before starting the calculations, it is worthwhile to reemphasize that the accuracy of the projection is highly dependant on the rates used. While the calculations are rather straightforward, accurate rates can often be a challenging task to determine. In particular, the cohort-component method needs survival rates, fertility rates, net migration rates, and the sex ratio at birth. These rates are more likely to be available for large regions. If the rates are not available for your study area, you may use a larger reference area that encompasses your study area. For example, if rate data are not available for Boone County, Kentucky rate data can be used since Boone County is part of the Commonwealth of Kentucky. From Chapter 3, we know that the 2000 rates for Boone County are made available through the Kentucky State Data Center (KSDC) at the University of Louisville. The KSDC survival rates, fertility rates, and net migration rates are gender-specific and cover 5-year periods. Therefore, we will make the population projection in 5-year increments.

The sex ratio at birth is obtained from the CIA World Fact Book for the United States.[1] It is important to note that this sex ratio represents a national average and may lead to significant calculation errors if the sex ratio in Boone County is much different from the national average. We should always try to derive the rates with local data.

All discussions regarding the Boone County cohort-component projections refer to the spreadsheet file "cohort.xls" (Fig. 8.2). The spreadsheet file "cohort.xls" contains a total of five worksheets. Four worksheets represent a 5-year population projection of Boone County: worksheet P00 – 05 contains the 2000 – 2005 Boone County population projection, and worksheets P05 – 10, P10 – 15, and P15 – 20 contain the projections for the 2005 – 2010, 2010 – 2015, and 2015 – 2020 periods, respectively. Each spreadsheet has three parts and is constructed identically to show the cohort-component calculations for a five- year period.

We start the 2000 – 2020 Boone County cohort-component projection by projecting the 2000 population to the year 2005. As displayed in worksheet P00 – 05, table 1 (Cells A2 through J25, e.g., A2: J25), contains the necessary survival rates, fertility rates, net migration rates, and sex ratio. More specifically, Cells A7: A25 indicate the 2000 population cohort breakdown by age, which applies to the female and male components of the model. Cells C7: E25 contain the survival rates, net migration rates, and fertility rates for the female age cohorts. Cells G7: H25 contain survival rates and net migration rates for the male age cohorts. The sex ratio is stored in Cell J7.

The second part of the P00 – 05 worksheet contains all the projections for the female population, shown in Cells A29 through N54. Analogously, Cells A56 through N82 contain the projections for the male population cohorts. Each column is labeled according to its content and numbered sequentially (see Fig. 8.3). For example, Column 1 is the age cohort and Column 2 contains the 2000 population. We will refer to the column number in following discussions. For a detailed

---

[1] http://www.odci.gov/cia/publications/factbook/print/us.html.

Figure 8.2 — Microsoft Excel - Cohort.xls

Age Cohort	Rates					
	Female			Male		
	Survival Rates* $_5Sr_x$	Net Migration Rates* $_5nm_x$	Fertility Rates* $_5ASBR_{x,i}$	Survival Rates* $_5Sr_x$	Net Migration Rates* $_5nm_x$	Sex Ratio**
1	3	4	5	3	4	
Newborn	0.9934			0.9924		1.05
0 - 4	0.9975	0.2130		0.9967	0.2130	
5 - 9	0.9992	0.1200		0.9988	0.1200	
10 - 14	0.9985	0.0214	0.0524	0.9972	0.0298	
15 - 19	0.9973	0.0213	0.3916	0.9929	-0.0022	
20 - 24	0.9974	0.3852	0.4917	0.9929	0.3505	
25 - 29	0.9966	0.2552	0.4917	0.9918	0.3211	
30 - 34	0.9953	0.1228	0.2878	0.9896	0.1624	
35 - 39	0.9932	0.1606	0.0864	0.9859	0.1552	
40 - 44	0.9891	0.0102	0.0095	0.9803	0.0493	
45 - 49	0.9635	0.1424		0.9709	0.0940	
50 - 54	0.9730	0.0675		0.9540	0.0766	
55 - 59	0.9570	0.0180		0.9256	0.0026	
60 - 64	0.9320	-0.0121		0.8830	-0.0121	
65 - 69	0.8970	0.0482		0.8236	0.0482	
70 - 74	0.8504	0.0747		0.7508	0.0747	
75 - 79	0.7653	0.0492		0.6392	0.0492	
80 - 84	0.6373	0.0131		0.4985	0.0131	
85+	0.3814	0.1432		0.2976	0.1432	

* Source: Kentucky State Data Center, http://ksdc.louisville.edu/kpr/pro/assumptions.htm
** Source: The World Fact Book, http://www.odci.gov/cia/publications/factbook/print/us.html

Figure 8.2   The cohort-component rates in spreadsheet format

Figure 8.3 — Microsoft Excel - Cohort.xls — 2000 - 2005

Female Cohort-Component Module

Age in 2000	Population $F_{x,2000}$	Survival Rates $_5sr_x$	Net Migration Rates $_5nm_x$	Fertility Rates $_5ASBR_{x,i}$	Adjusted Fertility Rates $_5aft_x$	Survive SF_{2005}	Deaths 00 to 05 DF_{00-05}	Migrate 00 to 05 MF_{00-05}	At Risk Female Pop. ARF_{00-05}	Births B_{00-05}	Live Births FB_{00-05}	Projected Population $F_{x,2005}$	Age in 2005
1	2	3	4	5	6	7	8	9	10	11	12	13	14
Newborn		0.9934								3,366		3,045	0 - 4
0 - 4	3,347	0.9975	0.2130			3,339	8	713				4,052	5 - 9
5 - 9	3,458	0.9992	0.1200			3,456	3	415				3,870	10 - 14
10 - 14	3,309	0.9985	0.0214	0.0524	0.2220	3,304	5	71	3,377	750		3,375	15 - 19
15 - 19	2,940	0.9973	0.0213	0.3916	0.4417	2,932	8	63	2,999	1,324		2,995	20 - 24
20 - 24	2,490	0.9974	0.3852	0.4917	0.4917	2,484	6	959	3,446	1,894		3,443	25 - 29
25 - 29	3,100	0.9966	0.2552	0.4917	0.4917	3,089	11	791	3,886	1,515		3,881	30 - 34
30 - 34	3,621	0.9953	0.1228	0.2878	0.1871	3,604	17	445	4,067	769		4,049	35 - 39
35 - 39	4,033	0.9932	0.1606	0.0864	0.0480	3,976	27	643	4,632	222		4,619	40 - 44
40 - 44	3,879	0.9891	0.0102	0.0095	0.0048	3,837	42	40	3,897	19		3,876	45 - 49
45 - 49	3,188	0.9635	0.1424			3,135	53	454				3,589	50 - 54
50 - 54	2,730	0.9730	0.0675			2,656	74	184				2,841	55 - 59
55 - 59	1,913	0.9570	0.0180			1,831	82	34				1,866	60 - 64
60 - 64	1,419	0.9320	-0.0121			1,323	96	-17				1,305	65 - 69
65 - 69	1,182	0.8970	0.0482			1,060	122	57				1,117	70 - 74
70 - 74	1,110	0.8504	0.0747			944	166	83				1,027	75 - 79
75 - 79	784	0.7653	0.0492			600	184	39				639	80 - 84
80 - 84	527	0.6373	0.0131			336	191	7				343	85 - 89
85+	492	0.3814	0.1432			188	304	70				258	90+
Total	43,492					42,092	1,420	5,050	26,296	6,383		50,187	

Figure 8.3   The female cohort-component model for Boone County, KY, 2000 – 2005

description on this data, please refer back to Chapter 3. But before we describe in more detail the individual calculations of a cohort-component model, we want to emphasize that there is no one correct way of setting up a cohort-component model in a spreadsheet. The sample Boone County model is designed for simplicity by placing all the cohort-specific calculations in the same row. This means that column 1 has the age for a specific cohort in the year 2000, the beginning of the projection period, and column 14 in the same row has the age for this cohort five years later in 2005, the end of the projection period. One difference from the model described in Chapter 3 is that we have added a row above the $0-4$ cohort, which now contains the projected number of newborns for the $2000-2005$ period. At the end of this period, these newborns make up the first $0-4$ age cohort in 2005. Columns 2 to 5 contain the survival rates, net migration rates, and fertility rates from Fig. 8.1, respectively.

Column 6 contains the adjusted fertility rate, which is the average of two consecutive fertility rates. For example, the adjusted fertility rate for the $10-14$ age cohort in cell F37 is calculated as the arithmetic mean of the fertility rates for the $10-14$ age cohort and the $15-19$ age cohort stored in cell E37 and cell E38, respectively. Thus, the adjusted fertility rate for the $10-14$ age cohort (cell F37) is calculated as:

$$= (E37+E38)/2 = (0.0524+0.3916)/2 = 0.2220$$

The adjusted fertility rates for other age cohorts (except the last one) are calculated in the same way. For the last cohort ($40-44$ age), the adjusted fertility rate is half of the fertility rate.

Column 7 contains the projected surviving population, which is calculated as the population in the Year 2000 (the beginning year of the time period, column 2) multiplied by the survival rate (column 3) for the same age cohort. For example, the surviving population of the $0-4$ age cohort, cell G35, is calculated as:

$$= B35 \times C35 = 3,347 \times 0.9975 \doteq 3,339$$

where, cell B35 is the 2000 population and c35 is the survival rate, both for the $0-4$ age cohort.

You may simply copy and paste the formula in cell C35 to all other cells in column 7 for the surviving population in other age cohorts.

Column 8 shows the number of deaths in the 5-year period for each age cohort. All deaths, except the first cohort of newborns, are calculated as the difference between the population in Year 2000 (column 2) and the surviving population in Year 2005 (the end of the 5-year period, column 8). For example, the value for the $0-4$ age cohort in cell H35 is calculated as:

$$= B35 - G35 = 3,347 - 3,339 = 8$$

Column 9 is the number of net migrations within the 5-year period, which is the product of the 2000 population (column 2) and the net migration rate (column 4). For the $0-4$ age cohort, the net migration in cell I35, is calculated as:

$$= B35 \times D35 = 3,347 \times 0.2130 = 713$$

The "at risk" female population, used to calculate births, is reported in column 10. You may notice that the calculation is only for the female population at reproductive ages, $10-44$. The population is calculated as the 2000 population minus half of the deaths and plus the net migration. For example, the population in the $10-14$ age cohort in cell J37, is calculated as:

$$= B37 - (0.5 \times H37) + I37 = 3,309 - (0.5 \times 5) + 71 = 3,377$$

The number of births is then calculated as the product of the "at risk" female population and the adjusted fertility rates, as shown in column 11. For instance, the number of births to the first female cohort at risk $(10-14)$ is calculated and stored in cell K37 as:

$$= J37 \times F37 = 3,377 \times 0.2220 = 750$$

The total number of newborns is calculated and saved in cell K54 using the spreadsheet function, as:

$$= SUM(K34:K52)$$

There is only one value in column 12 in cell L34. It is the number of female newborns, which is calculated from the total births in cell K54 and the sex ratio in cell J7. The formula is:

$$= K54/(1 + J7) = 6,283 / (1 + 1.05) = 3,065$$

Column 13 stores the projected population in 2005, the ending year of the period. The first age cohort $(0-4)$ in 2005 in cell M34 lists the number of all surviving newborn females for the period $2000-2005$ and is calculated as:

$$= L34 \times C34 = 3,065 \times 0.9934 = 3,045$$

where, L34 is the female newborns and C34 is the survival rate for the newborns. Now we can calculate the number of newborn deaths and save the result in cell H34 as:

$$= L34 - M34 = 3,065 - 3,045 = 20$$

For the remaining cells in column 10, the projected population in 2005 is calculated as the sum of the surviving population plus net migration. For example, the $0-4$ age cohort in 2000 will become the $5-9$ age cohort in 2005, shown in cell M35,

$$= G35 + I35 = 3,339 + 713 = 4,052$$

After we complete the rest age cohorts, we can get the total female population and save it in cell M54:

$$= SUM(M34:M52)$$

The value, 50,187, is the projected female population in Boone County in 2005.

The calculation for the male cohort component is similar to the female calculation, except that there is no need for calculations in columns 5, 6, 10, and 11, as, needless to say, men cannot give birth. The live male birth, stored in cell L62, is calculated as:

$$= K54/[1 + (1/J7)] = 6,283 \, / \, [1 + (1/1.05)] = 3,218$$

The total projected male population in 2005, 49,266, is stored in cell M82.

Now we have completed the 5-year projection. In the next worksheet, P05 – 10, all of the data is setup similarly. All the calculations follow the same procedure. The only additional step necessary is to fill in the 2005 projected female population in cells B35 through B52 and the projected male population in cells B65 through B82 in the worksheet. For example, the 0 – 4 age cohort female population (cell B35) is derived from the 2005 population projection:

$$= \text{“P00 – 05”!M34}$$

The last two age cohorts for the projected population is 85 – 90 and 90 + . These two cohorts need to be added together and saved in the 85 + cohort as the beginning year population for the next projection. For example, cell B52 is the 85 + female age cohort, is calculated as:

$$= \text{“P00 – 05”!M51} + \text{“P00 – 05”!M52}$$

Cell M51 in worksheet P00 – 05 contains the projected 2005 85 – 89 age female population and cell M52, the 90 + female population.

The rest of the projections for the 2005 – 2010 are exactly the same as the first 2000 – 2005 period projection. We may notice that the survival rates, fertility rates, net migration rates, and sex ratio are all the same. This reflects the assumption that those rates will remain constant during the projection period. This assumption is a necessity since we do not have estimates of future rates, only the rates from the year 2000. Keep in mind that this assumption of constant rates may introduce errors.

The P15 – 20 worksheet stores the final population projection in 2020. The female projections are in cells M34 to M52, and male projection, in cells M64 to M80.

We will conclude this section describing how to make **population pyramids** in Microsoft Excel. Generally, there are two ways of doing this: using the population data from the cohort-component model as we did previously, or using population as percentages. The latter is recommended if you are making comparisons with populations of other areas. In the exercise illustrated below, we will use the actual population data to construct a population pyramid.

Population pyramids are graphical presentations, usually double bar graphs, showing the sex-age structure of populations. They can be easily done within minutes using spreadsheet software. The starting point for a population pyramid is population data for one year, categorized by sex and age. In order to correctly label the population pyramid, you should also label all columns and rows accordingly. For instance, female and male are column headers in our example and the age-cohorts in five-year intervals are the row labels. To be able to have a meaningful "zero" in the pyramid with females to the left and males to the right on the graph you need to have the female population in negative numbers (see Fig. 8.4).

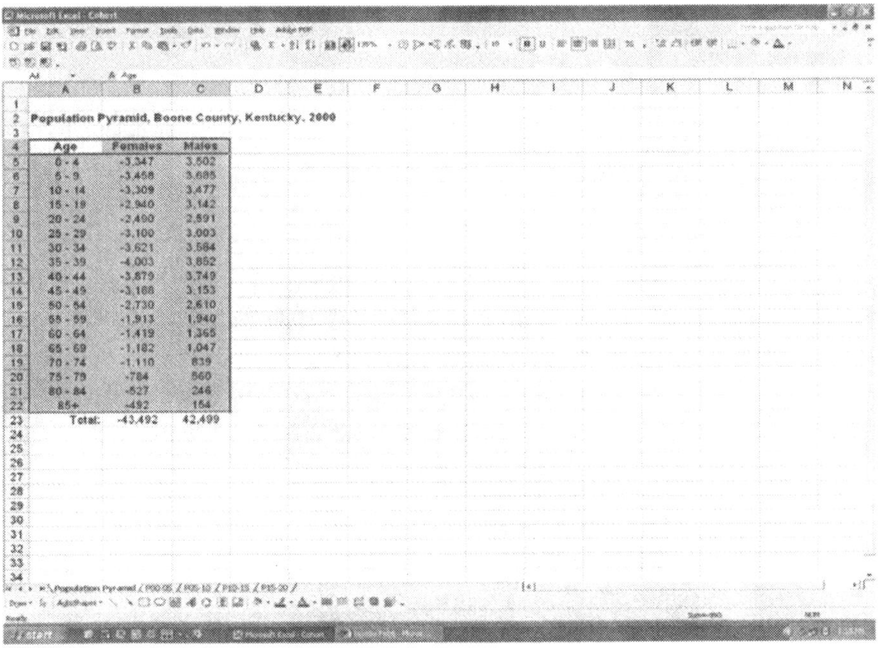

Figure 8.4   Spreadsheet setup for population pyramid, Boone County, 2000

Next, select the data for both females and males, including all sex and age category labels. In our example, simply select cells A4 through c22. Under **Insert** select **Chart** and a chart wizard will appear. Select **Bar** from the Standard Types tab and then select **Clustered Bar** on your right under Chart sub-type (Fig. 8.5).

You now follow the subsequent steps 2 – 4 until you finish the chart. Of course, you can customize your chart accordingly, but if not, you should get a chart that looks exactly like the one shown in Fig. 8.6.

The final step is to format the chart to get a visually appealing population pyramid. To do so, click on the vertical axis, right-click, and select **Format Axis**. On the Patterns tab, set Major tick mark type and Minor tick mark type to **None** and set the Tick mark labels to **Low** (Fig. 8.7).

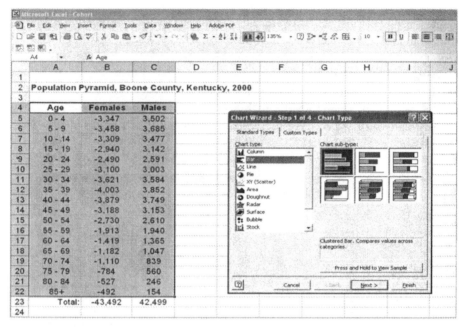

Figure 8.5   The bar chart type selection for a population pyramid

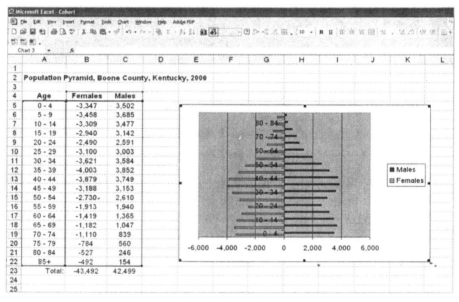

Figure 8.6   The "raw" population pyramid

The data series needs to be formatted in order to delete the gaps between the horizontal bars. To do so, double-click on either data series, or you can move the cursor over the bars, right-click and select **Format Data Series**. You should get a

dialog box labeled **Format Data Series**. Within the options window, make the
following adjustments: set the **Overlap** to 100 and the **Gap Width** to 0 (Fig. 8.8).

Figure 8.7   Formatting the vertical axis

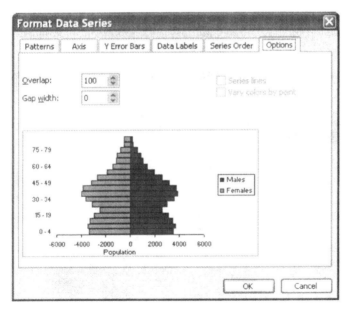

Figure 8.8   Formatting the data series

For formatting the horizontal axis, move the cursor over the horizontal axis,
right-click and select **Format Axis**. Within the **Numbers** dialog tab, select the
Custom number format on the left and the **0.0 Type** on the right. This will eliminate
the negative signs for the female numbers (Fig. 8.9).

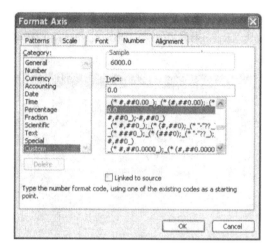

Figure 8.9   Formatting the horizontal axis

Technically, you are done making the population pyramid. The appearance of the population pyramid can be improved by modifying the chart options. For instance, you can change colors, change the labeling, remove the grid, etc. In our example, we got rid of the grid lines, we labeled the pyramid (e.g., population, female, male), and we colored the chart. The outcome produces a population pyramid that can be printed or copied and imported into other documents (Fig. 8.10).

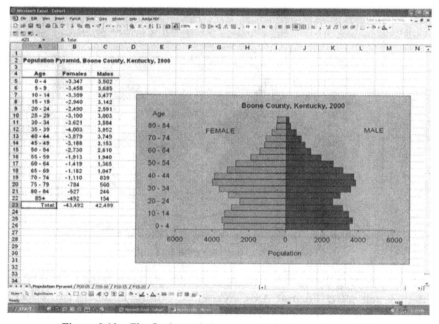

Figure 8.10   The final population pyramid for Bone County, KY

8.2   Case Study Two: Household Allocation

The population projection in Case Study One shows that the population of Boone County is expected to increase by 63,860 people. The land suitability analysis can provide a guide for determining if there is enough land to accommodate such growth, and if so, where would be the proper locations for the new residential development?

In allocating new households, it can be assumed that the proportion of new households in each census tract is related to the relative development potential of the tract. This assumption reflects the belief that the new residential development tends to grow outward from existing residential land. If an area has high-density development currently, it will likely remain high-density in the future. The development potential is the product of 2000 residential density and the available residential land, shown in the following formula:

$$P_i = \mathrm{Rd}_i \cdot \mathrm{Ra}_i \qquad (8.1)$$

where,

P_i — the residential development potential for census tract i;

Rd_i — residential density in census tract i;

Ra_i — available land for residential development in tract i.

The relative potential for a tract in a region of n tracts is then calculated as:

$$\mathrm{Pr}_i = P_i / \sum_{i=1,n} P_i \qquad (8.2)$$

where,

Pr_i — the relative residential development potential for tract i;

n — total number of tracts in the region.

With Pr_i, residential land demand can be allocated to each census tract proportionally. If the total amount of residential land demand is X, the residential land allocated to census tract i will be calculated as:

$$R_i = X \cdot \mathrm{Pr}_i \qquad (8.3)$$

A hypothetical example is used here to illustrate the process. Each census tract requires several calculations: Rd_i, residential density, Ra_i, available residential land, Pr_i, relative residential development potential, and finally, R_i, residential land to be developed.

From the U.S. Census web site, the 2000 census tract level population for Boone County can be downloaded. From the Census Bureau's home page (www.census.gov), click the **American FactFinder**, then choose the **Data SETS** to access Census 2000 Summary File 3 (SF 3) data. The census data are aggregated at different geographical levels, such as nation, state, region, county, census tract, and census block group. We will select the Census Tract level and download variable P1, total population.

Figure 8.11 is a map of the 16 Boone County tracts. There are many sources in the United States where you can get census tract boundary census files, such as the U.S. Census Bureau's Topologically Integrated Geographic Encoding and Referencing (TIGER) file. Special software is required to use the TIGER/Line files. Most Geographic Information System (GIS) software packages have the function to convert TIGER files to GIS data files. Many local governments have census tract boundary files that are much more accurate than TIGER files.

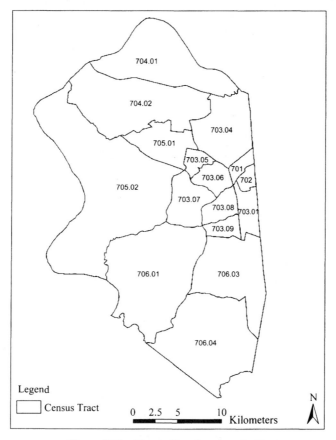

Figure 8.11   Boone County census tracts

Population data for the 16 census tracts are shown in Table 8.1. The first column lists the census tract name. The downloaded population data are stored in the second column. The third column is the size of census tracts measured in square kilometers. We may simply calculate population density for each census tract with the formula:

$$D = P / A \qquad (8.4)$$

where,

    D — population density, in persons/square kilometer;
    P — population, in persons;
    A — area, in square kilometer.

Table 8.1   Population density by census tract

Tract	Population (persons)	Area (square kilometers)	Density (persons/square kilometers)	Residential Land (square kilometers)	Residential Density (persons/square kilometers)
701	6,751	4.6	1,456	2.3	2,913
702	6,173	4.2	1,472	2.3	2,704
703.01	5,012	11.8	423	2.1	2,420
703.04	2,769	39.8	70	3.0	925
703.05	5,175	5.8	897	3.0	1,721
703.06	9,360	11.0	848	5.1	1,818
703.07	4,521	19.7	229	4.1	1,093
703.08	4,811	10.0	483	4.3	1,113
703.09	4,735	7.6	619	4.8	990
704.01	3,464	65.1	53	8.3	417
704.02	6,602	74.8	88	11.2	590
705.01	9,297	21.5	432	8.0	1,169
705.02	4,263	156.7	27	14.3	298
706.01	2,330	95.3	24	7.7	303
706.03	8,170	53.8	152	14.2	574
706.04	2,558	84.0	30	8.1	317
Total	85,991	666	129	103	835

For example, the population density for census tract 701 is:

$$D = 6,751 / 4.6 = 1,467 \text{ persons/square kilometers}$$

The density calculation results are stored in the fourth column in Table 8.1. However, there is a problem in the density calculation we just completed, because it does not consider land use. In fact, it is reasonable to assume that people only live on a portion of the census tract that is classified as residential land. Therefore, a more accurate calculation would be to identify the residential land in each census tract and calculate the population with the formula below:

$$D_{res} = P / A_{res} \qquad (8.5)$$

where,

D_{res} — population density, in persons/square kilometer;

P — population, in persons;

A_{res} — residential land area, in square kilometer.

In order to calculate D_{res}, it is necessary to know the amount of residential land in each census tract. The Boone County Planning Commission has prepared an existing land use data file in ArcGIS shapefile format. The amount of residential land can be determined by overlaying the land use shapefile with the census tract shapefile to derive the existing land use by census tract. The following paragraphs describe the procedure.

Launch ArcGIS and add the existing land use shapefile. We first need to know what categories in this file constitute residential land uses. By opening the land use file's attribute table, we can see that the "TYPE" field contains the land use symbol and the "USE" field has the description of the land uses (Fig. 8.12).

FID	Shape*	AREA	PERIMETER	TYPE	USE*
0	Polygon	344730396.11	651206.321	H	Water
1	Polygon	261740.973	2550.612	W	Woodland
2	Polygon	1825369.301	10458.752	W	Woodland
3	Polygon	203241.129	1927.446	RD	Rural Density Residential
4	Polygon	138194.121	1920.288	A	Agricultural
5	Polygon	337139.574	3897.198	RD	Rural Density Residential
6	Polygon	166597.906	1766.168	RD	Rural Density Residential
7	Polygon	285380.133	2902.295	A	Agricultural
8	Polygon	393759.852	2574.519	RD	Rural Density Residential
9	Polygon	213735.852	1972.938	RD	Rural Density Residential
10	Polygon	1423967.375	10552.351	A	Agricultural
11	Polygon	7076057.129	24628.503	A	Agricultural
12	Polygon	96635.355	1549.653	I	Industrial
13	Polygon	118904.078	1401.091	A	Agricultural
14	Polygon	662562.668	4663.798	A	Agricultural
15	Polygon	285198.151	2850.609	RD	Rural Density Residential
16	Polygon	637410.113	3682.015	RD	Rural Density Residential
17	Polygon	92535.055	1336.543	W	Woodland
18	Polygon	5516431.883	33986.917	A	Agricultural
19	Polygon	334155.711	2953.252	A	Agricultural

Record: 1 of 2843 Selected. Options

Figure 8.12   Attribute table of land use data

The ArcGIS "summarize" function can produce a table showing the unique land uses. We will create such a table with the following operations.

With the attribute table of land use open, right-click on the field title, **TYPE** and select the **Summarize** option. Click the + sign in front of the field **USE** and check **First** (Fig. 8.13). This will include the "USE" field in the output table. Specify the output table name and location and click **OK** to proceed.

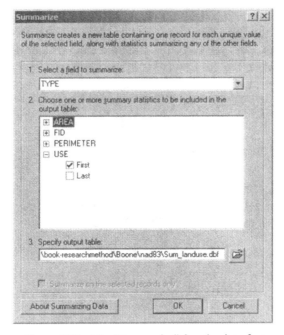

Figure 8.13   The "Summarize" function interface

The output land use type table is shown in Fig. 8.14. We can see that there are 14 different land use types. Among them, four are residential land uses:
(1) HSD—High Suburban Density Residential,
(2) RD—Rural Density Residential,
(3) SR—Suburban Density Residential, and,
(4) UD—Urban Density Residential.

OID	TYPE	Count_TYPE	First_USE
0	A	673	Agricultural
1	BP	6	Business Park
2	C	181	Commercial
3	H	5	Water
4	HSD	23	High Suburban Density Residential
5	I	68	Industrial
6	OS	56	Open Space
7	P	113	Public/Institutional
8	R	50	Recreation
9	RD	719	Rural Density Residential
10	SR	144	Suburban Density Residential
11	T	6	Transportation
12	UD	46	Urban Density Residential
13	W	753	Woodland

Figure 8.14   The output table of the "Summarize" function

Now we are ready to select the residential land from the existing land use data layer. From the **Selection** menu choose the option **Select By Attributes**. A selection window pops up. Enter the selection that includes the four residential land uses, as shown in Fig. 8.15.

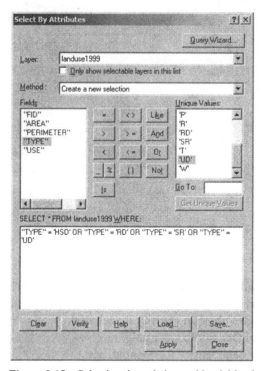

Figure 8.15   Selecting the existing residential land

Click **Apply** to proceed. Now you can see in the map window that the residential land uses are highlighted. Right mouse click the land use layer and select **Data** then **Export Data** to save the residential land use as a new shapefile. Name it "Residential" (Fig. 8.16).

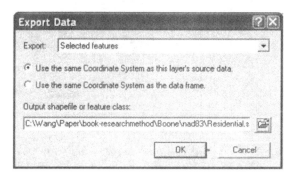

Figure 8.16   Exporting the existing residential land to a new file

The next step is to identify the census tracts where those residential land uses are located. This can be done with the GIS "Intersect" function. We will need to add the census tract layer to ArcMap. Then click the **ArcToolBox** button to show the ArcToolBox window. Under the **Analysis Tools**, click the + next to **Overlay** and select the **Intersect** tool. Add census tract and residential land use to the input feature list. Specify the name and location of the output file (Fig. 8.17). Click **OK** to proceed. In the output data file, a census tract ID is assigned to each residential land.

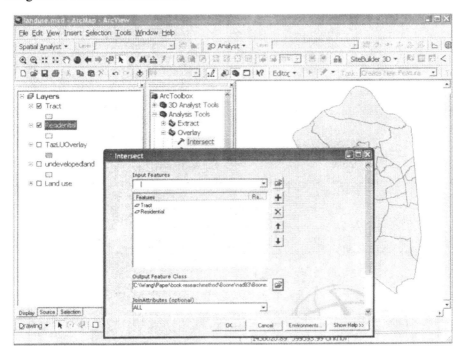

Figure 8.17   GIS "Intersect" function

Figure 8.18 illustrates the intersect function process. Part A shows the boundaries of three census tracts. Part B displays where the residential land in the area. After the residential land is intersected with the census tract, the tract ID is added to the land use data. As shown in Part C the corresponding census tract ID becomes part of the land use data layer.

In order to calculate the size of residential land in each census tract, we use the ArcMap **Summarize** function and select the option to sum the "Shape_ Area" field. Save the output as "sum_res_tract.dbf". Then we can convert the size in square feet to square kilometers.

The fifth column in Table 8.1 stores the residential land area by census tract. We can see that the residential area only takes a small proportion of the each census tract's land area. For example, residential land is less than one-tenth of the

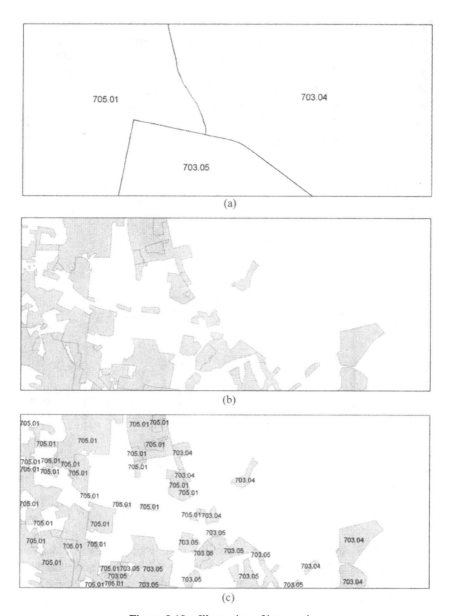

Figure 8.18 Illustration of intersection

(a) Part A: census tract; (b) Part B: residential land; (c) Part C: residential land by census tract

land area in census tracts 706.04. Census tract 703.09 has the highest proportion of residential land, which takes about 60 percent of the area. Consequently, the residential density calculated using residential land, is much higher than the density that is calculated with the whole census tract area (see Table 8.1). These revised residential density values are closer to the reality.

In Chapter 6, we created a land suitability map for Boone County. The land suitability analysis generates four categories for future residential land use. In order to calculate the amount of land suitable for development in each census tract, we need to overlay the residential land suitability data layer with the census tract data layer. Again, we can use "Intersect", the GIS overlay function to assign census tract ID to each land polygon.

Launch **ArcToolBox**. From the **Analysis Tools**, select **Overlay** and then **Intersect**. For the **Input Features**, add **Tract** and **Suitability**. Specify the name and location of the output feature file. Click **OK** to proceed. The output is a polygon feature file. Each polygon in the file has both the census tract ID and residential land suitability class ID. Use the **Calculate Areas** function to calculate the size of each polygon.

The suitable land by census tract is summarized in Table 8.2. The ideal approach for selecting developable land is to develop the most suitable land first. Therefore, let's calculate the relative residential development potential assuming the land in the most suitable category is used for the anticipated residential development. Table 8.3 shows that 18,736 people may move to the county without increasing the current density level by census tract. Since the forecasted population increase for Boone County is 68,865, 50,129 more than the most suitable land can accommodate, let's add more suitable and moderate suitable categories to the available land. The result is shown in Table 8.4. There are total

Table 8.2 Available land for residential development by census tract km^2

Tract	Most Suitable	More Suitable	Moderate Suitable	Less Suitable
701	0.08	0.00	0.00	0.00
702	0.05	0.00	0.00	0.00
703.01	0.70	0.11	0.00	0.00
703.04	0.29	0.11	0.25	0.00
703.05	0.91	0.71	0.01	0.00
703.06	1.82	0.72	0.01	0.00
703.07	0.59	7.14	1.04	0.05
703.08	2.86	1.74	0.03	0.00
703.09	1.31	0.43	0.00	0.00
704.01	1.17	7.56	2.12	0.04
704.02	3.08	5.76	0.88	0.02
705.01	1.62	3.12	0.08	0.00
705.02	0.01	2.58	2.58	0.02
706.01	0.59	2.30	1.40	0.02
706.03	3.44	3.87	0.10	0.00
706.04	0.14	6.08	1.73	0.00

Table 8.3 Population distribution assuming only most suitable land is converted to residential use

Tract	Available land for residential development, Ra_i	Residential density, Rd_i (persons/square kilometers)	Residential development potential, P_i (persons)
701	0.08	2,913	243
702	0.05	2,704	129
703.01	0.70	2,420	1,696
703.04	0.29	925	265
703.05	0.91	1,721	1,560
703.06	1.82	1,818	3,312
703.07	0.59	1,093	648
703.08	2.86	1,113	3,181
703.09	1.31	990	1,293
704.01	1.17	417	489
704.02	3.08	590	1,817
705.01	1.62	1,169	1,896
705.02	0.01	298	4
706.01	0.59	303	179
706.03	3.44	574	1,977
706.04	0.14	317	46
Total			18,736

of 71 square kilometers land in the moderate suitable or better categories, which can house 52,370 more residents using the current residential density. This amount of land is still not enough to accommodate the projected population increase.

Since the available land that is suitable for residential development is not enough to meet population demands at the present conditions, planning decisions need to be made to accommodate the population growth. These planning decisions may include:

(1) Increasing the residential density for the new development. As shown in the last column in Table 8.4, the population density has to be increased significantly (31%) in order to house the 68,865 population increase. Such increase will change the characteristics of the area.

(2) Modifying land use policy. Table 8.5 compares the amount of land available for residential development with the land available and permitted for residential development. We can see that for the most suitable category, 44% of the available land is permitted for residential development. The proportion is 17% for the more suitable category. To build homes for the forecasted population growth, the county may need to be ready to face various request of zoning changes.

Table 8.4   Population distribution assuming land in the most, more, and moderate suitable categories is converted to residential use

Tract	Available land for residential development, Ra_i	Residential density, Rd_i (persons/square kilometers)	Residential development potential, P_i (persons)	Relative residential development potential, Pr_i	Population (persons)	Density (persons/ square kilometers)
701	0.08	2,913	243	0.005	319	3,831
702	0.05	2,704	137	0.003	180	3,555
703.01	0.82	2,420	1,974	0.038	2,596	3,182
703.04	0.64	925	594	0.011	781	1,216
703.05	1.63	1,721	2,810	0.054	3,696	2,263
703.06	2.55	1,818	4,637	0.089	6,097	2,390
703.07	8.77	1,093	9,588	0.183	12,608	1,437
703.08	4.63	1,113	5,149	0.098	6,771	1,463
703.09	1.74	990	1,721	0.033	2,264	1,302
704.01	10.85	417	4,518	0.086	5,941	548
704.02	9.72	590	5,736	0.110	7,543	776
705.01	4.82	1,169	5,635	0.108	7,409	1,537
705.02	5.18	298	1,545	0.029	2,031	392
706.01	4.29	303	1,302	0.025	1,712	399
706.03	7.42	574	4,261	0.081	5,603	755
706.04	7.96	317	2,520	0.048	3,313	416
Total	71		52,370	1	68,865	

Table 8.5   Comparison of available land and permitted land

Suitability	Available	Available and Permitted	Percent of Permitted
Most Suitable	43	19	44%
More Suitable	245	42	17%
Moderate Suitable	168	10	6%
Less Suitable	2	0	10%
Total	458	71	

8.3   Case Study Three: Economic Impact Analysis

Boone County is home to the Cincinnati/Northern Kentucky International Airport, which is the hub for a major airline company. The importance of the airport to the local economy becomes apparent in Table 8.6, which lists 2001 employment

Table 8.6 Employment and industry output in Boone County, KY, 2001

NAICS Code	Industry	Output[1], X_i	Employment, E_i	Employment/ Output Ratio, e_i
11	Agriculture, Forestry, Fishing and Hunting	19.38	805	41.54
21	Mining	2.00	48	24.05
22	Utilities	216.15	313	1.45
23	Construction	353.13	4,072	11.53
31 – 33	Manufacturing	2503.71	12,151	4.85
42	Wholesale Trade	692.08	5,171	7.47
44 – 45	Retail trade	489.01	9,995	20.44
48 – 49	Transportation and Warehousing	2204.76	14,319	6.49
51	Information	201.26	1,420	7.06
52	Finance and Insurance	460.02	5,254	11.42
53	Real Estate and Rental and Leasing	264.57	2,653	10.03
54	Professional, Scientific, and Technical Services	169.35	2,612	15.42
55	Management of Companies and Enterprises	125.51	827	6.59
56	Administrative and Support and Waste Management	168.40	4,865	28.89
61	Educational Services	15.70	382	24.33
62	Health Care and Social Assistance	222.20	3,509	15.79
71	Arts, Entertainment, and Recreation	50.43	1,064	21.10
72	Accommodation and Food Services	277.12	6,562	23.68
81	Other Services (except Public Administration)	287.35	4,053	14.10
92	Public Administration	498.93	5,588	11.20
Totals		9,221.06	85,662	

(1) In millions of 2001 dollars. Source: Minnesota IMPLAN Group 2004.

by two-digit NAICS in Boone County. Not surprisingly, the Transportation and Warehousing (48 – 49) sector is the largest industry sector in Boone County at this level of aggregation, employing 14,319 people. Our case study involving economic impact analysis uses a hypothetical extension of this major airport as an exogenous stimulus to the county's economy. The extension will create 1,000 new jobs in the Transportation and Warehousing sector (48 – 49); this job expansion will allow for the evaluation of the local economic impacts result from the new jobs created.

The ultimate goal of an economic impact analysis is to trace a change in final demand (e.g., additional spending) through the regional economy and to measure the cumulative effects of that change in final demand. We will estimate the total economic impacts that these hypothetical 1,000 new jobs are expected to have with respect to total changes in output and employment. Therefore, using a multiplier framework for economic impact analysis will allow us to measure this total change in Boone County's economic activity—the direct, indirect, and induced effects. Multiplier analysis implies that the initial stimulus (e.g., the 1,000 new jobs) will produce additional economic activities once the additional flow of income and expenditures, which originate from the new activities in the Transportation and Warehousing sector, start circulating through the local service industries (indirect effects) and new income is spent in the local retail and service industries (induced effects).

To be able to measure total changes in output using the type II output multiplier model discussed in Chapter 5, we need to convert the initial change in employment (ΔE) into an equivalent initial change in final demand (ΔY). Assuming constant labor productivity, we can apply the employment/output ratio listed in Table 8.6. Remember, the employment/ output by industry is defined as Eq. (5.29):

$$e_i = \frac{E_i}{X_i} \qquad (8.6)$$

where,

e_i — employment/output ratio for industry i;

E_i — employment for industry i;

X_i — output for industry i;

i — industry sector, in our example, Transportation and Warehousing (48 – 49).

We assume a constant ratio of 6.49, meaning that Transportation and Warehousing needs 6.49 employees to produce an output of $1.0 million. We can rearrange Eq. (8.6) in order to solve for the expected initial change in final demand (ΔY) in Transportation and Warehousing:

$$\Delta Y = \frac{E_i}{e_i} = \frac{1,000}{6.49} = \$153.97 \text{ million} \qquad (8.7)$$

The result implies that an employment increase in Transportation and Warehousing of 1,000 people produces an expected initial increase in final demand for Transportation and Warehousing services of $153.97 million. This increase in final demand (ΔY) of $153.97 million is immediately met by an

405

increase in output in the Transportation and Warehousing services of an equal amount of $153.97 million. This is known as the direct effect and is made possible by the absence of any capacity constraints of Transportation and Warehousing services. Applying the multiplier framework also can provide an estimation of the indirect and induced effects, which in return enables the assessment the local economic impacts of this exogenous stimulus.

8.3.1 Building the Input-Output Table Using IMPLAN Professional 2.0

Our goal is to quantify the impacts of the 1,000 new jobs to the Boone County economy using the Input-Output multiplier framework. More specifically, we will use type II multipliers to assess local economic changes in industry output and employment following a change in final demand (ΔY) of $153.97 million dollars. Referring back to Chapter 5, type II multipliers assume that households are endogenous—in other words, households are treated in the same manner as industry sectors.

Commercially available software packages, such as IMPLAN Professional 2.0 by M.I.G., Inc. and the Regional Input-Output Modeling System (RIMS II) by the Bureau of Economic Analysis, are designed for economic impact analysis using input-output tables and social accounting matrices. However, using the software is like using a "black box" in that it will not show how the calculations are being done. Since constructing the input-output table is more complex than this book's intention, we will use the IMPLAN^{Pro} 2.0 software to build the Boone County input-output table. We will then export the table and do all manipulations and calculations necessary in MS Excel to enhance the transparency of the economic impact analysis.

Building the Boone County model using IMPLAN is a straightforward process once we have county data file, which must be purchased from M.I.G., Inc. The Boone County data used for this exercise is for 2001, the first year M.I.G., Inc. made data files available based on the NAICS code. Please note that the results are different from the economic base analysis from Chapter 4 due to the differences in the data with respect to the definitions of employment and time periods. Comparing this section's results with those from Chapter 5 is possible, but one must be aware that in Chapter 5 we used a highly aggregated input-output table to keep the amount of data manageable; while in this section, we go for a more disaggregated input-output table with 20 individual industry sectors in order to produce more detailed results.

Within IMPLAN, do the following to build an input-output table:[1]

---

[1] The IMPLAN^{Pro} 2.0 software is self-explanatory and very easy to use.

(1) Under the **File** menu, choose **New Model**. Name the regional model, "Bounty County 2001" and click **Continue**. Within the **Select Region** window, locate Boone County's data file(s) and click **Continue**. The model file created has an *.iap extension (e.g., Boone County 2001.iap).

(2) Depending on the size of the study area, several hundred industries may be identified. For instance, Boone County has 226 individual industries. The software allows you to aggregate industries according to the 2-digit or 3-digit NAICS code. Depending on your research focus, you can alternatively aggregate industries according to your own aggregation scheme. To aggregate the Boone County model, simply select **Aggregate** in the drop-down **Model** menu. On the next screen you can import the aggregation scheme from a library by clicking **Library**. On the library screen you will be asked to choose the aggregation scheme; for instance, the "2-Digit NAICS" used for this section's analysis. Once you choose "2-Digit NAICS", hit **Import** and then choose **Aggregate** and the software will aggregate all industries according to the 2-digit NAICS code. You can now close this window.

(3) The next step is to actually construct a model. To do so, click on **Model** then on **Construct** in the Boone County study area window and choose the multiplier you need for your analysis. To generate the social accounts and the predictive multipliers, select **Social Accounts** and **Multiplier** (make sure only the "Type SAM" box is selected in the Multiplier section). You should see that on the right side of this dialog window, all households are selected and included in the calculations of the multipliers. Click **Continue** to construct the Boone County model. The social accounts create a descriptive model and the multiplier option creates the predictive model. This window can now be closed.

(4) Once the model is constructed, you can print various reports by clicking the **Reports** tab. Reports are available for the study area, calculated multipliers, and other detailed information on industries and social accounts.

(5) Additionally, you can conduct an economic impact analysis by clicking the **Impacts** tab. We choose to export the data and use Excel rather then using the impact tool provided by IMPLAN Professional 2.0. Either approach will lead to the same results. You need to create an IMPLAN model through the multipliers. You also need to go to the reports tab and select the **Industry × Industry** tab. Run the **Industry by Industry SAM (Industry Detail, Aggregated Rows)** report. You do not need to save it. Running this report builds the tables needed to create the regional input-output table.

Unfortunately, the IMPLAN software does not provide you with an option that would allow you to export a ready-made input-output table in a spreadsheet format. However, each IMPLAN model can be opened with the Microsoft Access database program. Within MS Access, all data is available for building a regional input-output table or regional social accounting matrix. Open the IMPLAN model (*.iap file) with MS Access; you will see a screen like the one in Fig. 8.19.

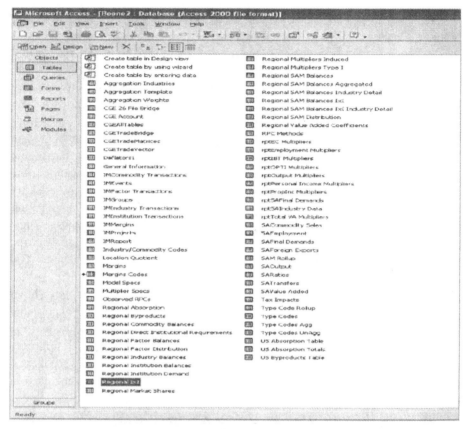

Figure 8.19   The IMPLAN[Pro] economic model in MS Access

Technically, all necessary information is now available for building the regional input-output table. However, it requires a good amount of time gathering and formatting all of the information from different tables. The Minnesota IMPLAN Group, Inc. offers a cross tab query on the internet (from ftp://plum.he.net/pub/ implan1/kb_files/create_ixi_sam_cross_tab.mdb) called "Create IxI SAM Cross Tab.mdb." Once this query is run, MS Access will organize the input-output table for you. However, you need to download the file and import the downloaded *.mdb file into Access. To do so, download the *. mdb file from the ftp site to your computer.

In Access, choose **Get External Data** and **Import** under the drop-down **File** menu. Locate your downloaded .mdb file, highlight it, then select **Import**. The query tab should be active; highlight the **Create SAM Crosstable** query then click on **OK** so that the query is imported into the Access Queries section. Now the query can be run in Access by double-clicking on it. Your result will be a raw social accounting matrix, which can be copied and pasted into a spreadsheet.

Some background on using Access is helpful to understand how to put the social accounting matrix together.

At this point, the only task remaining is formatting the "raw" social accounting matrix. This includes creating row and column headers and subdividing the matrix into sub-accounts as described in Chapter 5. Generally, there are no guidelines on how to format a social accounting matrix since there are numerous ways that it can be done. Also, you have to decide whether you do your economic impact analysis using the social accounting matrix or the input-output table. When using the input-output framework, you need to decide whether or not to treat households endogenously like industries (a closed input-output model). As described in Chapter 5, the social accounting matrix is an extension of the input-output framework. As such, the input-output table can be derived from the social accounting matrix now pasted and formatted in a spreadsheet. We decided to use the input-output framework, which is closed with respect to households. We also rearranged some rows and columns to put the final Boone County input-output table in a more user-friendly format. We want to emphasize that putting the input-output table into its final format is not an easy or straight forward task. It requires thoughtful planning, time and effort to get an input-output table that looks like the one provided in this chapter. The final, revised 20-sector Boone County input-output table used for the economic impact analysis in this section is shown in Table 8.7.

The Boone County input-output table in electronic format is also included. The first spreadsheet labeled "20 Sector Boone Cty I-O Table" in the Excel file "Input-Output Analysis.xls" contains the final, revised 20-sector Boone County input-output table.

The Boone County input-output table is divided into four sections. The highlighted endogenous account (upper-left hand section) contains twenty industry sectors plus one aggregated household sector. We have moved the aggregated household column, which originally is part of final demand, into the endogenous industry account. For deriving type II output multipliers, which account for induced effects, households must be treated endogenously like all other industry sectors. All other final demand figures from governments, investment, and exports is aggregated into one single column labeled "Final Demand (Y)". This will be the sector from where the exogenous injection originates. Another revision was made to the value-added accounts, which includes the rows below the industries. Value-added payments (i.e., employee compensation, proprietary income, and other property income) received by households are lumped together in the "Household" row. All other value-added payments are lumped into one single row labeled "Other Payments". The last row represents imports, the leakage of the regional economy.

Table 8.7   Boone County input-

NAICS	Industries	11	21	22	23	31 – 33	42	44 – 45	48 – 49
11	Agriculture, Forestry, Fishing and Hunting	0.63	–	–	0.08	12.38	0.00	0.00	0.01
21	Mining	–	–	0.02	0.00	0.05	0.00	–	0.01
22	Utilities	0.20	0.02	0.17	1.11	28.03	4.21	6.14	8.29
23	Construction	0.07	0.00	2.69	0.40	5.06	1.86	2.45	7.18
31 – 33	Manufacturing	1.33	0.08	2.85	44.65	378.25	15.88	8.42	112.95
42	Wholesale Trade	0.60	0.02	0.84	10.34	122.02	15.84	2.36	43.10
44 – 45	Retail Trade	0.02	0.00	0.11	26.40	5.17	4.41	5.72	14.08
48 – 49	Transportation and Warehousing	0.12	0.01	3.93	2.28	21.32	5.59	4.10	79.00
51	Information	0.02	0.00	0.32	1.92	7.04	3.78	3.19	11.22
52	Finance and Insurance	0.23	0.02	1.15	4.21	20.45	7.58	7.57	38.56
53	Real Estate and Rental and Leasing	0.63	0.16	0.68	4.50	35.26	13.50	20.06	51.36
54	Professional, Scientific, and Technical Services	0.09	0.02	1.61	8.83	25.31	13.38	12.36	36.78
55	Management of Companies and Enterprises	0.00	0.03	0.05	0.22	25.62	6.75	11.38	6.18
56	Administrative Support, Waste Management, etc.	0.02	0.00	0.58	2.70	8.46	11.89	7.59	45.95
61	Educational Services	–	–	0.20	0.04	0.63	0.73	0.36	1.04
62	Health Care and Social Assistance	–	–	–	–	–	–	0.00	0.12
71	Arts, Entertainment, and Recreation	0.02	0.01	0.05	0.18	1.72	0.74	0.44	0.69
72	Accommodation and Food Services	0.01	0.00	0.73	0.56	9.32	3.34	2.75	21.43
81	Other Services (Except Public Administration)	0.20	0.00	0.26	5.41	45.22	6.95	4.53	52.36
92	Public Administration	0.03	0.01	0.07	0.57	19.50	4.25	1.43	33.35
–	Households	4.64	0.48	59.72	100.77	465.45	198.90	161.00	583.64
	Other Payments	2.33	0.21	59.13	12.31	207.38	193.01	85.49	252.68
	Imports	8.13	0.91	80.67	124.51	1,049.00	177.66	140.76	797.99
	Total Supply-Inputs	19.33	1.99	215.78	351.99	2,492.60	690.25	488.08	2,197.94

output table (in 2001 million dollars)

	Endogenous Account											House-holds	Final Demand (Y)	Total Demand (X)
51	52	53	54	55	56	61	62	71	72	81	92			
0.00	0.00	0.04	0.00	—	0.12	—	0.02	0.01	0.58	0.01	0.01	1.75	3.69	19.33
—	—	—	—	—	—	—	—	—	0.00	0.00	0.00	0.01	1.91	1.99
0.55	0.74	4.92	0.33	1.02	0.83	0.07	1.76	0.36	4.71	2.92	0.88	39.32	109.22	215.78
0.58	1.27	3.37	0.28	0.85	0.25	0.36	1.15	0.29	2.06	2.02	4.26	(0.00)	315.56	351.99
6.64	2.19	2.19	2.36	1.55	2.77	0.22	10.99	0.68	23.26	25.32	4.31	156.06	1,689.68	2,492.60
1.62	0.40	0.49	0.47	0.21	1.04	0.09	3.57	0.20	8.76	5.74	1.34	59.27	411.95	690.25
0.26	0.34	1.70	0.39	0.00	1.74	0.01	1.12	0.12	2.15	5.65	2.78	198.09	217.82	488.08
0.64	1.72	0.79	0.65	0.06	0.72	0.05	1.55	0.13	1.34	1.52	0.43	16.47	2,055.55	2,197.94
5.26	1.83	0.99	1.04	1.24	0.74	0.09	1.28	0.20	1.13	1.49	0.34	13.36	144.32	200.79
1.40	62.86	5.01	1.13	0.19	1.31	0.14	4.24	0.43	3.32	2.44	7.00	99.36	190.22	458.80
4.01	8.42	10.76	3.26	2.96	2.71	0.86	10.75	1.22	11.23	10.24	2.97	45.79	22.86	264.17
4.01	7.01	3.73	3.13	4.28	2.07	0.13	3.70	0.66	3.22	3.33	1.85	10.29	23.31	169.08
0.30	1.34	0.18	0.16	—	0.95	0.01	1.15	0.13	0.38	1.11	0.01	—	69.53	125.48
1.36	2.55	6.79	2.93	0.08	3.66	0.20	6.03	0.51	1.82	3.95	1.40	4.93	54.60	167.98
0.10	0.26	0.08	0.07	—	0.18	0.46	0.20	0.20	0.05	0.83	0.04	9.85	(0.28)	15.04
—	—	—	0.01	—	0.01	0.00	0.72	0.00	0.00	0.01	—	220.35	0.10	221.31
1.56	0.49	0.25	0.40	0.02	0.23	0.02	0.23	2.19	1.14	0.52	0.02	28.81	10.30	50.02
0.52	3.11	1.47	1.32	0.01	1.10	0.04	3.02	0.10	1.85	1.41	0.07	105.89	118.29	276.35
1.85	1.38	1.85	0.93	1.73	2.46	0.11	2.24	0.44	2.63	3.33	1.83	92.17	57.63	285.49
1.85	4.26	2.30	0.48	0.24	0.37	0.03	0.53	0.09	1.10	0.90	0.44	187.57	239.33	498.70
64.59	157.23	78.15	85.85	58.98	74.99	5.56	76.10	23.06	90.24	82.30	226.64	134.64	352.63	3,085.55
33.50	64.90	83.89	20.74	15.21	23.41	2.13	18.83	7.95	31.41	43.15	136.84	1,005.42	666.89	2,966.80
70.19	136.51	55.23	43.15	36.84	46.32	4.47	72.15	11.04	83.98	87.34	105.27	685.09	1,216.80	5,034.01
200.79	458.80	264.17	169.08	125.48	167.98	15.04	221.31	50.02	276.35	285.49	498.70	3,114.45	7,971.90	20,277.52

8.3.2 Assessing Total Changes in Industry Output Using Type II Output Multipliers

The second spreadsheet labeled "Multiplier Calculation" demonstrates the step-by-step approach of calculating the type II output multipliers following the detailed description in Chapter 5. For simplicity (and without losing needed information), we have aggregated government, investment, and exports into one "Final Demand" sector.

Rows 2 – 30 contain the original input-output table for Boone County. It is a more disaggregated and thus more detailed table than the industry transaction table with households endogenous, shown in Table 5.10 of Chapter 5.

The derivation of the technical coefficient table, the "A matrix" in input-output jargon, is shown in rows 36 – 59. These technical coefficients are simple ratios derived by dividing the cell entries in the input-output table by their corresponding column totals. Accordingly, the column totals of the technical coefficient table of dimension 23×21 must add up to 1.0. The exogenous final demand sector is excluded from these calculations. For a more detailed description of the interpretation of these technical coefficients, please review Table 5.5 in Chapter 5.

Rows 64 – 84 contain the $(I-A)$ matrix similar to Table 5.6. In order to subtract the A matrix from an identity matrix I, i.e., $(I-A)$, a 21×21 identity matrix was created in cells Z36 through AT56.

The result of the last step, the inversion of the $(I-A)$ matrix, is shown in rows 88 – 108. Row 109 shows the type II multipliers. Please note that the row does not include the marginal household effects of row 108. The sum of all marginal multipliers, now including the households, is in row 110. This matrix of partial multipliers, commonly referred to as total requirements matrix, has been derived by inverting the $(I-A)$ matrix using the **Lotus 1-2-3 Help** Option in the Microsoft Excel **Help** menu as follows:

(1) Under Help, select **Lotus 1-2-3 Help**,
(2) Select **Data**,
(3) Select **Matrix**,
(4) Select **Invert**.

After clicking **OK**, a "Help for Lotus 1-2-3 Users" window should appear asking you to enter the range of data to be inverted and the output range for the inverted matrix. Follow these steps to invert the $(I-A)$ matrix:

(1) Place the curser into the field labeled "Enter range to invert" and highlight the entire $(I-A)$ matrix (B64: V84)

(2) Place the curser into the field labeled "Enter output range" and highlight the output range where you want to have the inverted matrix, i.e., (B88:V108). Note that the output range must be of identical dimensions, i.e., 21×21, to the input range.

(3) Click **OK** and you will get the final table including the marginal multipliers—the total requirements table—in the area specified under "Enter output range".

The final total requirements table is shown in rows 88 – 108. However, the final type II output multipliers are only the column sums of rows 88 through 107 and do not include the row with marginal multipliers labeled "households". For instance, the final type II output multiplier for the Transportation and Warehousing industry (value of 1.57) is listed in cell I109.

Now we can use the type II output multiplier table and calculate the expected local economic impacts that would result from an employment increase of 1,000 people in the Transportation and Warehousing sector. Knowing the change in the final demand (ΔY) of \$153.97 million, we can use the total requirements table—the $(I - A)^{-1}$ table—to calculate the expected change in output for all industries by applying the input-output multiplier formula expressed as:

$$\Delta X = (I - A)^{-1} \cdot \Delta Y \tag{8.8}$$

where:

ΔX — total expected change in output, including direct, indirect, and induced effects;

$(I - A)^{-1}$— the total requirement, or Leontief inverse matrix;

ΔY — the change in final demand, i.e., the exogenous stimulus.

The actual calculation is rather simple and straightforward. The example for this is shown in the spreadsheet labeled "Output Scenario". Again using the "Lotus 1-2-3 Help" menu, the total change in industry output (ΔX) is calculated by multiplying the total requirements matrix $(I - A)^{-1}$ by the final demand vector (ΔY) containing the exogenous stimulus. The individual steps in Microsoft Excel are:

(1) Under Help, select **Lotus 1-2-3 Help**,

(2) Select **Data**,

(3) Select **Matrix**,

(4) Select **Multiply**.

After clicking **OK**, a "Help for Lotus 1-2-3 Users" window appears again with now three fields to enter data. Do the following:

(1) Place the curser into the field labeled "First range" and highlight the total requirements matrix, i.e., (G3:Z22).

(2) Place the curser into the field labeled "Second range" and highlight the final demand column vector, i.e., (AD3:AD22)

(3) Move the curser into the field labeled "Output range" and highlight the array where you want the results to be. In our example, we chose (E3:E22).

After hitting the **OK** button, you should see the results of the estimated change in industry output in the specified cells of the spreadsheet; in our case, the output is placed in the cells (E3:E22). Figure 8.20 shows the result you should see when doing the actual matrix multiplications. Table 8.8 summarizes the results of the expected economic impacts on industry output following an increase in employment in Transportation and Warehousing of 1,000 people.

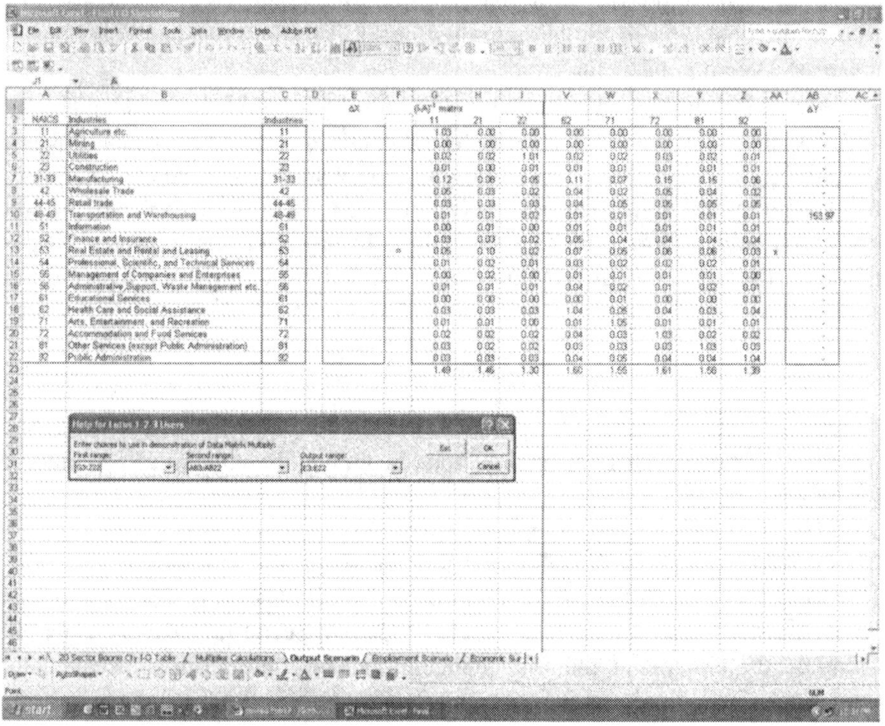

Figure 8.20   The economic impact calculations in Microsoft Excel

Please note that in order to show the entire matrix multiplication setup, we only showed eight out of twenty industry sectors in the total requirements table. As you can verify in the accompanying spreadsheet, the total requirements table has the dimensions of 20×20.

From Table 8.8, we can immediately see that:

(1) Output in Transportation and Warehousing will increase by $160.60 million. Of the $160.60 million, $153.97 million stems from the direct effects following an exogenous change in final demand attributable to the 1,000 new jobs.

(2) Besides Transportation and Warehousing, the largest beneficiaries of the exogenous stimulus are manufacturing ($16.31 million), public administration ($7.16 million), finance and insurance ($6.89 million), and real estate and rental and leasing ($6.79 million).

Table 8.8   Total change in industry output   million dollars

NAICS	Industries	ΔX
11	Agriculture etc.	0.14
21	Mining	0.00
22	Utilities	2.20
23	Construction	0.95
31 – 33	Manufacturing	16.31
42	Wholesale Trade	5.97
44 – 45	Retail trade	6.15
48 – 49	Transportation and Warehousing	160.60
51	Information	1.49
52	Finance and Insurance	6.89
53	Real Estate and Rental and Leasing	6.79
54	Professional, Scientific, and Technical Services	4.05
55	Management of Companies and Enterprises	0.94
56	Administrative Support, Waste Management, etc.	4.42
61	Educational Services	0.37
62	Health Care and Social Assistance	5.10
71	Arts, Entertainment, and Recreation	0.85
72	Accommodation and Food Services	4.42
81	Other Services (except Public Administration)	6.77
92	Public Administration	7.16
	Total	241.59

(3) Total change in output equals $241.59 million.

(4) The total change in output of $241.59 million can alternatively be calculated by multiplying the change in final demand of $153.97 million by the corresponding multiplier of 1.57 of Transportation and Warehousing, or:

$$\Delta X = \Delta Y \cdot OM_2 = 153.97 \times 1.57 = \$241.59 \text{million} \qquad (8.8)$$

While the estimated changes in industry output is the same as using the total requirement matrix, using the multiplier for calculating the total effects of a change in final demand falls short of identifying how this expected change in industry output is taking place in the Boone County economy.

8.3.3   Assessing Changes in Household Income

Calculating changes in income received by households uses the same total requirement matrix discussed above. The rationale of the type II household income multipliers is discussed in greater detail in Chapter 5. No calculations are necessary because the type II household income multipliers are provided in the $(I - \overline{A})^{-1}$ matrix, or total requirements table. The household row contains the type II household income multipliers, but the partial multipliers are not included in the income multipliers. For instance, the type II household income multiplier for Transportation and Warehousing, $HM2_{TW}$, with a value of 0.47, is listed in cell I108 on the spreadsheet labeled "Multiplier Calculations".

Household income multipliers are created to quantify the economic ripple effects that are produced from an increase in industry output—increased value added payments by industries leading to additional income received by households. Next, we can calculate the total change in income received by households that follows the exogenous change in final demand of $153.97 million. Again, using a type II multiplier indicates that households are treated endogenously in the same fashion as an industry sector.

Obtaining the type II household income multipliers for Transportation and Warehousing from the total requirements table (cell I108 in the total requirement matrix) enables us to calculate total expected changes in household income in Boone County as:

$$\Delta \text{ Household Income} = HM2_{TW} \cdot \Delta Y = 0.47 \times 153.97 = \$71.71 \text{million}$$

Or, household income will increase by approximately $71.71 million if demand for Transportation and Warehousing services increases by $153.97 million.

8.3.4 Assessing Total Employment Changes

The last part of this section on economic impact analysis shows how to estimate total changes in employment. We mentioned several times already that initially, employment will go up by 1,000. We also know that as a result of indirect and induced effects, total change in employment is expected to be much higher than the initial increase of 1,000 people. Now we must account for the direct, indirect, and induced effects to estimate the total employment change.

According to the section on household employment multipliers in Chapter 5, type II household employment multipliers are defined as:

$$LM2_j = \sum_{i=1}^{n+1} e_i \cdot \overline{\text{mult}_{ij}} \tag{8.9}$$

where:

$LM2_j$ — type II household employment multipliers;

e_i — employment/output ratio for industry i;

$\overline{\text{mult}_{ij}}$ — partial multipliers from the $(I - \overline{A})^{-1}$ matrix.

416

The starting point for calculating the type II household employment multipliers is the total requirements matrix of partial multipliers derived on the spreadsheet labeled "Multiplier Calculations". The multiplier definition shows that multiplying employment/output ratios for industries by the total requirements table will give us the type II household employment multipliers. The calculation of type II household employment multipliers is shown in a step-by-step approach on the spreadsheet labeled "Employment Scenario".

Row 2 (C2: W2) contains the employment/output ratios. Rows 5 through 25 (C5:W25) contain the direct requirements matrix $(I - \overline{A})^{-1}$ for industry i. And finally, row 29 (C29:W29) holds the type II household employment multipliers by industry. The calculation of the type II household employment multipliers follows the description of assessing the total change in industry output (ΔX) described above. Now, as "First range", we highlight row with the employment / output ratios (C2:W2); as "Second range", we highlight the total requirement matrix; and as "Output range", we highlight the array where we want the results to be (C29:W29).

From the final results in row 29, we can then obtain the type II household employment multiplier of 13.37. This means, that for every change in final demand of $1 million, employment is expected to increase by 13.37. Thus, knowing the change in final demand (ΔY) to be $153.97 million, we can calculate the change in total employment in Boone County as:

$$\Delta E = LM2_2 \cdot \Delta Y = 13.37 \times 153.97 = 2,059 \text{ jobs} \qquad (8.10)$$

Total employment is expected to increase by 2,059 jobs.

Alternatively, we could have used the employment multiplier for transportation and warehousing, which is defined as:

$$EM_j = \frac{LM_j}{e_j} = \frac{13.37}{6.49} = 2.059 \qquad (8.11)$$

We see that a change in final demand of $153.97 million which is equivalent to 1,000 new jobs would lead to a total of 2,059 new jobs using the employment multiplier and the change in employment of 1,000:

$$\Delta E = 2.059 \times 1,000 = 2,059$$

The outcome must be the same, whether we calculate total change in employment (ΔE) using the type II household employment multiplier $(LM2_j)$ knowing that final demand will change by $153.97 million, or using the type II employment multiplier $(EM2_j)$ knowing that employment will increase by 1,000 in transportation and warehousing. Using either multiplier, the estimated change in employment in Boone County is 2,059.

8.4 Case Study Four: Estimation of Trip Production and Trip Attraction

Let's assume that 400 of the 1,000 new jobs introduced in Case Study Three are directly related to Airport and the other 600 jobs are light industrial facilities. We will now estimate additional trips attracted to the work place that are related to the additional jobs. The Institute of Transportation Engineers regularly publishes trip rates for different human activities. Table 8.9 is an example of such rates for commercial airport and light industry.

Table 8.9 Trip rates for commercial airport and general light industrial

	Average Trip Rates per Employee	
	Commercial Airport	General Light Industrial
Weekday	13.4	3.02
Weekday A.M. Peak Hour	1.21	0.48
Weekday P.M. Peak Hour	1	0.51

The first row lists daily trip rates. The second and third rows are the rates for the morning and afternoon peak hour, respectively. From these rates and the number of employees, we can calculate the trips in Table 8.10.

Table 8.10 Trips attributed to the 1000 new employees

	Commercial Airport	General Light Industrial	Total trips
Number of employees	400	600	
Weekday	5,360	1,812	7,172
Weekday A.M. Peak Hour	484	288	772
Weekday P.M. Peak Hour	400	306	706

The result shows that on a weekday, we can expect 7,172 additional trips as a result of the 1,000 additional jobs. During the peak hours, we can expect 772 morning peak hour trips and 706 afternoon peak hour trips.

8.4.1 Trip Generation by Zone

In Chapter 7 we showed the trip generation and trip distribution for an area of four traffic zones. Let's now go through the calculation with an Excel spreadsheet. The file name is trips.xls. Figures 8.21 and 8.22 display the trip production portion of the spreadsheet.

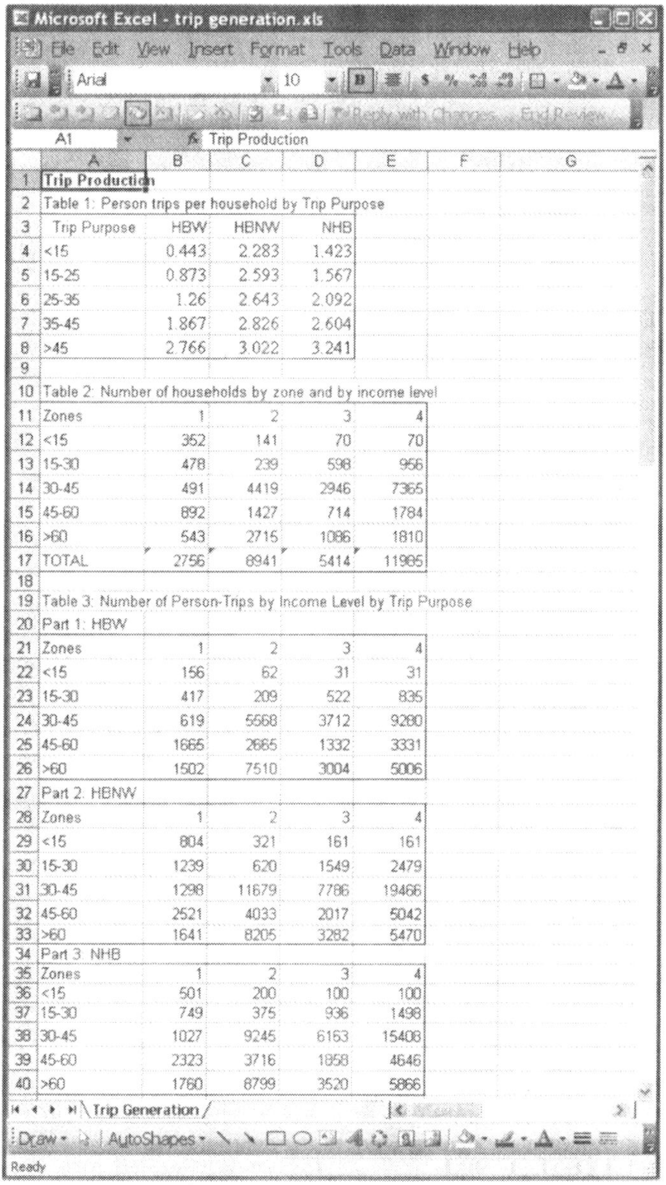

	A	B	C	D	E
1	Trip Production				
2	Table 1: Person trips per household by Trip Purpose				
3	Trip Purpose	HBW	HBNW	NHB	
4	<15	0.443	2.283	1.423	
5	15-25	0.873	2.593	1.567	
6	25-35	1.26	2.643	2.092	
7	35-45	1.867	2.826	2.604	
8	>45	2.766	3.022	3.241	
9					
10	Table 2: Number of households by zone and by income level				
11	Zones	1	2	3	4
12	<15	352	141	70	70
13	15-30	478	239	598	956
14	30-45	491	4419	2946	7365
15	45-60	892	1427	714	1784
16	>60	543	2715	1086	1810
17	TOTAL	2756	8941	5414	11985
18					
19	Table 3: Number of Person-Trips by Income Level by Trip Purpose				
20	Part 1: HBW				
21	Zones	1	2	3	4
22	<15	156	62	31	31
23	15-30	417	209	522	835
24	30-45	619	5568	3712	9280
25	45-60	1665	2665	1332	3331
26	>60	1502	7510	3004	5006
27	Part 2: HBNW				
28	Zones	1	2	3	4
29	<15	804	321	161	161
30	15-30	1239	620	1549	2479
31	30-45	1298	11679	7786	19466
32	45-60	2521	4033	2017	5042
33	>60	1641	8205	3282	5470
34	Part 3: NHB				
35	Zones	1	2	3	4
36	<15	501	200	100	100
37	15-30	749	375	936	1498
38	30-45	1027	9245	6163	15408
39	45-60	2323	3716	1858	4646
40	>60	1760	8799	3520	5866

Figure 8.21 Trip production calculation, Tables 1 – 3

The first table in Cells A3:D8 is a matrix of person trip rates by trip purpose and household income group. The columns represent the three trip purposes—Home-Based-Work (HBW), Home-Based-Non-Work (HBNW) and Non-Home-Based (NHB). The rows represent the five income groups. Please note that those numbers in the table are for illustration purpose. You need to search for the proper values for your study area.

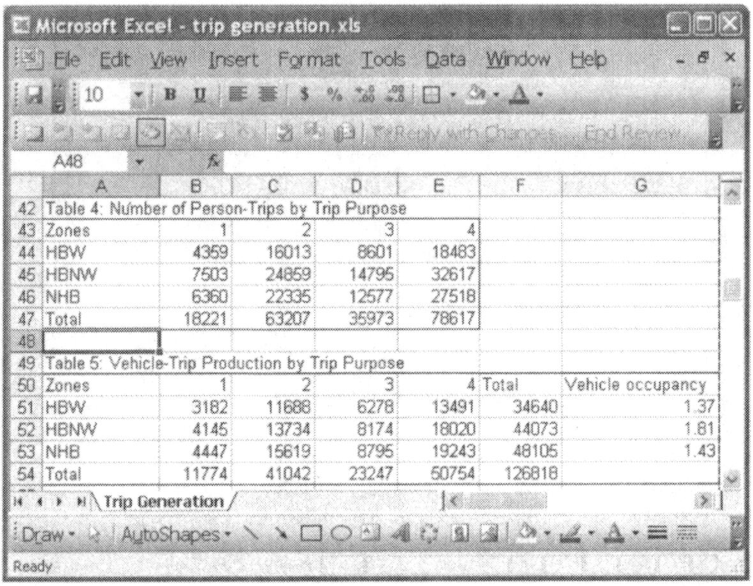

	A	B	C	D	E	F	G
42	Table 4: Number of Person-Trips by Trip Purpose						
43	Zones	1	2	3	4		
44	HBW	4359	16013	8601	18483		
45	HBNW	7503	24859	14795	32617		
46	NHB	6360	22335	12577	27518		
47	Total	18221	63207	35973	78617		
48							
49	Table 5: Vehicle-Trip Production by Trip Purpose						
50	Zones	1	2	3	4	Total	Vehicle occupancy
51	HBW	3182	11688	6278	13491	34640	1.37
52	HBNW	4145	13734	8174	18020	44073	1.81
53	NHB	4447	15619	8795	19243	48105	1.43
54	Total	11774	41042	23247	50754	126818	

Figure 8.22 Trip production calculation, Tables 4 – 5

The second table in Cells A11:E17 stores the number of households by income group in each of the four zones. From this table and the first table, we can calculate the person trips generated from each income group by traffic zone. The results are saved in a three-part table (Table 3, Cells A20: E40) since the calculations must be done for each of the three trip purposes separately.

Part 1 of Table 3 stores the HBW trips. For example, in Cell B22, the person trips from less than $15,000 income households in Zone 1 are calculated as:

$$= \mathrm{B4} \cdot \mathrm{B12} = 0.443 \times 352 = 156$$

where, B4 is the trip rates for Home-Based Work for less than $15,000 income households and B12 is the number of households in this category: HBW person trips generated by income groups in all zones are calculated this way and the results are saved in Cells A22:E26.

Similarly, home-based-non-work and non-home-based person trips are calculated and saved in Part 2 and Part 3 of the table.

The total person trips generated in each zone are derived by adding the number of trips from individual household income groups. Table 4 (Cells A43: E47) stores the trips by zone and by trip purpose. For example, the total HBW trips from Zone 1 are saved in Cell B41, which is calculated as

$$= \mathrm{SUM(B\$22{:}B\$26)}$$

where the trips generated by households in different income groups are saved in Cells B22:B26.

In Table 5 (Cells A50:F54), we convert the person trips to vehicle trips, using the vehicle occupancy ratios saved in the last column in Table 5 (Cells G51:G53). For example, the vehicle occupancy for HBW trips is 1.37, the HBW vehicle trips from Zone 1 (Cell B51) is calculated as:

$$= \text{B44/\$G51} = 4{,}359 \,/\, 1.37 = 3{,}182$$

where B44 is the total person HBW trips from Zone 1 and G51 is the HBW vehicle occupancy ratio.

We will proceed similarly for other trip purpose and zones in Table 5. This concludes the calculation for trip production. From the table, we can see the total trip production for each zone. For example, Zone 4 has higher trip production than other zones. When we examine the trip production distribution by trip purpose, we can see that Home-Based-Work trips take the smallest proportion of the trip production.

Now we can turn our attention to trip attraction. The trip attraction tables are stored in the same sheet, starting in Column I. Figures 8.23 and 8.24 display the tables in the trip attraction calculation.

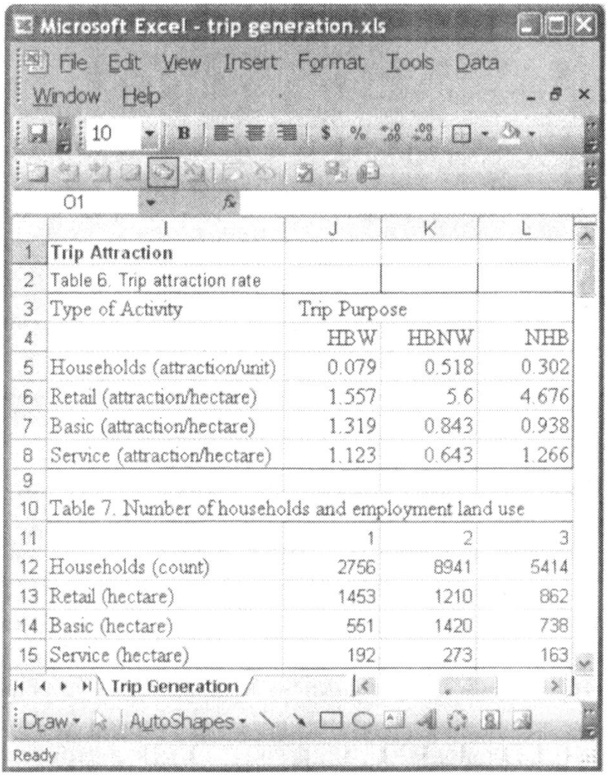

	I	J	K	L
1	Trip Attraction			
2	Table 6. Trip attraction rate			
3	Type of Activity	Trip Purpose		
4		HBW	HBNW	NHB
5	Households (attraction/unit)	0.079	0.518	0.302
6	Retail (attraction/hectare)	1.557	5.6	4.676
7	Basic (attraction/hectare)	1.319	0.843	0.938
8	Service (attraction/hectare)	1.123	0.643	1.266
9				
10	Table 7. Number of households and employment land use			
11		1	2	3
12	Households (count)	2756	8941	5414
13	Retail (hectare)	1453	1210	862
14	Basic (hectare)	551	1420	738
15	Service (hectare)	192	273	163

Figure 8.23 Trip attraction calculation, Tables 6 – 7

	I	J	K	L	M	N
17	Table 8. Trip attractions					
18	Part 1: HBW					
19		1	2	3	4	
20	Households	218	706	428	947	
21	Retail	2263	1885	1343	1587	
22	Basic	727	1874	974	1872	
23	Service	216	306	183	289	
24	Part 2: HBNW					
25		1	2	3	4	
26	Households	1428	4631	2804	6208	
27	Retail	8138	6778	4829	5708	
28	Basic	464	1197	622	1196	
29	Service	123	175	105	165	
30	Part 3: NHB					
31		1	2	3	4	
32	Households	832	2700	1635	3620	
33	Retail	6796	5660	4032	4766	
34	Basic	517	1332	692	1331	
35	Service	243	345	206	326	
36						
37	Table 9: Trip Attractions by Trip Purpose					
38	Zones	1	2	3	4	Total
39	HBW	3423	4771	2927	4695	15815
40	HBNW	10154	12783	8360	13278	44574
41	NHB	8388	10038	6565	10043	35033
42	Total	21964	27591	17851	28016	95423

Figure 8.24 Trip attraction calculation, Tables 8 – 9

Table 6 (Cells I3:L8) lists the trip attraction rates. There are four land use types used in the calculation. The attraction rate for residential use is calculated as trips per household and rates for non-residential uses are measured as trip attraction per square kilometer. For each household, we can expect the attraction rates to be 0.079 for HBW, 0.518 for HBNW, and 0.302 for NHB trip purposes. Similar to the trip production rates, these trip attraction rates are for illustration purposes. You must search for the rates that are appropriate for your study area.

The number of households and the amount of different land uses in the four zones are stored in Table 7 (cells I11:M15). The measure for residential attractions is related to the number of household units and size of non-residential land uses (i.e., measured in square kilometers). From the unit trip attraction rates and the land use amounts in these two tables, we can calculate the trip attractions and save the result in Table 8 (cells I19:M35). Similar to trip production, the trip attractions are calculated by the three trip purposes. The first part is for HBW, second part for HBNW and the last part for NHB trips.

For instance, in cell J20, the trip attracted by households in Zone 1, is calculated as

$$= \$J5 \cdot J12 = 0.079 \times 2,756 = 218$$

where, cell J5 is the trip attraction rate per household and Cell J12 is the number of households in Zone 1. The rest of cells in the row are calculated in the same way (K20:M20). The trip attractions for the non-residential land are the product of the attraction rate and land use area size. For example, the trip attraction associated to retail in Zone 1 is calculated and saved in cell J21 as

$$= \$J6 \cdot J13 = 1.557 \times 1,453 = 2,263$$

The trip attractions calculated by trip purpose for each zone (Table 8) are summarized in Table 9 (I38:M42). The trip purposes are organized by row of the table and zones, by column. For example, the Home-Based-Work trip attraction in Zone 1 is the total of all HBW trip attractions in Part 1 of Table 8 and is calculated as:

$$= SUM(J\$20:J\$23)$$

Cells in the last column (Cells N39:N41) of Table 9 store the trip attractions by trip purpose, which are calculated by adding the trip attraction for the same trip purpose from all zones. For example, the HBW trip attraction in Cell N39 is calculated as:

$$= SUM(J39:M39)$$

where, cells J39:M39 store the HBW trip attractions for Zones 1 through 4.

8.4.2   Trip Distribution by Zone

Now let's calculate the trip distribution among the four Traffic Analysis Zones using the gravity model below:

$$T_{ij} = \frac{P_i \cdot A_j \cdot F_{ij}}{\sum_{i=1,n}(A_j \cdot F_{ij})} \tag{8.12}$$

This model has the same structure as Eq. (7.13). We will first calculate the

Friction Factor between any two zones, F_{ij}. Then we will calculate the product of F_{ij} and trip attraction, $A_j : A_j \cdot F_{ij}$. Third, we will add ($A_j \cdot F_{ij}$) for all zones— $\sum (A_j \cdot F_{ij})$. Next, we will calculate the numerator of the gravity model: $P_i \cdot A_j \cdot F_{ij}$. Finally, we can calculate the trip distribution, T_{ij}.

Figures 8.25 and 8.26 illustrates the calculation procedure. We first switch to the Trip Distribution worksheet. Similar to trip generation, data and calculations are arranged in individual tables. Table 1, cells A3:F8, stores the result from the trip generation calculation data. The last column, F4:F7 are data from the trip production from each of the four zones. The last row, B8:E8 contains the trip

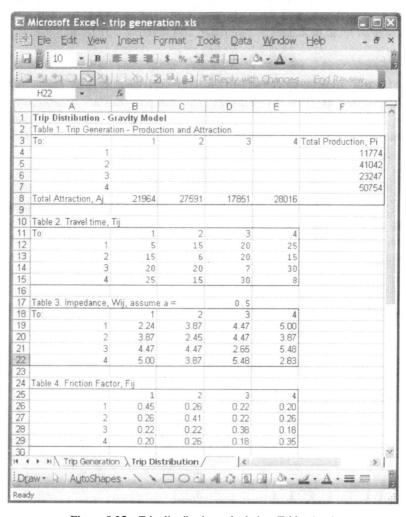

Figure 8.25 Trip distribution calculation, Tables 1 – 4

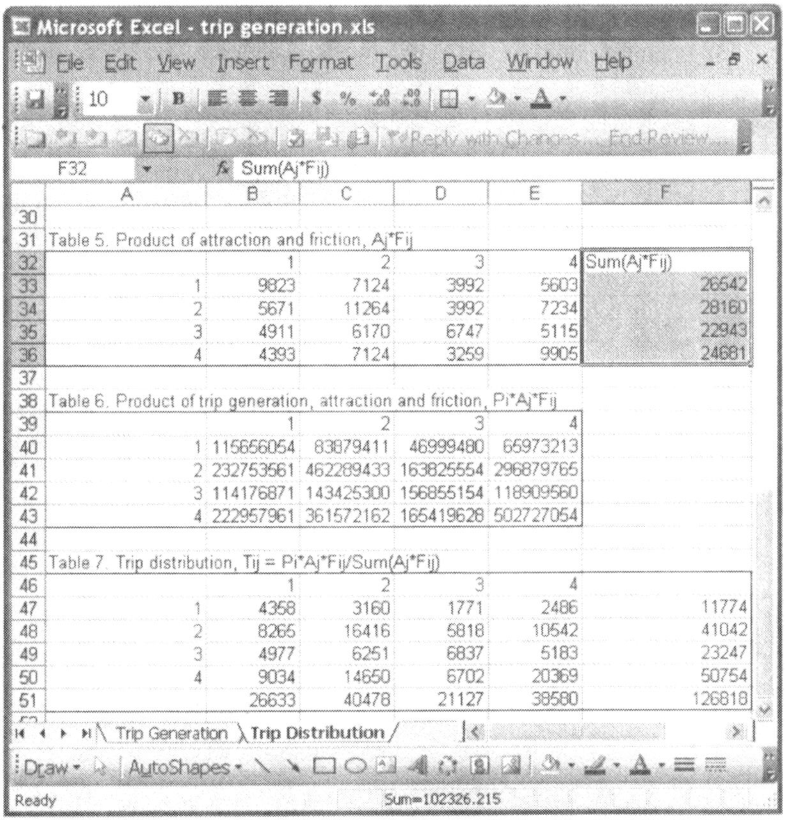

Table 5. Product of attraction and friction, Aj*Fij

	1	2	3	4	Sum(Aj*Fij)
1	9823	7124	3992	5603	26542
2	5671	11264	3992	7234	28160
3	4911	6170	6747	5115	22943
4	4393	7124	3259	9905	24681

Table 6. Product of trip generation, attraction and friction, Pi*Aj*Fij

	1	2	3	4
1	115656054	83879411	46999480	65973213
2	232753561	462289433	163825554	296879765
3	114176871	143425300	156855154	118909560
4	222957961	361572162	165419628	502727054

Table 7. Trip distribution, Tij = Pi*Aj*Fij/Sum(Aj*Fij)

	1	2	3	4	
1	4358	3160	1771	2486	11774
2	8266	16416	5818	10542	41042
3	4977	6251	6837	5183	23247
4	9034	14650	6702	20369	50754
	26633	40478	21127	38580	126818

Figure 8.26 Trip distribution calculation, Tables 5 – 7

attraction to each of the four zones. All values are linked to the corresponding cells in the "Trip Generation" worksheet. For example, cell F4 stores the trip production for Zone 1, which is calculated as:

= "Trip Generation"!B$54

We arrange the trip production as column and trip attraction in a row for easy calculation. Table 2 stores the trip time within each zone and between any two zones, measured in minutes. These numbers are for illustration purpose only. In reality, the travel time should be estimated from survey and actual measurement. The travel time is converted to zonal impedance using the formula:

$$W_{ij} = t_{ij}^{a} \tag{8.13}$$

where, t_{ij} is the travel time from Zone i to Zone j. We assume $a = 0.5$ and save the value in cell D17.

The impedance values are calculated using the constant, a, and the travel time, t_{ij}. For example, cell B19 saves the impedance within Zone 1,is calculated as

$$= B12\wedge\$D\$17$$

where, B12 stores the travel time within Zone 1 and D17 stores the constant, a. Also, we use the common formula discussed in Chapter 7 to calculate the friction factor, F_{ij}.

$$F_{ij} = 1/W_{ij} \qquad (8.14)$$

The results are saved in Table 4, Cell A25:E29.

Table 5 stores the calculation results $A_j \cdot F_{ij}$. The last column is the total for each of the four zones. $\sum (A_j \cdot F_{ij})$. In the spreadsheet, the calculation for Zone 1 is expressed as

$$= \mathrm{SUM(B33:E33)}$$

Table 6 stores the numerator of the gravity model. For example, Cell C40 is for trips from Zone 1 to Zone 2. That is, $i = 1$ and $j = 2$. The calculation is expressed as

$$= P_1 \cdot A_2 \cdot F_{12}$$

In spreadsheet, the calculation in cell C40 is

$$= \$F4 \cdot C33$$

where, P_i is stored in cell F4 and cell C33 stores $A_2 \cdot F_{12}$.

Finally, trip distribution of this four-zone area is calculated and stored in Table 7 (cells A46:F51). The calculation refers to Tables 5 and 6. For example, cell D47 is the trip distribution from Zone 1 and Zone 3. The calculation is expressed as

$$= D40/\$F33$$

where, D40 is the product of $P_1 \cdot A_3 \cdot F_{13}$ and F33 is $\sum (A_3 \cdot F_{13})$.

In the following step, we assess the impact of additional 1,000 jobs to the trip generation in this four-zone area. To simplify the calculation, we assume that the new jobs will increase the trip attractions in Zone 4 by 4%. We further assume that there is no change of trip production. This implies that some people who currently live in the four-zone will be taking the new jobs. First, we make a copy of the Trip Distribution worksheet. To do so, you need to select the **Move or Copy Sheet** option under the **Edit** menu. In the **Move or Copy** dialog window, check the **Create a copy** option and click OK (Fig. 8.27). A new worksheet, which is named **Trip Distribution (2)**, is created.

Figure 8.27   Copy an existing worksheet

You may remember that the trip attraction, A_{ij} and trip production, P_i are stored in the first table, Cells A3:F8. Now let's increase the trip attraction for Zone 4 by 4%. In Cell E8, apply the following formula:

$$= \text{"Trip Generation"!M42} \cdot 1.04$$

Now, the trip attraction from Zone 4 has been increased by 4%. We don't need to change any other values. The model has been rerun and appears in the new Table 7, cells A46:F51 (Fig. 8.28).

	A	B	C	D	E	F
44						
45	Table 7. Trip distribution, Tij = Pi*Aj*Fij/Sum(Aj*Fij)					
46		1	2	3	4	
47	1	4321	3134	1756	2563	11774
48	2	8181	16249	5758	10853	41042
49	3	4933	6196	6776	5342	23247
50	4	8891	14418	6596	20849	50754
51		26326	39998	20887	39608	126818

Figure 8.28   Trip distribution after an increase of 4% trip attraction from Zone 4

427

Table 8.11 compares the trip distribution before and after the 4% increase of trip attraction from Zone 4. The comparison shows that the actual trips attracted to Zone four is less than 4% from the original trip distribution. The reduction of trips attracted to other zones also varies. This is because the gravity model uses the relative trip attraction. Because we assume that there is no change of trip production, the additional trips attracted to Zone 4 reduce the trips attracted to other zones.

Table 8.11 Trip distribution comparison

Number		1	2	3	4	
	1	− 36	− 26	− 15	78	0
	2	− 84	− 167	− 59	310	0
	3	− 44	− 55	− 60	160	0
	4	− 143	− 231	− 106	480	0
		− 307	− 480	− 240	1,028	
Percent/90		1	2	3	4	
	1	− 0.8	− 0.8	− 0.8	3.1	0.0
	2	− 1.0	− 1.0	− 1.0	2.9	0.0
	3	− 0.9	− 0.9	− 0.9	3.1	0.0
	4	− 1.6	− 1.6	− 1.6	2.4	0.0
		− 1.2	− 1.2	− 1.1	2.7	0.0

8.5 Concluding Remarks

This book introduced some analytical methods planners may use in produce plans. Although the four aspects of planning analytical methods are introduced separately, the dynamic connection among them, for any given region, makes planning analysis interesting and challenging. You probably have noticed that numerous assumptions were made in any of the analyses. Although the discussion the assumptions' validity goes beyond the scope of this book, we would like you to remember those assumptions can significantly affect the analytical results.

When appropriately used, these analytical methods are valuable tools that can provide meaningful information about the past, present, and future of a community. There are many other methods available in addition to those introduced in this book. This book provides a foundation for you to be able to evaluate the function, outcome, and data requirements of the methods you may choose to use.

One of the key requirements in conducting planning analyses is high quality, site-specific data. However, sometimes planning decisions have to be made when such data are not available. Without the intention of substituting for local data, a user may choose to make informed estimates of the parameter values to use in analysis. Even though the results may not be the most accurate results possible, they can offer some initial guidance.

Planning is a field that reaches many aspects of both the natural and social sciences. We still know very little about the human-environment interaction. Very few analyses can provide results with a high level of confidence. However, this does not diminish the importance of these analyses. The analytical results can provide evaluations of the suitability of a method for a particular community and the limitations of the available data. Finally, they can direct additional data collection efforts. It is expected that the understanding of the analytical methods will help maintain data integrity and avoid the misuse of the methods. Users need proper training to understand the processes involved in any particular analysis, which is the overall intent of this book.

References

Brail, Richard K. 1987. *Microcomputers in Urban Planning and Management*. New Brunswick, NJ: Rutgers, The State University of New Jersey.

Cartwright, Timothy J. 1993. *Modeling the World in a Spreadsheet*. Baltimore, MD: Johns Hopkins University Press.

Huxhold, William E., Patrick S. Tierney, David R. Turnpaugh, Bryan J. Maves and Kevin T. Cassidy. 1997. *GIS County User Guide*. New York: Oxford University Press.

Kaiser, Edward J., David R. Godschalk, Richard E. Klosterman and Ann-Margaret Esnard. 1998. *Hypothetical City workbook*. Champaign, IL: University of Illinois Press.

Klosterman, Richard E. 1990. *Community Analysis and Planning Techniques*. Savage, MD: Rowman & Littlefield Publishers, Inc.

Krueckeberg, Donald A. and Arthur L. Silvers. 1974. *Urban Planning Analysis: Methods and Models*. New York, NY: John Wiley & Sons.

LaVergne, TN USA
10 August 2010
192688LV00001B/8/P